LINCOLN AND DAVIS

American Political Thought

EDITED BY

Wilson Carey McWilliams and Lance Banning

Brian R. Dirck

Lincoln & Davis

IMAGINING AMERICA, 1809–1865

 University Press of Kansas

Published by the University Press of Kansas (Lawrence,
Kansas 66049), which was organized by the Kansas Board
of Regents and is operated and funded by Emporia State
University, Fort Hays State University, Kansas State University,
Pittsburg State University, the University of Kansas, and
Wichita State University

Library of Congress Cataloging-in-Publication Data

Dirck, Brian R., 1965–
    Lincoln and Davis : imagining America, 1809–1865 /
    Brian R. Dirck.
        p. cm. — (American political thought)
    Includes bibliographical references and index.
    ISBN 0-7006-1137-1 (alk. paper)
        1. Lincoln, Abraham, 1809–1865. 2. Davis, Jefferson,
1808–1889. 3. Presidents—United States—Biography.
4. Presidents—Confederate States of America—Biography.
5. Lincoln, Abrahm, 1809–1865—Political and social views.
6. Davis, Jefferson, 1808–1889—Political and social views.
7. Nationalism—United States—History—19th century.
8. Nationalism—Confederate States of America—History.
9. National characteristics, American. 10. United States—
Politics and government—1861–1865. I. Title. II. Series.
E457.2.D57 2001 973.7'092'2—dc21 [B]   2001001784

British Library Cataloguing in Publication Data is available.

Printed in the United States of America

10 9 8 7 6 5 4 3 2 1

FOR MY PARENTS,

Larry and Dolores Dirck

Contents

Acknowledgments

This book began as a conversation with my adviser at the University of Kansas, Professor Phillip Paludan, over a hobo breakfast (extra cheese) at the Paradise Café in Lawrence, Kansas. He provided sage advice on the project that morning and has been enthusiastic in his support ever since. For six years he has been a patient and an incisive critic, coach, and adviser as well as a good friend. He deserves a great deal of credit for whatever of value may be found in this book.

Professor Angel Kwolek-Folland, currently the director of Women's Studies at the University of Florida, has likewise provided invaluable support, both for this project and for my academic career in general; I greatly value her friendship. Professors Jonathan Earle, Phillip Kissam, and Thomas Heilke of the University of Kansas also offered useful advice and commentary while serving as members of my dissertation committee.

Fred Woodward at the University Press of Kansas deftly handled the process of converting a dissertation into this book. His patience, expertise, and prompt attention to my various needs and concerns were absolutely indispensable. I also wish to thank UPK staff members Susan Schott and Melinda Wirkus, copy editor Claire Sutton, and the anonymous reviewers who provided me with detailed and incisive observations and critiques.

Many of my colleagues in the Department of History's graduate program at the University of Kansas read drafts of various chapters and offered helpful suggestions. I am indebted to Chris Boucher, Sally Julien, Marie Kelleher, Lisa Miles, Rusty Monhollon, Chris O'Brien, Jasonne Grabner O'Brien, Stephanie Roper, Lisa Steffen, and Laurie Stoff. Jay Antle, Mike Grant, Jim Leiker, Kristine M. McCusker, and Martha Robinson have been especially helpful; Martha in particular has helped me capture Lincoln's essential melancholy. All are good friends.

My colleagues at Anderson University have also been generously forthcoming with aid and support, not the least of which has been the creation of a congenial atmosphere at this university, where I have had the privilege of teaching since 1998. Douglas Nelson, chair of the Department of History and

Political Science, has been generously forthcoming with advice, suggestions, and friendship. Jaye Caldwell, Linda Chiang, Jacoba Koene, Paula Maris-Roberts, David Murphy, and Andrew Wisely read various parts of the book and offered useful comments. Our office secretaries, Dontie Edwards, Kristy Hadfield, Rebecca McCowan, and Joanna Sartwell, provided valuable clerical assistance. I am also indebted to my students at Anderson University, and at the University of Kansas, who have on more than one occasion taught me a thing or two about history and life in general.

I have benefited enormously from the aid of archivists and librarians during various stages of my research. The staff of the Watson Library at the University of Kansas was very helpful, especially in the Interlibrary Loan Department. Lynda Lasswell Crist, Mary Dix, Kenneth Williams, and the staff of the Jefferson Davis Papers at Rice University have patiently answered my questions and offered helpful advice; their many kindnesses extend to my days as an M.A. student at Rice University. Cindy Van Horn and the staff of the Lincoln Museum in Fort Wayne, Indiana, and the staff of the Mississippi Department of Archives and History in Jackson, Mississippi, were patient and helpful during my visits to their facilities. The staff of Bracken Library at Ball State University provided assistance during the latter stages of this project. Jill Branscum in the Interlibrary Loan Department of Nicholson Library at Anderson University helped me obtain several important research items.

I have also benefited from suggestions and criticisms offered by my colleagues in Civil War history. Emory Thomas has been an especially valuable critic and observer of this project. John M. Belohlavek, Ian Binnington, Vernon Burton, Donald Collins, Drew Gilpin Faust, David Herr, Wallace Hettle, Carl Moneyhon, George Rable, Ethan Rafuse, Anne Rubin, Brian Wills, and Steve Woodworth gave me useful input on various chapters. Vernon Burton's wonderful Southern history research group at the University of Illinois has been generously forthcoming with advice and hospitality. William C. Davis and Eric Walther graciously agreed to read the entire manuscript in its early stages and offered sage advice.

This is my first book, and it therefore seems an appropriate place to acknowledge some long-standing debts. Gregory J. Urwin, professor of history at Temple University, has been my adviser and friend for many years. He is a fine scholar and a peerless teacher, and his passion for history permanently infected at least one of his undergraduate students. Harold M. Hyman at Rice University introduced me to the wonders and possibilities of studying the politics, the law, and the higher intellectual meaning of the Civil War. Professors Norbert Schedler and Richard Scott, both of the Honors College at the University of Central Arkansas, provided early encouragement and support. I would also like to thank my close friend Glen Thurman, who patiently listened to my ramblings about Lincoln and Davis during many a fine dinner conversation, and Kristine M. McCusker, currently assistant professor of history at Middle Tennessee State University, whose friendship dates back to our first days together in the graduate program at the University of Kansas.

My entire family has been supportive of this endeavor. My parents have been unflagging in their love and encouragement. My wife Donna has patiently watched, waited, and suffered through the inevitable ups and downs of this book. She has also read every word and offered valuable comments, which is not a task every spouse would be willing to do. Most of all I would like to thank my children—Nathan, who was born about the time I began this project, and Rachel, born as it neared completion—for providing most welcome distractions from the sometimes taxing work of research and writing.

LINCOLN AND DAVIS

Introduction

In this book I offer an extended comparative analysis of the lives and careers of the two Civil War presidents, Abraham Lincoln and Jefferson Davis. How were they alike? How were they different? What were the precise sources of their differences and their similarities? These relatively simple questions have never been adequately answered.[1]

When historians have offered direct comparisons of the two men, Davis has usually been the horse chestnut to Lincoln's chestnut horse. "President Jefferson Davis of the Confederate States of America has always seemed somewhat poorly cast and colorless compared to his tragic opposite number," wrote one recent observer. James M. McPherson contrasted Lincoln's habit of "express[ing] himself in a clear, forceful manner" and his brilliant articulation of the war's meaning to Davis's "inability to communicate effectively." William C. Davis wrote that "Lincoln was Lincoln, a man of myriad quirks and failings, who yet governed his weaknesses," but "Davis was Davis, and was governed by them." In a widely read 1960 article, David Potter has summarized the prevailing wisdom that has gone largely unchallenged for nearly forty years: "It seems hardly unrealistic to suppose that if the Union and the Confederacy had changed presidents with one another, the Confederacy might have won its independence."[2]

In some respects this lopsided assessment of Lincoln and Davis is justified. Lincoln is rightly revered by millions of Americans as the Great Emancipator, the man who finally ended the execrable American practice of enslaving other Americans. Davis, on the other hand, defended the peculiar institution his entire life. He never questioned the wisdom or the morality of slavery, and he fought a war for its protection.

Davis lost that war, and Lincoln won; therein lies another reason why historians praise the Union president at his Confederate counterpart's expense. Lincoln's presidency is a model of effective political leadership. Davis was excoriated by many of his contemporaries and criticized by many modern scholars for his failure to provide adequate guidance for the Southern people at crucial moments during the war. Lincoln was decisive; Davis was weak; Lincoln was pragmatic and flexible; Davis was rigid and uncompromising; Lincoln was a master politician who was adept at negotiating the sometimes treacherous byways of democracy; Davis avowed his hatred of politics and in his repeated attempts to stand above the fray of parties and factions often proved unable to govern effectively.[3]

Victory and slavery are therefore the two key issues that lie at the heart of traditional assessments of Lincoln and Davis. There is nothing inherently wrong with this literature; it comprises some of the finest scholarly writing we possess on the war. But is there no room for other narratives, other ways of telling the stories of the Civil War presidents, which, while acknowledging the importance of victory and slavery, nevertheless ask different questions? That is my second purpose: to focus attention on each man's understanding of national identity—American, Confederate, and Union—in a comparative analysis that, while taking into account the twin Civil War shibboleths of victory and slavery, highlights different issues that have often been overlooked in previous studies of the two men separately and of the war in general.

Nationalism is not a new area of inquiry where Lincoln and Davis are concerned, but again, this literature is Lincoln-centered. Scholars generally see Lincoln as the embodiment of much that is good and admirable in the American national experience. With an eye toward his role as the Great Emancipator, David Potter has written that "Lincoln's own career illustrate[s] a humane nationalism with implications of universal value." James Rawley has stated simply that "Lincoln is the supreme nationalist in the history of the United States." Stephen Oates's popular and influential writings on Lincoln tend to collapse entirely his personal egalitarianism, his reading of the Declaration of Independence, and a nation founded on principles of liberty and equality. Most recently, the intellectual historian John Patrick Diggins has argued that Lincoln's understanding of the American experiment is fundamental to any nuanced understanding of the nation as a whole. Lincoln *is* America, or should be for any enlightened American mind.[4]

For at least the last fifty years Lincoln's status as America's preeminent nationalist has gone largely unchallenged.[5] Most Americans admire his robust defense of the Union, his commitment to preserving democracy, and his talk of America as the "last best hope of earth" for fulfilling the promise of human freedom. Those who came of age during the civil rights revolution of the 1960s praise his goal of placing the Declaration of Independence's agenda of personal liberty and racial equality at the heart of the American experience. Lincoln's concerns about the state of American democracy and the promise of a national "new birth of freedom" provide the driving narrative center in our modern storytelling about Civil War America, not Jefferson Davis's issues of states' rights, self-determination, and white Southerners' attempts to preserve America's racial caste system under a new Confederate mantle.

There is an extensive literature on Davis's nationalism, centered primarily on his responsibility (or lack thereof) for using his position as president to help create a viable, stable sense of Confederate nationalism. Some historians—Richard Bensel, Emory Thomas, and Raimondo Luraghi, for example—have praised Davis's efforts in this regard, seeing in him an effective political leader who oversaw the creation of a powerful, if short-lived, Confederate national government.[6] Others—most notably Paul Escott and Richard Beringer, with the latter's coauthors of *Why the South Lost the Civil War*—portray Davis in a far different light, as a man of limited political ability who could not take adequate steps to ensure popular loyalty to the Confederacy.[7]

These are fascinating issues, but they are wrapped so tightly around the pervasive matter of assessing praise or blame for the Confederacy's defeat that many other questions about the nature of Confederate nationalism go unanswered. Nor does this literature really challenge Lincoln's hegemony as the "supreme nationalist" who sets the primary agenda for our study of the national meaning of the Civil War. No one suggests that the story of the Davis administration's attempt to create a viable Confederate nation-state can or should supplant the primary narrative drive of modern Civil War literature: Lincoln's resurrection of a "house divided" and his morally admirable pursuit of emancipation as a defining national goal. Scholars treat this as the center of gravity of the Civil War. Davis's bout with Confederate nationalism is, at best, an interesting byway.

Beyond these issues, it is fair to say that much of the current literature on Lincoln's and Davis's nationalism is simply old-fashioned, rooted as it is in politics and institutions. When examining the two men's respective national identities, scholars have usually written straightforward political histories, asking questions about Lincoln's and Davis's policies, institutional structures, political ideologies, and party affiliations. The causal connections in this literature are relatively straightforward as well, with Lincoln and Davis making decisions about national politics and policy on the basis of the traditional motives of the democratic politician: the consolidation of power and the winning of popular elections. Few works draw broad causal connections between their national identity and the more subtle social, cultural, and psychological factors in their lives.[8]

In recent years, however, scholars who study nationalism have focused on issues somewhat different from the traditional mantra of politics and constitutionalism. Borrowing from Benedict Anderson's felicitous phrase, "imagined communities," we might term these "imagination questions." This new nationalism of the imagination sees loyalty to a nation as a matter of instinct as much as reason, psychology as much as politics. Its practitioners search for national identity in a wide variety of cultural and social settings: funeral rituals, national celebrations of dead patriots and military heroes, grassroots religious values, popular national fiction, religious and civic ceremonies, subtle variations of language and dialect—in short, a myriad of ephemeral phenomena where, according to Anderson, the "imagined community" of nationalism flourished among ordinary people. Nationalism is not an idea, it is an emotion, something more akin to a religion than to a political party or an institution.[9]

I wish to apply some of the methods pioneered by this new nationalist literature to Lincoln and Davis, for in doing so a new set of issues emerges that has rarely been examined for these two men. Rather than asking questions about how they approached American party ideology, political maneuvering, and public policy, I shall pose questions about how they imagined Americans themselves. When they looked for that grand abstraction, that imagined community called the American nation, what did they see? What were the psychological, social, cultural, and political factors that shaped their national imaginations? How much did they think they needed to know about what was in their fellow Americans' hearts in order to transact the nation's business? The issue here is not so much what Lincoln thought about slavery and race, for example, but what he imagined other Americans—particularly Southern Americans—thought about slavery and race, and how certain he felt he needed to be about their motives, interests, and perspectives on race and slavery to make common cause with them as Americans.

What emerges from this inquiry is a narrative that breaks from the traditional story arc whereby Lincoln is the American nationalist hero and Davis, the perpetrator of secession, its goat. Rather, the story is more like a rich conversation, a set of metaphorical Lincoln-Davis debates, perhaps, in which neither participant emerges as the clear victor and in which both have something important to say about the nature of American nationalism.

I have also found that this comparative narrative is integrative, collapsing antebellum and wartime thinking and blending political, psychological, and cultural factors in ways that traditional narratives about nationalism—with their straight, abstract causal lines involving only politics and abstract national ideas—have often failed to do. I have found myself looking for Lincoln's and Davis's nationalist imaginations in strange byways, relationships with their fathers, for example, and forging causal links that have been heretofore obscure or lost entirely. Thus we will see, in one instance, that Davis's experiences at West Point played a causal role in his national imagination that is on a par with his reading of John C. Calhoun and that Lincoln's law practice was a critical factor in the development of his American national identity.

In addressing these matters, I have deliberately chosen to minimize the issue of victory. An excessive focus on the final score obstructs a richer and more nuanced understanding of the game, and I have set aside the worthy but distracting and complex issues of leadership that an assessment of Lincoln's victory and Davis's defeat would require. I have also chosen to reconfigure slavery, not as a nonfactor but as one factor among the many social, cultural, political, and psychological components that made up Lincoln's and Davis's national identities. In doing so, I most certainly do not wish to be construed as having advanced the by now thoroughly discredited thesis that slavery was not a basic cause of the Civil War. I do wish to suggest that there are fruitful avenues of inquiry concerning Lincoln, Davis, and the Civil War whereby the matter of slavery and its demise may be at least temporarily placed to one side.

Besides offering the first comprehensive, comparative analysis of the two Civil War presidents, I also present a broad, extended argument for the value of balance in our understanding of Abraham Lincoln, Jefferson Davis, and the contributions each side in the Civil War made to the American conversation as a whole. A balanced narrative will give us a better sense of the boundaries and limitations of Lincoln's point of view (a perspective that has gone largely unappreciated by those who are obsessed only with the man's greatness) and the strengths of Davis's American and Confederate nationalism. Alike, and yet different, these two men engaged in a sort of ongoing, metaphorical conversation of their own on how one goes about fashioning and directing an American conversation in the first place. Few Americans can speak so tellingly to this issue.

Several methodological questions that have arisen during the course of this study merit attention here at the outset. First, do I mean to suggest that Lincoln's national imagination was the North's national imagination, or that what Jefferson Davis thought about these issues by definition reflects his fellow Confederates' point of view? Because these two men were wartime leaders, does this mean they were able to impose their visions on their people and that therefore to understand them is to understand Union, Confederate, and American nationalism? My thinking in this regard is traditional enough to believe that given their positions as presidents and men of influence, their ideas about national identity must have invariably had some larger impact on the ideas of those around them. But how far this impact might have extended is a question beyond the scope of this book. I shall advance arguments about the nationalist ideas of Lincoln and Davis and leave to a future project an assessment of how much their ideas in turn influenced political parties, legislators, voters, or soldiers in the field.

Second, there is the issue of context. In this era of social history's ascendance, the temptation is strong to reduce the lives of any historical figures to the particular cultural or social contexts in which they function. Thus it might be tempting to suggest that because Jefferson Davis's national identity invariably reflects some facets of his Southern political culture, he is therefore merely a product of that culture and that to explain him is to explain the South and vice versa. If we focus only on these broader matters, however, we lose sight of the creative role of the individual to shape and mold various environmental and cultural influences. Neither man should be reduced to such relatively simple common denominators of race, class, region, profession, or gender. Lincoln was a lawyer, for example, but he was both like and unlike other lawyers; Davis was a Southerner, but he was both like and unlike other Southerners. The recipes each followed may have been roughly similar for other Americans of their day, but each in turn was his own cook.

Third, may we assume that their speeches and letters accurately reflect their minds, given the fact that they were both politicians with explicit political agendas that affected their words and actions? Can we analyze a speech delivered by Lincoln, for example, and assume that his words do not reveal simply what his audience wanted to hear rather than what Lincoln himself privately believed? This is a problem endemic to any intellectual history, particularly one that focuses on pragmatic political men like Lincoln and Davis. I have no ready answer, except to point out that I have been struck by the lack of dissonance between their public and their private words. To a remarkable degree, their speeches and public documents seem very much in accord with their privately expressed thoughts. Indeed, I believe the strongest commonality between these otherwise extraordinarily different men was their fundamental honesty and frankness. In this vein, I have treated their public words as generally an accurate reflection of their private beliefs and their national imaginations.

Prologue

January 12, 1861. Washington, D.C.

His bedroom is dark. But lately he likes the dark. It dulls the pain, the rhythmic, throbbing mass of stings and hurts that plague his face, seeming to stretch his dry skin tighter and tighter across his cheekbone and jaw until even his teeth ache. "Neuralgia" is the term he prefers to use, but it is too short and limited a word to describe a malady that has kept him bedridden for almost two days.[1]

In fact the room is not completely unlit. It is late afternoon, and, as close as the shades are drawn, slivers of daylight still find their way around the sills, and he can see a fainter, yellowish glow from under the doorway. But he avoids the sunlight, that hot light with its hard edges. The light is like the pain; it is sharp and crouching, waiting behind the cool gray curtains. His mind is like the curtains, a collection of cold dark squares hastily arranged in front of the pain that threatens to blind him, as if he were staring into the sun. At times it does blind him; it breaks through and makes Davis wince and squint and even cry out, which is so unlike him.

"Won't you please try to eat something?" Varina had stood at the side of this same bed two winters ago. A plate of something had been in her hands, covered with a cloth through which wisps of steam escaped. He had been barely able to see her through a triangle of light that peeped under the bandage holding the cotton compress in place over his left eye. He scrunched open his right eye, the one that worked, and could see her round face contorted by a frown as she bit her lower lip. He knew that look, knew exactly what lay behind his wife's soft brown eyes. His mind's eye could clarify even what he could not clearly see; his wife was more than just worried, she was close to panic.

For a moment, just that fleeting moment, he forgot about that other eye, his pain. But then the pain came bellowing back, roaring like a wind. He almost could not hear his own voice over its roar and so nearly screamed at Varina. "No! I cannot!" and buried his face deep in the pillows.[2]

They had thought he might die, or at least go blind, that winter. Doctor Hayes called it a "procedenture of the pupil" and told him his eye might very well burst. There had been people in this room, always more people. Varina, of course, and Hayes, but also a local Washington surgeon, Doctor Stone, and Doctor Miller, the family physician. There were servants, his private butler, old army friends, Senate pages, and sometimes senators themselves.

In the light and in his one-eyed misery they had all seemed two-dimensional, flattened, their faces losing their features in the backdrop of light so that he could not tell exactly who they were or what they wanted. He remembered that feeling of confusion had been almost as bad as the pain, for he could never stand the sinking sensation he had always felt, somewhere near the base of his throat, when speaking to someone who suddenly seemed like a total stranger. He needed to look people full in the face, see what was behind their smiles, their frowns, their words. He needed to give them depth, three-dimensionality, lest they seem thin and flat as paper. Paper people could not be trusted.

Like William Seward, that fascinating, perplexing, damnable man. He had come bounding into the room nearly every day during that long winter, restless and frenetic, like a hungry terrier. The bandage was wrapped over both his eyes most of the time, so he could not see Seward, only hear his high-pitched voice as he happily recounted the latest political tilts on the Senate floor. "Your man out-talked ours," he would say; "you would have liked it. I didn't." Seward was uncouth, vain, petty, profane. At times he behaved like anyone but a U.S. senator. And of course his warmed-over abolitionist politics were all wrong.[3]

Yet this same facile creature, he who had declared war on the South and spoken of an "irrepressible conflict" between slave and free states, this sapper and miner against the foundations of the Constitution, this same man had been moved to tears in front of Varina over her husband's plight. She had later told him of a conversation with Seward, who with emotion choking his voice had said to her, "He must not lose his eye." Varina liked him, and she did not normally care much for her husband's political adversaries.[4]

What to make of the man? He had not really known. He sometimes liked Seward's company, as did Varina. But Seward was flat, he was superficial, and he even reveled in the fact. "Do you never speak from conviction alone?" Davis had once asked him. "Ne-ver," Seward replied. It did not even seem to be an issue of importance. At the time, Davis had simply shaken his bandaged head in amazement at Seward's words. "As God is my judge, I never spoke from any other motive," he had said to Seward. "I know you do not," Seward gently replied; "I am always sure of it."[5] What an odd man. But then that had been a strange, strange winter.

The days are more peaceful, now, or at least a bit less dramatic. The roaring of the eye has died away, leaving only a glassy appendage under his left brow, like a dead tree after a storm. It is now useless, almost an affectation, and he has never had much patience with ornaments. Varina is out for the afternoon, and the servants are elsewhere. But at times Davis finds he misses the people, for he has had fewer visitors these last two days. Someone comes in and lays the mail on his desk over in the corner but says nothing. Davis can't look at it anyway. Most of his Senate friends are elsewhere, dealing with matters that seem more important than one of Davis's stints in a sickbed. And Seward? Seward doesn't come around any more. Just as well, he supposes. A paper man.

His face tightens again; the neuralgia makes him wince. He instinctively reaches up to touch his face, to feel if it is actually throbbing. He thinks better of it. He raises his bony hand and looks at it in the dark, its long fingers, an age spot behind one knuckle, wrinkles that splay out like little cracks. At times he feels like little more than a collection of spots and wrinkles and cracks, crevices recording the slow passage of time over a battered body.

Battered but sturdy. He will turn fifty-three this summer. It is a ripe age. Or maybe "ripe" isn't quite the right word, implying as it does a growing, an organic flowering. No, he feels more like something that has been thrust into a fire, a series of fires that have melted away all the soft parts of him until nothing is left but this hard nugget of a man. The light, the hot light, has melted much of him, but perhaps he is better because of it. Perhaps he is stronger. It is cold comfort, but comfort nonetheless. He needs his strength for the work, and it is work for which he must be cold and hard. It is no small thing to break up one's country.

January 12, 1861. Springfield, Illinois

"Honorable W. H. Seward."

"Private."

"My Dear Sir."

What to write? He pauses, scratching his chin, still a little surprised at the scrutch, scrutch sound. The beard is only about a month old, and it still itches a little. He gives his jawbone a healthy scratch while he's in the neighborhood. He looks back down at the letter. It has not written itself.

Truth to tell, letters to Seward are relatively easy to write. At least Seward is getting what he wants, a cabinet post. State, no less. He looks for a moment out the window. The muffled buzz of human conversation penetrates the walls; someone is talking out in the hallway. It seems as if someone is always talking lately, that there are always several conversations going on around him at once, as if he were standing in a hotel lobby. President-elect Lincoln lives in a hotel of a world, and hotels are noisy places, thumps and bumps and rattles from rooms above and below. And they have that smell, the air is a thick stew of old and new aromas, stale and fresh, foods eaten, baths taken. In the grand dance of humanity, hotels are often the ballroom floor, weather-beaten but alive with movement. Lincoln loves hotels.[6]

"Your selection for the State Department having become public, I am happy to find scarcely any objection to it. I shall have trouble with every other Northern cabinet appointment." A little flattery for his new secretary of state. Your position was easy to fill, but the others are controversial. You are easy, they are hard. Seward will like that; it will fan his vanity. Lincoln pauses, smiling a little. He likes the stories he hears about Seward, how he takes his shoes off and warms his feet in the fireplace right in the middle of a dinner party.[7] It is the sort of thing Lincoln himself might do.

A little gust sweeps into the open window near him, carrying with it a swirl of faded brownish-black maple leaves that dance and swish across his desk. He brushes them onto the floor. Lately his life is a swirl, a gusty wind that carries dancing and swishing people. Friends, strangers, bare acquaintances alike, all mixed up together in a procession of faces and smiles and handshakes. This morning it was a wizened old farmer named Jones. The elderly gentleman rushed up to him and seized his hand, pumping it with his own calloused one, and recounted to all who were nearby how Abe had worked one of his fields thirty years ago at a dollar a day. Lincoln hates the diminutive "Abe," but he smiled and returned the handshake with warmth. He never cared for farming. Old Farmer Jones never knows it.[8]

At times they have strained his patience, the farmers and the well-wishers, old clients from cases so long ago he forgot who won, judges before whom he argued and pleaded, reporters, mostly from Chicago, looking for stories about the new president-elect, congressmen of greater or lesser import, and office seekers, always more office seekers. Last week it was a group of men from

Iowa, urging upon Lincoln an old army colonel to serve as postmaster general. A few hours later, he was compelled to listen to a former New Hampshire congressman recount his qualifications to serve as a collector of duties at the port of Boston.[9]

He heaves a sigh. But the truth is he loves the swirl of people, thrives on it, in fact. And a real swirl, too, frenetic and wild. He hates formal socials, where people dance only in carefully proscribed ways, cautiously dotting all their social i's and crossing their courtesy t's. He likes a cacophony of steps, even if the steppers occasionally tread on one another's toes. Lincoln chuckles. He's stepped on a few toes.

"I still hope Mr. Gilmer will, on a fair understanding with us, consent to take a place in the cabinet," he writes to Seward. "The preference for him over Mr. Hunt or Mr. Gentry is that, up to date, he has a living position in the South, while they have not." He needs a Southerner, but not too many Southerners. "I fear if we could get, we could not safely take more than one such man."

We cannot step on toes much anymore. Must be careful, be very, very careful. He pauses, looks at the half-finished letter, pen poised for the next sentence. His gaze wanders to his shirt sleeve. It is stained with little ink spots sprayed in a mist of black and gray nearly up to the button, residue of innumerable pen pricks on the lip of an inkwell. A lot of letters lately, mostly about the cabinet, that messy business. He has tried repeatedly to bring order to it in his mind's eye, imagining the cabinet positions as if they were a series of neat little cubbyholes. Put this one here, that one there. Fill that slot with this man from that part of the country. Don't alienate those people, or you are asking for it. Have got to help so-and-so, he did right by us in the election. It ought to fit all together, nice and neat.

But the nation just isn't like that now; it doesn't seem linear to him, neat and orderly. It is more like those leaves, or the ink splotches on what was once a clean white shirt. Matters are swirling, sometimes exhilarating, sometimes terrifying. "What is our present condition?" he wrote to a fellow Republican a few days ago. "We have just carried an election on principles fairly stated to the people. Now we are told in advance, the government shall be broken up, unless we surrender."[10] Sometimes he pictures a map of the United States, that familiar shape with its improbable sense of balance, riding like a stately ship. Then he sees the South, the lower stern of the ship ripped away, and the map loses its symmetry, it goes awry and becomes something else, something other than what it is supposed to be.

"I shall defer them as long as possible," Lincoln finishes his letter to Seward, referring to Cabinet appointments, "to avoid being teased to insanity to make changes." Teased to insanity. Yes, that is it. But isn't that democracy? "A republic if you can keep it," Benjamin Franklin once said. How true. It is no small thing to keep a republic; it is no small thing to keep a country.

Part One

EARLY

IMAGINATIONS

FATHERS

When Jefferson Davis was eight years old in summer 1816, his family sent him away from his home on the Mississippi frontier to attend St. Thomas College in Kentucky. His father Samuel Davis, a farmer of modest means, wanted his youngest son to receive a decent education, even at the high cost of sixty-five dollars per year and some marital stress, for Jefferson's mother opposed the idea. "I was sent on horseback through what was then called 'the Wilderness,'" he later recalled; "there were no steamboats, nor were there stage-coaches traversing the country." Samuel did not tell his wife about their son's journey until Jefferson was gone.[1]

It was an eventful trip. Jefferson met Andrew Jackson while traveling through Tennessee, an experience he never forgot. He seemed to do well at St. Thomas's, a Catholic institution. "I was the only Protestant boy remaining, and also the smallest boy in the school," he later said, and "the priests were particularly kind to me." Jefferson excelled at Latin and Greek, particularly for a child of his age, and he stayed for two terms. By summer 1817, however, his mother compelled Samuel to fetch her son home.[2]

Jefferson found his father in the fields when he arrived. Samuel "was a man of deep feeling, though he sought to repress the expression of it whenever practicable," his son recalled. But on this occasion the usually taciturn father abandoned all restraint and hugged Jefferson "with more emotion than I had ever seen him exhibit, and kissed me repeatedly." It was the only such outburst he ever remembered from his father.[3]

Jefferson expressed deep respect and devotion for Samuel, calling him a "silent, undemonstrative man of action" whose words "had great weight with the community in which he lived."[4] In truth, however, he must have harbored mixed feelings for this "silent, undemonstrative man" who eschewed overt affection and preserved an emotional distance from his family. Six years after embracing his son in a Mississippi cotton field, Samuel died. Jefferson was away at school in Kentucky again—this time at Transylvania University in Lexington—when he received the news. His reaction was stoical almost to the point of callousness, as he wrote mechanically to his sister that he had "lost a parent ever dear to me." Jefferson Davis rarely mentioned his father again.[5]

Samuel Davis and Thomas Lincoln would have found much in common. Both were hardworking small farmers who relocated frequently from place to place. Samuel moved from Georgia to Kentucky, to Louisiana, and finally to Mississippi.[6] Thomas Lincoln grew up in Kentucky; he was twenty-five when Samuel, ten years his senior, settled in an area of Kentucky not far away. The Lincolns had roots in Virginia and Pennsylvania. Thomas eventually moved his family to Pigeon Creek in Indiana and then to Illinois. Both Samuel and Thomas were community leaders in their way. Both valued education as a means for advancing their sons' futures. "Knowledge is power," Samuel wrote Jefferson in his last letter to him.[7] Thomas Lincoln might have said the same to his son Abraham, whose diligent pursuit of self-education has become part of American folklore. "As a usual thing, Mr. Lincoln never made Abe quit reading to do anything if he could avoid it," remembered Sarah Bush Lincoln, Abraham's sister. "He would rather do it himself first."[8]

Jefferson's relationship with Samuel was reserved, but Abraham Lincoln can only be described as fundamentally alienated from his father. If Thomas wished to see his son acquire an education, he also beat Abraham when he neglected farm chores for books. Abraham felt the back of Thomas's hand for other reasons as well, to the point that the boy sometimes "dropt a kind of silent unwelcome tear, as evidence of his sensations."[9] The two developed an edgy, strained relationship by the time Abe was a teenager. Thomas thought his son was lazy, impertinent, and irreverent. For his part, Abraham was dismayed by his father's lack of ambition, his financial carelessness, and his general ignorance. Thomas "never did more in the way of writing than to bunglingly sign his own name," Lincoln wrote.[10] This lack of education was almost the only characteristic Lincoln consistently attached to his father, along with a saying Thomas often quoted that stuck in Abraham's head: "If you make a bad bargain, *hug* it the tighter."[11] Abraham thought his father was indeed a bad bargain, but he did not follow Thomas's advice; rather, he moved as far away as he could, leaving the family farm while in his teens and never returning if he could help it. When Thomas lay on his deathbed in 1851, Abraham refused to visit him, writing his stepbrother that "if we could meet now, it is doubtful whether it would not be more painful than pleasant." He did not attend his father's funeral.[12]

Fathers like Thomas Lincoln and Samuel Davis were supposed to fill multiple roles in early America. As they moved in increasing numbers from farm fields to professions and businesses that separated them from the home and their children's presence, various commentators suggested they compensate by cultivating a closer, more intimate relationship with their children. They were to instruct their sons in the pragmatic business of earning a living, and they were to set examples of competence as breadwinners. They were also moral instructors, supplementing the role of the good "republican mother" by passing along to their sons lessons of thrift, industry, and ethical behavior. Fathers were essentially conservative figures in the sense that they preserved a secure, solid foundation within the family upon which the child would construct a stable self-identity and personal value system.[13]

Abraham Lincoln and Jefferson Davis idolized their mothers—and, in Lincoln's case, his stepmother—with a fairly straightforward, nineteenth-century sentimental adoration.[14] Their relationships with their fathers were a more complex, and in many ways a more revealing, matter. Samuel Davis and Thomas Lincoln affected their sons in a variety of ways, but they also left holes, empty spots in Abraham's and Jefferson's lives. Lincoln's contempt for his illiterate father is palpable, so much so that it is doubtful he felt his father could ever have anything worthwhile to teach him. In fact, Lincoln felt compelled to lecture his father occasionally on the values of hard work and prudence.[15] Samuel Davis may have been a more effective moral instructor for his children, but he was not a paragon of prosperity. When he instructed Jefferson to "use every possible means to acquire usefull [*sic*] knowledge" as the best path to prosperity, he did so as a penniless man who felt he had not adequately followed his own advice.[16]

Thomas's and Samuel's primary contribution seems to have been negative, examples against which their sons reacted. Lincoln's indulgent and kindly care for his boys—"had they sh[i]t in Lincoln's hat and rubbed it on his boots, he would have laughed and thought it smart," a friend irritably observed—was a marked contrast to Thomas's erratic, quarrelsome, and sometimes violent ways.[17] Davis named his son Samuel after his father, but he established a much different relationship with "Le Man," as he called the boy. "He was Mr. Davis' first thought when the door opened," his wife Varina recalled, "and the little fellow would wait as patiently as possible, sometimes a quarter of an hour, at the door to kiss his father first." Davis was also nearly Lincolnian in his permissive parenting; Varina remembered their daughter Margaret "would as soon as she could talk say, 'I wish I could see my father, he would let me be bad.'"[18]

Another consequence of Thomas's and Samuel's distant fathering lay in their sons' strong, almost overweening ambition for success.[19] Lincoln's law partner marveled at his seemingly bottomless desire to succeed, writing that Lincoln's ambition was "a little engine that knew no rest." Davis was no less driven; ambition and the desire for fame and recognition were key in his psychological makeup.[20] Ambition can be fed by a number of factors, and scholars have noted in both Lincoln and Davis a direct connection between their fathers' failures and their own energetic pursuit of success. In Lincoln this was a particularly pronounced trait. When as a teenager he fled the family farm in Indiana to pursue his fortune farther west, he fled Thomas Lincoln and the dirt-under-your-fingernails farming life that his father represented.[21]

Unlike Lincoln, Davis never spoke disparagingly of his father and seemed to bear him no enmity. Samuel Davis left his younger son a legacy of failure, however, whether Jefferson cared to admit it or not. Samuel himself acknowledged this. When Jefferson was fourteen his father traveled to Philadelphia in a vain attempt to recover a family inheritance that might have helped pay his debts. He was unable to do so, and in a sad letter to Jefferson shortly before he died he wrote that his life was ending with "mischiefs and misery." Samuel wrote Jefferson, "That you may be happy and shine in society when your father is beyond the reach of harm is the most ardent desire of my heart." His father's stark juxtaposition of his son's future happy life with his own death and subsequent release from care was not lost on Jefferson. When Samuel died a year later, Jefferson wrote his sister, "I lost a parent ever dear to me, but rendered more so (if possible), by the disasters that attended his declining years." One suspects that the twin images of Samuel Davis and economic ruin remained entwined in Jefferson's mind thereafter.[22]

This ambition pushed Lincoln and Davis into politics, putting them in a position to think, act, and feel nationally as they sought acclaim through the acquisition of national public offices. Even more important, they sought in the national arena the fathers they had not possessed in their homes. Lacking faith in their domestic fathers, Abraham and Jefferson sought strong and reliable father figures elsewhere, and this search proved to be the foundation of their national imaginations.

For Davis this figure was his brother Joseph, whom he often referred to affectionately as "Brother Joe."[23] Brother Joe was nearly twenty years older than Jefferson. He was a man of contradictory impulses, restless and ambitious yet soberingly serious, paternalistic to a fault yet often indifferent to others' feelings. Gifted with a first-rate intellect and what one contemporary referred to as "inquisitiveness of mind," he was a learned man, an intellectual, and a genteel Southern patriarch. This complex man became in many ways Jefferson's surrogate father.[24]

Joseph was a successful attorney, politician, and planter in Mississippi by the time his young brother reached adolescence. He had helped frame Mississippi's first constitution, he possessed a wide network of friends and political acquaintances, and his law practice was among the most lucrative in the state. His plantation, Hurricane, stretched for five thousand acres in a broad loop of the Mississippi River known as Davis Bend and was worked by over three hundred slaves. Here was an eminently prosperous breadwinner to set off against the failed fortunes of Joseph's and Jefferson's father. In a particularly poignant bit of irony, Samuel Davis was working on land owned by Joseph when he died.[25]

Joseph carried the model of the successful father/earner one step further by becoming Jefferson's economic benefactor. In 1835, he in effect gave Jefferson a twenty-three hundred acre plantation farther down Davis Bend, which Jefferson named Brierfield. Joseph's name remained on the property, however; and one is struck by the similarity between his paternalistic, proprietary supervision of his brother's property and the close, careful guidance offered by fathers over sons who lacked managerial and farming experience.[26] More than the successful breadwinner, Joseph was Jefferson's teacher and instructor. He taught him how to run Brierfield and, on the occasions that Jefferson was away from it, undertook its management himself. He passed on tidbits of information and advice concerning land management, crop prices, seasonal preparations, and other farming miscellany. Referring for example to some necessary labor in clearing land for growing oats and corn,

he wrote Jefferson not to overwork himself or his slaves during the hot summer season: "You Can judge better being on the Spot than I can, . . . I will
however Caution you against an error that I have too often committed . . .
an attempt at *too much*."[27]

There was more to Joseph's supervision, however. His instructions and
examples carried a broad moral dimension. He had quite definite ideas concerning the proper manner in which a Southern planter and gentleman
should behave. He was something of a paternal extremist, particularly where
slaves—whom he often referred to as "my people"—were concerned. Borrowing from the ideas of Robert Owen and other labor reformers, Joseph ran
his large slave population with a genteel racial benevolence that earned him
the reputation as the most lenient slave owner in the region.[28] "The less
people are governed, the more submissive they will be to control," Varina
remembered him saying, and he followed this maxim with a remarkably placid
ruling style at Hurricane. He created a mock trial system for slaves to mete
out punishments to other slaves. "Corporal punishment was not permitted,"
according to Varina, "except upon conviction of the culprit by a jury of peers.
The sentence was, even then, more often remitted than carried out."[29]
Joseph's slaves reportedly ran a "variety shop" and kept a significant portion
of their wages earned from outside labor. There is some evidence that Joseph
allowed these practices out of a genuine humanitarian impulse.[30] But the
truth is more accurately conveyed in Joseph's own words; this was benevolence in the name of power, generosity in the form of a somewhat looser than
normal racial leash.[31]

Joseph passed these ideas on to Jefferson, serving as his moral and intellectual instructor. He also gave his younger brother a stable family center
that was lacking in Jefferson's life after Samuel Davis died. Hurricane became something of a surrogate home for Jefferson, who spent his adolescence
and early youth attending a variety of academies, colleges, and eventually
West Point. Brother Joe's plantation gave Jefferson a semblance of a sense
of place, and if it was not exactly a haven it was at least a place he could go,
and one that he visited frequently throughout his life.[32]

Joseph was breadwinner, teacher, and conservator; he was the primary
father figure in Jefferson Davis's life. They were kin, and yet a close examination reveals a relationship oriented toward national issues and politics. A
primary manifestation of Joseph's breadwinner role in his brother's life was
to direct Jefferson firmly toward the political milieu within which he himself moved, the Democratic party. It was Joseph who eventually propelled

Jefferson into an active political career. Joseph himself stayed away from the political arena, in his lifetime holding only one office as state legislator. "In all these measures I am '*but a passenger*,'" he wrote Jefferson in 1838, concerning some pending state political battles, "and mean not [to] trouble myself about the Safety of the Ship."[33]

Joseph passed along to Jefferson not only his own unrequited love of political officeholding but also his political opinions and prejudices. Varina Davis later wrote of the "years of continuous study and calm comparison of opinions with a wise and decent man like his elder brother" as the primary impetus behind Jefferson Davis's long political career.[34] Joseph's letters were usually filled with political news and advice interwoven with family and personal matters. During a trip to Washington, D.C., in winter 1838, for example, Jefferson filled his older brother in on the doings of Congress and Joseph's hero John C. Calhoun, who, Jefferson wrote, planned to spark a debate by presenting "his resolution denying the right of the abolitionists to petition the senate." Jefferson hoped "that the discussion will be calmly conducted." Joseph responded by keeping Jefferson abreast of Mississippi's political developments and beseeched him to "send me any reports or Speeches that you may think worth the postage and any others that our members will Frank."[35]

Joseph did more than just pass along the political news; he acquainted his brother with states' rights, proslavery constitutionalism, and Southern political principles in general. He saw to it that Jefferson was well aware of what should and should not meet with the approval of a Mississippi planter. "Since I left Mississippi I have heard nothing [but] a continual din of Politicks," he wrote to Jefferson during a business trip to Lexington, Kentucky, in 1840. Joseph had met Cassius Clay aboard a steamboat and heard the fiery abolitionist hold forth for two hours on the "wonderful effect of reducing the number of slaves in Kentucky" and similar subjects. With the knowing wink of a mentor tutoring a willing student, Joseph wrote to Jefferson, "You may readily Suppose the feelings of any Southern man on hearing Such principles in Such a place." In a political and ideological sense Joseph wanted to see to it that Jefferson Davis was brought up right.[36]

American fathers were expected to provide a home, a physical space for their children to grow. Joseph the political father provided Jefferson the political space within which to grow: his library at Hurricane. Known simply as "the office," it was a large, book-filled room in which, as Varina put it, "the brothers sat when they were not riding their plantations, and talked of books, elementary law, of agricultural experiments [and] commented on the day's doings."[37] Here Jefferson "read aloud to his brother the Congressional debate," and Joseph introduced him to the writings of prominent American politicians and philosophers, particularly the Founders. Joseph's plantation library was stocked with the *Federalist Papers,* volumes of congressional debates, and the treatises from Greece, Rome, and Europe that had formed the context of the Framers' intellectual world.[38]

Joseph emphasized national politics, with national documents and books exuding an American point of view. Their thinking here was not particularly original. Davis imbibed from Joseph fairly standard political ideas for a Southern gentleman of his class and time. He learned to value an America that preserved local control, state sovereignty, and Southern autonomy. He revered the Constitution as a "sacred compact" and the Virginia Resolutions, with their paean to state sovereignty and localism, as final sources of political authority.[39]

Joseph gave his brother to understand that the American nation was a thing of abstraction, of high ideals far removed from the hurly-burly of everyday politics. The office was a place to hatch ideas, read debates, and ponder political and intellectual imponderables. It was a place where Joseph and Jefferson could retreat from the fluid, complex, and dirty relativism of politics and seek certain high, timeless ideas and principles. It was a place for preservation of ideas and values, a physical space in which Joseph acted the role of father by giving himself and Jefferson a solid, objective ground upon which to think and reason.

Joseph's office was a seedbed for Jefferson Davis's nationalism and the physical space in which he constructed his seminal ideas about what it meant to be an American. The legacy of this initiation possessed several facets. Fundamentally, Joseph passed along to Jefferson a love of politics on a high intellectual plane, coupled with a distaste for party politicking. Joseph's physical withdrawal from political matters was matched by an intensification of his detached, intellectual interest in political and constitutional issues. During the long hours of conversation and reading with Jefferson in "the office," Joseph gave to his brother a sense of national politics as a matter of carefully reasoned abstractions and polite, genteel debate. "He, like his brother Jefferson, could not comprehend any one differing from him in political policy after hearing the reasons upon which his opinion was based," Varina wrote of her brother-in-law; and he "was prone to suspect insincerity on the part of the dissenter."[40]

This was politics of the drawing room—the office—not the legislative chamber or party convention hall. Lincoln would never have been comfortable here, but it was the stuff of life for Davis. The office contained the cold, dry pages of the *Congressional Globe,* the julep served by one of "my people" wearing fine livery and a waxen smile, and Mr. Calhoun and states' rights laid out in logical precision. In many ways, Jefferson Davis never quite left Joseph Davis's office, imagining the national public square as a place of abstraction and deference in ways quite similar to the space and ideas his brother provided for him.

Lincoln had no equivalent of the office, and he lacked any such relationship as that of Joseph and Jefferson Davis. His family was more of a trial than a source of guidance. "You are not *lazy,* and still you are an *idler,*" Lincoln irritably wrote to his half brother—and by association his father—in 1848. "I doubt whether since I saw you, you have done a good whole day's work."[41] There is at least a grain of truth to the Lincoln myth of the self-made man, for he never found much to learn from his family, and no one stepped forward to act the part of a surrogate father.

As a result, Lincoln sometimes downplayed the value of fatherly relationships, discouraging young men from seeking out mentors and counseling self-reliance. He dismissed the time-honored practice of aspirant attorneys seeking the advice and counsel of older, established lawyers. He told others to follow his example by simply reading the relevant texts and drawing their own conclusions. "It is but a small matter whether you read *with* any body or not," Lincoln advised a young man named Isham Reavis who had asked to study law under him. "Get the books, and read and study them till, you understand them in their principle [*sic*] features; and that is the main thing."[42]

On the other hand, many people observed Lincoln's fatherly bearing toward others who were not family. He reminded friends and neighbors of a kindly old patriarch, even when he was still quite young, and he acted the part of fatherly mentor for many young men. Though dismissing Reavis's request he gave him little bits of sage advice, closing with the admonition, "Always bear in mind that your own resolution to succeed, is more important than any other one thing." The same Lincoln who told young lawyers to tough it out alone was "kind and tender to all members of the bar, especially the younger ones whom he always assisted."[43]

Lincoln was more ambivalent toward the father role than Davis, who seems to have slid rather easily into the part Joseph envisioned for him. Lincoln was not altogether certain whether he needed a father, real or otherwise.[44] But even as he rejected the notion of legal and political patronage and put as much distance between himself and his own father as he could, he found in the national realm father figures to fill the roles of breadwinner, teacher, and conservator in his life. He turned to two men: Henry Clay and George Washington.

Lincoln's admiration for Clay dated back to his youth. "He has constantly been the most loved, the most implicitly followed by his friends, and the most dreaded by his opponents, of all living American politicians," Lincoln rhapsodized in an emotional 1851 eulogy on Clay. Thomas had died a few months previously, and Lincoln had almost no reaction at all. The contrast between this response and his lengthy, heartfelt memorial for Clay is striking, and although there is no indication that Lincoln consciously weighed the relative value of the two men, one cannot help but notice the stark dichotomy between Thomas, the bad bargain who "could never do more than bunglingly sign his own name," and Clay, "whose eloquence has not been surpassed" and who had "the effective power to move the heart of man."[45]

Lincoln's eulogy suggested metaphorical father/son relationships between Clay the elder statesman and Lincoln and his generation. "Our country is prosperous and powerful; but could it have been quite all it has been, and is, and is to be, without Henry Clay?" Lincoln asked. Clay "apostrophised the names of Otis, of Henry, and of Washington," he wrote, and he drew analogies between Clay and Thomas Jefferson. Clay was born when America was born, Lincoln pointed out; "They have been companions ever since. The nation has passed its perils . . . the child has reached his manhood, his middle age, his old age, and is dead." In the national "family," Clay was for Lincoln a wise patriarch.[46]

Clay was also the model of a successful national politician to Lincoln the political aspirant. Much of this influence had to do with Clay's own origins as a humble man who used the political ladder to gain success and fame, as Lincoln wished to do. He could also see himself following Clay's example as a self-educated, self-made man. Remembering perhaps his own troubled attempts to gain an education for himself, he wrote that "Mr. Clay's lack of a more perfect early education . . . teaches at least one profitable lesson; it teaches that, in this country, one can scarcely be so poor, but that, if he will, he can acquire sufficient education to get through the world respectably."[47]

Lincoln frequently cited Clay's example as an eminent political success story, an accomplished winner in the legislative chamber and party caucus. "His political friends . . . repeatedly appealed to the people to rally under his standard, as a presidential candidate, as the man who had exhibited the power to . . . preserve the Union," Lincoln declared in 1854. And even though Clay never made it quite that far, his story as a principled yet successful political professional obviously was an inspiration to the young, ambitious Lincoln. Clay's life was his work, as it was to so many men of the early nineteenth century, and just as the successful Jacksonian father passed along to his son the business skills necessary to succeed in the world, so did Lincoln draw from this quasi father the professional lessons and example that Thomas had never provided.[48]

Clay was a moral teacher for Lincoln as well, on several levels, one of which was that most important of skills for a politician and lawyer, public expression. He was surely thinking of his personal standards of oratory and writing when he praised Clay's political speeches as a type of "eloquence [that] did not consist . . . of types and figures . . . but rather of that deeply earnest and impassioned tone, and manner which can proceed only from great sincerity and a thorough conviction of the justice and importance of his cause."[49]

Lincoln saw himself as the heir to Clay's vigorous nationalism and fervent devotion to preserving the Union and restricting the spread of slavery. In 1854 Stephen Douglas invoked both Clay and Daniel Webster as sources of approval in his decision to break the Missouri Compromise and simultaneously attacked Lincoln for violating Clay's principles by imperiling the Union in opposing Douglas's plans. Lincoln rushed to Clay's defense with the indignation of a natural descendant who had been wronged and denied his birthright. Clay and his cohorts "were greatly devoted to the Union," Lincoln declared; "to the small measure of my ability, was I ever less so?" Douglas was "trying to wrap himself up in the cloak of Henry Clay, a statesman in defence of whose principles [Lincoln] had battled all his life." Lincoln even went so far as to cite his and Clay's common Kentucky roots in an attempt to shut out Douglas the outsider and stated that "nothing but the most brazen impudence would dare to take the name of Clay on his lips, by a man so destitute of his principles."[50]

Clay was for Lincoln an effective father figure on two important levels, breadwinner and teacher. He provided a model of the successful professional politician, and he was a useful moral instructor in the realm of principles and politics. The nation and the Great Pacificator were inextricably connected in Lincoln's mind. But Clay was a distant figure; Lincoln had never met him. Unlike Davis, Lincoln had to search outside his immediate family for a person to fill these roles. There were also boundaries to Lincoln's idolization of

Clay, more so than any Davis seems to have felt concerning his brother. Lincoln raised no public objection when the Whigs chose William Henry Harrison over Clay as their presidential candidate in 1840 and Zachary Taylor over Clay again in 1848. He wanted his party to win those elections, and he knew Clay stood no chance of doing so.[51]

Lincoln's willingness to compromise on these political issues illustrates the limits of Clay's role as father figure. Clay provided an example of a political breadwinner, and he was a model of the self-made, self-educated man Lincoln believed himself to be. In the end, however, Clay lacked one important element of the father figure; he was not a conservator, a provider of fundamental stability. How could he have been? He was a calming influence in the rough political tumults of the early nineteenth century; he was a conciliator who brought together warring factions to achieve compromise and peace, but Lincoln could himself see that Clay's solutions to the passions aroused by sectionalism and slavery were at best temporary. Clay was a man who periodically calmed the national political waters, but he could not keep the storms from continually recurring.

Lincoln seemed to understand these limits, if perhaps only on an instinctive level. In his eulogy on Clay, he quoted at length the language of an unidentified "public journal" that seemed to give Clay the status of father/conservator. "On at least three important occasions, he has quelled our civil commotions," Lincoln quoted, "and in our last internal discord"—the crisis of 1850—"he left the shades of private life and gave the death blow to fraternal strife . . . in a series of Senatorial efforts, which in themselves would bring immortality." This language suggests the conservator, the father who achieves immortality by preserving future "sons" and their nation by permanently destroying his and their enemies. But then when he used his own words to describe Clay's career, Lincoln's emphases were quite different. He pointed out that Clay was a "party man" in a tumultuous political atmosphere, a player in difficult and hostile partisan wars rather than a supreme and immortal Lawgiver. Lincoln also pointed out that Clay had not slain once and for all the demons of disunion and strife over the meaning of human liberty; quite the contrary. For Lincoln, Clay's ideals of equality and liberty were high values of which the present generation had unfortunately lost sight. Clay's legacy was firmly set against those "who would shiver into fragments the Union" and against "a few, but increasing number of men, who, for the sake of perpetuating slavery, are beginning to assail and to ridicule the white man's charter of freedom—

the declaration that 'all men are created equal.'" "The like was not heard in the fresher days of the Republic," Lincoln believed.[52]

This Henry Clay was an important, wise man, but he had not really conserved anything; he had not performed an essential fatherly role of preservation for the American family. Lincoln admired the Great Pacificator, but he seemed to understand that pacification was a somewhat different matter from preservation, being less solid and objective. Clay had not given to Lincoln what Joseph had given to Jefferson, with his office and its physical space in which one attained objective truths and realities. For that Lincoln turned elsewhere, to the distant, abstract father figure of George Washington.

At the very time his relationship with Thomas was growing increasingly strained, Lincoln's favorite book was Parson Weems's *Life of George Washington,* with its characterization of Washington as the American moral archetype and its stories of George's father as a man who forgave misdeeds and who laid out garden plants to spell his son's name. The contrast between Washington and Thomas was stark and immediate for this young man. He kept a copy of Weems's biography on a small shelf between two logs in the Lincoln home, almost as a talisman against his father's abuse and failures. For the young Lincoln, "George Washington was the Greatest of all of them and was his Great favorite," according to a friend.[53]

As Lincoln grew older and became actively involved in the political controversies of his day, his opinion of the Revolution's legacy and the Founding generation grew to be somewhat more ambivalent. Like so many other public speakers and politicians, he enlisted "the Revolutionary patriarchs" to support his arguments, citing the Founders in speeches on the National Bank, the Mexican War, the Declaration of Independence, the Northwest Ordinance, and slavery in the territories.[54] On a more general level, however, he was uncertain as to whether the pursuit of personal fame, which he believed animated the Founders, was an adequate motivation for antebellum Americans living in a time when higher moral laws such as human equality were being broken.[55]

But this ambivalence seems not to have extended to the greatest member of the Founding generation. Lincoln expressed concern about that generation as a whole, and he wondered about the specific actions and ideas associated with specific Founders such as Hamilton, but such doubts rarely extended to the specific persona of Washington himself.[56] He tended to separate Washington from the other Founders. There was the Revolution and its luminaries; but then one cut above, there was George Washington.[57] In speeches supporting the National Bank, for example, Lincoln referred to him as "the immortal Washington," using language of timelessness he did not employ in the same speech for James Madison (or Henry Clay). He endeavored in the words of one spectator "to prove that Washington never done a wrong thing in his life" while using Madison simply to support the Bank's constitutionality.[58]

Washington performed for Lincoln, metaphorically and in the abstract, the task of father/conservator for the nation that Joseph Davis and his office performed in a more direct fashion for Jefferson Davis.[59] It was Washington, not Clay, whom Lincoln invoked as the ultimate authority for these values, an objective, final source of national moral authority, a conservator of stability, law, and order.[60] He later expressed indignation that what he took to be the simple, objective meaning of Washington's words could be twisted. "Let us be diverted by none of these sophistical contrivances," he declared in an impassioned speech at New York's Cooper Institute in February 1860, "such as invocations to Washington, imploring men to unsay what Washington said, and undo what Washington did."[61]

Undoing what Washington said and what he did—this carried implications of attempts to alter that which was permanent, changing that which should remain changeless and stable. Here was an invocation by Lincoln of Washington the father/conservator, an appeal to qualities that Henry Clay, for all his greatness, lacked. Several scholars have commented on the metaphorical father/son relationship Lincoln seemed to feel between himself and Washington.[62] Nor was he alone in this; Washington became an integral component of American mythology as a "Founding Father."[63]

These surrogate, distant fathers—Washington, Clay, and Joseph Davis—were an integral part of Lincoln's and Davis's sense of American identity. In Davis's case, Joseph created for his brother an environment in which Jefferson could envision a certain political milieu of state sovereignty, Southern localism, racial hierarchy, and deference, all constructed and defended in the abstract realm of parlor politics among gentleman who shared ties of principle. For Lincoln, Clay and Washington provided an objective grounding for lives lived in the rough-and-tumble national political realm that were at once principled and pragmatic. Davis's politics mirrored his brother's when he became a national figure. "I can have no relations to others which would interfere with those I bear to you," Jefferson wrote his brother, "and whoever is your enemy must needs be mine." For his part, when Lincoln engaged in the great political battles of the 1850s, he quoted Henry Clay so

frequently that many listeners, and some scholars, had trouble distinguishing Lincoln's and Clay's words.[64]

But in finding these father figures, Lincoln and Davis engaged in quite
different behavior, and in these differences we find planted the seeds of what
would eventually constitute two differing visions of America. Davis did not
have to engage in a concentrated effort of creation to conjure a fatherly figure from the distant past; Joseph was a constant, tangible presence in his
everyday life. The authority that Joseph wielded over Jefferson, and consequently the style that he communicated, was familial and immediate, the
stuff of close conversations between trusted and trustworthy men who knew
each other's hearts. Lincoln, on the other hand, had to conjure his national
fathers from distant individuals whom he had never met. Joseph was for
Jefferson a product of family ties and face-to-face relationships in relatively
intimate physical settings; Lincoln's fathers were acts of rhetoric. He was
compelled to re-create Clay and Washington's power and authority in the
spoken and written word, to make the distant seem close and the abstract
concrete, both for himself and his listeners.

Lincoln engaged in greater and more creative acts of imagination, based
in turn upon still other acts (Parson Weems knew nothing of the "real" Washington and did not much care to learn). He had to stretch his mind further,
work harder, to conjure the father figures of Clay and Washington. Does this
mean that because it required the greater effort, Lincoln's nationalism was
stronger? Perhaps. But at the very least, it would mean that, early on, Lincoln's
America (and the fathers within it) was largely a matter of rhetoric and abstraction while Davis's America was a matter of personal relationships, honed
in the closed space of his brother's office. Here lay the foundations for quite
disparate understandings of the American public square.

FRIENDS

        By the time he was fifteen, Abraham Lincoln had developed a facility for talking to whoever appeared in the countryside around his family's homestead at Pigeon Creek, Indiana. "If a man rode up on horseback, Abe would be the first one out, up on the fence asking questions," his uncle recalled. Lincoln became particularly adept at using his storytelling talents to enter into conversations with strangers. A childhood friend remembered that he "would go to the store of an afternoon and evening, and his jokes and stories were so odd, so witty, so humorous, that all the people of the town would gather around him. He would sometimes keep a crowd about him until midnight."[1]

    Lincoln carried these habits with him when he left Pigeon Creek in 1831 and set off for the raw little town of New Salem in Illinois. Whether by accident or design, he quickly placed himself in a position to become acquainted with a wide range of individuals. In a later age we might call this "networking," but there was in the young Lincoln little of the self-conscious, even cynical manipulation that the term now implies. He seems to have "networked" impulsively, by habit more than by design.

His wide-ranging choice of occupations put him in an excellent position to do so. Lincoln's first job in New Salem was as the clerk for the local election board, affording him a fine chance to meet the town's residents. He made the most of it. "When votes were coming in slowly, Lincoln began to entertain the crowd at the polls with a few attempts at storytelling," his law partner, William Herndon, wrote; "the recital of a few good stories easily established him in the good graces of all New Salem."[2]

Lincoln also carried a fondness for general stores with him to Illinois. He became "a sort of a Clerk" and later part owner of a store in New Salem, and he soon turned the place into a gathering point for anyone with a penchant for conversation. He frequented general stores throughout his early years in New Salem and Springfield. He had no particular affinity for the business (Lincoln was a terrible salesman), but he grasped the opportunity the stores afforded for introducing himself to others.[3]

His appointment as New Salem's postmaster, a job nobody else seemed to want, also gave him an ideal opportunity to see and meet the citizens of Sangamon County and the surrounding ones. Lincoln was renowned for his willingness to travel miles to deliver mail, wearing a hat stuffed full of letters he would distribute while he walked. The people of Sangamon County took these sojourns as evidence of his kindness, but they were at the same time opportunities for conversation among a wide circle of people.[4]

Stories of Lincoln's willingness to help his neighbors, his generosity toward others, and his honest, forthright demeanor abounded in New Salem, Springfield, and elsewhere.[5] When he offered to do chores for needy farm boys, or walked six miles to return six cents he had erroneously charged a customer, he was doing more than proving he had a good heart. He was also placing himself in a position to become known by sight and name to the entire region.[6]

He was motivated to meet people at least in part by his intense ambition.[7] But there was more to Lincoln's networking than his personal desire to introduce himself to great numbers of people. He also acted in a general way as a communications facilitator, a subtle mediator of interaction among the many friends and acquaintances he had made. This ability was evident in his business dealings. He was involved in many little informal and formal business transactions with his neighbors, acting as "official man for the whole Community, never charging one cent for his time and trouble," according to a neighbor.[8] He was a witness for a bill of sale, a guarantor of a small loan, or an attestant for a mortgage or a deed. A week before Christmas 1830 he appraised "an Estray Mare Taken up by Jonathan B. Brown"; a few months later he acted as witness for a "penal Sum of twenty Dollars" drawn up by James Eastep "for the conveyance of a certain tract or parcel of land" in St. Clair County willed to his wife by her deceased father. Relatively insignificant by themselves, taken together these transactions made Lincoln a sort of roving agent for economic interaction and goodwill.[9]

Lincoln's career in the state legislature also suggests a young man with a keen interest in creating new and better lines of communication in Illinois, clearly one reason behind his active support of legislation to move the state capital from Vandalia to Springfield, the former being inaccessible to much of the state because of its location. The Whig party's ambitious program of railroad construction and river improvements, which Lincoln strongly supported, likewise created more efficient means of interaction among Illinois's citizens.[10]

Lincoln was himself a line of communication of sorts. His letters to the many friends and acquaintances he had made in the region were vehicles for passing on news and information. His correspondence from the 1840s assumed a certain pattern in this regard, beginning with whatever personal business he wished to discuss and often ending with a few brief lines about the political or social doings to which he was privy. "The news here is . . . ," "The outline of things here are . . . ," or, on the other hand, "Nothing new here" were stock Lincoln phrases. At the same time, his letters served to connect his growing network of friends, acquaintances, and political contacts.[11]

To "all our friends—They are too numerous to be now named individually," Lincoln toasted at a formal dinner in Springfield during summer 1837.[12] It was an apt declaration carrying personal meaning for him, for by the time he was thirty years old he knew an extraordinary number of people. In one sense, there was nothing unusual in this; Tocqueville noted Americans' proclivity for forming associations with one another on the slightest pretext.[13] Lincoln's friendship-forming habits, however, were hardly typical. Had he been a farmer or farm laborer, he would have known a few of his neighbors. If he had been permanently established as a storekeeper, postman, or state-level politician he would have known a few more. Lincoln had done all of these things.[14]

He understood friendship as just such a loose network of acquaintances, a circle in which the bonds between him and his friends were founded on his storytelling, his humorous anecdotes, and the lively dialogues that he could almost effortlessly generate and use to set strangers immediately at ease.[15] It was a remarkably open and far-ranging network with relatively few limitations. He disliked the closed and rigidly formal social settings of the drawing room; he was not, as Herndon put it, "a society man."[16] Though Lincoln increasingly tended to associate with people whose party affiliations were, like his, with the Whigs, his friends were not limited by party loyalties.[17] Stephen Douglas, for example, frequented backroom conversations in the general store in Springfield where Lincoln held forth.[18] It was a circle of friends with a distinctly male tone, however. Lincoln felt awkward around women. "He always disliked to wait upon the ladies," recalled one observer from Lincoln's days as a clerk, preferring instead "to wait upon the men and boys." His conversations, stories, and anecdotes were largely ways of drawing other men to him, and the various circles he frequented to discuss politics and public events were almost exclusively male.[19]

Lincoln created this wide circle of friends for himself, but his own place within it was complex and contradictory. On the one hand, he was gregarious, trustworthy, and honest. Many people in New Salem, and later in Springfield, attested to his scrupulous integrity in business and everyday life. "I believed he was thoroughly honest," said one of the men who backed Lincoln's purchase of the general store. "He had no money, but I would have advanced him more had he asked for it." Hence the sobriquet "Honest Abe," which was attached to him during his residency in New Salem and followed him ever after.[20]

"Honest," however, carries multiple meanings. The word is associated with truthfulness and sincerity, but it can also carry connotations of frank openness, even a certain naïveté. In most cases, Lincoln placed his trust in reliable people. His relationship with Joshua Speed was a good example. When Lincoln left New Salem in 1837 to settle in Springfield, he arrived on a borrowed horse with all his luggage contained in two saddlebags. He knew Speed only vaguely. "He came into my store," Speed remembered, "set his saddlebags on the counter, and inquired what the furniture for a single bedstead would cost." When it looked as if Lincoln would be unable to afford neither the bed nor much in the way of living expenses, Speed offered to share his room with Lincoln. "Where is your room?" he asked. When Speed pointed upstairs, Lincoln "took his saddlebags on his arm, went upstairs, set them down on the floor, came down again, and with a face beaming with pleasure and smiles, exclaimed, 'Well, Speed, I'm moved.'" Joshua Speed quickly became a trusted and intimate friend.[21]

But sometimes Lincoln made friends a bit too quickly. In 1833, he entered into a partnership with William Berry, a serious business endeavor apparently based on nothing more than the two men's sociability and ambitious talk. Berry was a blowhard and a drunkard to boot, and Lincoln soon found himself saddled with all the debts of a bankrupt general store. He took years to pay off his and Berry's obligations. Lincoln's friends jokingly referred to this as his "national debt."[22]

For better or worse, rapid friendship was Lincoln's way during his early years in New Salem and Springfield.[23] He seemed willing and anxious to form associations with whomever he could, and he was "easy of approach and equally courteous to all." He began letters with "Friend Hull," "Friend Richard," "Friend Williams," habitually using the tag "friend" with close associates and bare acquaintances alike.[24] Nor was he afraid of the exuberant displays of physical prowess sometimes required to win friends on the frontier, displays with a lively air that gave the emotions of the moment full vent. He used wrestling and fighting matches as a way to gain acceptance among locals, who saw the demonstrations of bluster, pride, enthusiasm, and shame in physical contests as entirely appropriate and fundamental to the establishment of truly lasting friendships. Lincoln's famous encounter with the champion of a local gang called the Clary's Grove Boys offers a good illustration; he was "legged" by his opponent in violation of what he and many others thought were the accepted rules of wrestling. But he took this apparent foul play with good humor so that "from that day forward the Clary Grove boys were always his firm friends." Then at Wabash Point on the Mississippi River, Lincoln defeated a local wrestling champion, Daniel Needham, a feat that "rendered him forever popular with the boys of that neighborhood."[25]

This highly emotive sense of friendship meant that Lincoln could allow his feelings to get the better of him. He had a penchant for lampooning "those who provoked in any way his especial displeasure," according to Herndon. "If assailed [Lincoln] was merciless in satire," his law partner wrote, and "when driven to do so, used this weapon of ridicule with telling effect."[26] On one occasion, Lincoln ripped open an opponent's waistcoat to expose the man's gold watch, denouncing him as a "hard-fisted democrat." During another campaign encounter, Lincoln was given a tongue-lashing by a Whig-turned-Democratic opponent who also happened to own Springfield's first lightning rod. Lincoln delivered a blistering reply, stating that he would "rather die now than, like the gentleman, change my politics . . . and then have to erect a lightning-rod over my house to protect a guilty conscience from an offended God."[27]

Lincoln felt no apparent qualms about speculating on his opponents' "guilty conscience" and exposing what he believed were dark motives and intentions for all the world to see. He had few doubts about his abilities to do so. For him, the line between inner motives and outer deeds was short, obvious, and easy to find. In 1836 he publicly branded one of his critics "a *liar* and a *scoundrel*" and threatened to give his "proboscis a good wringing." In another dispute with a prominent Springfield Democrat, James Adams, Lincoln assailed Adams in a series of letters and handbills as someone who "stormed and raved till he hopes or imagines he has got us a little scared" and who wished to "tear, rend, split, rive, blow up, confound, overwhelm, annihilate, extinguish, exterminate, burst asunder and grind to powder" critics like Lincoln.[28] During one particularly testy exchange with a local Springfield Democrat who objected to such name-calling, Lincoln compared himself to a man who found a skunk in his henhouse. When the skunk protested that he was not in fact a skunk, the farmer replied, "You look like [one] . . . act like one, smell like one, and you are one, by God." Lincoln was confident that he could tell who the skunks were.[29]

If he was excessive in his denunciation of political critics, he also was given to flights of giddy rhetoric, a style Herndon rather charitably referred to as using "striking and lofty metaphors." In his address to the Springfield Washington Temperance Society, Lincoln described the temperance cause as "a living, breathing, active, and powerful chieftain, going forth conquering and to conquer" and declared "the trump of his conquerer's fame is sounding from hill to hill, from sea to sea, and from land to land, and calling millions to his standard at a blast." He finished one speech by declaring, "If ever I feel the soul within me elevate and expand those dimensions not wholly unworthy of its Almighty Architect, it is when I contemplate the cause of my country, deserted by all the world beside, and I stand up boldly and alone and hurling defiance at her victorious oppressors."[30] He was also prone to emotional excess in the opposite extreme. The same Lincoln who was so affable and boisterous also had a well-deserved reputation for moodiness and bouts of deep depression. The causes varied, from frustrated romance to simple loneliness, but whatever their source, Lincoln carried his private depressions with him into the public square for all his friends to see. He "dript melancholy when he walked," and nearly all his friends and neighbors noted his spells of deep despair, which seemed to take him almost to the point of suicide.[31]

Lincoln's demeanor could therefore be quite contradictory and subject to emotional extremes. Here was a young man who sometimes wore his heart on his sleeve and expected others to do the same.[32] There was still another side, however, to Lincoln. Those who knew him remarked on his penchant for quiet periods when he would seem utterly withdrawn from those around him. His first schoolteacher noted his habit of being "very quiet during playtime" and his "liking for solitude." Herndon referred to this quality as Lincoln's fondness for "deep meditation" and wrote that his law partner at these times would "dwell altogether in the land of thought."[33]

When he arrived in New Salem, Lincoln referred to himself in a sad way as "a piece of floating driftwood."[34] It was an interesting choice of words, for he spent much of his time in New Salem and Springfield drifting from one place and group of acquaintances to another, meeting many people but keeping nearly all of them at a discreet distance. Herndon wrote that Lincoln "was not peculiar or eccentric, and yet a shrewd observer would have seen that he was decidedly unique and original."[35] He never quite became a fully integrated part of his surroundings. He felt no particular fondness for the frontier or any of the mannerisms or lifestyles commonly associated with it.[36] During a time when the vast majority of his neighbors attended some established church, he avoided organized religion. Where alcohol was considered an indispensable part of everyday life, Lincoln was a teetotaler; yet neither did he join an organized temperance movement. In a state filled with farmers, the one occupation Lincoln never took up on a regular basis was farming. He would perform agricultural labor when necessary and on at least one occasion manned a plow to win the political support of several farmers. But he hated farmwork, and he kept this dominant way of life in Illinois at arm's length.[37]

His bookishness was also a major component in this separation from his network of friends and acquaintances. Lincoln read a great deal. He generally did not like fiction, and he gravitated toward works that emphasized detached, passionless, and unsentimentalized thinking. He read mathematical texts, works of geometry to improve his skills at abstract reasoning, and of course he read many works on the law. His intense reading habits established his reputation in New Salem and Springfield as a paragon of the intellect, as a purveyor of logic, reason, and rational discourse. The books played a part in his personal development, the formation of the inner man, but they were also part of his public persona. Neighbors often saw him walking along the streets reading, and he would carry books with him into the post office. An observer in the New Salem general store noted that he "would open his book which he always kept at hand, study it, reciting to himself; then entertain the company present without apparent annoyance from the interruption. . . . If the company he was in was unappreciative, or their conversation at all irksome, he would open his book and commune with it for a time."[38] Lincoln made the switch back and forth from introspection to gregariousness without apparent strain or even awareness that his behavior struck many as odd. "Occasionally he would become absorbed with his book; would stop and stand for a few minutes, then walk on, or pass from one house to another or from one crowd of men to another," according to a neighbor.[39]

Lincoln's bookish intellect made itself felt in his early speeches as well. His sometimes wild emotional stump oratory was offset by detached, sober analyses of relatively dry and passionless subjects like internal improvements, tariff rates, or the public debt. His intellect on these issues was formidable, and though he invested his economics with a high degree of passionate commitment, he avoided the overheated rhetoric that characterized his speech making on other matters. In general, Lincoln valued the power of reason equally with the power of emotion. "Did Mr. Lincoln rule himself by the *head* or heart[?]," Herndon asked years later. "He was great in the *head* and ruled and lived there."[40]

Herndon was right but only half so. From books to storytelling yarns, introspection to joviality, Lincoln's comportment in the circle of friends he created for himself was at once outgoing and brooding, passionate and calculating. The effect was disconcerting. His friends liked him, but they also found him a baffling man given to wildly contradictory mood swings. "Fun and gravity grew on him alike," one perplexed neighbor remembered. As a young man, he had created a wide-ranging and relatively stable circle of friends, but he had not been able to create a secure persona for himself within this circle.[41]

Jefferson Davis's circle was much different. Lincoln self-consciously created companionship and fraternity with his stories and witty anecdotes, but Davis's camaraderie was thrust upon him by the circumstances of his education and training at West Point. Lincoln made up his own rules of friendship; Davis found the rules already laid out for him by the mores of Southern society and the cold gray walls of a West Point education.

Samuel Davis died a poor man, but unlike Thomas Lincoln, Samuel had high aspirations for himself and his family that involved more than ordinary farming. His last letter to his son Jefferson is full of the sort of aphorisms about the rewards of hard work, thrift, and diligence that Lincoln seems never to have heard from his father. He called upon Jefferson to make a real effort, as he put it, to "shine in society." Samuel himself did not do so, never rising above the nebulous ranks of middling-level white Southern farmers, but he did instill in his sons and daughters a sense that they belonged in the Southern planter class.[42]

There were few respectable paths leading to the Great House. Davis's options as a middling white Southern youth who wanted to shine in society boiled down to two professions: the law or the army. At one time it seemed that he might unwittingly follow in Lincoln's footsteps and choose the former. While a student at Transylvania University in Lexington, Kentucky, Davis expressed his ardent desire to become an attorney like Joseph. He never said why. He does not seem to have done any serious coursework in the law at the university, which had a law "department" consisting of one professor. More influential perhaps was the example of several college friends who planned to enter the bar. Jefferson wanted to do the same and hoped to enroll in the law school at the University of Virginia upon graduation from Transylvania.[43]

Joseph had different plans for his brother. Maybe he took notice of the growing numbers of attorneys flooding the southwest during the 1830s and was discouraged about Jefferson's chances to make a go of it in a profession that was quickly becoming crowded and highly competitive. Or maybe Joseph doubted that his brother could sway a jury or judge, sensing what everyone eventually discovered about Jefferson Davis—that he was not good at persuasion or negotiation.[44] Whatever the reason, Joseph does not appear to have encouraged Jefferson's lawyerly ambitions, and in 1822 he used his considerable political influence in the Mississippi Democratic party to wrangle an appointment to West Point for his young brother. Jefferson dutifully bowed to his older brother's wishes, as he nearly always did, and packed his bags for West Point. He never became an attorney.[45]

When he arrived at West Point, the Academy was a relatively young institution. It had been created only twenty years previously by Thomas Jefferson, of all people, a man with a lifelong disdain for standing armies and professional soldiers. West Point would ideally correct what Jefferson considered the dangerous defect of European armies, restricting the professional officers' corps to the aristocracy. Jefferson's West Point was to admit any young man of merit, regardless of circumstances, and in so doing ensure that army and militia leaders would never constitute a closed, insulated cadre of potentially dangerous elitists. It was supposed to be an open, democratizing institution with roots in the national community and the mass of ordinary Americans.[46]

West Point did provide opportunities for higher education to many young men of middling and poor means, but it quickly lost the openness and unrestricted interaction with society Jefferson had envisioned. The school was cut off from the rest of the nation by geography and public indifference. "Barron loves solitude," observed an early Academy superintendent about one professor, "and at West Point he must have enjoyed it in supreme degree." By the time Davis arrived, the U.S. Military Academy was well on its way to becoming a secluded and constricted little world with its own self-imposed standards of conduct.[47]

Many of these standards were the informal rituals of initiation developed by cadets, who were themselves to induct newcomers into the cadre of Academy life, to weed out weak cadets. Like his other freshman comrades, Davis was immediately dubbed an "animal" or more often a "plebe" and required to undergo a variety of indignities and abuse. Plebes might have their clothes stolen, tent ropes cut during the annual summer encampment, or (a favorite trick) be suddenly yanked by their heels from their bunks while sleeping. Much of this was the relatively harmless pranksterism common among young men in such settings, but some of the more severe forms of hazing could constitute a fair amount of physical hardship and abuse.[48]

Enforcement of codes of honor and discipline by fellow cadets continued throughout Davis's stay at the Point, with varying degrees of levity. Mock trials were common, and they were at times fairly elaborate rituals in which upperclassmen accused plebes of various seriocomic offenses and "sentenced" them to death by shooting squad, only to rescind the punishment at the last moment. Upperclassmen also cornered cadets in classrooms when instructors were absent and gave them impossible assignments and problems in an attempt to unnerve weaker plebes.[49]

The common denominator in all these cadet-led rituals was their relative formalization; they became habits, with their own particular sets of standardized practices and expected responses. A mock trial involved the creation of a courtroom, replete with a court "president" and uniformed attendants. Hazing techniques were passed down from class to class.[50] It is not known how much of this treatment Jefferson Davis suffered. He surely endured (and perhaps inflicted) his share, for, like everything at West Point, hazing was a ritualized routine.

Superimposed over the cadets' own code of esprit de corps was a complicated rating system that measured and remeasured each cadet's conduct on virtually a daily basis. Introduced by West Point superintendent Alfred Thayer only five years before Davis's arrival, the Thayer System evaluated cadets through several layers of examination, the most prominent and ubiquitous one being the bestowing of demerits on cadets for everything from improper dress to absence without leave. Punishments also varied, from extra guard duty to expulsion, all determined by an eight-tiered system with its own logic—"mutinous conduct" rated ten demerits, for example, while a poorly made bed called for only one. Added to this were daily recitation exercises in the classroom, with each subject possessing its own ranking system, and yet another ranking system for each class based on that of a regular army infantry battalion with its own captain, lieutenants, sergeants, and privates.[51]

Cadet Davis was firmly embedded within this complex system of classification, categorization, and discipline. Indeed, almost the only surviving records of his stay in the Academy are the incessant fitness and competence reports, which in army officialdom constituted a rudimentary biography. In February 1826, for example, he was "distinguished for Correct Conduct" by having committed no offenses during that month. In March, however, he committed five unnamed offenses, and the month after that he committed four. The following June he performed sufficiently well to be appointed "Fourth Sergeant" of the "first company" for the upcoming annual summer encampment.[52]

West Point offered an experience for Davis very different from the general store gossip, stories, and colorful fare of Lincoln's early life among the Clary's Grove Boys, Berry's general store, wild stump speeches, and wrestling matches. Davis's community of West Point was more stately, more isolated, and more rigidly formalized, a collection of fitness reports, cadet rankings, and military etiquette. Observers in later years remembered Lincoln's life as an almost endless series of stories and anecdotes, but Davis's contemporaries noted his slow, stately growth into a young officer with a well-knit, soldierly demeanor. "Jefferson Davis was distinguished in the corps for his manly bearing, his high toned and lofty character," recalled one fellow cadet, and another described him as "a very stout, florid young fellow." Lincoln presented to his friends a confusing bundle of contradictory impulses; Davis, on the other hand, was what he seemed and no more.[53]

Davis's transformation into a soldier was not easy. West Point was such a closed community that it bred an inordinate number of squabbles, arguments, and hard feelings between young men and their superiors, who were thrown together in tense circumstances with few constructive outlets for releasing pent-up hostilities. The place seemed to encourage a binary, either/or mentality in its cadets, with the choices being either complete obeisance to a rigid hierarchy of rules or outright resistance. It was a community nearly obsessed with the rule of law, as defined by the code of military conduct and the judgments of superior officers. In Thayer's legal system, however, there was little room for negotiation or compromise.[54]

Davis was no exception here, and at West Point he was given unwelcome opportunities to indulge his taste for legal matters. In summer 1825, he and four other cadets "wandered too far" from the site of the annual summer encampment during a rainstorm and happened upon Benny Haven's, a tavern that had been catering to West Point cadets for years, despite Thayer's best efforts to shut it down. Davis and his friends were discovered by Captain Ethan Hitchcock and arrested. A year later on Christmas Eve, 1826, during a boisterous—and illegal—holiday party in the cadet barracks, Davis and nearly everyone else present got thoroughly drunk, and the same Captain Hitchcock tried to stop the merriment, only to be driven from the building with curses, clubs, and various projectiles in what came to be known as the "egg nog riot." Both the Benny Haven's visit and the egg nog riot resulted in courts-martial for Davis and the other offenders.[55]

Davis was quite the amateur attorney in these proceedings. He made use of his scant legal expertise to argue, for example, that the regulations regarding Benny Haven's were "ex post facto laws."[56] He also employed what he must have believed were sound courtroom techniques by minutely cross-examining witnesses. In this manner, he persuaded Captain Hitchcock to admit that he had not actually seen Davis with alcohol in Benny Haven's but had merely assumed from Davis's presence in the tavern that he must have been drinking.[57]

His court-martial stratagems in nearly every case were based on a central goal: getting the court to understand the wording of the regulations in question in such a narrow and confined manner that his actions and his compatriots' fell outside their boundaries. The precise wording of the anti-intoxication rules at West Point forbade cadets to enter a "public house" and "drink spirituous and intoxicating liquor." When asked whether he had seen a fellow defendant, Theophilus Meade, drinking "ardent spirits or intoxicating liquor" at Benny Haven's, Davis replied that he had not. He admitted having seen Meade drink "hard cider" and porter wine, but "of course I did not understand [these] to be spirituous liquors."[58] When pressed to defend himself, cadet Davis indulged in what became a lifelong penchant for construing as narrowly as possible the wording of rules and laws, particularly when doing so would advance his own position. Thus he told the court that it could not be proven that Benny Haven's was a "public house" under the strict understanding of the rules and argued that, since the cadets had not been proven actually to have purchased alcohol there, the mere fact of their having entered the place was irrelevant. Of course, everyone in the room knew why Davis and his friends had "wandered off" to Benny Haven's, and they certainly knew what Mr. Haven did for a living.[59]

In terms of the cases themselves, Davis's arguments were of marginal value, at best, for he was adjudged guilty in both instances. Ignoring his admonishment that "it is better a hundred guilty should escape than one righteous person be condemned," the judges in the Benny Haven's court-martial peremptorily sentenced him to be dismissed from the service, followed immediately by a recommendation, that was observed, that he be reinstated "in consideration of his past former good conduct."[60] The egg nog riot was a more serious matter, but Davis was spared the fate that befell several of his fellow cadets—permanent expulsion from the army with no recommendation of a reprieve—because he was not actually present in the room when the riot occurred, having been ordered to his own quarters by Captain Hitchcock, due to his obviously inebriated state. His drunkenness was enough to merit six weeks' arrest and confinement but no more. In any event, none of Davis's various legal stratagems allowed him to extricate himself entirely from blame or punishment.[61]

Davis's contemporaries and many subsequent scholars and observers have commented on his sometimes haughty legalistic hairsplitting as one of the man's most undesirable traits.[62] There is something deeper here worth examining, however, for it is within these proceedings that we can glimpse most clearly Davis's developing sense of the rules that govern behavior within a community. For Davis, and no doubt for his Academy peers, the code of army regulations was an objective set of guidelines among men whose sense of themselves as officers and gentlemen was by definition unimpeachable. The cadets were to be understood as being "righteous men," men of honor and duty. The rules did not make them so; they simply ratified the processes by which men of like sympathies and ideals had already become a homogenous fraternity of brother officers. Rules were designed to structure feelings or to channel pride, the giving of offense, or the feeling of shame. Thus Davis could react with a sense of outrage to the very idea of being court-martialed, declaring, "I cannot believe the Court would if previously acquainted with the circumstances have shown so little respect to my feelings as to have charged me (on such weak evidence) with conduct so contrary to principles of a soldier and a man of honor."[63]

In some ways Davis's circle of friends and acquaintances was every bit as diverse as Lincoln's, for at West Point, he was exposed to a variety of individuals. "Coming from every section and quarter of the country, [we] represent[ed] every degree of provincialism," wrote one cadet, and another described his West Point classmates as "a motley looking crowd."[64] But just as Lincoln's community relationships tended to explode outward, Davis's tended to collapse inward, as he compacted these many individuals into a tight little ball of military professionalism. "I behold myself a member though a humble one of an honorable profession," Davis wrote, and it was from within the boundaries of this military community that he drew most of his early and deepest friendships.[65]

The precise causal relationships within this sense of friendship were complex. Certainly a time-honored military tradition of esprit de corps was crucial in this regard. American military officers since the days of the Revolution had manifested a certain clannish quality. The very location of West Point allowed its students and faculty to foster a sense of distance and isolation from the world at large, which in turn was key in the development among the cadets of an exclusive professionalism.[66]

The fact that this was an all-male environment also played a crucial role. Both Lincoln and Davis moved in circles consisting largely of men. But Davis's West Point was far more the exclusive, all-male, tight fraternal circle than was Lincoln's circle of general store riffraff and the like.[67] Its social isolation depended on a prevailing masculine ideal of close, manly camaraderie among the cadets. In some ways, West Point reflected more general trends in antebellum American society, as American men gathered in small groups to form fraternal lodges that allowed them a temporary refuge from the ravages of a bustling nineteenth-century market economy. West Point possessed many similar attributes, as the trappings of its military lifestyle set its cadets apart, and somewhat above, the run-of-the-mill American male.[68] "The official garb is . . . primae facie evidence of the gentleman and scholar," wrote an anonymous observer of West Point cadets.[69] Davis indeed felt an almost rueful separation between himself and the world of civilians, writing after graduation in 1829 that "now I do not believe I could get along well with citizens."[70]

Regionalism may also have influenced Davis's sense of friendship, but here the evidence is more ambivalent. West Point was in some ways a Southern institution, with many Southern cadets.[71] There is little evidence, however, that Davis's status as a Southerner played an important role there; in fact there is little to indicate that at this stage of his life he had consciously constructed a regional Southern identity for himself at all. His sole reference to Southernness came in a plaintive letter to Joseph in winter 1825 asking for money and contrasting himself, and indirectly other Southern cadets, with the supposedly miserly Yankee cadets of the Academy. "I expect my pay generally to satisfy every demand, I hope entirely, which however depends entirely upon the company I keep," he wrote. "The Yankee part of the corps find their pay entirely sufficient . . . but these are not such as I formed an acquaintance with on my arrival, it having originated in the introductory letters I brought on with me; nor are they such associates as I would at present select."[72] Sectional squabbles and animosities were not unknown at West Point, but this sole reference to his Southernness is indicative at least as much of young Jefferson telling his older brother what he wanted to hear—Joseph being quite a bit more conscious of his Southern identity and the source of the "introductory letters" Jefferson had brought with him—than any highly developed regional self-identification on his part.[73]

Regionalism continued to play a muted role in Davis's thinking when he left West Point and entered the army. Many years later he claimed that he was torn between duty to the army and duty to the South during the Nullification crisis, but this may well have been sentiments colored by subsequent decades of sectional conflict, for he expressed no such feelings at the time. There is little evidence at this time that he thought of himself as a Southerner, or that he possessed any conscious regional identity.[74]

West Point and the army were the formative models of Davis's sense of himself and his relationships with others in his early years. In a literal sense, the Academy was his strongest source of friendship, as his closest friends were made there: Albert Sidney Johnston and Leonidas Polk, for example, remained comrades about whom he would brook no criticism. Though Lincoln in his early years had addressed even the most casual acquaintances as "Friend," Davis generally reserved the term for fellow West Pointers. He trusted these men as he would trust no other. "During all his life he remembered his old companions at West Point," Varina wrote.[75]

"By education, by association, and by preference I was a soldier," Davis later recalled, "then regarding that profession as my vocation for life." But there is also in his tone a lack of a real sense of fulfillment, of completeness, at West Point. A sad letter addressed to his sister toward the end of his stay at the Academy suggests this. "The four years I remained at West Point made me a different creature from that which nature had designed me to be," he wrote, drawing a distinction between himself as a soldier and the mass of ordinary people and suggesting that, had it not been for the army, "I might have made a tolerably respectful citizen."[76]

Like Lincoln, Davis grew into young manhood surrounded by a circle of acquaintances and friends who were a source at once of security and ambivalence. The nature of these circles differed with each man: Lincoln's rollicking collection of friends, held together by the glue of his eclectic personality, contrasted sharply with the carefully ordered, insulated world of Jefferson Davis's West Point. In these formative years each man would draw radically different conclusions about the ways in which compatriots and friends interacted and the meaning of camaraderie and fraternity. These differing assumptions would in turn create quite different foundations for their perception of that greater circle of "friends," the United States and its citizens.

JOBS

In early September 1836, Abraham Lincoln was formally granted a license to practice law in the state of Illinois. The event was anticlimactic; Lincoln had been an informal "attorney" to his New Salem neighbors for quite some time, helping them draft deeds, bills of sale, and other legal documents. Just a few days prior to acquiring his law license, for example, he had drawn up a will for a local farmer named Joshua Short. In the slapdash, highly informal environment of frontier Illinois, such practices were relatively commonplace.[1]

As Lincoln was more or less easing into his chosen profession, Jefferson Davis was easing out of his. While Lincoln officially hung out his shingle as a bona fide attorney, Davis was at home in Warrenton, Mississippi, an ex-lieutenant of dragoons. He had given his resignation to his commanding officer earlier, in spring 1835, but correspondence concerning his duties as quartermaster dogged him well into his civilian life. He resigned from the army for a variety of reasons: he had been embarrassed by a lengthy court-martial proceeding that did not exactly exonerate him of wrongdoing, he was concerned about the slow rate of promotion and low pay in the regular army, and, mostly, he wanted to resign from the dead-end career of an army officer and pursue a calling more lucrative and substantial. For Davis, and for Lincoln, entering (or leaving) a profession was a profound step with serious ramifications for how they understood themselves and the world around them.[2]

Lincoln never revealed exactly why he wanted to become a lawyer. Doubtless there were many reasons. He appears to have been fascinated by the public speaking aspects of a law practice, the logic of the law appealed to his analytical mind, and perhaps most important, the law was a good choice for a young man whose ambition was to enter political life and the public eye.[3]

Trials were grand theaters in the antebellum era where neighbors, friends, and strangers alike gathered to hear even the most mundane cases argued by frontier barristers, the more colorful and brash the better. Lincoln himself was attracted to the law by just such a courtroom speaker, the Indiana attorney John A. Breckinridge, who was renowned for his skills as an advocate in criminal law. Lincoln's neighbors remembered that he did his chores at night so he could hear Breckinridge hold forth in court the next day. Years later he told Breckinridge that "listening to your speeches at the bar first inspired me with the determination to be a lawyer." He acted on that determination by embarking on a lengthy, self-imposed course of reading in whatever legal books he could borrow or scrape up in New Salem.[4]

By the time he formally acquired his license as an attorney, Lincoln was fairly well prepared to practice law; and practice he did, litigating over four thousand cases in two decades of service in the Illinois bar. He enjoyed a wide range of interests and hobbies: history, economics, the theater, and of course politics. But he spent more time in and out of courtrooms and law offices than in any other pursuit. He spent several months of each year riding circuit up and down the Illinois countryside. He practiced law to make money; he did it to acquire social status; he made many friends and acquaintances in the Illinois bar; and he may or may not have found refuge from a bad marriage in his law practice. Whatever his reasons, he was a dedicated, tireless barrister. If politics was Lincoln's passion, the law was his center of gravity.[5]

When as a boy Lincoln stole into Indiana courtrooms to watch Breckinridge and other frontier barristers hold forth, he most likely believed the law to be a form of theater, and little else. But by the time he began pursuing serious legal study on his own, he seemed to have intuitively understood that being a lawyer involved much more than courtroom bombast. Attorneys might often be colorful, energetic figures who held forth before juries and judges like

trained actors. But trials were not wide open, scarcely controlled public displays. They were regulated by a relatively strict set of proscribed rules and
conventions concerning proper behavior and demeanor, more so than even
the state legislative chamber, where Lincoln got his first taste of politics.
Prominent in what he learned while studying law were highly technical procedures by which an attorney presented himself and his case properly: writs
of assumpsit, replevin, and so forth as well as techniques for framing written interrogatories, courtroom cross-examinations, appellate court briefs, and
the like.[6] These sometimes excessively technical legal proceedings were more
than just exercises in pedanticism; they were the conventions of behavior in
the public square that was the courtroom. As an attorney, Lincoln's bookishness was put to good use but with a purpose that was directed more toward the outer world than his earlier brooding intellectual reveries had been.[7]

Lincoln excelled here; he would come to master the courtroom.[8] Most
noteworthy here, however, is his manner in doing so. He was unusual in that
he generally avoided emotion-laden courtroom bombast. Young, politically
ambitious attorneys of the antebellum era normally indulged in "stump"
oratory before juries and audiences, the better to make a lasting impression.
As Lincoln grew into his law practice, his speeches became steadily less or-
nate, with fewer references to "hurling defiance at her victorious oppressors"
and the like. "His mode of speaking was generally of a plain and unadorned
character," according to a fellow lawyer; and other courtroom observers noted
his relative lack of "sticky sentimentality" in front of juries, his courtroom
tact, and his generally calm demeanor.[9]

This is not to say that Lincoln did not make passionate appeals in the
courtroom or that he entirely refrained from bringing his temper or his
emotions into the scene. He could grow incensed at uncooperative or dishonest witnesses. Herndon remembered that when his partner "got angry
at the bar . . . he was then ugly," looking "like Lucifer in an uncontrollable
rage." Lincoln certainly had a temper, but what is remarkable about his behavior in court is not how often he gave his temper free rein but how often
he did not do so. Such instances were rare, especially in the context of his
times.[10]

The flashes of temper Lincoln did exhibit in court seem to have been for
the jury's benefit. Some observers thought Lincoln had no taste for manipu-
lation or affectation in the courtroom. "He did nothing for effect and made
no attempt to dazzle the jury," remembered a fellow lawyer. But a careful
examination of his courtroom manner indicates that although he eschewed

the bombast and haranguing style of other antebellum American attorneys, he actually learned the art of affectation quite well. His more emotional outbursts at witnesses were often immediately followed by remarks to the jury, as when for example he forced a surgeon acting as an expert witness for the opposition to admit his large fee, then turned to the jury and, pointing to the doctor, "cried in a shrill voice . . . big fee, big swear."[11] He could use the aura of sober reason when necessary, but he could also manipulate a jury's feelings, and his emotional outbursts, rare though they were, suggest a man who had learned how to gauge their effect on the jury. In one case involving the pension of a Revolutionary War veteran's widow, Lincoln had written notes for his jury summation: "Revolutionary War. Describe Valley Forge privation. Ice. Soldier's bleeding feet. Plaintiff's husband. Soldier leaving home for army. SKIN DEFENDANT. Close."[12]

Here was a different persona for a man who not long before could quickly lose his temper without much thought of the consequences, who could be so oblivious of his relationships with others in his far-flung network of friends that he could bump blindly into neighbors while walking down a street reading a book or could impetuously threaten to wring an opponent's nose. The Lincoln of the general store, the post office, and the streets of New Salem seemed to give little or no thought to the impressions he made, and he had difficulty separating his private feelings from his public actions. The Lincoln of the quasi theater of the courtroom, however, learned to step back from his public persona of emotion and intellect, conviviality and reason, and carefully to manipulate both approaches as necessity required. He learned to create a lawyerly self-image, and he learned how to manipulate it to suit his needs.

He also found in the law an understanding of friendship involving more subtle, less emotive means than he had employed earlier. The law taught him that he should view friendship in ways that separated the private from the public, placed a higher value on outer forms than inner motives, did not presume an intimate understanding of another individual's point of view, and proceeded cautiously in matters of proof and absolute truths. As an attorney, Lincoln found out how difficult judgments about inner motives really were in a courtroom where witnesses, clients, and other attorneys often had something to hide. "You say Adams did go to Peoria with Bradshaw, but was not actually present when Bradshaw took the deed," he wrote a fellow attorney, "but by whom can we *prove* that he was not actually with him? This is the point."[13] In another case, Lincoln wrote that "the greatest difficulty of

all is the want of something definite to take proof about. . . . This matter harasses my feelings a good deal."[14]

Lincoln's law practice made him aware of the decided difference between
being right and being able to prove that to others. If a client had "the right
side," Herndon recalled, "Mr. Lincoln told him he had the right and the
equity. He then again patiently listened to what could be proved, and . . . he
would say, 'My friend—you are in the right but I don't think your evidences
are sufficiently strong.'"[15] This sensitivity to issues of proof and intent even
permeated Lincoln's attempts at poetry. In a poem "The Bear Hunt," he
describes a dispute over who should be awarded a dead bear's skin:

> But who did this, and how to trace
> What's true from what's a lie,
> Like lawyers in a murder case
> They stoutly *argufy*.[16]

Lincoln learned just how difficult it could be to determine truth from
falsehood, intent, and appearance in court, and he came to understand that
truth and intent could be easily hidden or twisted. Things were not always
what they seemed. He quickly found that reckless accusations without adequate proof and assumptions that he could easily discern a witness's or a
defendant's motives might easily backfire. In one early case, he told a jury
that the key witness for the defense was a liar and perjurer "who manifestly
prevaricates—manifestly attempts to cheat his conscience" because of a
minute inconsistency in the wording of the man's testimony. Lincoln lost the
case. By 1850 he knew better and went out of his way to avoid impugning
the motives of witnesses in the courtroom. In one speech involving conflicting testimony concerning a steamboat accident, for example, he told the jury
that they were to "try and reconcile them, and believe that they are not in-
tentionally erroneous, as long as we can."[17] Witnesses might mean well but
through carelessness or ignorance might present an image before a jury or
judge that could injure Lincoln's case. "I therefore, as one of your counsel,
beg you to fully refresh your recollection," he wrote a client. "If persons should
come about you and show a disposition to pump you . . . it may be no more
than prudent to remember that it may be possible they design to misrepresent you, and to embarrass the real testimony you may ultimately give."[18]

Lincoln came to see the lawyer's role in disputes as having at least as much
to do with facilitating negotiation and compromise as it did in arriving at an
understanding of some great, hidden truth. Earlier he had been willing to

rip open an opponent's waistcoat to expose his gold watch; now he was more willing to negotiate the opening of the waistcoat and suggest that doing so might be in the wearer's best interest. He had always had a tendency toward acting the part of referee and negotiator in New Salem and Springfield, helping settle disputes for neighbors.[19] Now the law gave him a certain impetus for resolving conflicts through negotiation, both in and out of the courtroom. Often these negotiations had less to do with rigid litigation procedures than simply with his standing as an attorney who could bring warring parties together. He recommended out-of-court settlements to his clients whenever practicable. "I understand Mr. Hickox will go . . . for the purpose of meeting you to settle the difficulty about the wheat," he wrote one client. "I sincerely hope you will settle it. I think you *can* if you *will.*"[20] He saw lawyers, in the best of circumstances, as neutral promoters of problem solving. "Discourage litigation. Persuade your neighbors to compromise whenever you can," he wrote in a set of notes for a lecture on the practice of law. "As a peacemaker the lawyer has a superior opportunity of being a good man."[21] The "good man" in this context was a facilitator, a conduit for conflict resolution rather than a person who held rigidly proscribed opinions.

The law also taught Lincoln how inadequate good feelings, kindness, and even family ties could be as methods of binding members of a community together. Throughout his career, he was involved in scores of acrimonious legal disputes between supposed close friends and family members. Contested wills, breach of contract, debtor/creditor disputes, dissolved business partnerships, broken marriages, custody disputes—he often saw the fragile nature of these seemingly heartfelt and sincere bonds. The lesson for Lincoln in many cases must have been how little estimates of an individual's outward appearance of trustworthiness and kindly feelings could mean and how useless it was to base feelings of friendship completely on a supposed understanding of another person's heart.[22]

He was not particularly cynical about this. He believed that honesty, trustworthiness, and other sentiments had an important part to play in the law, beginning with lawyers themselves. He had little patience with the popular belief that lawyers were inherently dishonest men, writing, "If in your own judgement you cannot be an honest lawyer, resolve to be honest without being a lawyer." But he understood the limits of honesty and friendship in a court of law, and he much preferred to keep legal matters and his own personal feelings separate. "As there is likely to be some feeling, and both parties are friends of mine," he wrote a fellow lawyer, "I prefer, if I can, to keep out of the case." Perhaps this increasing sense of the incompatibility between the law and sentiment explains the gradual cooling of his friendship with Joshua Speed. In 1846 Lincoln took on some legal business for Speed, and the correspondence between them suggests that the law crowded out feelings of friendship for Lincoln, who grew annoyed that Speed did not "precisely understand the nature and the result of the suit against you," and he rather coldly stated, "I must, in all candour, say I do not perceive how your personal presence would do any good in the business matter." Lincoln later informed another correspondent, "I am not a very sentimental man." And one law colleague recalled that Lincoln "handled and moved men remotely as we do pieces upon a chess-board."[23]

The shortcomings of sentiment left only adherence to the rules and procedures of the law itself as the fundamental guarantors of amicable relations in public. The law was an open-ended tool, a set of rules that helped people— good, bad, wicked, or saintly—come to agreed-upon arrangements. There is little evidence that before 1850 Lincoln saw an individual's personal morality as germane to legal settlements. Conscience, motive, intent—these mattered less than the legal procedures for a general practitioner like Lincoln, who became aware that there were often no absolute winners, and perhaps no absolute right or wrong, in the outcome of a trial.[24] "There are few things *wholly* evil or *wholly* good," he once remarked.[25]

Thus he could acquire the necessary legal acumen to try cases on both sides of moral issues. In an 1844 case, for example, he represented the interests of Polly Alger against her husband Addison Alger, who was accused of drunkenness, cruelty, and desertion; ten years later, he represented a dissolute husband, William Allen, against the claims for divorce by his estranged wife Phebe. In 1841 he used the Northwest Ordinance of 1787 to convince the Illinois Supreme Court that the presumption of the law must be in favor of freedom unless proven otherwise, subsequently gaining freedom for his African-American client; six years later, however, Lincoln defended the property rights of a farmer who had transported a slave to Illinois.[26]

The law created in Lincoln a sense of how individuals interact with one another, a sense different from what he had found in his loose network of friends and acquaintances in New Salem and Springfield. His law created and nurtured friendship, but not in the sense of close personal intimacy between strangers; the law taught him that this approach was highly suspect in a world where litigants concealed motives and defendants dissembled. Rather, the law promoted friendship in the sense that it provided rules of procedure, negotiation, perhaps even courtesy, for the amiable conduct of public business. It created a more viable and stable community.

The law also created for Lincoln a more viable and stable self. He became much more conscious of comportment. Only two years after becoming a member of the bar, he spoke in the Illinois legislature of his unwillingness to approach a bill in a manner that wore "the appearance of being a personal attack" on the bill's author. In one of his first speeches in Congress ten years later, he went out of his way to assure Democrats that during various critical remarks he made about pending legislation concerning postal contracts, "no assault whatever was meant upon the Postmaster General." He regretted "the impression which might have been created by the language he had used on a previous occasion," and added that he "had no desire . . . ever to be out of order—though he never could keep long *in* order."[27]

But Lincoln was steadily learning how to keep "in order" throughout the 1840s, and part of the process was distinguishing between remarks for private and public consumption. He wrote another Whig that "the Beardstown paper is entirely in the hands of my friends," but then quickly added, "don't speak of this." By the time he began to campaign for Congress in 1846, phrases such as "let this be strictly confidential," and "I address this to you alone" permeated his correspondence. "If any thing I have written *for* any body should be turned to your disadvantage, I could hardly ever forgive myself for the carelessness of so writing," he informed a political ally in 1849.[28]

At the same time, Lincoln dropped the overly exuberant epithet of "friend" with which he had begun many of his letters, and he allowed his old habits of assuming that he could immediately discern motives and intentions generally to fade away. In 1836 he could declare without reservation who around him was a liar and a fool, who was a "skunk" and who was not. A decade later, he wrote a friend, "In law it is a good policy to never *plead* what you *need* not, lest you oblige yourself to *prove* what you *can* not." He also scolded a newspaperman who had cast aspersions on his character and motives by suggesting that "he might, not without profit, learn . . . never to add the weight of his character to a charge against his fellow man without *knowing* it to be true." Lincoln began to draw distinctions between the inner feelings and the outward actions of political opponents and allies, criticizing a Democrat who "did *pretend,* that he *knew* [his constituents'] feelings, and that he fairly expressed them." He advised younger Whigs like Herndon to proceed with their careers, "never suspecting that anybody wishes to hinder [them]," for "suspicion and jealousy never helped any man in any situation." The underlying message here was that one could never know what one's political associates really felt in their hearts, and Lincoln informed Herndon that to dwell on this fact was useless and counterproductive, allowing one's "mind to be diverted from its true channel to brood over attempted injury."[29]

Lincoln also cultivated a calmer public image for himself. He wrote one political ally that he "appreciate[d] your desire to keep down excitement" and promised to "'keep cool' under all circumstances."[30] He did not usually give such assurances in his earlier days; his dominant mode of speaking increasingly became associated by observers with dispassionate, careful reason. He had always had a penchant for sober intellect in economic matters, but this quality became more and more identified with all his political speeches, even on partisan political matters. Newspapers described him as possessing a "cool judgement" and "a clear and cool, and very eloquent manner."[31]

He never lost his amicability, his storytelling abilities, or any of the other skills that were elemental to his first community of county roads and general stores, but he was careful about how much he revealed to others of himself. He was also careful about what he expected others to reveal to him. The various requirements and conventions of the law helped him achieve equilibrium between excessively exuberant and excessively stand-offish public behavior. Lincoln learned proper control of both emotion and reason and the value of keeping a certain distance between the private and the public, between intention and appearance.

Jefferson Davis learned very different lessons in places far removed from Lincoln's courthouses. After he graduated from West Point in 1828, he spent six years in the army. It was a lonely, rather peripatetic existence, driving some men to quiet despair (Robert E. Lee), others to drink (Ulysses S. Grant), and still others to seek a civilian occupation as soon as possible (George McClellan).[32] Few regular army officers were happy or content, and although Davis did nothing rash or desperate, he chafed at the inherent boredom of his chosen profession. "I am twenty-two and the same obscure poor being that I was at fifteen, with the exception of a petty appointment," he wrote.[33] His posts were a succession of lonely places. His first billet was Jefferson Barracks in St. Louis, then Fort Winnebago in Michigan, which he eventually left to help construct Fort Crawford and a sawmill on the Yellow River in the same area, followed by duty in Dubuque, Iowa.[34]

Davis was fascinated by the teeming variety of life he found in the West, particularly by the various Native Americans he encountered. "The Indians seemed to me to be legion," he told a friend, and he encountered members of the Sac, Fox, Osage, Pawnee, and Comanche tribes, among others. Davis regarded them with a fascinated yet detached eye, describing their lifestyles and behavior as interesting but discomfitingly alien. He later told stories about Indian dances and festivals, Indian children who behaved in what he thought were strange ways, and Indian adults who bet on horse fights and hunted and fished using methods he considered unusual.[35]

Such stories were the usual fare for whites who initially encountered the different Native American cultures of the West. For Davis, however, the white people he encountered were almost as peculiar as the Indians. In 1831 he was sent to Dubuque, Iowa, to help keep the peace between Indians and white miners. Davis found the latter to be a strange and in some ways intimidating lot. "He said that all these frontiersmen were armed to the teeth, believed themselves to be wronged, and were determined to resist any effort made to drive them out of the mines to the last extremity," Varina remembered. Davis described these men with much the same mixture of fascination and detachment he displayed toward Indians. "Their peculiarities were many in number," Varina wrote, no doubt paraphrasing her husband, "but their high qualities, their generosity, courage, industry, and good faith, inspired him with sincere respect."[36] Perhaps, but their West remained to Davis a strange and, in many ways, barbaric place. Western whites spoke a strange dialect, lived in strange houses, and indulged strange customs. "The frontier girls had few of the adventitious aids to modesty which we think so indispensable," Varina remembered her husband saying; "the white inhabitants in the West at that time were not less a noteworthy and picturesque population than the Indians."[37]

Just as Lincoln's law practice tossed him in the middle of all sorts of people as he rode circuit on the Illinois frontier, so Davis confronted much the same variety of people with the detached, sober perspective of a soldier and a West Point graduate who was used to orderly behavior in orderly places. He prefaced a report on the countryside surrounding Fort Winnebago with the comment, "I herewith transmit . . . the following remarks for which, were their imperfections less, I would offer the novelty of the Subject as an apology."[38] He moved through the West in a tightly controlled fashion. On only one recorded occasion did he simply roam about the countryside exploring. Otherwise, his encounters with the region took place in relatively structured military settings: patrols, expeditions, negotiations, and so forth. He was an army officer who held his surroundings at arm's length.

When Lieutenant Davis observed the countryside, he did so in the military context of reconnaissance and engineering, finding ways to classify and control the environment as quickly and neatly as possible. His report on the Fort Winnebago region was a detailed account of traveling and communications issues. "By land the distance to Fort Crawford is about 120 miles, a plain trace used by Waggons [sic] except about eight miles," he wrote. "Obstacles, the Fox River crossed at the garrison ferry . . . a deep marsh about 250 yards wide . . . thence no difficulty until the road inclines to the Ouisconsin." When describing the route from Winnebago to Fort Howard, he wrote, "obstructions, one deep marsh about 200 yards wide . . . three boggy bayoux and many deep ravines . . . the first half of the route uninhabited, the Second half very thinely [sic] inhabited." "All of the routes noticed lie in a country richly clothed with grass," he concluded, apparently as a reference to horse forage.[39]

His profession placed him in military posts that were carefully bounded and walled off from the surrounding countryside, like little oases of military order. Fort Crawford, for example, consisted of a courtyard surrounded by a tall wooden wall with only two entrances, both guarded. Fort Winnebago was a bit more open—it lacked a surrounding wall—but it was situated on bluffs overlooking the road it guarded, and its buildings were laid out in closed compounds encircling a central parade ground.[40]

Davis in the West was rather like a man stepping carefully across a raging river from one stone to the next, sometimes in a metaphorical sense, sometimes literally so. In winter 1831 while leading a scouting expedition he came upon a collection of wagons, stage coaches, and settlers stranded near a ferryman's cabin on one side of a frozen river. According to Davis, he organized the people present into an impromptu workforce and set them to building an "ice bridge." As Varina recalled the story, Davis "told them to keep a good fire in the cabin and set the men to hewing blocks of ice. . . . As each was set in position, water was poured over, which froze it in its place." If a worker fell into the water—as many no doubt did—"he was ordered to run into the cabin and turn round and round before the blazing log fire until dry." "Soon the bridge was pronounced safe," Varina wrote, "and the whole party of men, women, children, and vehicles passed safely over."[41]

Davis built a bridge to navigate a hostile space and a fire to conquer the inhospitable cold. The story could almost serve as a homily for his military life. His army existence was a collection of relative calm spots—various forts and military installations—surrounded by territory at once fascinating, difficult, and strange. After a few years the strangeness wore on him, and he began to wish for more ordered, safe places. "Naturally domestic in his tastes, he began to look forward longingly to establishing a restful home and to a more quiet life," Varina recalled.[42]

Davis found the army itself little more to his liking. He was uncertain about the character and reliability of many of his fellow soldiers. "The officers of the Post are like those of the army generally," he wrote his sister from Fort Winnebago in 1829; "[they are] men of light habits both of thinking and acting having little to care about and less to anticipate." On the other hand, he continued his close relationships with officers he had met at West Point, and he was generally solicitous, sometimes emotionally so, to enlisted men.[43] His army career was characterized by this sort of mental tug-of-war between his close friendships and doubts about the morals and talents of military men. Were they honor-bound, principled, and trustworthy, or were they merely career-minded opportunists or, worse, plodding mediocrities? The tug-of-war was at times fought out in a legal setting, for, as at West Point, Davis found himself involved in several court-martial proceedings.

The most serious such affair occurred in a pouring rainstorm at Fort Gibson on Christmas Eve, 1834. Lieutenant Davis absented himself from a miserably cold, wet morning roll call, believing the damp air might spark a renewed bout of the congestion and lung problems he had begun to suffer. When his commanding officer, Major Richard Mason, had Davis hauled out of his tent and dressed him down for failing to secure permission to miss the roll call, Davis, in what Mason later termed "a highly disrespectful, insubordinate, and contemptuous manner abruptly turn[ed] on his heel and walk[ed] off, saying at the same time, Hum!" Mason ordered Davis to turn around and face him, informing him that he was under arrest. Davis "stared Major Mason full in the face, without showing any intention of obeying the order of arrest." Mason repeated the arrest order, whereupon Davis, "in a disrespectful and Contemptuous manner, ask[ed]: 'Now are you done with me?'" and finally returned to his tent after Mason repeated the order a third time. He remained under arrest through the holiday season and into the first weeks of the new year.[44]

It was in itself a silly little incident, hardly worth the trouble it subsequently caused, but Mason insisted on bringing Davis up on charges of insubordination. The resulting trial took nearly a week to resolve. Davis undertook another elaborate, lawyerly defense of his actions, reminiscent of his performances during his West Point days. He argued that Mason had issued written, standing orders to the effect that officers might miss reveille in bad weather. He called numerous character witnesses who testified to his generally courteous bearing and attention to duty. He devoted considerable attention to that seemingly innocuous, at least to him, expression, "Hum!" that he had uttered. He told the court that "in such a word as 'hum' the tone and manner with which it is used must determine entirely the signification, to be mistaken as to the tone and manner is therefore to be mistaken in the meaning." He suggested that since Mason was not sure whether Davis had said it before, during, or after he turned on his heel and walked away, then he could not have known Davis's precise meaning.[45]

The absurdity of this exchange should not obscure its revelation of the ways in which Davis—and presumably many other regular army officers— understood the relationships within their little world. These relationships were so close, so intimate, that great meaning could be attached to the smallest words and gestures; a "hum" uttered at the wrong moment could have serious consequences among officers and gentlemen. Though rules and regulations were important, the bulk of his case was placed upon wholly personal terms: testimony as to his demeanor, his soldierly bearing, his status as a tried and true member of the brotherhood of army officers. Davis concluded his defense with a long speech in which he suggested that the whole matter should turn upon the personal injury done to himself, appealing not to abstract rules of reason or justice but to his reputation and his feelings. "An examination into the charges should wipe away the discredit which belonged to my arrest," he told the court, adding that "the humble and narrow reputation which a subaltern can acquire by years of the most rigid performance of his duty, is [of] little worth in the wide world of Fame, but yet something to himself."[46]

He won only a partial and ultimately unsatisfying victory. The court found him guilty as charged, except that it struck the words "highly disrespectful, insubordinate and contemptuous" from the charges, leaving only "conduct subversive of good order and military discipline." The court diluted even the impact of this language when it explicitly absolved Davis of any criminality.[47] It was not quite an exoneration. One can imagine the lawyer Lincoln counting such a ruling a victory, a halfway point that all parties, if not entirely happy, could at least live with. Davis, however, was not put together that way, and his ideal of the law allowed no such consolation; one was either right or wrong, either within the accepted codes and laws of military behavior or not. He seems to have been so dissatisfied with the verdict that he requested an extended leave of absence.[48]

By this time Davis was ready to move on. He had been involved in other clashes besides the Mason episode, and taken together these had given him a certain disillusionment with the peacetime army. He had once contemplated leaving the military for a more lucrative, and risky, position in a Mississippi railroad enterprise, until Joseph talked him out of it.[49] But now Davis was more determined to enter civilian life, and this time Joseph did not object. Davis stretched the leave granted him in the wake of the Mason affair into a lengthy absence from his post, followed eventually by his official resignation in May 1835.[50]

Davis may have left the army, but the army never left him. He remained close, lifelong friends with many officers, and he evinced an emotional concern for military men in general. "The humblest soldier could get an interview with him as readily as the greatest general," according to Varina, who wrote of her husband's "clinging memory and affection for his old profession."[51] The army gave him a sense of himself that placed a high premium on honor, duty, and personal fidelity to a code of conduct and a set of regulations. It gave him a sense of community that collapsed distinctions between public and private and placed a heavy emphasis on emotions, ranging from anger and pride to a sense of personal indignity and shame. Intimate friends (such as Albert Sidney Johnston) and vociferous enemies were the norm for Davis; those who knew him commented on this as a facet of his personality. He was "extreme alike in his attachments and aversions," noted one observer, and another asserted that he was "ardent in his attachments."[52] Lincoln, with his emphasis on reason in community relationships and his distancing of intent and appearance, had few very close friends or implacable enemies; Davis, with his veneration of emotional ties of affection among men in small groups, had both.[53]

HOMES

Lincoln and Davis were both honorable men—"honorable" in the broad sense of character and personal ethics. During several decades of public service, no hint of scandal ever attached to either of these two politicians. Both enjoyed well-deserved reputations for scrupulous integrity. "Honorable," however, carried more complex, nuanced meanings in nineteenth-century America. Honor meant adherence to socially proscribed rules of etiquette and a code of behavior concerning how one should conduct oneself properly in relations with others, particularly with members of the opposite sex. Community standards of honor required women to behave with chastity and humility and to defer to men and their opinions in public. Honor compelled men to run their households in a certain way, to behave with chivalry toward women, and to treat women as the weaker sex. Above all, honorable men and women had to keep a close watch on other members of the community, to be keenly sensitive to language, gestures, and phrases that might hint at an imputation of dishonorable or unworthy motives. Underlying this code was a dark foundation of violence, with honor sometimes dictating, from men, a physical public defense of character.[1]

Given Davis's reputation as a short-tempered Southerner, one might think that he was more likely than Lincoln to have stood on a dueling field at some point in his career. He subscribed to a code of honor, rooted in his military life and his Southern heritage, which could make him notoriously thin-skinned and sensitive to real or imagined slights. He habitually used the word in reference to a variety of matters personal and political—national honor, the honor of the South, Mississippi's honor, his family honor, and so forth. But for a man who was born in the antebellum South, with its thick patina of slave-owning brutality, Davis was not particularly violent. He was a charter member of the Vicksburg Anti-Dueling Society, albeit a moderate one, who wanted to water down some of the language in the organization's charter in such a way as to recognize that, in some cases, dueling was a necessary act.[2]

He came close to a duel on several occasions. At a Washington, D.C. Christmas party in 1847 he got into a passionate argument with fellow Mississippian Henry S. Foote, whom he intensely disliked, and the two men ended up tussling ignominiously on the floor like addled schoolboys. The scuffle nearly ended in a pistol duel before the combatants were separated, eventually calming themselves.[3] In February 1850 Davis challenged Senator William Bissell of Illinois to retract some disparaging remarks he supposedly had made concerning the military prowess of Mississippi soldiers. After a series of letters, which satisfied neither man, Davis asked Bissell to meet him at an unspecified location outside the District of Columbia (where dueling could result in their arrest) to settle the matter. In the end, cooler heads prevailed. Bissell's second, an Illinois Democrat, James Shields, met with Davis's representatives and negotiated a peace settlement whereby Davis withdrew his challenge and Bissell publicly acknowledged Mississippians' martial bravery. Probably both men breathed a private sigh of relief. Davis never came quite this close again to a violent confrontation on the field of honor.[4]

Lincoln knew Bissell well. They served together in the Illinois state legislature, and they later both joined the fledgling Republican party in Illinois.[5] Lincoln also knew James Shields. In fact, the closest Lincoln ever came to the "field of honor" involved an altercation with Shields. In summer 1842 an Illinois newspaper ran several pseudonymous letters about Shields, a prickly and rather vain sort, which mixed biting political satire and personal insult. "Dear girls," read one letter purporting to "quote" Shields directly, "it is distressing, but I cannot marry you all. Too well I know how much you suffer; but do remember, it is not my fault that I am so handsome and so interesting." When Shields angrily demanded the author's identity, Lincoln stepped forward, and in the process very nearly involved himself in a duel when Shields demanded "personal satisfaction." The affair was narrowly averted by a series of maneuvers initiated by the two duelists' seconds. It was embarrassing for Lincoln. "If all the good things I have ever done are remembered as long and well as my scrape with Shields," he said later, then "it is plain I shall not soon be forgotten."[6]

Honor may also have involved Lincoln in a far more permanent difficulty—it may well have prodded him into marriage. Herndon believed as much, unequivocally stating that Lincoln "married Mary Todd to save his honor, and in doing so he sacrificed his domestic peace." Lincoln's best friend, Joshua Speed, agreed. "Lincoln Married her for honor," he declared, "feeling his honor bound to her."[7]

Lincoln met Mary Todd at a party in 1840. She had been in Springfield for several months, visiting her sister, and had become one of the belles of the town. She was in many ways Abraham's opposite. "A bright, lively, plump little woman," Mary loved the society gatherings Lincoln detested, and she was skilled in the art of small talk and witty, cultured conversation that continually eluded him. She was the product of a rich Kentucky slave-owning family and had attended the best schools in the state (including Jefferson Davis's alma mater, Transylvania University).[8] She had a temper and a candid, rather harsh disposition; "My beaux have always been hard bargains," she once bluntly observed. Lincoln, who knew himself to be something of a "hard bargain" to most women, was captivated by Mary, and the two became engaged in fall 1840.[9]

But Mary Todd was not his first love. Several years before he met her, Lincoln had fallen in love with Ann Rutledge, the daughter of a New Salem taverner. Like Mary, Ann was smart, rather heavyset, and popular; unlike Mary, she was possessed of a fundamentally sweet disposition. "She had a gentle and kind heart as an ang[e]l," remembered a neighbor, and she was "beloved by ev[e]ry body." This included Lincoln, who courted her to the point that the couple were engaged to be married. But in August 1835 she contracted what locals called "the brain fever"—typhoid—and died.[10]

Lincoln was crushed. A friend described him standing guard over her final resting place, saying, "I can never be reconcile[d] to have the snow—rain and storms beat on her grave." Another recalled that he "would take his gun and wander off in the woods by him self. . . . This gloom seemed to deepen for some time, so as to give anxiety to his friends in regard to his Mind." This was a concern for many people in New Salem. "Some of his friends really thought he would go crazy," wrote one. Lincoln himself later admitted that "I run [*sic*] off the track. . . . I loved the girl dearly and sacredly."[11]

Herndon called Lincoln's affair with Ann the "'grand passion' of his life . . . the memory of which threw a melancholy shade over the remainder of his days." Though it is clear that Lincoln carried the memory of his grief with him ever after—during the war an old friend mentioned Ann to Lincoln, who replied somberly, "I did honestly and truly love the girl and think often— often of her now"—the experience does not seem to have effected a drastic or long-term change in his personality.[12] In much the same way that the law taught him how to create a social wall between public and private, intent and motive, so too did his instincts allow him to compartmentalize Ann Rutledge into a small, safe place in his soul, to be exposed on those rare occasions when the subject was broached but otherwise well enough left alone. Lincoln's spasm of near insanity may have been a quite sane response to this tragedy. Perhaps he used his madness, if madness it really was, as a sort of safety valve, a loud steam whistle of pain blowing out suddenly and sharply, to be replaced eventually by his normal calm demeanor.[13]

Lincoln had sufficiently recovered five years later to ask Mary for her hand in marriage, but that affair came to a crashing halt in winter 1841. Whether due to doubts about Mary, doubts about marriage in general, or simple panic, he suddenly broke off the engagement. In the process he suffered a guilt-induced bout of depression so severe that friends again feared for his sanity. Speed recalled removing "razors from [Lincoln's] room," and "tak[ing] away all Knives and other such dangerous things." Another friend simply stated that Lincoln "went Crazy as a Loon."[14]

At some point Lincoln came to believe that whether he really loved Mary or not, honor dictated that he follow through with the engagement. He worried that such a breach of faith might seriously harm his public reputation. Mary seemed to think so, for she told him he was honor-bound to follow through on his commitment to her. Lincoln gloomily agreed. "I shall have to marry that girl," he told a friend. And perhaps he could live with a less than rapturous marriage, after all. A few months previously when newlywed Speed expressed misgivings about his own marriage, Lincoln had written, "It occurs to me, that if the bargain you have just closed can possibly be called a bad one, it is certainly the most pleasant one . . . which my fancy can, by any effort, picture." Taking his own advice, he swallowed his misgivings and renewed his engagement to Mary.[15]

This decision may have ameliorated his depression, but his spirits did not rise too much. A few hours before the wedding, when a neighbor noticed him dressed nicely and asked where he was going, Lincoln replied, "to hell, I suppose."[16] "Hell" was a spartan, brief Episcopal marriage ceremony, attended only by a few close friends and kept secret from most of the town—a "policy Match all around," according to one observer. Abraham Lincoln and Mary Todd became man and wife on November 4, 1842.[17]

Three years later, Jefferson Davis and Varina Howell were wed in an Episcopal ceremony. The proceedings, as with the Lincolns, were rather simple: "my family, and some of his," as Varina later put it. The Lincolns spent their honeymoon in a Springfield hotel, after which Lincoln embarked on a fresh stint around the Illinois legal circuit. The Davises took a six-week tour of Mississippi, Louisiana, and New Orleans, where they met "a great many fashionable people," among them the uncle of the poet Oscar Wilde.[18] Varina took it all in with the enthusiasm of an eighteen-year-old woman. Her new husband was thirty-six, and a man far removed in personality and temperament from his teenage years.

Varina was not Jefferson's first love. Fifteen years previously he had met Colonel Zachary Taylor's daughter, Sara, at Fort Crawford in Michigan Territory. Sara was "refined, intelligent, sincere, and very engaging in her manners" while being "devoid of the least trace of stubbornness."[19] The young Mississippi lieutenant and the colonel's daughter were attracted to each other almost immediately. Davis's passion would have surprised some observers, who in later days took him to be a cold and heartless sort. "Oh! How I long to lay my head upon that breast which beats in unison with my own," he wrote her in December 1834; "neglected by you I should be worse than nothing and if the few good qualities I possess under your smiles yield a fruit it will be your's [sic] as the grain is the husbandsman's."[20]

Sara reciprocated her suitor's feelings, and soon they were engaged. An obstacle to their union emerged, however, in the form of Sara's father. Taylor liked Davis, but he adamantly opposed the marriage on the grounds that he did not want his daughter to endure the hard existence of an army wife. "His own wife and daughter had complained so bitterly," recalled one observer, that "he had once resolved that his daughter should never marry a soldier with his approval." Worse, Davis and Taylor had a falling out over a minor army matter that left their relationship frosty. But Davis persisted in his courtship and resigned from the army partly to appease Sara's father. When Davis became a civilian, Taylor relented. Jefferson and Sara were married in June 1835.[21]

Joseph Davis gave his young brother a kingly wedding gift: a plantation on the banks of the Mississippi River. Jefferson insisted on bringing his new bride there as quickly as possible. "I had no idea of leaving here before fall," Sara wrote her mother on her wedding day, "but hearing the part of the Country to which I am going is quite healthy I have concluded to go down this summer." They arrived in Mississippi in August, during the height of what locals called the "chill-and-fever season." The newlyweds contracted yellow fever or malaria—maybe both. At the very time Lincoln stood vigils in the rain over Ann Rutledge's grave, Davis sat, shaking with fever, by his stricken wife's bed. Sara died on September 15, four months after her wedding day.[22]

After Sara's death, Davis was overwhelmed with grief, but in a manner much different from Lincoln. Instead of Lincoln's sudden, violent spasm of near insanity, Davis began a long, slow inward contraction of his personality, his intellect, and his surroundings. He entered a period of semi-isolation on his plantation that lasted for nearly four years. He did travel a bit (and spoke more often of trips not taken) visiting relatives, friends, taking sight-seeing tours to Washington, D.C., New York, Baltimore, and Philadelphia. He even ventured overseas to Havana, Cuba, where he was nearly arrested for spying when he tried to sketch some of the city's old Spanish fortifications.[23]

These were mere interludes, however, to much longer stretches of isolation on his new plantation, "Brierfield," named in tribute to its dense matting of thorny underbrush. With a workforce of forty slaves, he devoted his energies to clearing the briars and making a home for himself. His days were spent "toughing it out," as he put it, supervising the slave labor that built a "cat and clayed" house in a grove of oak trees, constructed a steam mill, planted cotton and corn, and performed the myriad other tasks called for on a Southern plantation.[24]

Like his brother, Jefferson Davis carried kindly paternal racism to an extreme in his management of slaves. "We . . . stand in such a relation to that people as creates a feeling of kindness and protection," he once said; "we have attachments which have grown with us from childhood."[25] He never seemed to think that his slaves might wish to be elsewhere. He even believed in a sort of honor ethic for them, reminiscent of the military honor code among soldiers. "No matter who told him anything about his Negroes, he said, 'I will ask him to give me an account of it.'"[26]

It may be going too far to suggest that Davis might have deluded himself enough to believe that his Brierfield slaves wanted to be slaves. But there is such a lack of guilt, distrust, or suspicion in his public and private words on the subject that one suspects he intuitively saw in his "people" an emotive, small communal circle analogous to that which he had found in the military, a circle in which he bonded with them based on what he believed to be the soundness of their hearts, and they bonded with him based on their judgments of his heart. In making a comparison between free blacks in the North—"miserable, impoverished, loathsome from deformity and disease"—and slaves in the South, Davis said of the latter that "no hostility exists against them—the master is the natural protector of his slave, and public opinion, common feeling, [and] mere interest would not allow him to neglect his wants."[27]

While his days were spent caring for his "people" and supervising their work, his evenings were spent in Joseph's office at nearby Hurricane plantation, where the two brothers "occupied their evenings with conversations on grave subjects," usually politics. But Davis believed this to be more of a hobby, or at best an avocation. "You perceive that when I write of Politics I am out of my element and naturally slip back to seeding and plowing," he wrote a friend. And so Davis's life went, his mind on farming, locking itself within the relatively narrow borders of Davis Bend and his brother's office. This was his way of assuaging grief. "Sometimes a year would elapse without his leaving the plantation," Varina later wrote. "I am living as retired as a man on the great thoroughfare of the Mississippi can be," he wrote to a friend in summer 1840.[28]

Although Lincoln seemed able to wall off his grief, storing it in a separate area of a mind that was fairly adept at compartmentalizing, Davis allowed his tragic experience gradually to remold him, shaping him like running water slowly altering a riverbank. Whether from guilt—it was he who had insisted, after all, that his young bride accompany him south during the fever season—or deeply suppressed anger at the fate that had deprived him of Sara, or a sullen acquiescence in the cold reality of death, Jefferson Davis became a different man from his days as a dashing young West Point lieutenant. A certain stoic quality crept over him, and along with it an obsession with maintaining an air of dignified reserve. He now seemed humorless, gray, and cold, a man given to long hours of dry reading in his brother's library, to formulating detached constitutional abstractions, and to what some observers perceived as pettifogging legalism about the precise meaning of words.[29]

On the surface Davis seemed to be the sort who drew stern boundaries between his outward appearance and inner feelings, and yet in some respects the very opposite was true. Unlike Lincoln, Davis was unable to compartmentalize anything. He allowed Sara's death to change him, slowly but surely, in ways deep and lasting. He could not separate such a private tragedy from the other roles he played—planter, politician, and later, husband—because he wanted outward appearances and inner thoughts and feelings to mesh as closely as possible. "Every shade of feeling that crossed the minds of those about him was noticed," Varina later observed, "and he could not bear anyone to be inimical to him."[30]

Joseph allowed Jefferson to remain in his self-imposed isolation, but he apparently grew concerned about his younger brother's well-being. One suspects he brought Jefferson into frequent political conversations about current events, the Constitution, and American history as a way to keep his mind from becoming too narrowly focused on Brierfield, Davis Bend, and the planting season. Joseph took this one step further in 1843 when he apparently engineered the encounter between Jefferson and Varina Howell. Joseph knew the Howells well, and he asked Jefferson to deliver a message to Varina's family, hoping to foster an "accidental" encounter with Varina. The ploy worked. "To-day Uncle Joe sent, by his younger brother (did you know he had one?) an urgent invitation to me to go at once to 'the Hurricane,'" Varina wrote her mother. She added, "He impresses me as a remarkable kind of man," but "I do not think I shall ever like him as I do his brother Joe."[31]

Like Mary Todd, Varina Howell was given to expressing forthright, some might in her day have said impudent, opinions. She was intelligent and lively, with an independent mind, and her first recorded impressions of Davis provide perhaps the most accurate assessment of his character ever written. "He . . . has a way of taking for granted that everybody agrees with him when he expresses an opinion, which offends me," she wrote her mother. "He is the kind of person I should expect to rescue one from a mad dog at any risk, but to insist upon a stoical indifference to the fright afterward."[32]

Years later Varina copied this letter into her memoirs, with the sheepish comment, "So wrote this little miss of seventeen of the future hero and statesman!"[33] In her old age she seemed almost embarrassed by her own frankness (though not to the point that she refrained from reprinting her letter). Decades of marriage to Jefferson Davis may have caused her to become more circumspect, for she quickly found that her husband wanted no such opinions. He wanted a compliant, quiet, domestic spouse. "I was much gratified to see that you [have] been engaged in useful and domestic things," he wrote her in 1846. "However unimportant in themselves each may be, it is the mass which constitutes the business of life, and as it is pursued so will it generally be found that a woman is happy and contented."[34]

Davis wanted Varina doing the "useful, domestic things" common to a woman's world, and he effectively shunted her to the margin of his masculine domains. The "office," for example, (Joseph's and, presumably, Jefferson's) was a preeminently masculine space. Varina reflected the men-only atmosphere when she placed "the office" in direct juxtaposition to her own realm as she described Hurricane. "On the right-hand side of the hall were the drawing-room and the 'tea room,' where the ladies sat; on the other was a bedchamber and 'the office.'" Walking down the hallway many times, Davis received a continual tutelage in the gendered fraternity of politics as he turned left, away from "where the ladies sat" to the office where men discussed the public issues that to him mattered most. Occasionally a woman might be invited—"summoned" was the way Varina put it—to pick up the reading of congressional debates when Jefferson's eyes grew tired. "While I was there I often took my turn," Varina wrote, "and [I] greatly enjoyed their comments." She never referred to having joined in the conversation herself, however, acting merely as a bystander and reader. Here was an early, subtle education in both the presence and the absence of women from the realm of public affairs for the future president of the Confederacy, a replication in domestic miniature of the Southern male ideal of the *polis* at large.[35]

Varina learned submission in the office, but elsewhere there was friction. In the early years of her marriage she clashed with her husband, particularly when he entered public life, which meant long separations and loneliness for her, coupled with the common strains of marriage and motherhood. She did not like his sometimes salty language, she quarreled with his relatives, and she complained vaguely about what she called "the weary past and blighted future." She also committed a cardinal sin, at least according to Jefferson Davis: she apparently questioned his explanations for something he said or did. "I cannot bear to be suspected or complained of, or misconstrued after explanation, *by you*," he wrote Varina. He even told her once that she should take up horticulture and gardening; growing shrubs would be perfect for her "exacting and devoted temper . . . because no suspicion of ingratitude or faithfulness [faithlessness?] can exist towards them."[36]

Although he could not stand Varina's judgments concerning his character, Davis felt comfortable expounding at length on her character and giving her instructions for her proper deportment. "Be pious, be calm, be useful, and charitable and temperate in all things," he admonished her. When Varina clashed with Joseph Davis concerning the construction of the plantation home at Brierfield, Davis told her that as a woman, and most of all as his wife, she needed to avoid direct confrontations with others. "To be able to look over the conventionalisms of society, yet to have the good sense which skillfully avoids a collision is the power and practice I desire in my wife," he informed her; otherwise she would be commented upon unfavorably by polite society, "the fear of which would render me as a *husband* unhappy." Even Davis admitted that he carried this fear of acquiring a reputation as the husband of a difficult wife to excess, calling it his "morbid sensibility."[37]

It was a matter of honor, basically, a touchy subject among white Southern men. Southern honor required men to behave as masters of their realms, particularly their households; it required them to rule over their "inferiors," be they blacks, women, or poorer whites. Davis feared for his public reputation, and with it his social standing as a Southern planter, should his wife prove to be too forward or shrill by social standards. Lincoln salvaged his honor by marrying Mary Todd, and Davis tried to guard his by controlling his wife's outspoken opinions.

But Varina continued to offend his sensibilities during the early years of their marriage. Davis interpreted his wife's outbursts as simple willfulness, on which he blamed her "circumstances, habits, education, [and] combativeness." His response was to personalize their arguments; as with Sara's death, he allowed marital stress and strain to affect his personality. After one particularly tense fight, he left Varina at Brierfield while he traveled to Washington, D.C. He scolded her for causing him to go "alone from home; with body crippled, nerves shattered, mind depressed." He wrote Varina that she would be directly responsible for "destroy[ing] my sensibility . . . driv[ing] me for relief to temporary stupifaction, and vicious associations." Davis even told his wife she was ruining his always precarious health. "I had hoped your memory . . . would have grappled with substantial facts, and led you to conclusions, which would have formed for your future line of conduct suited to the character of your husband," he coldly admonished her, adding that "your course, if continued would render it impossible for us ever to live together."[38]

Varina did what many other young American women in her time must have done; she conformed herself to her husband's wishes. It would be going too far to suggest that she became a submissive wife, but the friction diminished as she learned to accept the consequences of being married to a public figure. She also learned to accept the consequences of being married to Jefferson Davis. She continued to offer her opinions but learned how to do so in ways her husband would find less abrasive. "I saw your very forcible little speech in partial answer to Mr. Hale's vituperations against slavery," she wrote him while he was in Washington in 1849. "It was a little too violent, more so than I would have liked to hear you be, however well deserved the censure might be." As to her loneliness, by 1852 she wrote, "I feel the want of you every hour," but then added, "I try not to be so selfish." In the postscript she added again, "Don't think me to [sic] selfish, but can you not come home[?]" Varina discovered how to couch her wishes in the more deferential tones of words like "little too" violent and "don't think me selfish." By the time Davis had fully embarked on his political career, Varina had become the dutiful politician's wife, and their quarrels seem to have subsided.[39]

Lincoln was never able to do so with Mary. Much has been written about the tribulations of the Lincoln marriage, though some of them have no doubt been exaggerated.[40] Yet there was a great deal of conflict between these two very different people, at least as much as in the Davis marriage, if not more so. Mary's irascible, unstable temper was the root source of their problems. "Lincoln and his wife got along tolerably well, unless Mrs. L[incoln] got the devil in her," remembered a Springfield neighbor.[41]

Their life together began on a difficult note when the Lincolns moved into a Springfield boarding house, the Globe. While Lincoln was away for long periods riding the circuit, Mary remained in this ramshackle hotel, enduring the raucous company of her (mostly male) neighbors, the incessant hammering and clanking of a nearby blacksmith shop, and eventually the tribulations of pregnancy and childbirth. The Globe was the very sort of place where Lincoln had spent his bachelor years, and he would have thrived on its hustle and bustle. Mary did not.[42]

The Lincolns eventually moved to a house located near the center of Springfield and within easy walking distance of the courthouse and Lincoln's law office. It was a modest little home, somewhere between rich and poor, like the Lincolns themselves. Abraham brought with him the slovenly habits ingrained from thirty-something years of informal living. He lounged about the place wherever he was most comfortable, reading books and newspapers on the floor and in the hallways. He displayed what Mary thought were execrable table manners and sometimes answered the door in his shirtsleeves. "I'll trot out the womenfolk for you," Lincoln once said to a caller, much to her horror.[43] Raised in a rich Southern family with all the attendant order and comforts of a plantation home, she was shocked at his behavior.[44]

There were other problems as well. Like Davis, Lincoln was away from his home and family for long periods of time, and, like Varina, Mary was terribly upset by this. "She always Said that if her husband had Staid [sic] at home as he ought to, She could love him better," one neighbor said. Alone for long stretches of time while her husband rode the law circuit, burdened with the care of a growing family and household, perhaps it is small wonder that Mary was often short-tempered.[45]

Mary could irritate neighbors, friends, and servants alike, many of whom found her to be "troublesome," "hysterical," "uncontrollable," or just plain "cranky." If neighborhood rumors were accurate, she sometimes carried her frustrations to the point of physical violence. During one imbroglio over a fireplace Lincoln allowed to burn low, Mary struck him in the face with a stick of wood, injuring his nose so badly that he showed up in court the following day with a large bandage on his face. On another occasion she hit him because he purchased the wrong type of meat for their breakfast, and on still another she chased him down a Springfield street with a knife.[46]

Lincoln responded to these problems in several ways. One neighbor remembered him pushing Mary back into the house after an argument, exclaiming, "Now stay in the house and don't disgrace us before the eyes of the world." But his more typical reaction was a disarming calm, or even a laugh in the face of one of Mary's outbursts. "Lincoln paid no attention . . . would pick up one of his Children and walked [sic] off," recalled a neighbor.[47]

On most occasions, he chose the better part of valor and simply retreated. Sometimes he would walk the streets and alleys of Springfield until late at night, waiting for Mary's temper to subside, or he would show up at friends' homes and remain as long as he could. He once stayed after supper at a friend's house until eleven o'clock at night, remarking, "Well I hate to go home." Most often, he ended up in his law office, sleeping on a six-and-a-half foot couch well suited for his lanky frame. Herndon wrote that he would sometimes find Lincoln already there when he arrived in the morning, a sure indication "that a breeze had sprung up over the domestic sea, and that the waters were troubled."[48]

Davis more or less commanded Varina to change, but Lincoln did not take this sort of approach with Mary. "He always meekly accepted as final the authority of his wife in all matters of domestic concern," Herndon observed, and Lincoln "exercised no government of any kind over his household." He possessed a fundamentally passive personality anyway, but in the presence of Mary's opinions and temper he could be almost submissive. Once, when a worker who was engaged in some task at their home needed to cut down a shade tree, he went to see Lincoln to ascertain his wishes. Lincoln asked the man whether he had asked Mary for her opinion. When the man replied that she wanted the tree removed, Lincoln exclaimed, "Then in God's name cut it down clean down to the roots."[49]

Davis compelled changes in his wife's character—or at least Varina's outward demeanor—but Lincoln did not try to do so with Mary. Accounts of their domestic disputes almost always stress Mary's role as the aggressor; it seems never to have occurred to Lincoln to try to change her behavior by taking charge of his household or by leaving home for an extended period of time, or by pursuing the strategies Jefferson Davis employed with Varina. Aside from an occasional scolding concerning Mary's squandering of money, Lincoln appears to have had surprisingly little to say about his wife's manifest character flaws.[50]

Indeed, neighbors and friends noted that it was Mary, not Abraham, who constantly tried to alter her spouse's behavior. She was particularly scornful of his often slovenly dress and manners, constantly berating him for his frayed cuffs, awkward mannerisms, and other such shortcomings. Jefferson Davis confessed to a "morbid sensibility" concerning his wife's effect on their social standing; Mary's sensibilities concerning her husband's behavior were quite "morbid" and often excessive. Lincoln responded with a shrug. "Mary is having one of her spells," he would say, and he tried as best he could to stay out of her way.[51]

Theirs was a rocky union, a source of unending gossip and concern among Springfield's citizenry, and yet, like the Davis marriage, it survived, and perhaps even grew stronger as the years passed. Both marriages, though not idyllic, were for the most part functional, and sometimes even passionate and romantic. "Hubbin would kiss the paper he sends to his wife, but is in the midst of men," wrote a self-conscious Davis; "I send a kiss upon the wires of love and feel earth, air and sea cannot break the connection."[52] Varina wrote to her mother that "Jeff. . . . is so tender, and good" and "such a dear good fellow."[53] Lincoln often referred to his wife affectionately as "Molly," and Mary later remembered that "it was always, music to my ears, both before and after our marriage when my husband told me, that I was the only one he ever thought of, or cared for." Mary's possibly selective memory aside, there was at least some music in the Lincoln marriage, enough to facilitate the creation of a large family, of whom Lincoln was quite proud.[54]

At the very least the two marriages endured, and for a long time. They endured in different ways, however, and for different reasons. The differences reflected the disparate personalities of the two wives but perhaps even more so of the two husbands, men who approached married life from very different angles. Davis demanded, and eventually got, a submissive wife, and so their marriage lasted. Lincoln allowed Mary to give her emotions full vent and worked around the consequences as best he could, and so their marriage lasted. They danced different dances, the Lincolns and the Davises.

They did so in part because they approached matters of control and persuasion differently. Davis possessed a more domineering personality, a temperament accustomed to commanding soldiers and slaves. Lincoln, on the other hand, was a fundamentally passive man, a compromiser when at all possible. The series of retreats, circumventions, and reunions that made up so much of his married life were artful, if taxing, acts of negotiation.

Underlying this difference of temperament were more subtle differences in the presumptions Lincoln and Davis brought to any relationship at this point in their lives. Lincoln's approach to Mary was part and parcel of a worldview that was careful not to presume any great knowledge about what animated a person's spirit or governed a person's actions. He behaved as if women in general, and Mary in particular, were a mystery, not to be gainsaid or solved but carefully handled or evaded, as circumstances warranted. Lincoln never tried to solve the riddle that was his wife; to do so would have required an intimate knowledge of her innermost thoughts, fears, and anxieties. He was unwilling to attempt this. He "distanced himself physically and emotionally" from Mary, according to historian Michael Burlingame, and "invested most of his psychological capital in his career as lawyer and politician."[55]

Davis, on the other hand, presumed to know what was in Varina's heart, just as he presumed to know what was in the heart of his Brierfield slaves. "Without hearts there is no home," he once wrote. Ever the benevolent paternalist, he believed that anyone he took into his inner circle of Brierfield had to know that he had their best interests in mind and that he could tell at all times what those interests were and how an honest soul would react to his ministrations. He wanted his wife to have a heart that "beats in unison with my own." This was what a home meant for Davis: a place where he could peacefully assume that he knew what those around him thought and felt, where he could see "happy, truly affectionate faces," where he could form "associations of friendship and kindly feeling."[56]

Whether this is the sort of home Jefferson Davis actually possessed at Brierfield—surrounded by slaves who learned at least to fake contentment and a wife who learned to couch her opinions in circumspection—is debatable. Lincoln may have had much the unhappier home, but he never deceived himself as to what he had and what he did without.

SPEECHES

        Davis and Lincoln embarked on political careers at roughly the same time during the late 1830s and early 1840s. Politics was the surest route to fulfill the ambition that lay buried deep in their psyches, and by the 1840s they wanted renown and fame as national political figures, having set their sights on acquiring national offices to fulfill this desire.

    Both men spent much of their early political careers campaigning in the various towns and farming communities around their homes. They appeared at political clubs, social gatherings, rallies, and events of every shape and size. On October 6, 1843, for example, Lincoln spoke at a barbecue in Jacksonville, Illinois, where he "took up the three prominent principles of the Whig party—the Tariff, a sound and uniform National Currency and the Distribution and proceeds of the Public Lands."[1] A month later, Davis appeared at a Democratic party rally in a Vicksburg hotel to expound his views on various state economic matters. Responding to a three-hour address by a prominent Mississippi Whig, Sargeant Prentiss, Davis "in a speech of thirty minutes successfully replied to the principal controversial points in [Prentiss's] address."[2] Such gatherings were the stuff of political life in Jacksonian America, and at first glance it is difficult to find much difference between Lincoln's and Davis's experiences in ostensibly "Northern" or "Southern" (or "western") settings. Both were compelled to do this political grunge work, addressing relatively small, local gatherings, sometimes in a debate format, sometimes as a leader of the party faithful.

But Lincoln and Davis immersed themselves in very different political ideologies. Davis seems never to have given any thought to becoming anything other than a Democrat. He once said he had been "bred in the paths of Democracy," and he was quite right. It was the party of choice for his family, most of his region, and his brother Joseph. He was "always a democrat [whose] political conduct had been guided by the principles of the democratic creed," as he told an audience in 1848. He had never abandoned the party or "doubted its correctness," and he "knew of no name more sacred" than the Democratic party, "nor of any that he would more readily bear."[3]

Lincoln, for his part, was almost reflexively a Whig. That party's emphasis on economic development, his own distaste for the farming life that formed the backbone of Jacksonian Democracy, and his admiration for the Whig leader Henry Clay combined to push him firmly into the Whig camp. Even as he threw in with the Whigs, he knew a good many Democrats; he probably knew more Illinois Democrats than Davis knew Southern Whigs. Nevertheless, his political associates and contacts were overwhelmingly Whig. He was quite pleased with this political pedigree. "I belonged to the whig party from its origin to its close," he proudly wrote in 1860.[4]

Lincoln turned to politics almost instinctively, pursuing political office in a slow upward climb from New Salem postmaster to state legislator to, briefly, Illinois congressman. He built up his political résumé one handshake at a time; Davis took advantage of his social standing and his brother's high political contacts in Mississippi. After a brief stint as a state presidential elector, he became a viable, and eventually successful, congressional candidate. "I have mingled but little in politics and . . . have an arsenal poorly supplied for a campaign," he confessed to a Democratic party leader in 1844.[5] Lincoln was like a chugging, grinding engine, working his way doggedly up the political ladder from below. Davis was rather more like a person presented with a political career ready-made, his military title, social status, and family contacts having given him advantages Lincoln never knew.

This is not to say that Davis was not compelled to work for his political living. He worked in the guise of numerous speaking engagements, before audiences large and small, throughout the Mississippi countryside. Here lay a common ground with Lincoln: both men became by necessity prolific political speechmakers.

When addressing an audience, Lincoln was renowned for his animated style. He typically began a speech slowly, haltingly at first, until he warmed to his subject, "gradually fixing his footing, and getting command of his limbs, loosening his tongue, and firing his thoughts." He was fond of dramatic arm and hand gestures or an occasional sharp snapping of his head and neck to emphasize a point. Sometimes he would bend his knees, then nearly leap upward, gesticulating with outspread arms for emphasis. Combined with his unusual height and generally gawky appearance, his mannerisms could leave an indelible impression, sometimes more so than his actual words.[6]

It is always difficult to tell with any public figure what is artifice and what is "genuine" (if indeed there is any firm distinction between the two). Lincoln may have been Honest Abe, but he was a devotee of theater and Shakespeare, and he had learned in courtrooms the value of performance. Thus, even though his peculiarities in style and delivery simply may have been manifestations of his equally peculiar personality, it is also likely that they were calculated to impress his audience. "If Mr. Lincoln studied any one thing more than another and for effect it was to make himself understood by all classes," remembered one observer. Perhaps he displayed a set of idiosyncracies guaranteed to make a lasting impression even on people who might not have easily followed his sometimes complex political arguments.[7]

Davis, on the other hand, was often described in terms denoting distance and formality. He was a talented orator—at this stage in their careers as talented as Lincoln—but his speechmaking style was different. When he gave his reply to Prentiss in Vicksburg, an audience member described him as a "classical and chaste speaker." He was frequently called "proud," "honorable," "elegant," "deliberate," and "calm" in appearance and demeanor. As one sympathetic onlooker commented, Davis's "manner is formed after a highly intellectual, pure, but unimpassioned model. He addresses the reason, the judgement, the intellect; but he has no word for the passions." A political opponent was less charitable, remarking that Davis displayed oratorical powers that "resembled . . . a schoolboy declamation."[8]

Even those friendly to him noticed his inability (or unwillingness) to really arouse his audiences. "Could he only animate the perfect, but somewhat inanimate statue of his eloquence with some of the strong outlines of passion," remarked an observer, could he only "enlist the feelings and captivate the imagination, he would rank among the foremost of our Mississippi ora-

tors." Dispassionate, unemotional argument was his natural political disposition, honed by long hours of lofty conversation in Joseph's office where he
need not cajole or persuade or assume any other pose to sway a brother with
whom he never disagreed or the invisible black servants whose opinions did
not matter to him. In this sense, Davis may have been more unaffected—
more "honest"—than Lincoln. Davis was genuine in his stiffness; he was
unable to seem.[9]

Aside from style, Lincoln and Davis differed greatly in the substance of
their early political speeches. Belonging to different political parties with often
diametrically opposed policies and philosophies, they of course espoused quite
different positions on many of the major national controversies of their day.
Lincoln was generally well disposed toward the establishment of a National
Bank; Davis believed his party's leader, Andrew Jackson, had been entirely
correct to wage a political war on that institution. As a good Democrat, Davis
abhorred protective tariffs as a violation of the "most liberal principles of
commerce," which ensured "the freest exchange of the products of different soils and climates"; Lincoln, along with other Whigs, signed petitions
calling on Congress to create tariffs as a means to "prevent excessive impor-
tation of goods, and excessive exportations of specie." In this and other such
matters the two men usually followed the orthodoxy of their parties.[10]

Both men also spoke often about local politics, where economic issues
predominated. Lincoln was the Illinois prophet of "internal improvements,"
constructing river improvements, canals, roads, and railroads in an effort to
make his state into a capitalist entrepreneur's dream. "Illinois surpasses every
other spot of equal extent upon the face of the globe, in fertility of soil, and
in the proportionable amount of the same which is sufficiently level for actual cultivation," he declared in 1839. He believed the vast potential of these
natural resources could be realized only with an ambitious, state-sponsored
program that revamped (or created from scratch) an economically viable
infrastructure. To that end, he was one of the architects of an ambitious
multimillion-dollar internal improvements program passed by the state legislature in 1835, a program with nearly utopian economic visions of Illinois
bound together and with the wide world by a web of canals, railroads, and
highways. An economic downturn in 1837 dashed these hopes and plunged
the state deeply into debt, but Lincoln clung to the program to the very last.[11]

Interestingly enough, in light of his strict constructionism and general
aversion to internal improvement schemes, Davis too made a strong case in
his early speeches for government funds (in this case federal money) to be

spent improving the harbors and waterways of his region. He made his case in a different context, however, arguing that coastal improvements along the Gulf of Mexico were indispensable to the nation's defense. There was also a hint of the sectional friction that later animated so many of his speeches. "Having made such appropriations for the benefit of other portions of the Union, inability has not been the cause of this failure in duty towards us," Davis argued, "a failure which is aggravated by the recollection, that throughout the whole period of our federal existence, we have contributed, as consumers, to the revenue, in a higher ratio than that of our representatives in the halls of legislation . . . and therefore our claim to a share of those appropriations to which we are all entitled, is something stronger than our representative rate."[12]

But Davis's primary economic focus in Mississippi concerned banking, an ostensibly dry subject that nevertheless created troubling and emotionally charged controversies. He spoke for his party's agricultural roots and distrust of banking in general. He declared it to be a general rule "that the few borrow, the many hold the notes of the Banks; it surely must be elsewhere than in the ranks of the Democracy that advocates are to be found, contending for the exemption of the few, by sacrificing the rights of the many."[13]

Davis had a lot to say about these matters and did so in several speeches during the mid-1840s. Overall, however, he devoted relatively little time to local politics in his early speeches. He spent more time discussing issues of national concern, and his speeches could serve as a primer for the great American controversies of the day: the annexation of Texas, the Oregon dispute with Great Britain, the creation of a sound national currency, and the best means of distributing public lands in the West.[14] This is perhaps an eloquent statement about the vitality of Jacksonian America's political culture, but it also indicates the immediate upward arc of Davis's political ambitions.

Lincoln tended to be much more locally focused on issues vital to Springfield and to Illinois. This was no doubt a function of his stint in the Illinois state legislature, a level of political service that Davis did not experience. Nevertheless, Lincoln also had a great deal to say about national issues and national policies in his early political speeches. In May 1844, for example, he appeared at an evening gathering at the statehouse in Springfield to discuss President John Tyler's attempts to annex Texas. Lincoln argued that such a move "at this time upon terms agreed upon by John Tyler was altogether inexpedient."[15]

Beyond such pragmatic policy matters, Lincoln also spoke to the big picture, the state of the American experiment. He did so many times during the Civil War, of course, in words at Gettysburg and before the Capitol rotunda, which would remain deeply etched in the nation's memory. But this was not yet the Lincoln of "four score and seven years ago" or "with malice towards none"; he still lacked that eloquence, that voice leavened by the devastation of war. During the early years of his career, however, he did have something to say about where he believed America was going and what it should be, most notably in a remarkable address before a Springfield oratory society.

Oratory clubs, or Lyceums, were popular in the Jacksonian era. Approximately four thousand American communities sponsored debate and lecture clubs that hosted regular sessions on topics ranging from personal hygiene to American foreign policy. Audiences flocked to such gatherings in an age when popular democracy was thought to include the wide dissemination of public knowledge on every conceivable topic. Lyceums fed both a populist public's thirst for knowledge and the ambition of upwardly mobile professionals seeking a name for themselves. When Lincoln was twenty-seven years old, he made one of his first attempts at a formal address before one such club, the Young Men's Lyceum of Springfield, with his speech, "The Perpetuation of Our Political Institutions." Here he addressed matters of American nationalism more ephemeral (but no less important) than protective tariffs or monetary policies.[16]

Lincoln opened the Lyceum address with a romantic wordscape of the American continent. "We find ourselves in the peaceful possession, of the fairest portion of earth, as regards extent of territory, fertility of soil, and salubrity of climate," he said. At the same time, Americans were blessed with a Constitution and form of government "conducing more essentially to the ends of civil and religious liberty, than any of which the history of former times tells." Lincoln believed his generation owed a profound debt of gratitude to the Founding generation, which had made this possible. "Theirs was the task (and nobly they performed it) to possess themselves, and through themselves, us, of this goodly land; and to uprear upon its hills and its valleys, a political edifice of liberty and equal rights."[17]

As good as the times were, however, Lincoln saw clouds on the American horizon; he feared the instability and chaos of 1830s America. He told his listeners that a "growing disposition to substitute the wild and furious passions, in lieu of the sober judgement of the Courts" pervaded America. "This mobocratic spirit, which all must admit, is now abroad in the land," profoundly troubled Lincoln as a sign of a deepening and dangerous hostility toward government in particular and law and order in general. The nation stood in little danger of conquest from foreign enemies; rather, the true danger for America's institutions lay within: "If destruction be our lot, we must ourselves be its author and finisher."[18]

This internal threat took two forms. First, Lincoln conjured the image of an American Caesar who might arise to destroy the liberties of the American people. He would be a "towering genius" who "disdains a beaten path" of glory and power and instead "seeks regions hitherto unexplored" for self-gratification and ambition. Lincoln's Caesar was a bundle of emotional extremes, all brought out into the open. He "scorns," he "thirsts," he "burns," he "seek[s] the gratification of [his] ruling passion." These emotions could be destructive, or they could be constructive; certainly passion was necessary, for those who lack it, according to Lincoln, "belong not to the family of the lion or the tribe of the eagle." He recognized, too, that every person harbored dangerous feelings, referring to "the jealousy, and envy, and avarice, incident to our nature." Problems arose when those feelings took on a public form in the guise of "some man of lofty genius."[19] Some scholars have suggested that Lincoln was talking about himself when he spoke of this Caesar, projecting upon this imagined figure the warring impulses of ambition and conquest within himself. I think it is more likely that he was speaking of a figure much simpler and less murky: Andrew Jackson, perhaps, with Lincoln betraying his Whiggish mistrust of a strong executive.[20] But it is interesting to note that Lincoln here suggested that public displays of emotion could be potentially dangerous and destructive forces to the smooth operation of the American polity.

Lincoln's second internal danger was that of unrestrained mob violence. He was disturbed by a spate of lawlessness then making newspaper headlines across the country, and he recited a litany of recent violent behavior in Mississippi, St. Louis, and Illinois. Lynchings and vandalism were "awfully fearful in any community," and his answer was an appeal to rationalism as the only safe way for Americans to conduct themselves. He equated the law with logic and reason, and he told his audience that only adherence to both could safeguard Americans from the dangers of "the mobocratic spirit" or a dictator. "Cold, calculating, unimpassioned reason, must furnish all the materials for our future support and defence," he declared.[21]

Lincoln's Lyceum address contained a variety of themes and subthemes, but underlying it was his fundamental antipathy toward open and unrestrained emotionalism in American public life, whether from a Caesar or from the people themselves.[22] His was an antipathy, however, that was shot through with confusion. His appeal for reason was in fact quite emotional, asking that "every American pledge his life, his property, his sacred honor" to the support of law and order. He wanted, in effect, a passionate oath by all Americans not to let their passions sway them. He wanted what he called a "political religion," to which "the old and the young, the rich and the poor, the grave and the gay, of all sexes and tongues, and colors and conditions, [would] sacrifice unceasingly upon its altars." The root value of this almost evangelical political faith, however, would be "unimpassioned reason."[23]

Lincoln also appeared to be uncertain as to whether one might actually be able to discern clearly an individual's motives or true intentions. On the one hand, he suggested quite plainly that he knew what feelings animated his American Caesar: "Distinction will be his paramount object." At the same time, however, he pointed out how hard it was to judge what really lay in the hearts of strangers. "Good men, men who love tranquility" were just as susceptible to the "mobocratic spirit" as "the lawless in spirit." Furthermore, when mobs did take the law into their own hands, how could they really be sure they were punishing the wicked and protecting the innocent? Referring to a recent lynching of several gamblers in Vicksburg, Lincoln said that he had no love for the gamblers themselves, being a "portion of the populace that is worse than useless in any community." He warned, however, "When men take it into their hearts today, to hang gamblers, or to burn murderers, they should recollect, that, in the confusion usually attending such transactions, they will be likely to hang someone who is neither a gambler or a murderer."[24]

In the end, it is difficult to see whether Lincoln wanted an America based on sentiment, emotion, and intense feelings or whether he wanted the roiling emotions that he believed resided in every American's breast to be buried beneath a public facade of sober calculation. The imagery of political religion suggested that only a public square in which individuals openly proved their worthy motives and sentiments, as he put it, by "swear[ing] by the blood of the Revolution, never to violate the least particular of the laws of his country" could function properly.[25] Yet his recognition that all human beings possessed base and selfish impulses, and his appeal to reason alone as the foundation of the law, suggested the utility of subsuming emotion and sentiment, of drawing a sharp line between the private and the public and not inquiring too closely into the hearts of one's fellow Americans.

We see in the Lyceum address all the elements of his sometimes confused sense of self and the community around him. But in this instance, he painted these problems as pertaining not to himself, or to his circle of friends, but to the nation as a whole. And the only answer, the only means by which Americans could nurture reason, control emotion, and promote stability was the law. "Let reverence for the laws, be breathed by every American mother, to the lisping babe, that prattles in her lap—let it be taught in the schools, in seminaries, and in colleges—let it be preached from the pulpit, proclaimed in legislative halls, and enforced in courts of justice," he exclaimed.

Lincoln had been a licensed attorney for about a year when he gave the Lyceum address, and already his chosen profession had become more for him than simply a matter of courtrooms and litigation. It permeated American life, it created the conditions of American liberty, and it bound the American community together. "While ever a state of feeling," such as reverence for the law, "shall universally, or even, very generally, prevail throughout the nation," he said, "vain will be every effort, and fruitless every attempt, to subvert our national freedom."[26] Such attempts could come from a Caesar or from mob violence, he believed; the law, and the national identity bound up with it, would prevail and preserve order. It could do for the nation as a whole what it had done for him personally and the communities in which he practiced.

With this speech, Lincoln stood on a mountaintop, as it were, surveying the American landscape around him and offering a mulifaceted commentary that owed at least as much to his own personality as it did to any political or party ideology. Historians have sensed the importance of the Lyceum address, and they have exhaustively analyzed it in an attempt to plumb the depths of Lincoln's psyche. On a basic level, however, the speech is about just what Lincoln stated from the outset: America. And it reflected where he stood as a young lawyer on matters of community and social relationships, be they personal, local, or national. Banks, tariffs, and the like could be debated within the context of a thriving polity. What could not be debated, for Lincoln, was the need to keep excessive emotion out of the American public square, the need to avoid assumptions about other Americans' motives, and above all the universal necessity for all Americans, whatever their region, party loyalty, or political persuasion, to swear fealty to the rule of law.

Davis gave no equivalent of the Lyceum address in his antebellum political career; he did not stand aloft and peer over the tops of the mundane political and policy issues of his day to offer such a sweeping commentary on the American landscape. It is tempting to make this divergence from Lincoln an invidious commentary on their relative stature. Lincoln was the "great man"-in-the-making, who could sense, even at a young age, the calling to define and shape the American experiment; Davis was merely an ordinary Southern politician. But Davis gave no such speech because it was simply not his style. Lincoln was more given to the act of stepping back, of pausing for a moment to look about him and grasp the meaning of what he saw, whether it was the state of American society at the time of his Lyceum speech or later on the state of American ideals in the Gettysburg Address. Davis preferred the more classical mode of constructing a discourse, with his more abstract, quiet ideas about such matters as the state of the American community imbedded within the myriad parts of his arguments. Like Lincoln, Davis possessed certain assumptions about what it meant to be an American in the 1840s. Lincoln may have stood briefly on a mountaintop in the Lyceum address, but Davis formed such opinions and attitudes while toiling away at various policy matters as a Mississippi representative in the U.S. Congress.

When he first entered Congress in 1845, his constituents could not complain that he neglected his home state or its citizens. Only four days after he was sworn in as a new member of the House, he wrote a letter to Secretary of the Navy George Bancroft requesting a midshipman's position for a young Mississippi applicant. "Allow me to add that (if I am not misinformed) we of Mississippi have had less than our proportionate share of Navy appointments," he rather boldly informed the secretary. Bancroft complied with Davis's wishes, and the state of Mississippi had a new and outspoken advocate in Washington, D.C.[27] Over the next few months, he acted the part well, seeking a variety of favors and boons for Mississippi applicants.[28]

At the same time, Davis was quite willing to expand federal authority on matters near to his heart. His first resolution in Congress attempted to expand the army's education system by looking into the "expediency of converting a portion of the forts of the United States into schools for military instruction." He also helped lay the groundwork for a new national institution, sitting on the committee that established the Smithsonian Institute as a body that "tended to the increase and diffusion of knowledge among men" and was therefore all to the good. His remarks on the Smithsonian to the House have a distinctly nationalist ring: "Knowledge was the common cement that was to unite all the heterogenous materials of the Union into one mass."[29]

The same man who so forthrightly defended the principles of state sovereignty on the floor of Congress was simultaneously given to expressions of ardent, even jingoistic nationalism, speaking in lofty tones of American national character in a way he would never employ in his later days as a spokesman for Southern grievances. "The will to do, the soul to dare, the patriotism which will bear every sacrifice belongs to the American people," Davis said. It was a "national character" that was "bounded by no class or geographic section." Elsewhere he spoke of "the versatility, the convertibility, of the American mind" and "the energy and restless spirit of adventure which is a characteristic of our people." When a controversy arose concerning the disposition of public property in newly annexed Texas, Davis wanted its very identity submerged within that of the United States. "Her glory was now the glory of the Union," he said; "her people were our fellow citizens, and their deeds of chivalric daring were our boast as much as theirs."[30] He also consistently and passionately denounced sectionalism, declaring unequivocally that "my thoughts, my feelings, are American." He tended to point fingers toward the North in this regard, saying in effect, you are the sectionalists, not the Southerners. The hypocrisy of this point of view aside, it is most interesting to note the flowery, almost bombastic language this future secessionist used to convey his patriotic feelings. "In our hearts, as in our history, are mingled the names of Concord and Camden, and Saratoga, and Lexington, and Plattsburg, and Chippewa, and Erie, and Moultrie, and New Orleans, and Yorktown, and Bunker," he told Congress in 1846. "Grouped together, they form a record of the triumphs of our cause, a monument of the common glory of our Union."[31]

Davis was an early and enthusiastic American expansionist, and although this was by no means rare for a Southerner of his time, he cast his expansionism in nationalistic, not in sectional, terms. He took umbrage with the suggestion that westward expansion was a Southern issue only, and his endorsement of it generally as "extend[ing] the 'area of freedom' until we had reached a point where man was no longer capable of self-government," had a distinctly nationalistic ring to it. When he called for American involvement in Cuban affairs, perhaps even to the point of outright seizure of the island, he did so in terms of national security, declaring that "the very necessity of defending the United States requires that we should take whatever steps should be necessary always to secure the freedom of the great point of exit and entrance to a large portion of the American coast."[32]

Jefferson Davis the representative was therefore at once a spokesman for Mississippi, the South, and the United States. Certainly his brother's influence pushed him toward adopting strict constructionist and states' rights arguments, but he had also spent enough time in one of the few national institutions of antebellum America, the army, to possess a strong nationalistic streak. It was not unusual for white Southerners to take contradictory positions on issues of local, sectional, and national power, depending on their relative political expediency and their value in protecting slavery and white supremacy. But Davis was different. He thoroughly despised politics even as he became a politician, calling Washington "that hotbed of heartlessness" and disparaging what he termed the "agitation of politicians." At times he seemed almost ashamed of his profession, writing to his nephew, "It has been my misfortune to witness in my political course but little of that elevated statesmanship of which it would give me pleasure to speak to a younger relation." There is throughout Davis's speeches a ring of sincerity in this regard. Given a choice, he wanted to practice the high and principled politics that he and his brother discussed in the office at Hurricane, a politics reflecting the honorable and gentlemanly policies of a former soldier. He wanted "elevated statesmanship," and he wanted a politics not of heartlessness but of genuine sincerity as to principles and values.[33]

Davis's oscillation between localism and nationalistic patriotism in his early political speeches therefore suggests a genuine confusion, a lack of any clear center of gravity. But this of itself is a revealing indicator of his sense of American identity at this stage in his career. The careful hierarchy of priorities and constitutional values so evident in his later thinking—from state to region, and last, to the conditional Union—is nowhere to be found in the 1840s because at this point he drew no rigid distinctions between local, state, and national communities. The question of whether or not the president of the Confederacy was fundamentally an early states' rights enthusiast or an early nationalist is moot: he was both.

Davis placed himself firmly in the state sovereignty, Calhoun camp early on. "To all which has been said of the inherent powers of this Government, I answer, it is the creature of the States," he said, and "as such it could have no inherent power." But these ideas were not for him corrosive; quite the contrary. Davis believed that Americans bonded as a community around these sacred constitutional principles. Just as Lincoln, somewhat contradictorily, wanted Americans to make a passionate commitment to the passionless rule of law, Davis expected a heartfelt, nationwide commitment to the very state sovereignty and strict constructionist principles that would someday tear the nation apart. "State sovereignty, unshorn of its attributes, and private interests freed from undue interference; mutual advantage must bind the people of our Confederacy perpetually together," he said. Calhounian constitutionalism's later centrifugal effect on the American polity should not obscure the fact that in the 1840s, Davis genuinely believed that these ideas were the glue that bound the nation together. They were not simply ideas about the protection of Southern sectional interests or of slavery; for him these ideas created "harmony" and "fraternity" within the Union.[34]

Davis talked a lot about the balance of power, between states, between sections, between nations; and many of his state sovereignty arguments are grounded in these issues. Power for him was a matter of policy, of deciding for example whether a river in Indiana ought to be given equal consideration with a harbor in Louisiana, where federal appropriations were concerned. But these matters of power and the interminable debates concerning proper allocation of resources within the federal orbit—this was not American identity, this was not American community for him. "The southwestern and western States have passed from infancy to manhood, their attachment to the Union growing with their growth," he said in a speech on internal improvements in March 1846; "and now it is proposed by works of internal improvement to bind them to the Confederation." He found this proposition insulting. "Sir, they need no bonds save those of fraternal feeling," he declared."[35]

This was the essence of Americanism for Davis: feelings, fraternity, an emotional sense of cohesiveness within the family that was the Union. He often used familial metaphors for the American community in his speeches. When speaking of Texas's admission into the Union, he said, "Texas had been a member of our family; in her infancy, had been driven from the paternal roof. . . . She now returned, and asked to be admitted to the hearth of the homestead. . . . The generous sympathy, the justice of the family, threw [the door] wide open, and welcomed her return." Elsewhere he referred to Massachusetts and Virginia as "stronger brothers of the family," and he called frontier Americans "our western brethren." Conversely, he described sectionalism as producing "family strife and destruction."[36]

Close bonding among people bound by a sense of honor and brotherhood and by adherence to well-articulated rules of constitutional behavior that all Americans of good faith must recognize to secure harmony and peace in the nation—this has a distinctly West Point flavor, the flavor of a man used to thinking of communities in terms of comradeship, fraternity, and cheerful obedience to clearly defined rules of conduct, whether army regulations or state sovereignty constitutionalism. It was also a common facet of the South's political culture that white Southerners often conceptualized political relationships in familial, face-to-face terms.[37] Through a combination of his military training, his personality, and his regional identity, Davis revealed in his early speeches a man who imagined an American community rooted largely in the heart.

Lincoln thought more in terms of the head. He used no metaphors of "fraternity" in his Lyceum address. His only references to the Union as a family pointed to the rather distant connections of ancestry, what Lincoln called "duty to our posterity, and love for our species in general." Davis the West Point graduate and soldier believed Americans were bound by an emotive, highly idealized affinity to common values and a sense of community. Lincoln the lawyer thought that Americans were bound by a rational fidelity to the law and that the sentiment that ideally bound the national community together—civic virtue and so forth—"must fade, is fading, has faded." Lincoln distrusted the viability of the very qualities Davis required in a vital national community.

Part Two

SECTIONAL
IMAGINATIONS

PATRIOTS

When Davis dictated two brief autobiographical sketches from his sickbed in 1889, he was quick to mention his family's combat record in both. "My father . . . served in the War of the Revolution," he said, "first in the 'mounted gun-men,' and afterward as captain of infantry during the siege of Savannah." He was quite proud of this, and also of his brothers' service during the War of 1812. Three served while one remained, and Davis took pains to illustrate that this was no reflection on his family's honor: "A county court . . . ordered a draft for a certain number of men to stay at home. This draft stopped my brother . . . making him the exception of my father's adult sons who were not engaged in the defence [sic] of the country during the War of 1812."[1]

Davis's West Point education and frontier service in the regular army might be expected to have given him an insider's perspective on war, but this was true only to a limited extent. Military subjects were actually subordinated to engineering and mathematics at the Academy, and during his tenure in the army, Davis saw little combat. He was away from the army on furlough during the Black Hawk War of 1832, when the Sauk chief Black

Hawk led an armed uprising on the Illinois frontier. Davis may have returned just in time to witness the war's last skirmish, the Battle of Bad Axe, in which he played no significant role. He did act as Black Hawk's guard, escorting the Native American prisoner during his trip to a military prison at Rock Island, Illinois. Black Hawk described him as a "young war chief," but in fact Davis had seen very little war of any kind and did not during the rest of his stay in the army.[2]

Like many professional soldiers, Davis probably wanted at least to taste combat, but he did not romanticize war itself. When many of his country-men called for war with Great Britain over the Oregon boundary dispute in 1845, Congressman Davis spoke soberly about the possibility, describing as "heresy" the notion that "war is the purifier, blood is the ailment, of free institutions." The future president of the short-lived Confederacy admitted that "it is true that republics have often been cradled in war, but more often they have met with the grave than the cradle."[3]

Yet at the same time Davis interpreted his nation's founding through the lens of war, suggesting that the Revolution was the defining American com-munity experience. His particular reading of the Revolution had the British visiting "outrages upon the northern Colonies," after which Southerners rose to their defense. "Sympathy, fraternal feeling, and devotion to principle, brought the South to your side in your first step to resistance," Davis told Congress. For him, war cemented the Union by bridging what he apparently believed was a natural gap between North and South. The Revolution formed "a record of the triumphs of our cause, a monument of the common glory of our Union. What southern man would wish it less by one of the northern names of which it is composed [?]"[4]

When Lincoln wrote his own autobiography in 1859, he did not dwell on any ancestral military prowess, probably because he knew relatively little about his own genealogy.[5] He took pains to separate his family from even the suggestion of combat. "My paternal grandfather . . . was killed by In-dians," he wrote, then added, "not in battle, but by stealth, when he was labor-ing to farm in the forest." Others might have dressed up this incident into something smacking of martial bravery, but not Lincoln, who never was much impressed with the drums and trumpets of warfare and felt a lifelong abhor-rence of violence in general.[6]

Nevertheless, he could evoke romantic images of war when the need arose, and like Davis he saw that shared experiences of war had helped shape the Revolutionary generation's sense of community. Lincoln believed eighteenth-century Americans were able to redirect at Britain the negative emotions—"jealousy, envy, and avarice"—that might have otherwise destroyed any nascent American nationalism. Military service created positive national memories and shared experiences. "At the close of [the Revolution], nearly every adult male had been a participator in some of its scenes," he said in 1838. "The consequence was, that of those scenes, in the form of a husband, a father, a son or a brother, a living history was to be found in every family . . . a history that could be read and understood alike by all."[7]

Not that Lincoln himself had much personal experience with such matters. His family does not seem to have passed down war stories, and he failed to generate any of his own. The closest he came to combat was marginal involvement in the Black Hawk War. When Black Hawk led his followers into Illinois, Lincoln volunteered with many other young men in the state and, to his immense joy, was elected captain of a company. They were "a whole souled hard set of men," and he wasn't much of a captain. He was unable to curb his men's profligate drinking habits, and at one point his superiors made him wear a wooden sword for two days as punishment. When he himself violated military rules by firing a musket in camp, he was relieved of his sword (the real one) as well as the musket. Lincoln was fourteen miles away when the Battle of Bad Axe occurred, stationed near the town of Dixon—as close as he ever came physically to Jefferson Davis or (prior to the Civil War) to combat.[8]

Lincoln was not much of a soldier, but he appreciated the impact of war on a community. Both he and Davis worried that the unifying nationalism of the Revolutionary experience had worn thin during their time. Davis believed the corrosive agent was sectionalism. "If envy, and jealousy, and sectional strife, are eating like rust at the bonds our fathers expected to bind us, they come from causes which our southern atmosphere has never furnished," he declared. He called for the "remembrance of the petty jarrings of today" to be "buried in the nobler friendship of an earlier time." Northerners should keep alive the flame of revolutionary ardor, keep the familial spirit created by the Revolution permanently intact. That some of them might not spoke to a failure of (Northern) character.[9]

Lincoln thought the community spirit of the Revolutionary War was fading away naturally. The passion produced by the conflict with Great Britain "must fade, is fading, has faded, with the circumstances that produced it." The passions of war and revolution "were a fortress of strength; but, what invading foemen could never do, the silent artillery of time has done." It was unreasonable to expect otherwise. "Like everything else, [the Revolution] must fade upon the memory of the world, and grow more and more dim by the lapse of time. . . . Their influence cannot be what it has heretofore been."[10]

He had less faith than Davis in the abiding sense of national fraternity forged in war. There is more than a little irony here, considering Lincoln's future role as the president who would use war as an instrument of national unification. War would someday remake him as it remade America during his time, but the antebellum Lincoln was a lawyer who only briefly sampled military life and wanted no more. Davis, on the other hand, was trained for war, then rejected that training to pursue the life of a Mississippi planter. He returned to the army again in 1846, when America declared war on Mexico over a dispute about the precise location of Texas's southern border, among other things. The ensuing conflict gave a baptism of fire to several future luminaries of the Civil War: Robert E. Lee, Ulysses S. Grant, and Thomas J. Jackson as well as Jefferson Davis. For Lincoln, the Mexican War seemed likely to spell the end of his fledgling political career; for Davis, it proved to be a watershed event.

Davis had served only six months in the House of Representatives when hostilities broke out with America's southern neighbor in May 1846. Like many other Americans, he saw the war coming, discussing the possibility as early as February of that year. "The most delicate and difficult of questions, the adjustment of a boundary between us [and Mexico], remains unsettled," he pointed out.[11] The caution he expressed in his public statements concerning an armed clash with Great Britain was largely absent in his statements about Mexico. He sounded jingoistic and belligerent, declaring that Americans "have borne more of insult and outrage on our citizens by Mexico, than England ever has, or ever will be permitted to perpetuate." Referring to several clashes between American and Mexican vessels, he said, "Our citizens have been robbed, our vessels seized and condemned. . . . Our treaties have been broken, and in innumerable instances the property of our citizens confiscated." He wrote to a Vicksburg newspaper on the day Congress declared war, "Let the treaty of peace be made at the city of Mexico, and by an Ambassador who cannot be refused a hearing—but who will speak with that which levels walls and opens gates—American cannon."[12]

Many white Southerners, particularly from Davis's region in the southwest, were spoiling for a fight, believing that new slave states could be carved out of territories seized from Mexico.[13] There were political plaudits to be won here as well. A war record was a prized possession in the South. John A.

Quitman, a Mississippi fire-eater and a future governor of the state, exulted that his goal was to enlist in the army and receive "a major general's baton, fairly won on the field of battle, or a Mexican grave!"[14]

Davis was not quite as outspoken—or as crass—as Quitman, but he was certainly not immune to such considerations. He had a war record, of a sort, as a West Point graduate and army veteran, but he was not an insider in Mississippi's state militia organization where social status and quasi-military standing converged in the state's social and political culture. The militia had never accomplished much in a real martial setting, but then again, Davis hadn't accomplished much either. Mississippi journalists could not even get his army rank right, variously referring to the former army lieutenant as "captain," "major," and "colonel."[15] He knew how useful a military title might be and how nondescript his army career had been to that point.

At the same time, Davis may also have been having, if not second thoughts, at least rumblings of irritation concerning his new profession of politics, particularly in direct juxtaposition to his old profession. "I do not claim to possess all the qualifications necessary for a representative," he said during a speech in May 1846, "but know there are very many in which I am deficient."[16] He thus acted as a congressional expert on military matters, "a friend to the army," and throughout his brief stay in the House he presented himself as one who spoke for the military establishment. Moreover, he suggested that he knew not just the interests but the hearts and minds of military men. "Those who have served in the army approach me as a former associate," he wrote President James Polk, regarding one military appointment. Davis wanted a West Point man to be given the post, and he told Polk that the army officer corps would feel the same way, stating that he could be understood as "knowing thus intimately their feelings."[17]

Davis always needed to think that he was part of some special circle, some close community whose members had a sentimental attachment to him as a comrade and leader. It helped if this circle could be set off in stark contrast to some malevolent, dangerous "other"—the frontier outside the confines of Fort Crawford, for example, or, later on, the hostile antislavery North's rising majority imperiling the slave South. In the House of Representatives he believed he spoke for an embattled military community of honorable men against the indifference or sometimes outright hostility of politicians who did not understand military affairs. While Congress scrambled to put together an army to face Santa Anna, Davis could not help gloating a little. He "rejoiced at the evidence now afforded of a disposition in this House to deal justly, to feel generously towards those to whom the honor of our flag has been intrusted. . . . Too often and too long [have] we listened to harsh and invidious reflections upon our gallant little army."[18]

He received a jarring reminder of how different the army and politics could be during a series of exchanges with Abraham Lincoln's future vice president over the value of a military education. On May 28, 1846, with the Mexican War only two weeks old and with skirmishes already breaking out between the contending armies near the Texas border, Davis delivered a speech praising the army's successful defense of an American fortification near Matamoros. Singling out William Sawyer, an Ohio congressman who had criticized West Point graduates, Davis said he "hoped now the gentleman would withdraw those denunciations." He invited Sawyer to consider the strength of the American fortifications at Matamoros, which were constructed by professional soldiers, and "then say whether he believes a blacksmith or a tailor could have secured the same results." Sawyer happened to have once been a blacksmith and took offense at these remarks, but it was Andrew Johnson, a Democrat from Tennessee—and a tailor—who chose to make of Davis's speech a public brouhaha. For days after Davis spoke, Johnson blasted him as a part of the "illegitimate, swaggering, bastard, scrub aristocracy, who assumed to know a good deal" and who disparaged the honest labor of ordinary Americans. Davis tried repeatedly to assure Johnson and his fellow congressmen that he had meant only to uphold the honor of West Point and had meant no disrespect for tailors, blacksmiths, or anyone else. Johnson ignored him and gleefully took the opportunity to sing the praises of tailors everywhere, starting with Adam, who "sewed fig leaves together." The recorder for the *Congressional Globe* wryly observed that "the debate, in all its stages [was not] of an entirely pleasant nature."[19]

Davis wanted to escape the likes of Andrew Johnson and rejoin the brotherhood of soldiers. "My position here [in Congress] forces upon me the recollection of all which is due to those who sent me here," he wrote, "yet I look to the movements of our forces on the Mexican border with a strong desire to be a part of them."[20] The feeling proved irresistible, and soon he was positioning himself to be given command of one of the new volunteer regiments. "Jeff promised me he would not volunteer," Varina wrote her mother, "but he could not help it, I suppose. . . . If it comes to the worst I *can* bear it, but god only knows how bitter it is to me." She admitted that she had "cried herself stupid" over the matter, to the point that Davis believed his wife might be physically ill or even emotionally disturbed.[21]

Despite Varina's objections, Davis lobbied hard for the opportunity to serve with the army in Mexico. "My education and former practice would, I think, enable me to be of service to Mississippians who take the field," he wrote to a Mississippi newspaper, no doubt for public consumption.[22] The competition was fierce, for there would be only one regiment from Mississippi, and many men wanted the post as its colonel, including several distinguished and high-ranking officers in the state militia. In the end Davis's lobbying efforts and his West Point training proved decisive, and he was elected by the regiment as its colonel. He quickly wrapped up his personal affairs in Washington and departed for Mississippi and his new command in July 1846.[23]

On the trip to Mississippi he carried with him a book on military tactics, chattering away happily to his distraught wife about "the mysteries of enfilading, breaking column, hollow squares, and what not." He generally entered upon his new duties with the energy and enthusiasm of a former army officer returned to the fold.[24] Still, it must not have been a particularly comfortable position for him. He knew many of the men, particularly the officers, one of whom was Varina's brother, but there were many he did not know.[25] And this was a Mississippi organization, representing a state Davis called home but that nevertheless remained largely unknown to him. He had spent large portions of his adult life elsewhere: at Transylvania University in Kentucky, West Point, various frontier outposts in the north, and Washington, D.C. His life at Brierfield had been notable for its isolation, and when he left the plantation he usually visited areas outside the state's borders. Davis's speeches on the Mississippi hustings and his Democratic party affiliation, not to mention Joseph's influence, had given him contacts in the Mississippi gentry, but the truth is that he was as likely to disparage his state as praise it. He once belittled the education he had received in Mississippi grammar schools during his childhood, and while in the army he wrote his sister that "dissipation [was] less common [among his fellow soldiers] than among the citizens of Mississippi."[26]

Mississippi was not, then, quite the cherished homeland for him. Indeed, at this point in his life, he had no such place. He valued emotional, personal, heartfelt bonding of the sort he believed he had with fellow West Pointers and soldiers, but he had not yet deposited these feelings in any one place. Soldiers, Southerners, wife, relatives, and even slaves—all were generally on an even plane for him; Mississippi, the South, and America were all generally equal.

For their part, the men of the First Mississippi felt no particular affinity for him. Many had voted for Davis, as much for his West Point credentials as anything else, but many others had not. He also was quick to establish a reputation as a strict disciplinarian, causing grumbling in the ranks. "Some complaints have been uttered against you for the severity of training," Joseph wrote him.[27]

The training at first seemed pointless, for after the regiment disembarked at Brazos, St. Iago, Mexico on August 2, the men spent the next few weeks huddled in miserable tent camps waiting for riverboat transportation to join Zachary Taylor's command. Worse, the regiment's arms and ammunition were slow in arriving. Over one hundred men in Davis's command were ill, and many of the rest were increasingly annoyed at his insistence on drilling and strict West Point–style discipline. The men chafed at the inactivity. So did Davis, who wrote the secretary of war, "We have met delay and detention at every turn."[28]

The situation soon changed. The First Mississippi joined Taylor's army on August 31, and Davis enjoyed a warm reception from his former father-in-law. Davis's regiment was absorbed into Taylor's command and found itself marching on the fortified Mexican town of Monterrey. Here they received their first taste of fighting. Ordered into battle near a fortified Mexican position, La Teneria, Davis's regiment was directed to attack the enemy (by none other than John Quitman, who fairly won his glory, along with a serious leg wound), and the First Mississippi helped drive the Mexican troops from their position with a dramatic full-tilt assault through what Davis called a "galling fire." During the rout that followed, the First Mississippi's colonel was in the very thick of the pursuit, personally taking prisoners at swordpoint and helping direct his men to overtake the fleeing Mexicans. The First Mississippi acquitted itself well. Davis later wrote that the Battle of Monterrey "verifies an opinion I have always entertained, that for incurring hardships with an unflinching will . . . the best soldiers are *gentlemen*."[29]

Davis's gentlemen were given another chance to prove their mettle seven months later when Santa Anna marched against Taylor with a force that outnumbered the Americans by nearly three to one. Arranging his army behind hastily constructed fortifications at the town of Buena Vista, Taylor refused Santa Anna's demands for surrender, and fighting commenced on February 22. The First Mississippi saw action the following day, when it was ordered to reinforce a shaky American flank. Davis's men did so with élan, repulsing several Mexican infantry and cavalry assaults that might otherwise have routed Taylor's entire army. "The contest was severe," Davis later wrote, "the destruction great upon both sides." Buena Vista was painful for him as well. A Mexican bullet struck him in the right foot, wounding him so severely that at the end of the day he had to seek the assistance of an army surgeon.[30]

The wound effectively ended his Mexican War service and his stint as the Mississippians' commander (whose twelve-month term of enlistment was due to expire, anyway). Davis was sent home to recuperate. He spent the next few months hobbling painfully about on crutches and picking pieces of lead and boot leather from his ankle. The healing process was frustratingly slow. "I hoped by this date to have been able to leave home free from the inconvenience and disagreeable exposure of hopping on crutches," he wrote a friend in July 1847. "My foot has not improved much and though just now its appearance is flattering I have been so often disappointed that I await further evidence."[31]

The pain and inconvenience aside, it was not such a bad thing to return home a wounded warrior. Many people in the United States suddenly found much to like in a war that would eventually cripple Santa Anna and soon add large chunks of territory to the nation's western marches. They had convinced themselves that this was a noble endeavor, and they were looking for a hero. They found one in the hobbled colonel of the now renowned "Mississippi Rifles." Davis was showered with praise and honor, particularly in his own home state and region. A Natchez newspaper described his reception as "one long ovation." During a homecoming parade in New Orleans, flowers were thrown at his feet from throngs of female admirers, one of whom shouted, "There goes our lion-hearted Davis." This "gratified Colonel Davis exceedingly," according to a reporter.[32] The spirit of the day affected the Mississippi legislature, which first appointed Davis to serve out the remaining months of the late Senator Jesse Speight's term and then made the appointment for the full six years.[33]

He had become a hero to the nation and in particular to his own men. The grumbling about excessive attention to drill and military discipline had long since vanished, replaced by a glowing admiration for his qualities as a combat leader. "Davis is a gallant fellow," remarked one man, and another reported that "Col. Davis was in the front and head of the battle from the opening to the close, cheering onward the men by his cool, pleasant, fearless, and confident manner." Davis knew how to lead, and he knew how to inspire his volunteer soldiers. "I announced to the men my conviction of the ease with which we could storm the place," he later said of the Monterrey siege, "by saying that twenty men with butcher knives could take it." His men loved such talk, and they responded well.[34]

For his part, Davis heartily reciprocated, acquiring a proud, affectionate feeling for the First Mississippi. He had always been keenly interested in seeing the regiment establish a reputation that would make it stand out among all the others in Mexico. Before setting out from Washington to take command of the regiment, he had met with Cadmus Wilcox, a young West Point cadet. Davis informed Wilcox that he wanted to arm the men with rifled muskets rather than the usual smoothbores. When Wilcox asked why, Davis replied, "If armed with the ordinary infantry musket it would be but one of many regiments similarly armed; but with the rifle, besides being more effective, there would probably be no other body of men so armed, and it would be known and referred to as the Mississippi Rifles, and, consequently, would be more conspicuous."[35]

Davis expressed none of the doubts that had assailed him in his regular army days about his men's character or performance of duty. "Our boys bore all without a murmur," he wrote proudly, "and only seemed eager for a renewal of the conflict."[36] He consistently described his regiment's service in emotive terms, as a matter of the heart rather than reason. It was emotional bonding and feeling, even more than training and drill, that made good soldiers. "Individual courage, sustained by a sense of individual responsibility— the mind kindling beneath a consciousness of personal dignity and personal character—this is the feeling that, when excited, exalts the commonest man into the soldier," he told a New Orleans audience, adding, "there is not a volunteer before me who will not tell you that his heart beat proudly on the morning of Buena Vista." His Mississippi volunteers prevailed in battle because "they it is who have a high spirit of honor . . . and with that spirit the immortal mind asserts its power, bides the toil and suffers without fatigue, [and] mocks the danger and death." In an especially lofty flight of rhetoric, he told the citizens of Natchez that he would return the regiment to its home state "melted down from that terrible engine of power, disciplined Mississippi courage." This was remarkable language from a man who only a few months previously had been known for his austere, dry speaking style.[37]

His model regarding military leadership was similarly based on emotion, expressed repeatedly in his praise of Zachary Taylor. The general was a "godfather to the sons of Mississippi," Davis said, and he described Taylor's ability to lead men into battle in highly emotional language. Telling a crowd in Raymond, Mississippi, of how Taylor visited him when he was wounded, Davis said of his commanding general, "The firm determination on his brow seemed struggling with an expression of deep sorrow for the brave fellows who had fallen and those who were yet to bite the dust." He took from his observations of Taylor, as well as from his experiences with the First Mississippi, the lesson that military men must stir their soldiers' hearts to lead effectively.[38]

Davis implicitly connected his unit's service to the South in that he gave nearly all his speeches in Southern cities; for the first time he was actually getting to know the region, and its people were getting to know him.[39] The war helped him identify with the nation and his region; but by far the most profound change was his attitude toward his home state. Prior to 1848, he had been largely indifferent and even hostile toward Mississippi, but Monterrey and Buena Vista had melded men and state together in his mind.

Davis frequently described the glory of his regiment and the glory of the state in nearly identical terms. "It has been the high fortune of the Mississippi Regiment to add by their valor and conduct at Monterrey, another chaplet to the honor and chivalry of our State," he told a Mississippi crowd. He also tried to elevate, at least rhetorically, his regiment's service above the rest of the American command and declared that he was proud of his effort "to preserve our distinct organization, our state individuality." "Our Mississippians at the siege of Monterrey did much more than they have received credit for," he wrote a friend in late 1846. "Our services [should] have been noticed not as part of a Brigade but as the fact was, a Regiment often acting independently."[40]

Through the service of the First Mississippi, the state became a land of heartfelt reverence for Davis, what he described as "the home of his affections, his interests, his hopes."[41] His conceptualization of combat had created, perhaps without Davis himself fully realizing it, an emotional bond with his state where little had previously existed. It is perhaps no coincidence that he felt a refreshed attachment to Brierfield; after the war he finally turned what had been a half-finished project into a thriving plantation, and he took up gardening—a most fundamental way to involve oneself with a patch of ground—on a regular basis.[42]

Davis employed a nice turn of phrase in 1852 that accurately described these assumptions. Speaking to a group of college students in Oxford, Mississippi, he said, "To you the young men of Mississippi and the eleves of her University I look for the protection of her rights, from you I expect such a keen sensibility to her fame and her honor as sons feel for their Mother and that community of sentiment which gives us strength."[43] "Sons feel for their mother" and "community of sentiment which gives us strength"—a great deal of Jefferson Davis's worldview is packed in that little phrase. West Point, the regular army, and Brierfield were sources of such heartfelt emotions for him, small little circles of intimate relationships among like-minded individuals with the same values and principles, the same heart. Yet Mississippi had become the strongest inner circle, for through the First Mississippi it could combine together in one place so many of the disparate threads that made up Davis's life to this point: the honor code of military service, the life of the Southern planter, a sense of place and of duty, and a budding political career.[44]

It was this sense of Mississippi as an inner circle of friends that laid the foundation for his political principles as a constitutional theorist of state sovereignty and as a Southern sectional spokesman. Davis in many ways became a Southerner and a Mississippian through his Mexican War experiences.[45] When he returned to Congress in 1847, he exhibited more consistent signs of a Southern identity. He began to refer to himself as a "Southern man" and felt he could speak authoritatively on the Southern mindset and Southern attitudes. He was also more steady and self-assured in his states' rights arguments. He began to abstract from his appreciation of Mississippi a consistently state-centered constitutional ideology. "The Federal government can have no other powers than those derived from the Constitution," he asserted confidently in July 1848. "It is the agent of the States; has no other authority than that which is delegated. . . . It is not to suppose that the sovereign States, when forming a compact of union, would confer upon the agent of such compact a power to control the destiny of the States."[46]

At the same time, his more ardent declarations of fidelity to the American national community faded but did not entirely diminish. He drew a direct connection between military service and American nationalism, saying, "When our country called us, we went, as dutiful children, to her defense."[47] He still had a soft spot for national military expenditures, opposing even John C. Calhoun at one point to vote for the raising of new regiments. But expressions of nationalistic patriotism began to be heard less frequently from the Mississippi senator, certainly much less so than the frequent hymns of praise he sang to Mississippi.

While Davis had lain wounded in the army surgeon's station following Buena Vista, he could have seen not far away the body of John J. Hardin, colonel of the First Illinois Volunteer Infantry. Hardin was an Illinois Whig and fellow congressman (and yet another Transylvania University alumnus) who had withdrawn from a close congressional race to command a regiment of volunteers. Hardin had rushed headlong into a Mexican assault during the confusion of battle; he died during a fierce hand-to-hand struggle, not far from where Davis stood commanding his Mississippians. Davis later praised Hardin as one of the men who "gave themselves to their country" and declared that "their country will do them eternal honor."[48]

Hardin was a longtime political rival of Abraham Lincoln; the two men knew each other quite well. Hardin had a law practice in Springfield, which brought them into frequent contact. He had been one of the men who helped settle peacefully the near-duel with James Shields, and he had corresponded with Lincoln on various Whig political matters. Lincoln competed with Hardin for the party nomination that would virtually guarantee the winner a congressional seat from one of the few "safe" Whig districts in Illinois. When Hardin withdrew from the race to go to war, his departure ensured that Lincoln would be nominated and thus elected to Congress. "From the state of my own residence, besides other worthy but lesser known whig names . . . one fell," Lincoln said in a speech before Congress in July 1848, "and in the fall of that one, we lost our best whig man."[49]

Lincoln waxed eloquent about the sacrifice of Hardin and other Americans on the fields of battle in Mexico. He referred to Buena Vista as "that fearful, breathless struggle . . . where each man's hard task was to beat back five foes or die himself."[50] Already he demonstrated a knack for evoking the sacrifice and valor of men on battlefields where he himself had not stood. But the circumstances here were much different from what they would be fifteen years later at Gettysburg, for he praised Hardin's battlefield courage in a war he did not support.

Lincoln was at best a lukewarm expansionist, and like most Whigs of his day he painted the world in largely moralistic terms of right and wrong behavior.[51] Thus he was deeply troubled by what looked to him uncomfortably like an American land grab with a shaky moral foundation, and for the Democrats he believed it might be "a war of conquest brought into existence to catch votes." Jefferson Davis saw in the successful American defense of the Matamoros fortifications a vindication of West Point military expertise; Lincoln saw there little more than an example of American callousness. "It is a fact that Fort Brown, built opposite Matamoras [sic], was built . . . within a Mexican cotton field, on which, at the time the army reached it, a young cotton crop was growing and which crop was wholly destroyed, and the field itself greatly, and permanently, injured, by ditches, embankments, and the like," he fumed to one reporter.[52]

Lincoln was particularly disturbed by the suspicious circumstances surrounding the war's origins. Polk had told Congress that Santa Anna's army had attacked an American army patrol on "American soil," purposely leaving the vague impression that the Mexican president was spearheading an invasion to retake all of Texas; in fact, the skirmish that began the war occurred on a strip of land whose ownership was in dispute. Lincoln and many other Whigs felt they had been hoodwinked and the nation stampeded into a declaration of war without knowing all the facts. On the floor of Congress, he demanded to know precisely where Santa Anna's assault had taken place. In what came to be known as the "spot" resolutions, Lincoln called on the president to inform Congress "whether the particular spot of soil on which the blood of our *citizens* was so shed, was, or was not, *our own soil,* at that time."[53]

As the war progressed, Lincoln increasingly tended to focus on the president's motives and behavior, and in doing so he lapsed into earlier speaking habits of making Polk's private motives and feelings a fit subject for public comment. In a fiery speech before the House of Representatives on January 12, 1848, he declared that the president was "deeply conscious of being in the wrong—that he feels the blood of this war, like the blood of Abel, is crying to Heaven against him." He accused Polk of starting the war and "trusting to escape scrutiny, by fixing the public gaze upon the exceeding brightness of military glory. . . . He plunged into it, and swept *on* and *on,* till . . . he now finds himself he knows not where." Lincoln thought the president was incompetent, or mean-spirited, or probably both. "His mind, tasked beyond its power, is running hither and thither, like some tortured creature," he said. "He is a bewildered, confounded, and miserably perplexed man." He told Congress that "my way of living leads me to be about the courts of justice," and Polk reminded him of a lawyer with a weak case who employed "every artifice to work round, befog, and cover up, with many words, some point in the case, which he *dared* not admit, and yet *could* not deny." Perhaps Polk reminded Lincoln of the American Caesar in his Lyceum speech, or perhaps his desire to make a lasting impression in Congress caused him to give vent to earlier habits. Whatever the cause, he had not engaged in this sort of speculation on the state of an opponent's conscience for a long time.[54]

He expected great things from this speech. "I wish you to know I have made a speech in Congress," Lincoln wrote a fellow Whig. "I want you to be *enlightened* by reading it." He was disappointed. Not only was the Whig press's reaction muted, but Herndon informed Lincoln that "murmurs of dissatisfaction" were evident among party members in Illinois who thought his remarks were unpatriotic and, by implication, excessive. The Democrats criticized Lincoln's words almost as a matter of course, but their manner of doing so must have suggested to him the impropriety in particular of his assault on Polk's motives, which one Democratic editor labeled a "base, dastardly and treasonable assault."[55]

Lincoln found himself backpedaling, reassuring anyone who would listen that his criticisms of Polk in no way implied a lack of patriotism or support for American soldiers. Democrats ridiculed him as "spotty" Lincoln and charged that he refused to vote for appropriations to feed and clothe American troops in the field. Lincoln bristled at the charge: "A careful examination of the Journals and Congressional Globe shows, that [I] voted for all the supply measures which came up, and for all the measures in any way favorable to the officers, soldiers and their families."[56]

Lincoln was never quite so careless with his language afterward. Six months later, he took the floor to criticize Polk's stance against appropriations for internal improvements. The difference in tone was striking, for Lincoln tried hard to avoid personal assaults on the president or on any other Democrat, telling the House Speaker that he "desire[d] to do nothing which may be very disagreeable to any of the members." Thereafter he engaged in no speculations as to the state of Polk's mind and soul; indeed, he said very little about the president at all.[57]

Lincoln was given an added impetus toward caution in this regard by the nomination of Zachary Taylor as the Whig candidate for president in 1848. He supported Taylor's nomination because he thought the old man's status as a war hero, even in a war he loathed, would give the Whigs a serious chance of success in capturing the White House. "Our only chance is with Taylor," Lincoln wrote a friend. "I think he would make a better [president] than Polk, or Cass, or Buchanan, or any such creatures, one of whom is sure to be elected, if he is not."[58]

But neither Lincoln nor anyone else knew exactly what Taylor's political principles were. Lincoln was compelled to support a candidate whose personal views on nearly every meaningful public issue were a mystery. His now habitual separation of appearance and motive, private and public, stood him in good stead as he fashioned his pro-Taylor arguments. He did so by suggesting in various ways that Taylor's private character was of little concern to voters: the only issue was his outward behavior. Democrats "are in utter darkness as to his opinions on any of the questions of policy which occupy the public attention," Lincoln told members of Congress in July 1848. "But is there any doubt as to what he will *do* on the prominent questions, if elected? Not the least." In fact there was considerable doubt in most Americans' minds, including Lincoln's. "I hope and *believe* Gen. Taylor, if elected, would not veto the [Wilmot] proviso," Lincoln said in a speech before Congress. "*But* I do not *know* it." In the end, he was reduced to arguing that Taylor's principles were no more vague than those of his opponents, and he contended that the general operated according to the "great principle" of "allowing the people to do as they pleased with their own business."[59]

These were weak arguments, but the point here is not Lincoln's facility for propping up a candidate with nondescript political values. It is the way in which he tried to separate Taylor's privately held opinions from what he would actually "do if elected" to public office. He assailed Democrats who suggested that a vote for Taylor was an endorsement of the man himself and all his beliefs, saying that this was a "plausible, though pernicious deception."[60] Lincoln used this strategy to get around the rather sticky point that he was heartily endorsing the candidacy of a military hero from a war he despised, suggesting that any American might well offer his services for the public good of the country in wartime while perhaps harboring private feelings that the war itself was a bad idea. "It is sufficient for him to know that his country is at war with a foreign nation," Lincoln said, and "to bring it to a speedy and honorable termination . . . without enquiring about its justice, or anything else connected with it."[61]

Lincoln was cutting against the grain of popular opinion in this regard, for Taylor had been nominated with the idea that voters would assume such a fine military man possessed a sterling and upright personal character, with no outward declarations of policy ideas or principles required. Accordingly, the Whigs trumpeted Taylor's military leadership and bearing at every opportunity. Lincoln, on the other hand, offered few allusions to Taylor's military record or to the private veracity and honor that it implied. Indeed, he said relatively little about the man himself at all. His goal was to separate Taylor's character from his presidential bid.[62]

Ultimately, Lincoln was both gratified and disappointed. Taylor ascended to the White House, and Lincoln went home after a single term in Congress to resume the life of an Illinois attorney. He had pledged to serve only one term so that other Whigs might take their turn, and he was less pleased with the life of a congressman than he had expected he would be.[63]

Nevertheless, he informed Herndon that he would stay for a second term if his party saw fit to let him do so.[64] But there was no movement to reelect him. This response could be attributed at least in part to his antiwar speeches, which had bothered some Whigs and elicited only lukewarm praise from others.[65] Lincoln was surprised by this; he had quarreled a bit even with Herndon. "You fear that you and I disagree about the war," Lincoln wrote him. "I will stake my life, that if you had been in my place, you would have voted just as I did."[66]

His political future seemed dim. He had campaigned vigorously for Taylor, and he expected to share in the spoils of a rare party presidential victory; he was sorely disappointed. Passed over for higher office himself, he bombarded the new administration with recommendations and suggestions concerning who would be the proper Whig appointees to federal jobs in Illinois. Taylor's men ignored him, for he was merely a one-term congressman with little standing outside Illinois. "In my present condition, I can do nothing," he sadly informed a political ally.[67]

Had Lincoln known Davis, he might have reflected sourly on the fact that the Mississippian, a lifelong Democrat, carried more influence in the second (and last) Whig White House than he himself ever would. Taylor wrote several long letters soliciting Davis's advice on politics. "It will afford [me] always much pleasure to hear from you no matter how often you may write," Taylor informed him, "and your views on political as well as other subjects will be read with much interest and no doubt with profit."[68] Davis papered over the different party affiliations that separated him from Taylor, and he expressed unreserved confidence in him as a military leader and as a president. "As soldiers we have learned to reverence him for his military judgement," Davis said in July 1847. "Our hearts are bound in sympathy with his."[69]

By the time of President Taylor's death in 1850, Lincoln and Davis were traveling in quite different directions, politically and personally. Davis had begun a decade of service in the Senate that would see him rise to the top of his party's hierarchy; Lincoln returned home to Illinois and the relatively obscure life of a trial lawyer. The Mexican War had made the former the "hero of Buena Vista"; at the same time, the latter had become "spotty" Lincoln.

Yet in one respect the Mexican War affected both men, and the nation, with equal impact and result; it forced a reckoning with a peculiar American institution, whose ramifications and evils had gone unchecked and unnoticed for far too long. In August 1846 Jefferson Davis's friend and fellow Democrat David Wilmot introduced his famous rider on an administration appropriations bill requiring all territory won from Mexico to remain free of slavery.[70] Davis angrily declared that the proviso was an affront to "every prospect of public peace, general interest, and the benefit of the territorial inhabitants."[71] Lincoln said the Wilmot Proviso "created a great flutter," but "it stuck like wax"; and he proudly proclaimed, "I voted for it at least forty times, during the short time I was [in Congress]."[72] The Revolutionary War, both Lincoln and Davis believed, had been a unifying, nationally reaffirming experience. The Mexican War, with its introduction of Wilmot's proposal onto the national political stage, would in the long run prove to have entirely the opposite effect.

DECLARATIONS

On the morning of March 6, 1857, Chief Justice Roger B. Taney read the majority opinion in the case of *Dred Scott v. Sanford* to onlookers packed in the dark little basement room that served as the Supreme Court's chambers. Wrinkled and pale, with white hair flowing to his shoulders, Taney was "old, very old," according to one observer; "the infirmities of age [had] bowed his venerable form."[1] The opinion was fifty-two pages long; reading it took a long time for the seventy-nine-year-old man, to the point that his words in the end faded away to a barely audible whisper.[2]

However weak it may have seemed, that parched old voice pronounced doom on African Americans, abolitionism, and the fledgling Republican party. In addressing this lawsuit of Dred Scott, an army physician's slave who sued for freedom because he had been transported from a slave state to free territory, Taney read white Southern racism directly into the law by refusing Scott's right to bring any legal action in an American courtroom. African Americans like Scott "had no rights or privileges but such as those who held the power and the government might choose to grant them," the chief justice declared, and he pointedly asserted that whites had never seen fit to grant blacks much of anything. Blacks had long suffered under an "inferior and subject condition" and enjoyed none of the guarantees of freedom and equality contained in the Declaration of Independence, in which it was "too clear for dispute that the enslaved African race were not intended to be included." Going further, Taney directly attacked the position of Republicans and other antislavery Americans that slavery should be excluded from the territories by arguing that slaves, as a species of property, fell under federal protection and as such could be carried anywhere in the Union or its western marches. Thus any restrictions on slavery in the West—the Missouri Compromise line, popular sovereignty, or any future action from a (presumably) Republican Congress—were by definition unconstitutional. In the space of two hours, Roger Taney tried to sweep all the antislavery pieces off the American political gameboard and declare the proslavery South the winner in sectional controversies stretching back to the nation's founding.[3]

Proslavery Southerners were delighted with the boon they received from the Supreme Court. Jefferson Davis was quite satisfied with Taney's opinion, since it substantially validated views on the Constitution, slavery, and property rights that he had often expressed. During a speech to the Mississippi legislature in fall 1857, Davis made a passing reference to *Dred Scott,* pronouncing himself "happy" that his constitutional arguments "had since received the sanction of the Supreme Court of the United States." In later speeches he dismissed the fear that *Dred Scott* would nationalize slavery as a "palpable . . . absurdity," and he told congressional critics of the decision that since they themselves had averred to the Court as the final authority on the status of slavery in the territories, they should find a way to live with the result. After the war he was less charitable, referring to "Northern agitators" who "flouted, denounced, and utterly disregarded" the *Dred Scott* case and its perpetrator, "a man eminent as a lawyer, great as a statesman, and stainless in his moral reputation."[4]

When Taney read his opinion Lincoln was in Springfield, attending to the demands of an increasingly busy law practice. Business was flourishing at the firm of Lincoln and Herndon. He and his partner handled a wide variety of cases, ranging from divorce to debt collection, in courthouses all over central and western Illinois. Much of his practice was still of the nickel-and-dime variety, small cases for relatively small fees, but he was also handling litigation for important and well-heeled clients like the Illinois Central Railroad. Lincoln was by this point a comfortable and fairly prosperous attorney, and although he kept alive his passion for politics, the law dominated much of his daily life.[5]

But political issues increasingly intruded upon legal affairs, and his letters to clients and other businessmen sometimes suddenly switched from matters of litigation to matters of politics.[6] Along with the flurry of legal paperwork, Lincoln found time to scratch out some notes for a speech he was to deliver in Chicago on the occasion of that city's Republican nominating convention for municipal officers. A new member of a new party, he groped for words to describe adequately what he was doing in this company. The Republicans had "formed and manuvered in the face of the disciplined enemy," he wrote, and stood as the embodiment of the "sentiment, opposed to the spread, and nationalization of slavery."[7] He might have had Roger Taney in mind, for the general gist of the *Dred Scott* opinion was widely rumored prior to its public release.

Before 1857 Lincoln had taken a wholly uncritical position on the Supreme Court's power to settle constitutional questions, that is, when he took notice of the Court at all. He had enlisted the Court's aid during early speeches supporting the Whig position favoring a national bank. "The Supreme Court—that tribunal which the Constitution has itself established to decide constitutional questions—has solemnly decided that such a bank is constitutional," he said in an 1839 speech, adding that the Court's opinion "ought to settle the question—ought to be conclusive." Four years later he co-authored a campaign circular that simply declared that the Supreme Court was "the most enlightened judicial tribunal in the world."[8] Lincoln probably put little thought into these casual references to the Court, sharing with many Americans of his day the vague and largely untried assumption that it was, if not exactly infallible, at least a satisfactory repository of final constitutional wisdom. The Court, after all, was but one component of a general legal machinery in which Lincoln had great faith. And this faith in the American legal system and its institutions was the foundation of his sense of community and his sense of self.

In the late 1850s, however, he found this faith severely tested on a variety of fronts, perhaps most tellingly by the infamous *Dred Scott* decision. Lincoln seems casually to have believed that the Supreme Court was incapable of such behavior; hence there is a tone of incredulity in his pronouncements concerning the decision. "What would be the effect of this, if it should ever be the creed of a dominant party in the nation?" he wondered, and he shuddered at the answer: that "the whole community must decide that not only Dred Scott, but that *all* persons in like condition, are rightfully slaves."[9] If Lincoln's antislavery principles left him as outraged as anyone in the North, his faith in the law made it difficult to follow the *New York Tribune*'s dismissal of the *Dred Scott* opinion as possessing "just so much weight as . . . the judgment of a majority of those congregated in any Washington barroom."[10] Although he would develop constitutional arguments stressing the capabilities of the president and Congress to interpret the Constitution for themselves—and thus void the *Dred Scott* decision when the opportunity arose—at no point did he trivialize the Court or the impact of its behavior. Legal institutions mattered too much for him to do so.

But *Dred Scott,* along with other proslavery activities, did test Lincoln's faith. The context of this test was a personal value system that had previously gone largely unchallenged. He had created for himself a paradigm, rooted in the law, that seemed to explain fairly well both how communities worked, how America worked, and his own place within the larger schemes of both. But the perceived perversion of the law by men like Roger Taney suggested shortcomings in his understanding of American identity and community.

These were shortcomings Lincoln never fully articulated as such. He did not consciously set out a new theory of American identity to replace his old one. But the emotional element of alarm, of defensiveness, of betrayal even, in his political observations of the time suggest an almost subconscious feeling of crisis. He sounded uncharacteristically defensive. "Everywhere in the ranks of the common enemy, were old party and personal friends, jibing, and jeering, and framing deceitful arguments against us," he wrote in his speech notes. Proslavery apologists were a "disciplined enemy" given to "persistent misrepresentations." They "assailed, sneered at . . . [and] hawked at" the principles of the Founding Fathers.[11] Here was an agitated, uncomfortable Lincoln.

Agitation seeks rest, and discomfort looks for solace. In the 1850s Lincoln groped toward both, and in so doing he subtly reconfigured his understanding of American identity. Lincoln the lawyer who had avoided looking into others' hearts now needed some reassurance that his compatriots' hearts were not, as Taney would have it, crusted over with racism. He needed a new way of perceiving his fellow Americans. The essential premises would remain the same, but their repository would be different—in a new party, in a new habit of speaking politically, and perhaps chiefly in a new reading of an old, venerated American document.

Even as Lincoln picked up the pieces of his law practice following his brief absence in the House of Representatives, Americans from various backgrounds and persuasions began to coalesce around a new political organization based on a polyglot ideology of republicanism, abolitionism, nativism, and free labor economic practices. Its adherents were a mixed bag. Some were disaffected Democrats who had abandoned the party of Jackson for various reasons. Others were nativists who found their dislike of immigrants to be unpalatable in a Democratic party that depended in some districts on Catholics, the Irish, and other immigrant votes. Many were refugees from the wreckage of what was once the old Whig party, now destroyed by a combination of sectional divisiveness and general incompetence.[12]

Lincoln was not a founder of this new party. He seems to have first been aware of its existence sometime in 1854, when antislavery Republicans meeting in Springfield added his name to their central organizing committee. They apparently did not inform Lincoln of this decision, which resulted in some embarrassment for him, as it would for any politician in a region where antislavery agitation was just barely tolerated in most quarters.[13] He must have found this annoying and in the process hesitated to involve himself in the early birth pangs of the new party in Illinois. But by 1856, with Whiggery so obviously dead beyond hope of resuscitation, he moved toward formal membership in the Republican party as it began to organize itself into a viable entity in Illinois. In spring of that year he attended a convention of Republican party organizers in Decatur, Illinois, and thereafter remained a committed and steadfast member of the party.[14]

When Lincoln finally did cast his lot with the Republicans, he did so with gusto, quickly becoming an acknowledged leader of the party's Illinois organization.[15] He did so because the new party's free labor, Free-Soil ideology was quite compatible with his personal point of view, and it gave him a good vehicle from which to launch a run for the Senate in 1858. Along with these matters, however, was his need for a party that could reassure him that they at least had their hearts in the right place where slavery was concerned. "Our cause . . . must be intrusted to, and conducted by its own undoubted friends— those whose hands are free, whose hearts are for the work—who *do care* for the result," Lincoln told a Republican gathering. He believed he had found such friends and such hearts in the Republican party.[16]

But the Republicans, as with any broad-based political organization, were prepared at times to welcome into their fold members whom Lincoln considered suspect as to motives and intentions. The most dramatic and disturbing illustration of a political party's limitations was offered by none other than Stephen Douglas, when for a brief time in 1856 prominent Republicans considered welcoming the Little Giant into the party. Douglas had watched his popular sovereignty program go seriously awry in Kansas when proslavery extremists in the territory used violence, intimidation, and voter fraud to elect a proslavery convention, which in turn created an extremist proslavery constitution. When the Buchanan administration formally recognized this series of frauds as the territory's legitimate government, Douglas broke with his president and called for new elections and a new constitutional convention, both of which would reflect Kansas's Free-Soil, antislavery majority. This stand delighted many Free-Soil Republicans, including influential easterners like the *New York Tribune*'s editor Horace Greeley and the eastern political boss Thurlow Weed, who began calling for their new party to embrace the Little Giant as a way to split the Democratic party and to nurture a powerful new friend in the Senate.[17]

Lincoln was incredulous. "What does the New York Tribune mean by its constant eulogising [sic], and admiring, and magnifying [of] Douglas?" he wrote a fellow Republican in late 1858. "Have they concluded that the republican cause, generally, can be best promoted by sacraficing [sic] us here in Illinois? If so, we would like to know it soon; it will save us a great deal of labor to surrender at once." Lincoln was a shrewd political observer and organizer, and he was not usually averse to working with political opponents to secure some desired end, but the idea of extending Republican membership to Douglas was too much. To Lincoln's way of thinking, Douglas's motives were suspect and his heart was definitely not in the Free-Soil cause. "His whole effort is devoted to clearing the ring, and giving slavery and freedom a fair fight," Lincoln argued. "With one who considers slavery just as good as freedom, this is perfectly natural. . . . But [Republicans] think slavery is wrong [and] it ought to be prohibited by law. . . . Upon this radical difference of opinion with Judge Douglas, the republican party was organized. There is all the difference between him and them now as there ever was."[18]

The adopt-Douglas movement was short-lived, but it pointed up a basic weakness in political parties as a guarantor of one's good intentions, particularly the Republican party, which embraced so many diverse interests and points of view. Lincoln understood the impulse to draw a powerful national figure like Douglas into his new party's ranks. "I think [Republicans] ought not to oppose any measure merely because Judge Douglas proposes it," he wrote.[19] He called for party unity on principles rather than on political expediency, though, and if there were a conflict between the two, principles must win. "Stand with anybody that stands *right*," he had told old-line Whigs four years earlier when they hesitated to break party ranks and identify themselves with abolitionists. "Stand with him when he is right and *part* with him when he goes wrong." Lincoln's experience with pro-Douglas Republicans had taught him that past a point, party loyalties could be a limited means in identifying who was "right" and who was not.[20]

Lincoln found a second, more negative approach to explaining and understanding the presence of Americans who might disagree with him over the evils of slavery. It was an answer as old as American politics itself: a conspiracy theory. Davis indulged in this sort of reaction to explain what he saw as the growing abolitionist menace in the North. Lincoln turned to conspiracy theories as well, to explain how some of his fellow Americans had gone seriously awry. In this sense, the murky world of conspiracy formed its own photonegative, imagined community in Lincoln's thinking, where Stephen Douglas would again figure prominently.

During the 1858 senatorial race, Douglas first leveled conspiracy charges at Lincoln. To use a modern term, Douglas tried to create a "character problem" for Lincoln. He accused him of being a closet abolitionist whose secret scheme was to deliver up Illinois to the likes of Joshua Giddings, Salmon Chase, "the Negro Fred Douglass," and other "Black Republicans." Lincoln wanted to "cover up and get over his abolitionism," he told his listeners, but Douglas would not let him get away with it.[21] He insinuated that Lincoln was a wily political manipulator who did his dirty deeds by shady backroom deals and subterfuge, who wanted to "cheat the American people out of their votes" and "conceal from this vast audience the real questions which divide the great parties."[22] Lincoln was a political skulker who, like all such "little Abolition orators," went around and "lectured in the basements of schools and churches."[23] He was, in other words, a man whose intentions, motives, and sentiments were suspect; thus, any of his public acts must likewise be suspect.

In leveling these charges, Douglas continually suggested that he was privy to Lincoln's innermost plans, his private motives, indeed the very state of his soul. Phrases such as "Mr. Lincoln thinks," "he intends," "Lincoln knows in his heart," and "Lincoln knew better" permeate Douglas's speeches.[24] "Lincoln has a fertile genius in devising language to conceal his thoughts," Douglas said, but he, the Little Giant, could penetrate Lincoln's facade and expose his various subterfuges.[25] "If Mr. Lincoln is a man of bad character, I leave you to find it out," he said. But the Little Giant wasted no opportunity to give his listeners a strong push in the right direction.[26]

Lincoln gave as good as he got. Responding to Douglas's reading of an earlier speech Lincoln had made, he replied, "When I made my speech at

Springfield, I really was not thinking of the things he ascribes to me at all."[27] In the same vein, he denied that Douglas could have any proof of his trying to abolitionize the Whigs or anyone else: "I can only say again that I am placed improperly—altogether improperly, in spite of all I can say—when it is insisted that I hold any other view or purpose in regard to this matter."[28] In a later speech, he said, "I understand this is an imputation upon my veracity and honor," but "I do not know what [Douglas] understood by it." And he coldly told his listeners that "if the Judge says that I do *not* believe [in a proslavery conspiracy], then he says what he does not know," for Douglas could not have any idea what Lincoln believed or did not believe.[29]

In these instances Lincoln's point was not only that Douglas was ill-informed but also that the very premise of his accusations was faulty. Douglas could not know what Lincoln's inner motives really were and, at any rate, one's inner motives were far less of an issue than one's outward actions and public activities. "I do not state a thing and say I know it, when I do not," he declared, and Douglas should be very careful to do the same.[30]

But Lincoln leveled a series of conspiracy charges of his own. He accused Douglas of involvement in a scheme to nationalize slavery and to "plant the institution all over the nation, here and wherever else our flag waves."[31] He focused on the recent *Dred Scott* decision, suggesting that it was the first step in a plan to make it illegal for states as well as territories to exclude the peculiar institution, and he accused Douglas, President Buchanan, Supreme Court Justice Roger Taney, and eventually the leaders of the Democratic party of being the executors of the plot to do so.[32]

Most scholars see little difference in Lincoln and Douglas here; both seem to be equally intent on swapping conspiracy charges to prove the other a liar and a fraud. Yet there are subtle differences in what each man was saying and the way he said it. Where the *Dred Scott* conspiracy charge was concerned, Lincoln carefully drew a distinction between knowing and implying what Douglas thought. "I do not say that I *know* such a conspiracy to exist," Lincoln said, "I reply that I *believe* it."[33] Douglas presumed to speak of what Lincoln knew and thought and intended; Lincoln time and again carefully qualified his remarks to avoid any such implication. In one speech, he said that Douglas "thinks" and then quickly added, "he says at least"; in another, he said that Douglas was "afraid" of the "amalgamation of blacks and whites," but then he said, "perhaps I am wrong in saying he *is* afraid."[34]

Whenever Lincoln leveled charges of conspiracy and duplicity at Douglas, he did so by inference and innuendo. He danced around these accusations with all the finesse of an attorney who knew how to avoid direct and reckless charges. "Senator Douglas regularly argues against the equality of men," he mused in some notes for a speech he never gave, "and while he does not draw the conclusion that the superiors ought to enslave the inferiors, he evidently wishes his hearers to draw that conclusion." In the very next paragraph, Lincoln turned "evidently" to an absolute certainty, writing that "it is impossible to not see that the common object" of Douglas and his party was "to subvert, in the public mind . . . all men are created equal."[35] Lincoln never publicly aired this sentiment, however, and he tried to avoid such stark statements concerning Douglas's motives and conspiratorial intentions.

Even on those rare occasions when Lincoln crossed the line and actually accused Douglas of holding bad or unworthy motives, he immediately drew back from the implication that he himself was engaged in Douglas-like speculations on the state of his opponent's mind and soul. During their debate in Galesburg, Lincoln came as close as he ever would to castigating Douglas's motives openly. Douglas had in an earlier speech recoiled in mock horror at Lincoln's circumspect suggestion that Douglas and his supporters had forged some false Republican documents and leaked them to local newspapers. In Galena, Lincoln told his audience that Douglas had become "somewhat exasperated" at the term "forgery." He then turned and said directly to Douglas, "Yes, Judge, I did dare to say forgery . . . I do dare to say forgery when it's true." The Lincoln supporters applauded, shouting, "Hit him again," and "Give it to him, Lincoln." But then Lincoln quickly retreated, accusing Douglas of starting the whole affair and saying, "I do not wish to push this matter to the point of personal difficulty."[36]

Lincoln's care in casting shadows on Douglas's motives was such that at times he unwittingly turned his own arguments into logical absurdities. For example, during one of many heated exchanges over Douglas's involvement in a conspiracy to make slavery national, Lincoln stated, "I think I argue fairly (without questioning motives at all) that Judge Douglas is most ingeniously and powerfully preparing the public mind for [a second *Dred Scott* decision] when it comes."[37] How could he make such an accusation without imputing Douglas's motives, and how could Douglas have conspired to make slavery national without being motivated to do so? Lincoln did not say.

At the same time, Lincoln poked fun at Douglas's preoccupation with the state of his soul and his inner motives. Referring to Douglas's charges of a conspiracy between former Democratic senator Lyman Trumbull and himself, Lincoln joked, "I have no doubt he is *conscientious* in saying it. . . . I know there is no substance to it whatever. Yet I have no doubt he is *'conscientious'* about it." The audience roared with laughter. "I have a right to claim that if a man says he *knows* a thing," Lincoln continued, "then he must show *how* he knows it. . . . It is not satisfactory to me that he may be 'conscientious' on the subject."[38]

Lincoln walked this thin line between suggesting that Douglas's motives might be suspect and leveling outright accusations against him with mixed results. And yet it is remarkable that he tried to walk that line at all, in a day and age when politicians regularly accused one another of having the souls of blackguards and thieves. Lincoln's listeners, and most scholars since, took these carefully worded inferences of Douglas's poor behavior to be simply examples of Lincolnian humor and sarcasm.[39] No doubt this is at least partly true, but there is an alternative explanation: that Lincoln meant exactly what he said. He was circumspect in denouncing Douglas's intentions and his inner purposes because he believed that it was inappropriate for Americans to do so when analyzing one another's public deeds. "I will not charge upon judge Douglas that he willfully misrepresents me," Lincoln once said, and by the same token he tried to soften his own inferences.[40]

Conspiracy theorizing was useful for Lincoln only to a point. Indeed he was not very good at it. This was not necessarily because of any sense of delicacy or fairness to Douglas, but because his sense of how people ought to interact in the national public square precluded that sense of certainty that is central to any successful conspiracy story. Conspiracies work when they explain what has previously been inexplicable and when they do so with a ring of finality and inevitability. A conspiracy theorist must convince his listeners that he can see directly into the dark hearts of those who are hatching secret plots, that he and his theory can tear aside the veil of dissembling and reveal the truth. Lincoln was never comfortable doing so.[41]

Joining and helping organize the Republican party was one approach to the problems the crises of the 1850s posed for Lincoln; constructing conspiracy theories was another. Both helped him make sense of these events; both approaches had their drawbacks and limitations. Lincoln was also groping toward a third approach, one centered on the interpretation of a sacred American document.

As the sectional crisis deepened, Lincoln increasingly invoked the Declaration of Independence, a document about which he had said relatively little prior to this point.[42] He said that Jefferson's document contained "the very fundamental principles of civil liberty"; it was "the fountain whose waters spring close by the blood of the Revolution," "our old and only standard of free government," and "that immortal emblem of humanity." The Declaration was his personal, core value; "my ancient faith" as he once put it. "I have never had a feeling politically, that did not spring from the sentiments involved in the Declaration of Independence," he told a Philadelphia audience on the eve of the war.[43]

His heightened consciousness of the Declaration during the 1850s reflected in part a general renewal of interest among the various antislavery factions that combined to form the Republican party. It was an explicit part of the first Republican platform, and key Republican leaders like Salmon Chase and William Seward used the document to denounce proslavery policies. Lincoln chose to focus so strongly on the Declaration partly because many other Americans of his day were doing so.[44]

His decision was not nearly so natural or inevitable as it may have seemed, however. His initial response to the slavery problem was to think in terms of courtroom logic. He made but a glancing reference to the Declaration in his early antislavery musings, writing that "*most governments* have been based, practically, on the denial of equal rights of men. . . . *Ours* began, by *affirming* those rights." He sensed that perhaps the place to look for a moral high ground in the slavery controversy was not so much to the Revolution as it was to reason based on general moral principles. After all, a great many people laid claim to the legacy of the Revolution, some of whom directly and passionately disagreed with Lincoln on what the Declaration was and what it meant. By making it the center of gravity for his antislavery arguments, he ran the risk of shifting the entire problem to a debate over the historical meaning of the Revolution; here he was on contested ground, for many persons in positions higher than he—Roger Taney, for one—believed the document had nothing whatever to do with racial equality or slavery. He left himself open to some sharp criticisms from political opponents like Stephen Douglas, who slashed mercilessly at Lincoln's "preaching up this same doctrine of negro equality, under the Declaration of Independence."[45]

Lincoln had spent a significant portion of his adult life making careful, lawyerly arguments. He would not have taken risks before a jury without a very good reason, and in the same vein he required a better reason than his own private convictions about the Revolution's meaning when he turned to the Declaration of Independence. Citing the Declaration was not necessarily a self-evident and natural act. It was risky, and he needed good reasons for doing so.

He had many such reasons. The Declaration was an expression of his almost religious reverence for the Founding Fathers, it was an outward manifestation of the core economic values he held concerning Americans' commitment to entrepreneurial liberty and free enterprise, and it was the chief symbol of America's role in world affairs as a beacon of equality.[46] The Declaration signified all of these values for Lincoln, but it was also a solution to the problem of how one took the measure of one's American neighbors when they were of necessity strangers. Lincoln's conspiracy theory served to reveal what had gone wrong in his American community, but the Declaration served to illustrate how these ills could be put right.

Part of this approach lay in Lincoln's particular reading of American history. He saw the Declaration as the touchstone of the Revolution, evidence that the Framers disliked slavery and sought to plant the seeds of its eventual eradication by using those words "all men are created equal" in a document that needed no such ringing affirmation of human equality to achieve its short-term end of declaring independence from Great Britain.[47] He tended to collapse the Declaration, the Union, and the Constitution, as if all were the products of the same moment and the same mind.[48] The Declaration "has proved an 'apple of gold' to us," he mused in some notes for a speech. "The Union, and the Constitution, are the picture of silver, subsequently framed around it." Many scholars have taken this to mean that Lincoln was holding the flawed Constitution and its legal/political system up to the higher moral standard of the Declaration.[49] This is true; Lincoln often stated that the Declaration was a high goal toward which Americans, their nation, and their Constitution must always try to strive.[50]

But the process worked both ways; he was also pulling the Declaration "down" to the Constitution. The Constitution was the preeminent American legal document, and Lincoln in a broad sense wanted the Declaration to be a legal document as well.[51] He suggested this metaphorically when he told an audience that if Douglas and the Democrats wanted to exclude African Americans from the Declaration, "Let them come up and amend it," or, on another occasion, when he said, "If that declaration is not the truth, let us get the Statute book, in which we find it, and tear it out!"[52] Lincoln was here bringing the Declaration onto familiar ground, his world of statutes, amendments, court cases, writs, and other legal documents.

Legal documents were negotiating tools for Lincoln, malleable but tangible and practical instruments that were useful in achieving equitable settlements of community disputes. He saw the "apple of gold " as being under negotiation. In purely personal terms, he himself may have fallen short of egalitarian perfection. "I have no purpose to introduce political and social equality between the white and the black races," he said. "There is a physical difference between the two, which in my judgement will probably forever forbid their living together upon the footing of perfect equality."[53] His admirers have explained these statements by suggesting that he had to tell audiences what they wanted to hear to get elected.[54] But we have no way of judging his intent; he may have meant what he said, or he may not.

The more revealing point is that Lincoln said these things, and then, in the very next breath, asserted his commitment to the Declaration of Independence, all the while showing no sense that the two were incompatible. Immediately after asserting that there was a "physical difference between the two races," he told his listeners that "there is no reason in the world why the negro is not entitled to all the natural rights enumerated in the Declaration of Independence." During a speech denouncing the *Dred Scott* opinion, he declared, "There is a natural disgust in the minds of nearly all white people, to the idea of indiscriminate amalgamation of the white and the black races," and he ridiculed Douglas's charges of race-mixing by saying, "because I do not want a black woman for a slave I must necessarily want her for a wife." He immediately followed this assertion with the statement that "in her natural right to eat the bread she earns with her own hands without asking leave of anyone else, she is my equal, and the equal of all others."[55]

Critics who would accuse Lincoln of hypocrisy, or of a limited definition of equality, miss an important point: for Lincoln, the Declaration was not a tool for prying open white Americans' innermost racial prejudices and feelings. He saw no evidence that Americans any time soon would relinquish their racial biases; he may not have yet been willing to do so himself. Nor did he think the Founders were unrealistic utopians; "They did not all at once, *or ever afterwards,* actually place all white people on an equality with one another," and "they did not intend to declare all men equal *in all respects.*" The Founders "meant to set up a standard maxim for a free society, which should be familiar to all, and revered by all; constantly looked to, constantly labored for, and even though never perfectly attained, constantly approximated."[56]

These are high principles, a constitutionalism of lofty aspirations.[57] Less noticeable perhaps than the high end that Lincoln envisioned, however, was the lowly beginning he needed: agreement among all Americans that the *words* of the Declaration carried an implicitly egalitarian message, even if the ramifications and meanings of that message had not yet been worked

out. It is remarkable how often his arguments over the Declaration centered
not so much on the ideals of a free society but on how the specific language
of the document was read or misread—in his words, how unscrupulous or
misinformed individuals "mutate[d] the fair symmetry of its proportions."
"Our progress in degeneracy seems to me pretty rapid," he wrote Speed in
1855. "As a nation we began by declaring 'all men are created equal.' We
now practically read it, 'all men are created equal, except Negroes.' When
the Know-Nothings get control of [the Declaration], it will read, 'all men are
created equal, except negroes, foreigners, and catholics." He elsewhere referred to the Declaration as "the noble words which you are all familiar with,"
presuming a broad communal knowledge, and implicitly, a consensus on their
meaning. "I should like to know if taking this old Declaration of Independence, which declares that all men are equal upon principle and making exceptions to it where will it stop[?]" he asked a crowd in Chicago. "Suppose
after you read [the Declaration] once in the old fashioned way, you read it
once more with Judge Douglas' version," Lincoln said in another speech; "are
you really willing that the Declaration shall be thus 'frittered away?'" Quoting a proslavery apologist from Virginia who had declared he had never seen
two men who were equal and could therefore prove the "sage aphorism" of
the Declaration untrue, Lincoln suggested that in the days of the Revolution, everyone had known what those words "all men are created equal"
meant. The Virginian's remarks "sound[ed] strangely in republican America.
The like was not heard in the fresher days of the republic." On another occasion he quoted a supporter of the Kansas-Nebraska Act as proclaiming the
Declaration a "self-evident lie," and he was astonished that no one had challenged these words. "If this had been said among Marion's men, Southerners though they were, what would have become of the man who said it? . . .
If it had been said in Independence Hall, seventy-eight years ago, the very
doorkeeper would have throttled the man, and thrust him into the street."
As Lincoln later told another crowd in Monticello, Illinois, he "only wanted
that the words of the Declaration of Independence should be applied" as the
Framers intended them.[58]

For Lincoln a proper interpretation of the Declaration's specific language
mattered, whatever individuals felt in their hearts about race or slavery.
Unlike many abolitionists, he did not wish a religious conversion; he did not
call for repentance for an aching racist heart. He was not, like Jefferson Davis,
presuming to be able to pierce outer veils and reveal inner motives. As he
himself pointed out, one could hold that blacks were inferior and at the same

time subscribe to his reading of the document. "I as well as Judge Douglas am in favor of the race to which I belong having the superior position," he said; "but I hold that, notwithstanding all this, there is no reason in the world why the negro is not entitled to all the rights enumerated in the Declaration of Independence."[59] But Lincoln did insist that *some* reading of the Declaration as containing such rights, for all mankind, was nonnegotiable; otherwise, it "is of no practical use now—mere rubbish—old wadding left to rot on the battlefield after the victory is won."[60]

The best immediate analogy here again is a legal writ, a courtroom document. As an attorney, Lincoln dealt every day with legal papers, the words of which had to be rooted in a general consensus by both parties and the court, even if the circumstances, intentions, and so forth remained variable. Justice often consisted in locating an objective meaning to these words, and proof of good or bad behavior was often established first by a close understanding of the words in an interrogatory, a writ, or a cross-examination. The Declaration was Lincoln's proof that all the participants in the American enterprise at least agreed on the rules of conduct in the national courtroom and on the overarching, abstract goals of justice and equality, even if the outcome of specific cases was still uncertain.

The Declaration offered a way for Lincoln to provide an imagined link among his fellow Americans. It allowed him some room to speak to matters of the heart and to resume some of his earlier habits of speaking to the inner motives not of those whom he thought of as adversaries but of Americans who he believed were his fellow neighbors: he once called the Declaration "the electric cord . . . that links the hearts of patriotic and liberty-loving men together."[61] And one of his chief criticisms of Douglas and the Democrats' reading of the Declaration was that in making it indifferent to slavery, "they must penetrate the human soul, and eradicate there the love of liberty."[62] But it is important to note that in thus denouncing Douglas, Lincoln did not necessarily want to "penetrate the human soul" himself. At times he seemed to think he would find "tendencies to liberty and ultimate emancipation" there, at other times, not. He did not want to use the Declaration as a means to plumb these depths, however.

Scholars have long understood that the Declaration was important to Lincoln on many personal and political fronts, but one front that was perhaps primary was his Americanness. The Declaration solved, at least temporarily, certain key problems for Lincoln's nationalism in the 1850s. As the sectional crisis escalated, he found himself wondering whether the American strangers of his community were too strange, too removed, and too distant. Did not a people who produced the *Dred Scott* decision call for some sort of soul-searching, some measure of the common sentiments that was necessary for the nation to function and to progress? By calling for a commitment to the Declaration's language of equality, he could assure himself that his fellow countrymen's hearts were at least nominally in the right place. By 1860, Lincoln—as Davis once did—could speak of shared sentiments and "that fraternal feeling which has so long characterized us as a nation." He did so in the context of the Declaration, a document that embodied the "great principle or idea . . . that kept this Confederacy so long together."[63]

Davis clearly did not share in Lincoln's reading of the Declaration of Independence. He did not directly dispute the antislavery reading of "all men are created equal"; he simply ignored it. Lincoln's eyes rarely strayed below the document's preamble, with its ringing assertions of equality, but Davis never strayed above the body of the document—the long list of grievances asserted as a right of revolution by Jefferson. "The Declaration of Independence recognized the right of secession under circumstances of oppression and injustice," Davis said, declaring that he wanted "to see the man who would come forward with arguments to show that if a country has a right to secede from an oppressive government . . . why States had no right to secede from the federal government under similar circumstances."[64] He too described the Declaration as a "power above the Constitution." His golden apple in the silver frame was not equality but self-determination and secession, "that inalienable right which was asserted by the Signers . . . and of which the people of the States had not been deprived."[65]

Lincoln is said to have been the passionate Unionist, invoking the "mystic chords of memory" that all Americans can hear. His attachment to the Union was profound, but this quality should not obscure his ability to separate emotion from reason and private from public considerations. If he wanted all Americans to hear the "mystic chords," he knew there were limits to how far he could go in ascertaining whether this was indeed the case. He wanted a nation that agreed that slavery was wrong, just as Davis wanted a nation that agreed slavery was right. During the 1850s, both men faced the possibility that many of their fellow Americans might not live up to these different standards of national sentiment.

PARTIES

Jefferson Davis's first public encounter with Stephen Douglas occurred in April 1848. Both men had begun their first term of office in the Senate that spring, and it did not take long for Douglas to embroil himself in a verbal tussle with his Southern colleagues. While arguing about a bill that would reimburse property owners for damages caused by proslavery riots, Douglas expressed sympathy with Southerners' fear of slave rebellion and race warfare. Davis immediately rose to correct him, declaring, "I have no fear of insurrection . . . our slaves are happy and contented." He coldly informed Douglas, "We are able to take care of ourselves."[1]

Although they tried to maintain an air of civility and party unity—they were both Democrats, after all—their relationship began to deteriorate from that point. In repeated clashes on the Senate floor, Davis disputed Douglas's understanding of American history, Mexican history, the Constitution, civil law, the Wilmot Proviso, the Missouri Compromise, the Compromise of 1850, the nature of American frontier life, the people of the states of Texas, Illinois, Mississippi, the North, the South, and the navy and the army.[2] He called into question Douglas's veracity, his ethics, and even his sanity.[3] In the 1880s

Davis strongly hinted that Douglas, with his "empty, baseless theory" of popular sovereignty, was responsible for causing the Civil War. Varina was less restrained, privately castigating Douglas as "the dirty speculator and party trickster, broken in health by drink," and adding in an uncharacteristically scathing tone, "water is going to be introduced into [Washington, D.C.], and I trust with a view of . . . sparing his wife's olfactories Douglas may wash a little oftener."[4] The proprieties of public life notwithstanding, one suspects that her husband's feelings were similar.[5]

Lincoln and Stephen Douglas got off on the wrong foot permanently some twenty years earlier. As a young state legislator in Illinois during the early 1830s, Lincoln helped kill a proposal sponsored by fellow representative Douglas to carve a new county out of Lincoln's own constituency; in the process, Lincoln accused him and his fellow Democrats of "discourteous" tactics that were a "departure from the rules of etiquette." In 1839 Lincoln added his name to a letter addressed to a Chicago newspaper editor, implying that Douglas was involved in voter fraud and asking the editor to find proof that Douglas's ballots were signed by minors, "unnaturalized foreigners," and other "illegal voters."[6]

There was always tension in Lincoln's dealings with Douglas, and vice versa. During one early encounter, for example, Lincoln read aloud to an audience from a biography of Martin Van Buren to disprove an assertion Douglas had made, whereupon Douglas became so incensed that he grabbed the biography from Lincoln and threw it into the crowd, shouting, "Damn such a book!"[7] Lincoln described Douglas as "the *least* man I ever knew," whose speaking style was filled with "shirks and quirks," and he gleefully passed on to a friend a choice bit of gossip about a street fight between Douglas and a newspaperman. "The whole affair was so ludicrous," Lincoln wrote, "that . . . everybody else (Douglas excepted) have been laughing about it ever since."[8] On another occasion, Lincoln wrote a friend, "The Democratic giant is here, but he is not now worth talking about." Lincoln's lifelong motto was "in politics there are short statutes of limitations," and he generally prided himself on maintaining amicable relationships with political opponents. His denigration of Douglas, mild though it was, suggests that the Little Giant irritated him more than usual.[9]

Lincoln and Davis were barely aware of each other during the 1850s—Lincoln made a few passing references to Davis as a spokesman for proslavery Southerners, but Davis never seems to have mentioned Lincoln at all prior to his nomination for the presidency in 1860. Both men, however, were keenly aware of Stephen Douglas.[10] By the time Douglas propelled himself onto center stage in the growing sectional drama by brokering the political deals that led to the Compromise of 1850, Lincoln and Davis could have found some common ground in their dislike of the Little Giant and his policies. Indeed, both men defined a significant portion of their own political careers in the 1850s against the backdrop of Douglas and his policies. They did so in different ways, but they both saw in him a concrete, tangible manifestation of their own private hopes and fears concerning race, slavery, and the role these issues should play in the American conversation.

From the time Lincoln and Douglas settled in Springfield during the 1830s, they were constant competitors, in politics, in the law, and perhaps even in love, as the Little Giant possibly had been a suitor for Mary Todd. It was one of the few battles Douglas lost, for in most other respects he quickly outstripped Lincoln, vaulting from attorney to judge to congressman to serious presidential aspirant by 1852. Lincoln watched his success with a touch of envy. "The Judge is a giant," he remarked sarcastically, while he himself and his friends "are but common mortals."[11]

Douglas's forte became congressional politics, the intricate give-and-take of national legislative policymaking. He placed himself squarely in the center of the most controversial political debates of the day, controversies swirling around the issue of slavery. He did not particularly want to become entangled in the increasingly complex and dangerous political web of slavery. He disliked the peculiar institution, but he did not want that dislike to assume overriding importance in his political career. He wanted the whole subject out of the national arena—his arena—and placed in the states, where "the people . . . [could] settle the question within their limits." Yet time and again he was the point man for slavery matters in Congress, as that issue became entwined with his most cherished political ambitions. Here, then, was high politics, policymaking on Capitol Hill, not in the courtroom.[12]

Douglas was the lawyer turned politician; Lincoln was the politician turned lawyer. "While a member of Congress . . . Lincoln seemed to lose all interest in the law," his partner William Herndon recalled, but when Lincoln returned from Washington in 1848 he threw himself into his law practice with renewed vigor. It was probably the busiest time of his legal career. Besides taking up his regular sojourns on the Illinois circuit once again, he represented several large business and railroad interests and on a couple of occasions traveled out of the state to conduct legal business.[13]

This was a nuts-and-bolts law practice, the sort of gritty legal work Douglas had quickly and gladly left behind. Lincoln tried cases in nearly every available venue and in nearly every available area of the law. Rather than dealing with the lofty political parchments and refined debates in the *Congressional Globe* that constituted the professional paperwork for Senator Douglas (and Senator Davis), Lincoln was awash in a sea of writs, deeds, drafts, interrogatories, bills of sale, and other workaday legal documents. "I have at last found time to draw up a Bill in your case," he wrote a client in a typical case. "Get from the Recorder's office a copy of Cole's deed to Campbell, mark it thus . . . then fill properly the blank date in the bond."[14] As always, Lincoln was constantly aware of the distance between what could be proven in a court of law and what could not, and paperwork often constituted the essential difference between the two. "If you wish me to do anything further on the case you would better get up your evidence of title and send it to me," he wrote one client.[15] During one complex case in 1853, he expressed his exasperation over a missing piece of vital evidence. "But the great difficulty of all is the want of something definite, to take proof about," he wrote his client; "without a bill of particulars . . . any proof that I can possibly take, will be wide of the mark. . . . This matter harasses my feelings a good deal."[16]

The high politics of slavery had little presence here; in fact, slavery was not much of an issue in Lincoln's life at all before 1852. There were elements in his background that made him fundamentally averse to human bondage. Thomas Lincoln apparently despised slavery, and its existence in Kentucky may have been a factor in his decision to move the Lincoln family to freer soil in Indiana. At the same time, he worked his son so hard and treated him so wretchedly that Abraham developed a half-conscious but intense aversion to forced labor of any kind. "I have always hated slavery, I think as much as any Abolitionist," he told a Chicago audience.[17]

His racial views seem to have been on the more enlightened side of the norm for whites of his day, but not extremely so. Frederick Douglass later said that Lincoln was "the first great man that I talked with in the United States freely who in no single instance reminded me of the difference between himself and myself, on the difference of color." Lincoln was capable, however, of employing humor that carried racial overtones. While serving as a postmaster in New Salem, he wrote a sham letter from a black woman to one of his more annoying customers "saying many funny things about opossums, dances, cornshuckings, etc." In 1852 he called Democratic presidential candidate Franklin Pierce a cross between "hunksterism and free

soilism"—a reference to nicknames given to proslavery and antislavery factions of New York's Democratic party—and he then quoted a ribald poem
about "Sally . . . a bright Mullatter." Lincoln stated that "should Pierce ever
be President, he will, politically speaking, not only be a mulatto, but he will
be a good deal darker one than Sally." This sort of racial humor was not
unusual, particularly for southern Illinois.[18]

On the whole, Lincoln's early views on race and slavery, like these jokes,
were spontaneous, half-conscious, and fairly typical of white Americans
during his time. He did not give race relations or slavery much serious thought
before the 1850s.[19] Why should he have? His direct contact with African
Americans and the peculiar institution was sporadic. It had little presence
in the dominant factor of his life, his law practice. He litigated only a hand-
ful of cases that had anything to do with the institution, a drop in the bucket
of tort, corporate, and criminal cases he handled.[20] His few recorded observations of slavery during the 1830s and 1840s revealed a tinge of antislavery
feeling, but little else. He felt pity for a chain gang of slaves he saw while
visiting New Orleans, and he helped introduce a measure in the Illinois state
legislature that declared slavery to be "founded on both injustice and bad
policy."

Yet the resolution followed up this indictment of slavery with an even
stronger indictment of abolitionists as tending "rather to increase than abate
[slavery's] evils."[21] Lincoln did not particularly like abolitionism, a movement he viewed as a dangerous disruption of peace and stability. He hated
slavery "as much as any Abolitionist," but this did not necessarily mean he
supported their cause of immediate emancipation, or more especially the
tactics they employed in the name of that cause. In his Lyceum address he
virtually equated abolitionism with mob rule while ignoring a well-publi-
cized act of mob violence—the murder of Elijah Lovejoy—perpetrated upon
an abolitionist.[22]

Beyond the issue of law and order, abolitionism posed a deeper problem
for Lincoln in that it was predicated on assumptions concerning community
interaction that were the opposite of the premises Lincoln had learned in
the law: separation of intent and action, motive and appearance, private and
public. Much of abolitionism, particularly of the more radical headline-
making variety, demanded the collapse of these very distinctions. Harriet
Beecher Stowe's sentimentalist approach called for a moral measure of the
law based on a personal, highly emotional inner conversion by all Americans.
William Lloyd Garrison's burning of the Constitution was a rejection of the

core values contained in the American legal system. Lincoln knew how to use emotion as a tool in the courtroom, to manipulate the feelings of a jury, a judge, and an audience. But his professional training had led him to distrust the introduction of feeling and sentiment as the fundamental basis of policymaking and legal reasoning and particularly to eschew the probing of his neighbors' innermost moral convictions of the sort Stowe, Garrison, and other abolitionists envisioned.[23]

Of course, not all antislavery reformers were abolitionists, and not all attempted to penetrate their neighbors' souls. To that extent, Lincoln was friendly with the more temperate antislavery Whigs and later on, Republicans, lawyers like Salmon Chase and Charles Sumner, who tried to effect antislavery ends through legal means. Lincoln had faith in the procedures of law, the processes by which one carefully measured men's outer actions and behaved accordingly, and he was suspicious of the introduction of practices into the courtroom, or into the public square, that required deep inquiries into one's inner convictions on matters like slavery and race.[24]

There was, paradoxically, another side to his point of view. Strangers his neighbors may have been, but buried beneath this perception was a subtle assumption on Lincoln's part that these strangers could remain so with little danger of community disruption because they agreed on certain basic principles. Americans who shared little else in common could at least agree on the efficacy of the legal system, for example, and to abide by a court's rulings. Lincoln's profession required him to harbor fundamental, unspoken assumptions that strangers did have some common ground; otherwise anarchy would prevail, and he feared anarchy. Where slavery was concerned, he did not want to plumb the depths of his neighbors' feelings because, at bottom, he harbored an unarticulated assumption that they must generally believe as he did, that slavery was fundamentally a flawed institution. "The great mass of the nation have rested in the belief that slavery was in course of ultimate extinction," he said and frankly stated that he "believed that everybody was against it."[25]

This included white Southerners, and here Lincoln possessed a curious blind spot, curious because he himself was Southern by birth and often touted his understanding of the Southern mind. But even as white Southerners grew increasingly alienated from their Northern neighbors, and increasingly recalcitrant in their support of slavery, Lincoln professed his belief that they thought just as he and most Northerners did on the slavery question: that it was an unfortunate institution and a moral blight on the nation. Southerners "are just what we would be in their situation," he told an audience in Peoria, Illinois. "If slavery did not now exist amongst them, they would not introduce it." He presumed that those strangers south of the Mason-Dixon line were not so strange as to disagree with what he held to be universal principles, so universal that one need not search for their presence in every individual.[26]

Silence on slavery was therefore entirely consistent with his imagined America of strangers, friendly enough so that he did not have to ask what their beliefs were and strangers enough so that he did not want to. Before 1850 slavery and race simply had not exercised any special influence in Lincoln's imagination at all.

This situation changed as the new decade began, however, and as he settled back into his law practice. Among the letters and documents to clients and other lawyers concerning court judgments, writs, wills, and deeds, slavery and its attendant national crises began to appear during the early 1850s. One can sense in Lincoln's correspondence that the peculiar institution was a growing irritant, a condition triggered chiefly by the actions of Stephen Douglas.

The first vestiges of Lincoln's unease over slavery appeared in 1854, an eventful year for slavery issues. The peculiar institution was beginning to dominate national headlines, and Lincoln could not help but notice this. His own party was showing signs of splitting along sectional lines, and the vexing matter of slavery's existence in the territories was a subject of ongoing debate in Congress and elsewhere around the country.[27]

Sometime during that summer Lincoln felt moved to compose some random musings on the injustice of slavery. One such argument set out his telling observation that "although volume upon volume is written to prove slavery a very good thing, we never hear of the man who wishes to take the good of it, *by being a slave himself.*" The second paper was written in the classic form of a legal problem, what would later be called a "hypothetical" by professional attorneys. "If A. can prove, however conclusively, that he may, of right, enslave B.—why may not B. snatch the same argument, and prove equally, that he may enslave A.?"[28]

The effect is nothing so much as that of a courtroom address, a series of arguments to be put to a client defending slavery on trial before the bench and bar of Illinois or, in this case, the court of public opinion. One can imagine Lincoln seeing himself pointing an accusing finger at a proslavery apologist on the stand, all the while with one eye to the effect on the national "jury." "You say A. is white, and B. is black. It is *color* then. . . . Take care. By this rule, you are to be slave to the first man you meet, with a fairer skin than your own."[29] This was a scenario composed in Lincoln's head for himself and (apparently) for no one else, but its form suggests two key characteristics of his thinking on slavery: he viewed the issue through the lens of the law and his courtroom experiences, and he set out from the beginning to see slavery not as an issue of private personal revelation but of its effect, defense, or prosecution before the community at large.

Lincoln was finding that an antislavery moral temperament and an unquestioning faith in ordinary political and legal processes were becoming mutually incompatible. Stephen Douglas first illustrated this tension with the passage of his bill organizing Kansas and Nebraska on the basis of popular sovereignty in 1854. In one blow he repealed the Missouri Compromise and opened the possibility of slavery's spread into any new territory where it was supported by a popular mandate. He also aroused a lethargic Lincoln from his political slumber. Taking his disappointing congressional term as a sign that his political future might be limited, Lincoln had largely removed himself from the political arena during the first years of the 1850s. He kept informed through his Whig contacts, but that party was already well along the road to its eventual disintegration. He had ample motivation to devote the bulk of his time and energy to his law practice. Douglas's Kansas-Nebraska Act changed this and sent Lincoln back into the political fray during summer 1854, when he made several speeches in and around the Springfield area denouncing the "great wrong and injustice of the repeal of the Missouri Compromise" wrought by the act and its subsequent "extension of slavery into free territory."[30]

Lincoln had sound policy reasons for opposing Kansas-Nebraska. He accused Douglas of subverting the will of the Northern people by repealing the Missouri Compromise without their consent. Lincoln saw the compromise line as a nearly sacred political pact, engineered chiefly by his political father, Henry Clay, that kept slavery isolated, limited, and hence on the road to eventual extinction. He also accused the Little Giant of subverting the will of the Founders by passing a law that negated the antislavery principles of the Northwest Ordinance. And he had good moral reasons; he thought Douglas was trying surreptitiously to introduce slavery into free territory by what Lincoln considered a sham commitment to democracy through popular sovereignty.[31]

But Lincoln's fundamental reaction was that of shock and surprise in the face of a law he believed to be unprecedented in its attempts to nationalize human bondage. Herndon described his reaction as emotional and even volatile. "In the office discussions he grew bolder in his utterances," he later wrote, and he remembered Lincoln declaring that "the love for slave property is swallowing up every other mercenary position." He called the act "grand, gloomy, and peculiar, wrapped in the solitude of its own originality." He was disturbed by the possibility that the bill could make slavery the norm and freedom the exception, but he was perhaps more stunned to learn that there were Americans who really did not agree with him that slavery was fundamentally a moral evil perpetrated on a people instead of a matter of property with little intrinsic moral content. For Douglas and his supporters to pass the Kansas-Nebraska Act, Lincoln told an audience, they must believe that slaves were not really men. "If we admit that a Negro is not a man, then it is right for the government to own him and trade in the race, and it is right to allow the South to take their peculiar institution with them and plant it on the virgin soil of Kansas and Nebraska." But if blacks were human beings, "then there is not even the shadow of popular sovereignty in allowing the first settlers upon such soil to decide whether it shall be right in all future time to hold men in bondage there."[32]

Until this point Lincoln seems to have believed that at the very least, even white Southerners believed blacks were human beings; now he was not so sure. His friendly American strangers could be bad strangers with bad motives and bad sentiments, and they were making morally execrable public policy in the name of dehumanizing a people. Douglas and others like him were not to be trusted, even if they did nothing technically wrong. Lincoln's unwillingness to peer into the hearts and motives of other men was being put to a severe test, for surely it was incumbent upon law-abiding antislavery men to do so where Douglas and supporters of the Kansas-Nebraska Act were concerned. Their actions were almost unimaginable for Lincoln.

Conversely, it was necessary for men whose hearts were in the right place to combat the Douglases of the world. Lincoln suggested as much in a letter he wrote to the Illinois Democrat John M. Palmer in September 1854: "You know how anxious I am that this Nebraska measure shall be rebuked and condemned everywhere. . . . You are and have always been *honestly* and *sincerely* a democrat; and I know how painful it must be for an honest, sincere man, to be urged by his party to the support of a measure, which on his conscience he believes to be wrong." Lincoln urged Palmer to follow his heart. "You have had a severe struggle with yourself, and you have determined *not* to swallow the *wrong*," Lincoln wrote, and he believed Palmer should publicly express the dictates of his conscience. The Kansas-Nebraska Act led him to a response he was not in the habit of making: speaking of the inner motives, inner struggles, and moral qualms of a stranger.[33]

The Kansas-Nebraska Act exposed the limits of Lincoln's American identity, an identity that had at its roots a belief that the forms of the law, if followed, would create the bonds necessary for the smooth functioning of any community, local or national. As a lawyer, he was compelled to think in these terms. He could be personally detached as to a client's or a witness's private motives, and he had to develop, as a practicing attorney, a certain sense of distance from the outcomes in court proceedings. He would win cases, he would lose cases, sometimes bad men would get away with bad things, and good men would be wrongly punished. But he found he could not afford this point of view where slavery was concerned; even if all the legal formalities and legislative procedures had been attended to, slavery possessed a deeper moral significance. "It is wrong . . . [to allow slavery] to spread to every other part of the wide world, where men can be found inclined to take it," he said; "this *declared* indifference . . . I cannot but hate." But "hate" had no place in his America; it got in the way of the detached, impersonal forces of reason he had extolled in his Lyceum address.[34]

The chief source of such "declared indifference" was the Little Giant and his doctrine of popular sovereignty. Douglas saw popular sovereignty as an expression of democratic values, but Lincoln saw it as an instance of moral lassitude; and he criticized Douglas for his seeming indifference to the moral implications of slavery. "When he invites any people willing to have slavery, to establish it, he is blowing out the moral lights around us," Lincoln said; "when he says he 'cares not whether slavery is voted down or voted up' . . . he is in my judgement penetrating the human soul and eradicating the light of reason and the love of liberty of this American people."[35]

Lincoln was not being entirely fair to Douglas, whose private views on slavery were disapproving and in fact not very different from Lincoln's.[36] The practical effects of popular sovereignty, as Lincoln understood it, were a basic amoralism in the name of majoritarian democracy. He seemed mystified by Douglas's apparent inability to grasp his point of view. On a more fundamental level, however, Lincoln was mystified by Douglas's behavior and by the behavior of any American who seemed not to care whether slavery was right or wrong. He was so mystified, in fact, that he began to believe that Douglas *did* care, only in the sense that he cared enough to believe slavery was morally right and had engaged in a secret scheme to aid its spread.

This belief was a powerful subtext to Lincoln's famous "House Divided" speech delivered in Springfield in June 1858. Lincoln did not merely assert that "a house divided against itself cannot stand" or that the "house" would become either all slave or all free. He argued that Douglas and others were engaged in an active, secret plan to rebuild the house in slavery's image:

> Let anyone who doubts, carefully contemplate that now almost complete legal combination . . . compounded of the Nebraska doctrine and the *Dred Scott* decision . . . [and] let him study the history of its construction, and trace, if he can, or rather fail, if he can, to trace the evidences of design, and concert of action, among its chief bosses, from the beginning. . . . We cannot *know* that all these exact adaptations are the result of preconcert. But when we see a lot of framed timbers, different portions of which we know to have been gotten out at different times and places by different workmen—Stephen, Franklin, Roger, and James, for instance—and when we see these timbers joined together, and see they exactly make the frame of a house or mill . . . we find it impossible to not *believe* that Stephen and Frank and Roger and James all understood one another from the beginning.[37]

It is interesting to note that Lincoln names "Stephen" first in his indictment of the four major Democratic "builders." It is even more interesting to note a degree of confusion in Lincoln's thinking here: he accused Douglas of being both indifferent to slavery and actively engaged in its promotion and growth. The confusion stems from Lincoln's own thinking. His understanding of the American community had been predicated on a belief that strangers could and usually did reach essentially moral decisions when engaged in public business. Follow the rules, keep within the guidelines of the system, and the outcome would be, on the whole, equitable. Defend a client to the best of your ability—creditor and debtor, defendant and accuser, slaveholder and runaway slave—and let justice take its course. To carry Lincoln's own metaphor a bit further, he believed that the American "house" was safe even when the builders did not know one another, and he assumed that the final product would be a good house.

Yet Lincoln could see another, dangerous point of view in Judge Douglas, but what was that point of view, exactly? Was it the face of an amoral national polity that would pursue policies like popular sovereignty to their bitter end, even if those ends were unjust? Was Douglas akin to a prosecuting attorney who sends a man to the gallows knowing he is innocent but who merely tells himself that the rules had been followed? Then again, perhaps Douglas's point of view was not amoral but immoral. Was he using popular sovereignty to cover over his proslavery tracks? Perhaps he was more akin to the lawyer who conspired with the judge and members of the jury to cheat a client and subvert justice. As the decade wore on, Lincoln did not know what manner of American Douglas was; he only knew that he did not like what he saw.

Douglas and slavery illustrated the limitations of Jefferson Davis's world-view as well, but in a different way. By 1848 Davis was a rising star in the Democratic party, a war hero who was gaining recognition around the country as a leading spokesman for the South in national affairs. Some were calling him the heir to John C. Calhoun; others believed he was possibly presidential timber. The Jefferson Davis of 1848 seemed an ideal middling Southerner, a man who would of course have no truck with abolitionists but who had little contact with Southern fire-eaters and other proslavery extremists, either.[38]

His loyalty to his state and the South were firmly entrenched, and though he had previously spoken little about either, he now unhesitatingly expressed his affection and camaraderie. He referred to Mississippians as friends and fellow citizens, and a newspaperman reported Davis referring to his state as "the land where he was reared . . . the home of his affections, his interests, and his hopes," and declaring that "as a Mississippian, his highest allegiance was to the State." Davis waxed eloquent about Mississippi in an almost romantic fashion. Acknowledging that he had spent a great deal of time away from it, he nevertheless asserted that "the State recurred in his mind." He offered vivid testimony to the close connection between his state and his war service, telling one audience that "whether crouched in the grass or deep morass, or on the more open field" in Mexico, "his memory had still wandered back to his parent State—to the days of his childhood—for in Mississippi he had always hoped to make a home."[39]

At the same time, Davis felt he could speak with confidence as a Southerner about the region's needs, hopes, aspirations, and general state of mind. He referred often to Southern "interests," Southern "rights," and Southern "institutions" as well as to the "stout hearts and strong arms of the southern people." He was aware of the interdependence and migratory ties between different Southern states; he once referred to Georgia as "the mother of Mississippi," and he told fellow Mississippians that South Carolina and Mississippi should look to each other "for support and sympathy."[40]

Meanwhile, Davis remained a staunch Democrat, and his faith in that organization as a bastion of Southern and slaveholding rights grew along with his stature in the party. His loyalty to the Democracy was strong enough to compel an unsuccessful run for the Mississippi governorship in 1851. Davis did not want the job. He enjoyed being a senator, and his health, always precarious, was particularly shaky just at the time he would be needed on the stump. But the party needed him, so he ran and lost. The defeat did him no lasting political harm and may even have strengthened his standing as a Southern spokesman in certain quarters, for the few speeches he did give concerned primarily Southern rights and principles. The campaign demonstrated a high degree of self-sacrifice in Davis where his party was concerned.[41]

He advertised his standing as a "party man . . . [who] had been bred in the paths of Democracy and never deviated from them." At the same time, however, he fell back on old-fashioned republican rhetoric about the evils of party factionalism. He resolved the apparent contradiction by declaring his belief that the Democracy's principles were national principles and vice versa—good Democrats were good Americans. "Party consultation and party organization are the means, not the end," he wrote. "Principles alone can dignify a party." Loyalty to the Democrats, the South, and the Union could at times become nearly indistinguishable to him. One reporter observed Davis declaring unequivocally that he "believed the principles and measures of the democracy to be essential to the preservation of the Union, and to the prosperity and security of the southern planting States."[42]

By 1850 slavery was becoming the issue that might split the party, but Davis had not yet contributed to this problem. His public pronunciations on slavery had to this point been the bland, self-assured statements of a man comfortable with human bondage and secure in the belief that his "people" could mean him no harm. Slaves were happy and content, and so were their masters. "I have no fear of insurrection," he said. His people "are rendered miserable only by the unwarrantable interference of those who know nothing about which they meddle," in other words, abolitionists. Otherwise, the peculiar institution was neither troubled nor troublesome.[43]

Prior to 1848, then, Davis's loyalties and his assumptions had not been placed under any real pressure. He could be at once a fervent nationalist and a state sovereignty enthusiast, a believer in national authority and strict construction of the Constitution, a stern critic of Northern sectionalism and a guardian of Southern rights and interests. Varina, Joseph, his "people," white Southerners, Democrats, and Americans, to a greater or lesser extent, were all bound to him. Brierfield, Davis Bend, Mississippi, the South, and

America, to a greater or lesser extent, were all the sort of emotive, intimate communities he idealized. Those ideals had not really been tested any more than Lincoln's pre-1850 views on race and slavery had been.

Davis had begun to take note of Northern antislavery sentiments as early as spring 1848. When a senator from New Hampshire introduced legislation to pay for damages incurred by an antislavery newspaper editor during a proslavery demonstration in Washington, D.C., several Southern representatives angrily rose to block the bill and defend proslavery interests, Davis among them. "Is this District to be made the field of abolitionist struggles[?]," Davis asked, and he responded with an intemperate burst of secessionist rhetoric previously quite out of character for him. "If the fire is to be kindled here with which to burn the temple of our Union," he declared, "here let the conflict begin. I am ready."[44] His anger was palpable, or perhaps it was shock, of the same sort that Lincoln felt during the Kansas-Nebraska controversy. Several months later, Davis began his remarks on the issue of Oregon's admission as a free state with the query, "Shall jealousy, discord, and dissension—shall political strife, for sectional supremacy—be permitted to undermine the foundation of our republican fabric?" The question seemed more incredulous than rhetorical.[45]

Two years later the Compromise of 1850, the brainchild of Henry Clay but in the end a Douglas measure, landed as another bombshell on Davis's political landscape.[46] He objected to what he saw as a one-sided policy, which gave Northerners the right to vote slavery out of existence in the West, admitted California as a new free state, and limited proslavery Texas's boundary claims while giving the South only a reinvigorated fugitive slave law that he saw as essentially redundant, since it was for him a Southern constitutional right. "We are called upon to receive this as a measure of compromise!" he angrily exclaimed. "Is a measure in which we of the minority are to receive nothing, a measure of compromise?"[47]

Davis viewed Douglas's Compromise of 1850 as more than just a poorly considered matter of policymaking; it struck directly at the heart of fundamental matters of American rights and the bond of Union between Northerners and Southerners. Much of this reaction stemmed from Davis's views on the Missouri Compromise. "When slavery was excluded from the country north of 36" 30' it must be recognized south of that line," he declared. There was some confusion as to whether the Compromise of 1850 actually eradicated the Missouri Compromise line once and for all, but Davis seemed to have no doubts on this score. The line itself was a matter of some ambivalence for him; at times he viewed it with skepticism as a way of hemming the South in and keeping it from sharing in the wealth of the West. He saw it less as a matter of geography, however, and more as a violation of a sacred trust, a spirit of family and fraternity that he believed lay at the heart of the American community. The men who crafted that line "were some of the wisest statesmen and purest patriots of that period," and he believed the Compromise of 1850 was a denigration of their patriotism and of the spirit of sectional cooperation.[48]

Even more seriously, Davis saw the 1850 compromise as a violation of Southern constitutional rights, no small matter to him. Unlike Stephen Douglas, who could take up or leave constitutional arguments as political exigencies dictated, Davis saw that document as a touchstone of American values, a repository of basic American truths, which his countrymen would tamper with only at their peril. Focusing his ire on the arguments by compromise supporters that Mexican antislavery laws should remain in force in California, thus effectively forever barring slaves and slaveholders from its soil, Davis claimed that the Constitution's privileges and immunities clause had been violated. "We only claim that there should be an equality of immunities and privileges among citizens of all parts of the United States; that Mexican law shall not be applied so as to create inequality between citizens," he said. For Davis, the entire Constitution was a sectional Bill of Rights, establishing equal moral and political standing among slaveholders and nonslaveholders, Northerners and Southerners.[49]

Davis had worked this philosophy out in the office with Joseph long ago, when the two brothers could relax for an evening of convivial politics and perusal of the Constitution and the *Congressional Globe,* where no opposing viewpoints or challenges were likely to be offered to their interpretations of the Constitution and its meaning. Davis had assumed that his reading of property rights, Southern rights, and the Constitution were objective truths. Americans might occasionally stray from their meaning, but in the end they had but one meaning, final and irreproachable. Before 1850 he had been given little reason to question this: in his brief stint in the House and from his experience in the Senate he had witnessed disagreements, of course, but not on matters so profound and unimpeachable as Southerners' property rights and federal protection of those rights.

As Lincoln did in 1854, Davis in 1850 saw the Republic as jeopardized by bad men whom he had not heretofore considered to be capable of such behavior. He was profoundly shocked by the behavior of Southerners and Northerners alike during the ratification fight over the compromise. He believed his fellow Southern representatives had sold out their constituents by voting for a measure that would ultimately destroy slavery. Davis castigated Henry Clay as a slaveholder who had "dashe[d] down those . . . barriers against encroachment" upon Southern rights by reopening the old debates over slavery in the District of Columbia and by asserting that slavery could never really be established in the West. He was also disturbed by the divisions of opinion among the Southern people in general, and he appealed to his Southern neighbors "to cease wrangling among themselves—to form a common platform on which all can unite—to cease calling each other harsh names."[50]

But he was particularly incensed at fellow Democrats like Stephen Douglas. Northern Democrats were "no longer worthy of being called 'allies of the South,'" he told a Southern audience, referring with particular anger to several Northern senators' support of a provision barring slavery from the Oregon territory. Chiefly, Davis was upset with Northerners as a whole, and it was during the compromise battles that he first began consistently grouping Northerners together in his mind as a separate community with its own agenda and interests. Davis saw hatred of slavery, and by implication of the South, as a factor unifying previously disparate elements in the North and melding them into a new and dangerous sectional community. "The power of the anti-slavery shibboleth," as he referred to it, was "to fraternise men of the most opposite opinions on other subjects."[51]

Davis saw abolitionism not just in its pragmatic political and moral manifestations; he cast it in terms of its emotional impact on white Northerners. The movement gave them "a thirst for political dominion"; it caused "excitement" and a "bubbling cauldron." When he supported attempts by some Southern congressmen to suppress antislavery petitions, he did so in the name of suppressing the dangerous emotions such petitions aroused. "The right of petition . . . may yet be carried to such an extent that we are bound to abate it as a nuisance," he said. Antislavery petitions were more than just a nuisance, however; "They disturb the peace of the country; they impede and pervert legislation by the excitement they create."[52]

Abolitionism, in other words, was creating in Davis's mind a new and dangerous element—an implacable abolitionist North. There was "some feeling at the North against the South," and it was such emotion that he believed formed the core of a new and disturbing Northern sectionalism.[53] He believed the Northern agenda was nothing less than sectional domination, the creation of a "Union of concession instead of the Union as formed by the founders of the Constitution." The North had "secured the majorities in all the departments of the government," he claimed, and its purpose was to use the power of government to make the South "slaves of a superior power." He began to see signs of a growing abolitionist conspiracy in the North to kill slavery, and he hinted that these two entities, the North and abolitionism, were essentially interchangeable, referring at one point to the North as "the abolition States."[54]

The compromise was Davis's wake-up call, in much the same way that the Kansas-Nebraska Act aroused Lincoln four years later: it produced an irritant, a twitch, which grew stronger in prompting Davis's political behavior. It threw his various loyalties, state, South, Democrats, and Union, into question. Before 1850 he had not drawn sharp distinctions between any of them, and he was content to think of each as deserving of his loyalty equally. Now he was not so sure.

Stephen Douglas was at the root of this uncertainty. He was a Democrat who had backed a measure that bartered away the slaveholding rights of other Democrats. He was a Northerner who had endorsed a compromise inimical to the rights of Southerners. He was an American whom Davis believed was engaged in trimming the constitutional rights of other Americans. In Douglas, Davis saw the specter that would increasingly haunt him and other Southerners in the years to come: the power of an expanding, exuberant, sometimes belligerent North that cared nothing for slavery or the South and that would someday overwhelm both the peculiar institution and its defenders with sheer numbers and economic might. There was real fear here and an increasing defensiveness about the South's decreasing numbers and power. "In truth, sir, we are rapidly approaching to that state of things [when] the rights of the minority will be held at the mercy of the majority," Davis told a Senate colleague.[55]

In this regard he reflected the general anxiety of a beleaguered South.[56] Many Southerners feared the North, and Davis was no exception. "I feel it is as if the grain sheaf should oppose the sickle to oppose the dominant majority," he declared, "who can, and we have reason to believe will, crush any proposition which will . . . be substantially for the benefit of the South."[57] Unlike many more radical Southerners who had never placed much faith in the Union, Davis's alienation and separatist sentiments were born of dashed hopes that the Union was a collection of people whose hearts were in the right place. He needed an America based upon his—and what he believed to be true American—sentiments of loyalty and friendship. Like many white

Southerners, he personalized political conflict, making party strife and policy debate tests of personal regard between Northerners and Southerners.[58] He needed a Union that was the same comfortable, friendly community that Mississippi, Brierfield, his "people," and the South had become. It was a need that, to Davis's dismay, remained unfulfilled.

He rooted this need in his particular reading of history. As his disenchantment with the North grew, he frequently referred to the time of the Revolution and the nation's founding. He saw the Revolution as a special moment when Northerners and Southerners came together and created a nation by creating a meeting of the hearts. According to Davis, it was the South, not the North, that had made most of the requisite sacrifices for the movement toward independence and afterward the formation of a peaceful, stable national government. "Virginia had a title to the Northwest territory, older than the confederacy," he pointed out in one example, but it relinquished that title through its "patriotism . . . generosity, confidence, and anxiety to perpetuate the confederation." Davis even went so far as to claim that the Revolution had been an essentially Yankee war. "When the mother country violated the rights and interests of the Northern colonies, the Southern people, like brothers made the quarrel of the North their own," he claimed.[59]

The Constitution had been created to ratify this meeting of the hearts between Northerners and Southerners, to "draw closer the bonds of union." It was a pragmatic instrument, a guarantor of the nation's security and prosperity. For Davis, however, it was also a statement of heartfelt bonding, "a perpetuation of fraternity by Union of the states." Such fraternity carried with it certain duties owed by one family member to another. "The Constitution did not create the institution of domestic slavery," he pointed out, but it did create "legal and constitutional obligations to surrender fugitive slaves" and otherwise to protect slave property.[60]

The North had reneged on the Revolutionary compact; it had given vent to the darker sides of its heart. Davis referred to Northerners as the South's "pride-swolen [sic] neighbors" and abolitionists as people "dead to every feeling of patriotism."[61] Davis's ethic of honor, born of his military service and his Southernness, was evident here, as he posited antislavery aggression in terms of an affront to the slaveholding states' collective honor. Northerners wanted to "fix an odium" upon the South and its institutions, he stated. They had "wronged and slandered" the South, and he informed fellow senators that "we who represent the southern States are not here to be insulted on account of the institutions we inherit."[62]

The Union was therefore becoming not only a dangerous but a dishonorable and degrading place for Davis and his fellow Southerners. At first he believed that if Southerners stood united against abolitionist aggression, then Northerners would come to their senses. This was an intellectual matter, but it was also emotive; Northerners would come to feel how deeply they had wronged their brothers. "My hope then is that the united voice of the South will reach the ear of the North, and that the common interest, the good sense, the patriotism, the national pride, the respect for the constitution which characterise the mass of the people will . . . stop this car of sectional strife . . . with all its freight of disunion."[63]

But Davis increasingly despaired of relying on the South's friends in the North. With Northerners shifting their hearts away from their duties to the South, he turned to the Democratic party as a possible alternative. If Northerners in general would not remain members of the Union community of sentiment, at least Northern democrats might.

These hopes were dashed by Stephen Douglas. The Kansas-Nebraska Act and its doctrine of popular sovereignty were the sticking point between Douglas and proslavery Southerner Democrats like Davis. Lincoln saw popular sovereignty as a veiled attempt to make slavery national, but Davis and his brethren saw it as a policy designed to hem slavery in and slowly destroy it. From a constitutional point of view, Douglas's theory violated protected property rights by allowing a mere popular vote to keep the institution from being introduced into territories where it lawfully ought to be allowed to go. For Davis this was a direct violation of the Constitution, which conferred a positive duty on Congress to protect all property rights on American soil.[64]

From a personal point of view, Douglas had made the Democratic party a fallen organization, espousing principles that Davis and other Southerners could not condone. Douglas obviously did not have his heart in the right place, Democrat or not. The Little Giant seemed more and more like a lodge brother who had strayed. Worse, Douglas's political maneuvers were wrecking the Democratic party, a "community" Davis hoped would preserve the peace. He especially wanted Douglas to see that his popular sovereignty doctrine, his actions in regard to Kansas, and his bid for the Democratic presidential nomination in 1860 were dividing the party. Davis remonstrated with him as if he were an apostate from the party of believers, saying that Douglas was "full of heresy." When Douglas told his fellow senators that he was defending the principles of the Democratic party, Davis derisively answered, "That party might as well cry out, 'Save me from my friends.'" He accused Douglas of personally killing the party's chances in Illinois and elsewhere as well as waging a "war upon the Democratic organization" in general.[65]

Davis led the fight against the principles of popular sovereignty being inserted into the party platform, and he led the fight against Douglas himself. A few days before Christmas 1859, he felt compelled to explain himself in a long and sometimes acrimonious speech on the floor of the U.S. Senate.[66] The speech was full of military metaphors from this former army officer and secretary of defense. The imagery is significant, for Davis saw the Democratic party rather like a military unit, a closely knit community of people whose loyalty should be above reproach and with motives clearly and easily understood. "I desire no divided flag for the Democratic party," he declared, nor did he seek to "depreciate the power of the Senator [Douglas] or take from him any of that confidence he feels in the large army [of Democratic supporters] at his back." But, he said, "I prefer that his banner should lie in its silken folds," because, at bottom, Douglas led a minority faction that threatened to upset the necessary harmony of interest and feeling that should pervade the party.

Davis downplayed the platform fight in 1859 over popular sovereignty, even though he had led the Southern delegates in their efforts to insert a plank offering what he termed "the simple declaration that negro slaves are property, and . . . recognition of the Federal Government to protect that property." "The fact is I have a declining respect for platforms," he said. Instead, he cut right to the heart of the matter: he did not trust Douglas. "I would sooner have an honest man on any sort of a rickety platform you could construct, than to have a man I did not trust on the best platform which could be made." In this backhanded slap at Douglas lay the true issue for Davis: he needed to be able to imagine the men in a community like the Democratic party as good men, with honorable intentions and principled motives. Party platforms, then as now, were matters of appearance, outward manifestations of party harmony. Davis wanted more than this, however, and he believed the voters did too. What Davis needed, and what he thought Americans in general needed, was a good man, and Douglas was not that man.[67]

At the same time, Davis was incensed at Douglas's suggestion that he, not the Little Giant, was destroying the Democratic party. When Douglas commented on the divisive effects of Davis and other Southern Democrats' "petty controversies in regard to African labor," Davis lashed back by informing Douglas that Southerners' principles were at once Democratic principles and the principles of the Constitution. He further suggested that Douglas was pandering to "the mere bidding of popular prejudice" with popular sovereignty doctrines that were "a delusive gauze thrown over the public mind."[68]

Throughout these exchanges, Davis averred that he could see what Douglas's true inner motives were; he could pierce the veils that hid his heart much the same way he claimed he could do with Varina. He believed Douglas was an unscrupulous political operator with no principles other than those that might get him elected to higher office. At one point Davis sarcastically stated that he "admire[d] the ingenuity with which [Douglas] escaped from his attitude of hostility" to the Democratic Buchanan administration; "It was ingenuity, however, at the expense of other qualities more valuable." On other occasions, Davis made it quite clear that those "other qualities" were honesty and a forthright devotion to the principles of the Democratic party. After one testy exchange, Davis leveled an accusation, then said to Douglas, "Wriggle out of that one, if you can." Davis believed Douglas did more than his share of "wriggling" and thus was not to be trusted.[69]

Moreover, Davis was convinced that Douglas's questionable actions were quite intentional. The Little Giant was not merely wrongheaded or impolitic but immoral. For example, Davis wrote an angry note in fall 1859 to a Maryland newspaperman, John Hess, concerning a speech by Douglas on "popular sovereignty in the territories," which Hess's paper had printed. Davis claimed Douglas's "extracts are so partial as to misrepresent the position which I then and have ever since held." Douglas had purposely misrepresented Davis's opposition to popular sovereignty; "The comment which Mr. Douglas makes," Davis wrote, "perverts the position which he had full opportunity to know was held by myself and others."[70]

Douglas was nonplussed by Davis's assaults. He wished Davis would simply swallow his arguments for the good of the party and said he would not accuse him of "not [being] a good Democrat" simply because of these intraparty disagreements. Douglas told everyone that Davis had a problem with him personally, rather than with his ideas or principles.[71] Although Davis publicly declared that he bore Douglas no personal ill will, Douglas had a good point. Propriety may have compelled Davis to declare on occasion his friendship with Douglas, and the two men could work together when party politics or Senate business made collaboration a necessity.[72] But in the end, Davis consistently and repeatedly treated Douglas as an apostate who placed personal ambition ahead of the health of the party and, eventually, the country.

As with Lincoln, Douglas's actions provoked in Davis the shock and surprise of someone who simply had never imagined he would encounter such a person or such behavior. Both Lincoln and Davis had created for them-selves an America that rested upon assumptions affording a degree of personal comfort. In Lincoln's case, his imagination had allowed him to exercise a degree of control over disparate and sometimes conflicting facets of his own personality. Davis's imagination allowed him a value system that could reconcile the inherent and tragic contradictions of slavery—they were not slaves, they were his "people"—and that could allow him to claim close allegiance to a state, a region, and a nation after he had spent so much of his early life in the peripatetic existence of an army soldier.

Their viewpoints may have offered the two men a high degree of personal meaning and resolved contradictions, yet they did contain contradictions and unresolved issues. If the paradox of Lincoln's point of view was his unspoken assumption that Americans were strangers and yet agreed upon certain things—like slavery's essential injustice—then the paradox of Davis's perspective was that hidden beneath his presumptions of sentimental unity was a constant need to be reassured that such sentiments did in fact exist. He needed his neighbors to give constant reassurances of their right thinking and right feeling. Lincoln was comfortable enough in his presumptions that he sought no such assurances.

Douglas—and, in the long run, the white South—gave Lincoln a rude awakening, illustrating that there were some Americans who were not necessarily repelled by the idea of human bondage. His response was twofold: Douglas's behavior propelled Lincoln back into politics and compelled him to search for some means by which to explain the actions of wayward citizens like Douglas and to test the soundness of fellow Americans on the moral issue of slavery.

Davis eventually embraced secession, but not because his nationalism was weak. Quite the contrary: his disillusionment with the North pushed him toward separation precisely because his Unionism had been so strong, strong enough to be based on the same presumptions that his loyalty to his state and his region had been. Before 1850, he confidently believed the Union was bound together on the same intimate, emotive basis as West Point, his plantation, or the state of Mississippi. His response fell so low because his expectations concerning the Union had been so high.

INSURGENTS

   A little over a year before Lincoln's election as president, Senator Davis exhibited what some observers thought to be his growing prickliness on matters related to Southern rights by writing a polite but terse note to the editor of the *New Orleans Delta*. The paper had just published in full an essay circulated nationwide by Stephen Douglas, and Davis wrote to dispute Douglas's arguments on several technical points of territorial law and the status of slavery in the Mexican cession. Douglas "perverts the position which he had full opportunity to know was held by myself and others who participated in the debate" on territorial law, Davis claimed. The editor was a strong Douglas supporter but apparently admired Davis as well, for a month later Davis wrote him again to thank him for making "some kind, and very gratifying allusions to myself." Davis was about to depart for Mississippi, the fall session of the Senate having ended some days earlier. The date was October 13, 1859.[1]

  Davis was probably en route to his plantation home when, five days later, his future favorite general stormed a brick arsenal in the little Virginia town of Harpers Ferry, killing ten men and capturing seven others, including the leader of an attempt that had been intended as the opening round of a white-led slave rebellion. When Robert E. Lee took John Brown prisoner, he probably had no idea who he was. In all likelihood Davis had never heard of Brown either, even though he had made a bit of a reputation for himself by staging some bloody raids against proslavery settlers in Kansas.[2]

Like Davis, Lincoln was also traveling during fall 1859. After losing the Senate election of 1858 to Douglas, he had begun thinking about a possible bid for the Republican party's presidential nomination in 1860, and to that end he had embarked on a series of speaking tours in western states outside Illinois: October found him in Wisconsin, where he attacked Kansas-Nebraska, *Dred Scott,* and popular sovereignty before mostly Republican audiences. He was back home in Springfield when Brown's raid took place. He said nothing about Harpers Ferry until a month later, when he took a brief tour of Kansas prior to the election of territorial officers in that troubled territory. He called the raid on Harpers Ferry "a violation of the law and . . . as all such attacks must be, futile as far as any effect it might have on the extinction of a great evil."[3]

Years later Davis wrote that Harpers Ferry itself was of no particular importance, a botched enterprise led by "a fanatical partisan leader." Davis had little to say that was bad (or good) about Brown himself.[4] He saw the raid as evidence of a deeper sign, "a startling revelation of the extent to which sectional hatred and political fanaticism had blinded the conscience of a class of persons in certain states of the Union."[5] In a series of resolutions introduced by the Mississippi senator in winter 1860, Davis made an oblique reference to the Brown raid when he denounced "open covert attacks" on slavery by antislavery Northerners who had engaged in "a manifest breach of faith and a violation of the most solemn obligations."[6] He drew a direct connection between Republican rhetoric and John Brown's actions. Quoting a speech by Republican abolitionist Caleb Cushing on the floor of the Senate in January 1860, Davis asked, "Was it possible for any one to have thrown out an invitation to John Brown and his followers, broader than this?" He denounced this and similar speeches as "the language of one who instigates insurrection, who seeks to carry war into neighboring States."[7]

When the Senate decided to appoint an investigative committee to look into the Harpers Ferry raid, Davis was appointed as one of its members. He told a Washington newspaperman that "prominent individuals" had been associated with the attack, and he apparently believed that a little digging would unearth a conspiracy that would embarrass the North and bring the

Republican party crashing down.[8] Denouncing the raid as "an act which stands out prominently as the first . . . of those violent proceedings which can only be considered civil war," Davis called upon his congressional brethren to "inquire to the bottom" concerning the possibility of any conspiracy behind Brown's actions.[9]

Davis became the Senate's point man in this inquiry. He received correspondence from Northern citizens concerning the attack, and he conducted the questioning of several key witnesses at the committee's hearings. He voted for a resolution calling for the arrest of any person who failed to come forward with information concerning the raid, and he often led the fight waged by Southern senators to expand the scope of the committee's proceedings.[10] In the end he was forced to admit that the raid was "simply the act of lawless ruffians." But he continued to see John Brown as evidence of a general ill will toward himself and his fellow slave owners by many people in the North.[11]

The Harpers Ferry raid, and subsequent revelations that Brown had received aid from prominent Northerners—including some with connections to the Republican party—initially placed Lincoln on the defensive. During the Leavenworth speech, he professed admiration for Brown's courage but reminded his audience that "no man, North or South, can approve of violence or crime." Brown was in his grave by this time, and Lincoln stood on a spot not far away from where, five years previously, Brown had hacked five people to death with swords along Pottawatomie Creek. "Old John Brown has just been executed for treason against a state," he said. "We cannot object, even though he agreed with us in thinking slavery wrong."[12]

Lincoln admired Brown's principles and his antislavery convictions, but he had to walk a careful line between this admiration and an unintentional endorsement of the man's violent behavior. During a second speech in Leavenworth on December 5, Lincoln said he sympathized with Brown's hatred of slavery, even though the old abolitionist was in all probability insane.[13] He denounced Brown as an "insurrectionist" and portrayed him as a symptom of a general decay in Americans' ability to settle their differences peacefully.[14]

Lincoln rejected Democratic charges of Republican backing for Brown as "an electioneering dodge."[15] "The democrats cry John Brown invasion," Lincoln said; "we are guiltless of it, but our denial does not satisfy them."[16] But he worried about the uses to which any possible connections between his party and the raid might be put by Democrats eager to paint him and his cohorts as abolitionists and anarchists. When Davis's Senate investigating committee was unable to establish a direct connection between the Republicans and John Brown, Lincoln exulted over what he viewed as a complete exoneration of his party from any wrongdoing. "If any republican is guilty in that matter, you, the democracy, either know it or you do not know it," Lincoln said. "If you do know it, you are inexcusable not to designate the man and prove the fact. If you do not know it, you are inexcusable to assert it, and especially to persist in the assertion after you have tried and failed to make the proof."[17]

He deeply resented any implication that Republicans had been even indirectly responsible for the raid. When Stephen Douglas declared in spring 1860 that there was a direct causal relationship between antislavery rhetoric and Harpers Ferry, and in so doing introduced a bill calling for congressional action against insurrection and treason, Lincoln smelled a threat to Republicans' free speech rights (and future political prospects). Quoting at length from Douglas's speech equating John Brown and antislavery words, Lincoln angrily declared, "I conceive the real object of [Douglas's] proposed bill was to put down republicanism; to prevent republican meetings and shut men's mouths!"[18]

During his widely publicized address at New York's Cooper Union in February 1860, Lincoln pressed these points home, denouncing the Democrats for demagoguery and for shamelessly exploiting the Brown raid for political gain. To Lincoln, attempts to use Harpers Ferry as a weapon against the Republicans were at best futile and, at worst, a threat to the political process itself. "And how much would it avail you, if you could, by the use of John Brown . . . break up the Republican organization?" he asked Democrats. Antislavery sentiments would remain in the North regardless of the party. "There is a judgement and a feeling against slavery in this nation," he pointed out. Democrats and fire-eaters would simply destroy the very process that might be used to resolve differences in a reasonable manner: "How much would you gain by forcing [antislavery sentiment] . . . out of the peaceful channel of the ballot box, into some other channel? . . . What would that other channel probably be? Would the number of John Browns be lessened or enlarged by the operation?"[19]

Lincoln's response to men like John Brown and to events like Harpers Ferry was on a fundamental level precisely what his use of the Declaration dictated; he drew a careful separation between Brown's intentions—the old man meant well—and his actual behavior, and he suggested that one did not excuse the other. He seemed to expect that for Southerners this would be enough: if he excoriated Brown outwardly, it would mean far more than any praise of Brown's inner soul.

But for Jefferson Davis it most certainly was not enough; he wanted the very concession Lincoln and others like him would not give; a disavowal of Brown's sentiments as well as his deeds. Davis believed there was a direct line from one to the other; bad hearts spawned bad deeds. On the surface, Harpers Ferry was evidence of a Republican conspiracy to foment rebellion; in Davis's eyes, it revealed something much deeper: the disintegration of the American community, the only sort of Union to which he could be committed. If it were gone, he would compact his expectations and his beliefs into the smaller and more comforting space that was Mississippi. There at least he knew that his neighbors shared his principles and ideals.

Long before Brown assaulted the U.S. arsenal at Harpers Ferry, Davis's faith in his fellow Northerners and in the Union was steadily waning. From his heartfelt pronouncements of national patriotism during his early years in Congress, he had become by 1859 a man who, in the vernacular of the day, "calculated the value of the Union." As early as 1849 he wrote to a Mississippi journalist that Southerners were bound to the Union "by associations of past, by historic pride, by duty and by love," but this could change "if its terms are violated" or "its band broken."[20]

The Union had become little more than a utilitarian device, a limited tool designed only to perform certain tasks that the states could not do themselves. For Davis it was no longer a community of intimate friends connected by emotional ties of honor and principle. He now likened America to a "mercantile or comanufacturing partnership," in which "the participants came together . . . to abstain from the separate exercise of certain powers, which they agree to entrust to the management and control of the union."[21]

What were those "certain powers"? The federal government dealt with foreign governments and exercised control over the nation's tiny army and navy. It facilitated the free flow of commerce between the states by maintaining and repairing major rivers. Above all, it extended legal protection to American citizens traveling with their slave "property" in areas "beyond the municipal power of the states," chiefly unsettled territories, where Davis wanted an even playing field for "the white man coming from the North, and the white man coming from the South."[22] These were significant grants of power, illustrating that he was not completely oblivious of the needs and prerogatives of the federal government.[23]

But references comparable to a "character of the American people" became increasingly rare in Davis's speeches. Suspicions he had sometimes voiced concerning the motives and reliability of Northerners grew stronger, until he came to deny there was any such thing as an American community at all.[24] His fundamental litmus test for loyalty to the Union was that the federal government should never operate as if it represented a single "people." According to Davis, Americans were not a people, and the United States was not a "community" in any meaningful sense of the term.

Davis spoke not as a fire-eater who had never placed much value in the Union, or even as a strict Calhounian who had believed only in a nation of disparate state sovereignties; rather, he denigrated the notion of an American "people" almost sadly, as a man whose disillusionment was so profound because his expectations had once been so lofty. Throughout his speeches and writings of the late 1850s runs a continual reference to the Union as a "fraternity," with the term denoting a particularly pure and virtuous sort of community that Northerners in their wickedness had violated. He referred to "anti-slavery agitation" as disturbing "the fraternity and peace of the Republic," and he accused Northerners of engaging in a form of treason by inviting foreign agitators—referring to British abolitionists—to shame the South and further disrupt the harmony of the Union.[25]

His adherence to Calhounian orthodoxy grew steadily stronger as his belief in the Union fraternity waned; in a sense, he constitutionalized his disappointments. Thus the Revolution became for him an act of thirteen separate communities, not one. The Revolutionary War "closed with the recognition of the independence, not of the confederacy, but of each state severally as a sovereign community." Further, "The delegates to the convention of 1787 represented, not *the people of the United States* in mass . . . but *the people* of the several states, *as states*." This was not a convention of the sort that affirmed fundamental values such as support for slavery, forming states from territories and a "people" from mere inhabitants. Davis insisted that the phrase "we the people," in the Constitution's preamble, "was certainly not intended to convey the idea that the people of the American continent . . . constituted one political community," and he denounced the "monstrous fiction" that the United States was "one people" as having "not an atom of fact to serve as a basis."

Davis thought that none of the powers legitimately exercised by the federal government could create such a community. Washington, D.C.'s regulation of diplomacy and defense, according to him, did not automatically give it the power of sovereignty, which was the essential attribute of a people. The power to govern major waterways and rivers was designed to bind together the various "products and . . . institutions of the several States," not individuals. Nor did the power to oversee settlement of the territories of itself create a people. Each separate state community had made different decisions where slavery was concerned, and he was keenly aware of the fact that his and his fellow slave owners' sentiments were not shared nationwide. Legal protection of slavery was necessary, but this did not mean the federal government could exercise the sovereign right of choosing whether or not slavery would continue to exist for the entire country or whether it was morally right.[26]

Davis described America as a "confederation of sovereigns," and a "union of these states," but he rarely used the term "American people."[27] When he did, the circumstances were almost always such that any connotation of unity or homogeneity was diluted. When he referred to "the people of the United States" in the Senate, he immediately followed the phrase with state sovereignty or sectional qualifications.[28] As early as 1852, during an address he delivered to college students in Oxford, Mississippi, where he stated that he would "endeavor to present to you my idea of the character proper to a citizen of the United States of America," he strongly urged them to stay at home in Mississippi where they belonged and reiterated his constitutional argument that there was no such thing as "we the people."[29]

Assertions that treated different areas of the country as distinct and unfamiliar are scattered throughout Davis's speeches and correspondence, for he had come to believe that only states—and to a certain extent, regions—imposed enough homogeneity on their residents to be termed a "people." He set South Carolina off against Massachusetts, New York against Mississippi, and, of course, North against South. He tended to look upon Americans from one state or region who ventured into other areas as something akin to foreigners. Thus he accused Stephen Douglas of "set[ting] a bad example" by delivering speeches on Davis's home turf in Mississippi and irritably remarked, "I trust it will be the last time."[30] He even proposed that the electoral college be abolished as an unwarranted intrusion into each state's political activities. Most important, he wanted Northerners to mind their own business where the peculiar institution was concerned. Davis informed Northern senators, "If slavery be a sin, it is not yours."[31]

A statement Davis made in 1858 neatly summarizes this perspective on the Union. While traveling north by steamboat to begin a speaking tour in

New England, he described his fellow passengers as "a mixed company" made up of "citizens from many states of the Union."[32] For him, America was like that steamboat, a land with a "mixed company" of very different communities. They shared the same space, and they shared the same interest in keeping the ship afloat and headed in the right direction. These circumstances did not constitute ties of loyalty or sentiment however, and they could get off the boat whenever they wanted.

Increasingly, Davis and others interpreted this view as an exposition of Southern rights and regional identity. His sense of regional identity, rather weak in his early years, had now become quite strong, and he was described in many quarters as the new "Calhoun of the South." As early as 1847 he had written to a friend that it "might become necessary to unite as southern men" in the Democratic party, because of the "extensive defections . . . among Northern Democrats" concerning "Southern institutions and southern rights." He hoped it would be unnecessary to engender such a sectional split within his party, believing that Northern Democrats would "show themselves worthy of their ancient appellation" and remain sensitive to Southern needs.[33] In the wake of the Compromise of 1850, he had called for a Southern convention to "point out the guarantees and safeguards, which the South is entitled to." He spoke increasingly of the "rights of the South," "Southern citizens," and the "people of the South." He wanted Southerners to unite in the face of enmity displayed by "our pharasaical brethren of the North."[34]

But the common interest of Southerners in protecting slave owners' property from Northern abolitionists was not quite the same thing to Davis as the close bond of values and loyalties that constituted his ideal community. He saw a Southern community in rather practical terms, as a careful calculation by each Southern state concerning where its best interests lay. Any decision made by Mississippi concerning its interests was binding on Davis, irrespective of what the rest of the South might do. He had no divided loyalties in this regard, as he made clear in an 1851 speech when he said that Mississippi's "honor was the first consideration" in any secession scheme. Mississippians "should endeavor to meet the other Southern states," he told his audience, "and confer as to the best means of repelling aggressions. . . . If the Southern states cannot and do not join Mississippi in her efforts for Southern rights, then Mississippi will have given them fair opportunity." He hoped that any move by Mississippi toward defiance and secession "will be sustained by general action of the South," but if not, his primary loyalties were with his state, and the rest of the South could do what it wanted.[35]

He did not necessarily expect unanimity among Southern states and in fact saw the interests of some being pitted against others, particularly where slavery was concerned; it was not quite as strong a unifying factor in the South as it was in Mississippi. For example, Davis denounced the provision of the Compromise of 1850 that called for tougher fugitive slave laws as "a policy only for those slave States bordering upon the free states." He believed fugitive slaves were a problem only in such border areas; the real need for the Deep South, as he saw it, was elbow room to expand into new western territories. He bitterly denounced the border states as abandoning the concerns of the "planting states" in supporting a compromise that restricted the expansion of slavery's domain for the sake of recovering a few runaways.[36]

Indeed, Davis spent as much time complaining about the South as praising it. "The cause of the South, I regard as prostrate, for the present," he wrote a friend. "It is not now to be hoped, that the position taken by the Southern states . . . can now be maintained. Virginia and Georgia have abandoned their ground [and] the other Southern states, with the exception of South Carolina, seem utterly indifferent." He often criticized Southern "deserters" who would not stand with other Southerners and defend the region's interests during the battles over the Compromise of 1850 and other important pieces of national legislation. "The fact was," he said, striking a dejected note, "the South's own members neglected, in one solid body, to speak out manfully and boldly; some deserted their ranks, and the North reaped the advantage."[37]

By the time of Harpers Ferry, Davis's faith in the Union had largely vanished. He had hopes for the South, but even he realized how thin a reed Southern nationalism really was without some sort of dramatic, galvanizing event to pull Southerners together and awaken them to what he considered to be violations of their sacred rights. "They cannot be brought to act harmoniously together, in advance of the experience which, in a few years more, will enlighten all minds," he wrote. He firmly believed that a crisis was coming, but in the meantime, he could not count on the South—and certainly not on the Union anymore—as a community to ground his principles and beliefs.[38]

In the end, Mississippi commanded his ultimate loyalty, more so than the Union or even the South. Perhaps his state's fundamental appeal to Davis was its supposed homogeneity. Despite the diversity of peoples contained within its borders, he frequently referred to its residents as a single entity. A "people" was more than a mere collection of individuals occupying the same physical space. For Davis, a people was a homogenous, united, and harmonious polity, and state boundaries were expressions of that harmony.

Thus did he understand the process of state formation, as a creation not of a political entity but of a community with certain shared values. According to Davis, a territory would undergo a period of emigration, during which time settlers would, under the guarding eye of the federal government, bring their different ideas, principles, and institutions together and, through some unidentified process, create of themselves a "people" who had made crucial decisions about matters such as slavery, much in the same way soldiers were molded to the ideals of military honor. Then these settlers would form a constitutional convention, where "calmly and deliberately . . . equally uninfluenced by headlong passion or unmanly fear," they would make the decisions about value and principle that would bind them together as a community. They would exert the "right of a people . . . to determine what their domestic institutions should be." Once this happened, "the inhabitants of a territory became citizens of a state"; they became a "people."[39]

He wanted Mississippi's citizens to think in such a manner, to act as one community and to speak with one voice wherever possible.[40] He emphasized his own statewide vision on all matters, great and small. He would not exploit internal differences within Mississippi, even when it might have been in his interest to do so. Early in his political career, for example, Davis declared his opposition to construction of a proposed naval base in Memphis, seeking instead to relocate the project to a site on Mississippi's Gulf Coast. A Vicksburg newspaper noted that "if he were more of a politician (using the word in its odious sense) . . . he would hardly jeopard[ize] the support he will receive from the strong Democratic counties in the North of this State, which, of course, feel a deep interest in the success of a Navy yard at Memphis." The idea that one section of Mississippi might actually feel more in common with another state than with fellow Mississippians never seemed to have occurred to him.[41]

If Davis emphasized his allegiance to the whole Mississippi community, he generally expected the whole community to give its allegiance to him. He was hurt by charges that he showed favoritism to any one area of his home state; it was "mortifying" for him to hear "that any section of the state should assume the attitude of opposition to me under the idea that one part of Mississippi is less dear to me than another." He was also miffed over criticism of his opposition to the Compromise of 1850, telling an audience of Mississippians that "he did not expect, after serving them in the best manner that he could . . . to return home to the people of Mississippi and have to feel it necessary to come before them and argue the very questions that he had discussed with the Northern freesoilers and opponents of Southern institutions."[42]

This rather arrogant presumption was a central facet of his personality, observed by friends and enemies alike. Edward Pollard, a Richmond newspaperman who despised Davis, wrote that "he spoke as one who would not brook contradiction, who delivered his statements of truth as if without regard to anything said to the contrary." He expected deference from his slaves, from his wife, and from those whom he considered beneath his intellectual and social standing.[43] He also expected deference from his constituents, for whom he would in turn offer public service and unquestioning loyalty. The classic American debate over whether a political representative should exercise his own independent judgment or simply act as a conduit for his constituents' will was largely a moot point for Davis. He often expressed his willingness to be bound by the wishes of Mississippi's voters, but he did not really expect to be questioned about his judgment or decisions.[44]

When he was criticized, Davis tended to blame "outsiders," people whose hearts were not really with Mississippi. After a speaking tour of the state in 1851, he wrote to a friend that his community's sentiments were in "great confusion," some supporting his stand against the "Northern aggressors" and some not, a situation he blamed on a pervasive "Yankee influence." In public speeches he qualified a call for Mississippi's unity by appealing only to those who "permanently identified with the State." Such appeals did not apply to "those who were transiently resident amongst [us]," whom he described as outside agitators, "strangers," and even "vampires . . . who lived amongst [us] for what they could make then returned to their homes in the North." He did not expect real differences of principle among the people of Mississippi.[45]

Davis particularly expected consensus concerning the efficacy and necessity of slavery. Like most white Southerners, he viewed slavery as the foundation of Southern social unanimity.[46] This pattern began with the slaves themselves. He believed slavery was a reciprocal relationship between master and slave; the former received service and deference, the latter was civilized and Christianized, rescued from a supposedly barbaric state. This "real identity of interest," as he put it, benefited all Mississippians, black and white, and so bound all together.[47]

It was on this basis that Davis consistently defended slavery as a benevolent, unifying factor in Mississippi. He told a packed assembly of Mississippians who gathered in May 1849 to condemn the latest antislavery rumblings from the North that he was "gratified to observe the vigilance and unanimity of the people . . . upon a question which involved both the feelings and interests of the whole community."[48] Differences on this crucial issue were unnatural and dangerous, especially in the face of growing Northern hostility toward slavery. "Mississippi disapproved of the first act of aggressive measures" by these abolitionists, he confidently told a crowd in 1851, and Mississippians were "united—firmly united."[49]

Davis expected all Americans to feel the same way about their own home states. He abstracted his feelings for Mississippi into a general theory of state sovereignty constitutionalism, which he saw as the only moral basis for American government. He told an audience in Corinth, Mississippi, that "the allegiance of each citizen was due to the state of his residence." In this sense, his devotion to Mississippi was not unique or accidental but part of the larger constitutional structure that defined American citizenship as being bound directly to the states. "The only political community—the only independent corporate unit—through which the people can exercise their sovereignty is the state," he wrote; a state was the only place in which "they have community existence."[50]

Each of these "independent corporate units" was by definition a distinct community. As such, all states represented like-minded persons with similar values and principles: New Yorkers thought as other New Yorkers just as Mississippians thought as other Mississippians. Uniformity of opinion within a state's borders was important for Davis; he felt that any government, especially a state government, in order "to afford the needful protection and exercise proper care for the welfare of a people, must have homogeneity in its constituents."[51] He did not qualify this statement by suggesting unity on issues like slavery or the interpretation of the Constitution, leaving the impression that he expected a fundamental uniformity on a broad range of issues and principles. Thus, if a government required a homogenous community, then a homogenous community required a strong government to carry out its sovereign will. "The power to govern, as an absolute, ultimate authority, remains in the States," he told fellow senators in 1848. The governments of these unified constituencies could exercise almost unlimited control over their own institutions, "leav[ing] every independent community to determine and adjust all domestic questions as in their wisdom may seem best." He called this "the great principle of community independence," which he believed was an integral part of American constitutionalism.[52]

By "domestic questions," Davis meant slavery. He seems to have remained essentially comfortable and confident with the peculiar institution throughout the 1850s, and he apparently assumed that other Mississippians were unambivalent about it as well. As abolitionist assaults increased, he felt compelled to press it forward as the focus of the debate and to make it a centerpiece of his state sovereignty constitutionalism. In a series of resolutions submitted to the Senate in 1860, he told Northerners that "no change of opinion or feeling on the part of the non-slaveholding States of the Union" would "justify . . . open and systematic attacks" on the institution of slavery in those states where no such change had occurred. Davis had good reasons for wanting to keep decisions concerning the propriety of human bondage exclusively within the state. Slavery was safest when left in the hands of Southern state legislators, governors, and judges, who generally were slave owners themselves and who would therefore hesitate to strike any blows against the peculiar institution.[53]

There was much more to this approach than a slaveholder's opportunism, however. Davis's state sovereignty constitutionalism was an expression and an abstraction of what had become a deep, abiding, and uncompromising devotion to Mississippi. It was for him a homogenous entity, a "people" with the emotive, sentimental bonds that constituted a true community. As such, it was his final refuge, his root equation of loyalty. His devotion to it was unquestioned in a way that his loyalty to the Union and the South were not. He announced without hesitation on numerous occasions that his first duty was to Mississippi, "for good or for evil," and despite what the rest of his nation or section did.[54] "Mr. Davis eloquently vindicated the loyalty of Mississippi," Varina wrote. "His State was fortunate in her champion. On this theme never once did he utter an uncertain note."[55]

Mississippi was Davis's answer to the crises of community and national loyalty he had confronted since Stephen Douglas had introduced his compromise and during the stormy years that followed. Faced with the question of where his loyalties lay, he turned them around and around in an ever-tightening circle until only Mississippi remained as a source of final, unequivocal, completely uniform set of principles and feelings that he held and that he believed the people whom he would completely trust also must hold. Fear, mistrust, and suspicion marked this move toward his state and away from his country, it is true, but there were also more proactive, positive factors involved, high expectations of heartfelt bonding and community that he felt had simply vanished. The "fraternity essential to the existence of our Union" was gone, he said in 1861, and he would seek that fraternity elsewhere. In the end, secession was not so much a breakdown of Davis's nationalism as a removal of the values and expectations he had placed in the Union and a subsequent relocation of his feelings to a different community. When Lincoln was elected, Davis promised to "hug [Mississippi] to his heart" should secession come. That was what he did.[56]

Lincoln simply would not have fathomed this romantic attachment Davis felt for his state. To Lincoln, a state was just a place, and he was not much given to romanticizing physical spaces, be it his law office, his home, or Illinois. "What is this particular sacredness of a State?" he asked incredulously. "If a State, in one instance, and a county in another, should be equal in extent of territory, and equal in number of people, wherein is that State any better than the county?" The difference in Lincoln's nation-centered constitutionalism and Davis's state sovereignty creed was rooted in more than just power or political expediency or even opinions about slavery; the difference also lay in a fundamentally divergent approach by both men to the nature of community and communal bonding.[57]

Placing a great divide between Lincoln and Davis, and many like them, was the fundamental question of means, of the ways in which Americans did or could converse about high moral values. Americans like Lincoln and Davis could and had agreed to disagree over slavery: what they could not abide was their inability to agree on how they would disagree, as strangers or as sentimental brothers and sisters.

Part Three
WARTIME
IMAGINATIONS

10

PRESIDENTS

A few days before her husband was inaugurated as the nation's sixteenth president, Mary Lincoln found herself frantically searching for a new seamstress to join the White House staff. She needed someone to help her appear well dressed and fashionable before an elitist Washington social set that was already clucking with disapproval at the thought of the supposedly rough-hewn Lincolns mingling in the upper circles of the capital's society. Before they even reached Washington, the rumor mill had typecast Mary as an ill-bred western bumpkin, despite the fact that she hailed from a wealthy and genteel Kentucky family. The new First Lady was determined to prove herself (and her husband) to be cultured and socially refined, and she intended to look the part.[1]

Among the applicants who came to the White House for an interview was an African-American woman, Elizabeth Keckley, a forty-three year old former slave who had resided in the nation's capital since purchasing her own freedom in 1855. She had acquired a local reputation as an excellent seamstress and was recommended to Mary as a suitable possibility to meet her needs. When Keckley was shown into Mrs. Lincoln's room, the First Lady asked her,

"Mrs. Keckley who have you worked for in this city?" Keckley replied, "Among others, Mrs. Senator Davis has been one of my best patrons." Mary was impressed and hired her on the spot.[2]

Elizabeth Keckley worked for Varina Davis during the "secession winter," 1860–1861. She liked Varina, and Jefferson Davis too, whom she described as "a thoughtful, considerate man." Keckley was struck by the number of distinguished visitors to the Davis home. "Mr. Davis occupied a leading position," she later noted; "his house was the resort of politicians and statesmen from the South. . . . The prospects of war were freely discussed in my presence by Mr. and Mrs. Davis and their friends." She apparently found a bit puzzling this habit of openly contemplating war in front of a servant, and an African American at that.[3]

"Lizzie, you are so very handy that I should like to take you South with me," Varina said at one point during the sectional crisis. After telling her seamstress that she was certain there would be a war, Varina insisted, "You had better go South with me. I will take good care of you. Besides, when the war breaks out, the colored people will suffer in the North. The Northern people will look upon them as the cause of the war, and I fear, in their exasperation, will be inclined to treat you harshly." Elizabeth later wrote that she took Varina's offer seriously. Neverthless, as she wrote in her memoirs, "The more I thought the less inclined I felt to accept the proposition so kindly made by Mrs. Davis. . . . I preferred to cast my lot among the people of the North."

Assuming Keckley was not being extraordinarily disingenuous, her reaction to Varina's proposal might seem surprising. To modern ears it sounds odd that a former slave would even consider voluntarily relocating south and farther away from the side that, although not yet embracing emancipation, still carried better guarantees for her freedom and liberty. Not only did she consider the possibility, but issues about slavery and African Americans' status in the South apparently played little role in her thought processes; rather, she made a quick (and, as it turned out, accurate) survey of the North's ability to win a war with the South. "I knew the people of the North to be strong," she later wrote, "and believed that the people would fight for the flag that they pretended to venerate so highly."[4]

Varina's offer is perhaps equally surprising. Did she expect Elizabeth voluntarily to return south of the Mason-Dixon line? Perhaps she really believed the white Southern bromide about their section's benevolent racial attitudes. In truth, manumitted slaves like Keckley faced a precarious position in the slaveholding South, where their free status caused suspicious whites to view them as possible instigators of slave revolts. Under these circumstances, free black Southerners were often the targets of efforts at imprisonment, expulsion, and reenslavement. Keckley's chances of once again becoming someone's "property" increased with every southward step she took.[5]

Varina's offer reveals much about the mind-set she shared with her husband during those chaotic early months of 1861. The choices they faced were fairly simple, binary questions of communal identity. Did the Davises identify with the North or the South? Would they choose the old Union or the embryonic new Southern nation? The storied Mason-Dixon line created an imagined boundary between two places, across which Americans like the Davises might now step and become something else. Of course, these choices were fraught with emotional and political baggage, and no one—not even the latter-day "Calhoun of the South," Jefferson Davis—made the mental and physical journey across the line lightly. But the choices seemed fairly clear; indeed, Davis came to see crossing the great divide between North and South, Union and Confederate, as a way of simplifying the complexities of sectional politics, of "putting our house in order, by the resumption of the powers needful to provide for our own protection."[6]

Keckley's calculations reveal a movement in rather the opposite direction by many others whose sectional loyalties were not so clear-cut. National loyalty was a messy, gray, difficult area for African Americans, border state whites, nonslaveholding Southerners, white Northerners like Mary Lincoln with kinship ties to the South, or white Northerners like her husband who never really possessed much of a regional identity and found it difficult to understand how regionalism could supersede the Union for some Americans.

Every American in 1860 crossed a mental (and often geographic) divide and reconfigured his or her community loyalties to fit the temper of extraordinary times. This was no less true for Lincoln and Davis, but added to their particular situations was a transition to the presidency. By 1860 both had become, to a greater or lesser extent, national figures. Everyone knew Jefferson Davis as a veteran senator and bona fide Mexican War hero who would most likely lead the Southern charge out of the Union should secession come. Lincoln did not possess quite the national stature of Davis, but he was well known as the man who dueled verbally with Stephen Douglas for a seat in the U.S. Senate in 1858; and his "House Divided" speech had made him many friends (and enemies) outside Illinois. Nevertheless, these two national or quasi-national figures were now making the great leap to the two nations' highest executive positions. They were heirs to the presidency, Union and Confederate, which required a readjusting of many aspects of their private lives, including their national imaginations.

Mary Lincoln wasn't the only member of the Lincoln circle who was apprehensive during the days leading up to Lincoln's inauguration. Keckley commented on the tense atmosphere in Washington as she took up her new White House job. "The streets of the capital were thronged with people," she remembered; "never was such deep interest felt in the inauguration proceedings as was felt to-day; for threats of assassination had been made, and every breeze from the South came heavily laden with the rumors of war." She found crowds of excited, nervous people milling about at Willard's Hotel, where the Lincolns had been staying. If Keckley attended the ceremony, she would have seen sharpshooters posted on rooftops ringing the Capitol and details from the army guarding key city crossroads. A covered wooden walkway protected the president-elect from assassins' bullets as he entered the Capitol, and a battery of cannon guarded Capitol Hill.[7]

Americans had never seen anything quite like it. Normally a presidential inaugural was a chance to celebrate national unity, beginning with the tradition, rarely broken, that the defeated candidate should accompany the new president to the swearing-in ceremony in a show of bipartisan support. Lincoln kept this tradition; despite his private disdain for outgoing president James Buchanan, the two shared a carriage ride to the swearing-in ceremony. Lincoln even allowed lifelong rival Stephen Douglas to hold his hat while he delivered his inaugural address.[8]

Presidential inaugurals were expected to be displays of such political healing; they were nationalizing rituals in a country that boasted few truly national events. But Lincoln's inaugural was unique in its circumstances and its implications. With its sharpshooters, covered walkways, and batteries of cannon, the inaugural's tone and its tense atmosphere spoke more to the imminent threat of national disharmony.

Then again, Lincoln's inaugural journey from Springfield to Washington, D.C., was in many ways uniquely his own. The idea of a grand political procession, a metaphorical discovery of the nation by a president-elect as he traveled to his new home in the nation's capital, was not new. George Washington used his 1789 trip from Mt. Vernon to Philadelphia as a nationalizing tool; he understood that the thousands of diverse people who lined the roads, provided enthusiastic escorts for his carriage, scattered flowers in his path, and erected patriotic arches for his passage were discovering themselves, as Americans, even as they discovered their new president.[9]

Lincoln was well aware of the precedent Washington had created. In his famous farewell speech to his Springfield neighbors, he invoked the memory of the Founding Father and used words similiar to those Washington had spoken at a farewell dinner given in his honor by his Virginia neighbors.[10] But during his own twelve-day, nineteen-hundred-mile trek across America, Lincoln did something rather different.[11] He let Americans get a good look at him, but more to the point he used the inaugural trip to discover America, or rather, a multitude of Americas.

Many historians, and not a few of his own contemporaries, pointed out that Lincoln was one of the most inexperienced presidents in American history. This is true. Prior to 1860, he had held only one national office, his brief two-year stint in Congress. He had never held an executive office of any kind. But the issue goes deeper. His national imagination lacked experience as well. However well developed and robust his nationalism may have been before 1860, it was nevertheless a product of a man who had lived most of his adult life in one state and who had infrequently ventured beyond its borders. His national imagination was indeed a product of his collective experiences with family, friends, Illinois neighbors, fellow lawyers, judges, and clients, which in turn formed the substance, the vocabulary for a way of imagining an America he had not really seen.

Now, however, that America was right in front of him, staring him in the face as he rode eastward from Springfield. The nation was no longer quite the ephemeral, imagined community that he could conjure simply by using his personal experiences—diverse in their way, but still relatively provincial— as a normative starting point. The United States of America was immediate, expectant, placing the burden of the hopes, fears, and needs of millions of people primarily and directly upon his shoulders. During his inaugural journey he saw in the most concrete sense the nation he had heretofore only imagined; in the pale, waving hands of well-wishers lining the railway, in the pleasant or hostile or deceptively passive upturned faces of strangers pressing at the back of his train, in the requests for favors and offers of advice with which he was already being inundated.

Here was a great swirling blizzard of a nation, and its effect on the new president-elect was profound. In reading accounts of Lincoln's trip to Washington, D.C., one gets the sense of a man who was to a certain extent stunned by the sheer magnitude of his great national burden and who was struggling mightily to get control of the thousands of details, ideas, policies, and people showering down upon him. "He is now public property, and ought to be where he can be reached by the people until he is inaugurated," New York's political boss Thurlow Weed observed. Weed was right, but the burden of being public property, national public property, at that, taxed Lincoln's powers of endurance. At one point, his friend Henry Ward Lamon remembered, Lincoln wearily exclaimed, "I wish . . . that this thing were through with, and I could find peace and quiet somewhere."[12]

Lincoln delivered at least fifty speeches in cities and towns spread across five states: not only the major cities of Indianapolis, Cincinnati, Cleveland, Columbus, Pittsburgh, Philadelphia, New York, Albany, and Buffalo but also obscure little hamlets like Frazeysburg, Coshocton, Newcomerstown, Wellsville, and Silver Creek. In a show of political harmony, he insisted that the many welcoming committees that visited his train should be bipartisan in nature, with Democrats as well as Republicans, and he spoke often of the essential unity of the country. "I suppose that here, as everywhere, you meet me without distinction of party, but as the people," he told a cheering crowd of onlookers in Poughkeepsie, New York.[13] But however much he may have wished for unity, what he in fact confronted at every turn was diversity, on a national scale. For Lincoln, the journey, in a literal and symbolic sense, was an act of complexity, a refracting of his national imagination.

One immediate manifestation of this diversity was to make him more self-aware, more cognizant of his image and the effect his behavior might have on those around him. His law practice had done so in the 1840s and 1850s, teaching him the value of erecting barriers between his innermost thoughts and feelings and the world around him. His newfound status as president-elect deepened these tendencies, for now his behavior impacted an entire nation. Lincoln the Shakespeare and theater devotee stood in 1861 on a national stage before a national audience; and though he did not contract a case of stage fright, he was suddenly and keenly aware that there were more faces in the crowd and the footlights were much hotter.

As he moved closer to Washington, that fishbowl of a city where he and his family would be subjected to withering scrutiny, he became more conscious of his physical appearance. There was the famous matter of his beard, which he grew with the purpose of covering an otherwise homely face and lending just a bit more dignity to his lank, sallow features. An oft-repeated and favorite quip during the trip was his comic statement to a given crowd that "I have stepped out upon this platform that I may see you and that you may see me, and in the arrangement I have the best of the bargain."[14]

But this awareness of appearance went far beyond the superficial matter of facial hair. Lincoln had to worry about the impression of impropriety before a possibly critical American audience. Following the time-honored American tradition that presidential candidates should be neither seen nor heard, for example, he was forced to reject nearly all requests for a personal appearance during the presidential campaign. "Your kind invitation I suppose I must decline," he wrote in a rather sad tone to Zachariah Chandler in August 1860, who had invited him to attend the Michigan State Fair. "It is the opinion of friends, backed by my own judgement, that I should not really, or apparently, be showing myself about the country." To a secretary of the Republican National Committee, he wrote, "I am invited to a horse show, at Springfield, Mass., beginning, I believe, on the 4th of September. Would it *help* or *hurt* our cause if I were to go?" Apparently he was advised to avoid even this mundane public appearance, for he declined the invitation.[15]

After the election, Lincoln developed the habit of separating himself as a man from his persona as president. "I do not believe that you extend this welcome—one of the finest I have ever received—to the individual man who now addresses you but rather to the person who represents for the time being the majesty of the constitution and the government," he told one audience. This was a useful political ploy for Lincoln, who wanted to smooth away some of the jagged animosities generated by the election and to place matters on the higher plane of national unity and patriotism. But it also indicated his growing need to create an acceptable presidential figure that he could present before a national audience to generate a patriotic, nationalist response.[16]

Lincoln became aware that for the first time in his life, his words, his behavior, even the use of his name by others had national ramifications. His actions as president could impact political decisionmaking in places far removed from the familiar grounds of Illinois. "My name *must* not be used in the Senatorial election, in favor of, or against anyone," he told Weed, some of whose followers had intimated that Lincoln might use his patronage powers to help put the *New York Tribune*'s editor Horace Greeley in Congress. Lincoln was surprised to learn that a few passing remarks of "kindness towards Mr. Greely" [*sic*] could so easily snowball into an unintentional political endorsement. "It is very strange that such things should be said by any one," he wrote Weed.[17]

As such little incidents educated Lincoln about the subtleties of being a national figure, he grew steadily more cautious in what he said and how his words might be construed. Lamon recorded that, early on, Lincoln had resolved to attain the "object of speaking and saying nothing" to the crowds lining the route. He admitted to members of the Pennsylvania legislature that his speeches "were rather carefully worded. I took pains that they be so." In response to numerous requests from audiences along the route to Washington to speak on the subject of secession, he often begged off by saying that he wanted time to prepare his remarks carefully on that potentially explosive subject. "It is naturally expected that I should say something on that subject," he admitted to an audience in Pittsburgh, Pennsylvania, "but to touch upon it at all would involve an elaborate discussion of a great many questions and circumstances, would require more time than I can at present command, and would perhaps unnecessarily commit me upon matters which have not yet fully developed themselves."[18]

Lincoln's always reticent nature became still more pronounced. When he told his private secretary John Hay of his intention to resupply the garrison at Fortress Monroe and "then go down to Charleston and pay her the little debt we are owing her," Hay wrote that he "felt like letting off an Illinois yell. . . . I begged the privilege of scattering an intimation of the coming glory through the host, but [Lincoln] quickly said 'Not yet.'" When Hay or other friends and advisers sometimes pressed him too far on sensitive matters, he would simply reply that he was "shut pan" on the matter. Lincoln's friend Alexander McClure found the new president's reticence exasperating, writing that during a typical talk with Lincoln on policy matters he would find that "when the conversation ended I had no more idea as to the bent of his mind than if I had been conversing with the Sphinx."[19]

In many respects Lincoln's attitude was justified, for he knew his actions were being monitored by Americans who bore him ill will. "I have *bad* men also to deal with, both North and South," he believed. Even after he arrived in Washington, he was apprehensive of just how close these bad men were. "While I write this I am, if not in *range,* at least in *hearing,* of cannon-shot, from an army of enemies more than a hundred thousand strong," he wrote in September 1861.[20]

Years of experience in the rough-and-tumble world of Illinois politics had left Lincoln with a perceptive sensibility to the subtle politics of appearance, and when his political arena became national that sensibility became an even more valuable asset. When rumors surfaced during the campaign that he had been a member of the nativist Know-Nothing party, he vehemently denied the charge and supplied political allies with the information needed to refute such claims. "That I never was in a Know-Nothing lodge in Quincy [Illinois], I should expect, could be easily proved," he wrote, "and now a word of caution. Our adversaries think they can gain a point, if they could force me to openly deny this charge. . . . For this reason, it must not publicly appear that I am paying any attention to the charge."[21]

But sometimes this "shut pan" attitude could push Lincoln a bit over the edge. "Let no eye but your own see this," he concluded in a letter to Congressman Lyman Trumbull and then rather sheepishly admitted, "not that there is anything wrong, or even ungenerous, in it." He marked much of his correspondence "confidential," on matters great and small. He cautioned one correspondent, "Please do not make this public" in a letter that merely recited the bare facts of his career in the Illinois state legislature. He made a similiar request to a young man whose family had once lived near the Lincoln homestead in Illinois and who had asked him for a bit of family history. He berated his running mate Hannibal Hamlin in an uncharacteristically cross tone for a relatively harmless slip of the tongue concerning Republican prospects in Maine. Hamlin had been quoted as having predicted that the party might lose a couple of congressional seats and would win the governorship only by a slim majority. Lincoln admonished him: "Such a result as you seem to have predicted . . . would, I fear put us on the downhill track, lose us the State elections in Pennsylvania and Indiana, and probably ruin us in the main turn in November."[22]

The president-elect had come to realize that the eyes of a great many people were upon him, and he was acutely conscious that those eyes belonged to strangers, many more strangers than he had ever known, even in his general stores, his courtrooms and state legislative chambers, and the streets of New Salem and Springfield. Some he felt as the cold stares of Americans who had already begun to demonize him and his party. He was painfully aware of this new, possibly ugly addition to his national community. "You suggest that a visit to the place of my nativity might be pleasant to me," he wrote to a Kentuckian in June, 1860; "indeed it would. But would it be safe? Would not the people Lynch me?"[23]

Even those Americans who were not openly hostile were at least apprehensive about a national future fraught with uncertainties. Lincoln's imagined community of America was calm and rational from the perspective of a circuit lawyer and Illinois legislator. But from the vantage point of an embattled president-elect, presiding over a disintegrating nation and rumored to be in danger of his very life, the America he imagined as he confronted scores of people was a a tense and anxious place.

President-elect Lincoln saw the secession crisis in overtly emotional terms. In his correspondence and speeches during the secession winter he referred to the present "excitement" against Republicans in the South, the "irritation" white Southerners felt at the presence of a federal garrison in Fort Sumter, the "restless" attitude of South Carolinians, and the "distraction of the public mind" at the thought of civil war. Rebellion was caused by "ill feelings" in the South among those who were stricken with a sense of "apprehension" at the prospect of a Republican president. "I certainly am in no temper, and have no purpose to embitter the feelings of the people of the South," he wrote one man. On the other hand, he believed that secessionists were engaged in a systematic "debauching of the public mind," and he called upon Americans to resist such blandishments and to remember the spirit of the Founding Fathers, who eschewed "passion, ill-temper and precipitate action."[24]

Lincoln understood that "the condition of the country . . . is an extraordinary one, and fills the mind of every patriot with anxiety and solicitude." He appealed to alternate emotions of calm and sober reflection to combat this rising tide of nervousness and fear. "It is a consoling circumstance that when we look out there is nothing that really hurts anybody," he told members of the Ohio legislature. "We entertain different views upon political questions, but nobody is suffering anything. This is a most consoling circumstance, and from it we may conclude that all we want is time, patience, and a reliance on that God who has never forsaken this people." To Southerners he offered reassuring observations: "You are as good as we. . . . You have as good hearts in your bosoms as other people, or as we claim to have."[25]

Never before had Lincoln referred to the nation in such starkly emotive terms. Here was a new line of thinking in his national identity, whereby Americans needed emotions and the heart to remain steadfastly American. In his Lyceum address he had expressed reservations about appeals to emotion as a way of stitching together the fraying seams of the national fabric, and he had studiously avoided overt emotionalism in his law practice and in much of his public life. But face-to-face now with a nation—rather than with a jury or a cohort of Illinois voters—and beset by a profound national crisis, he rediscovered emotion and appeals to the hearts of his fellow Americans.

In a speech before his Springfield neighbors right after the election, Lincoln had referred to Americans as "brothers of a common country" and to the national "bonds of fraternal feeling." As he made his way toward Washington he increasingly used such Davisonian language, appealing to "that fraternal feeling which has so long characterized us as a nation" and reassuring Americans that "I bring to the work an honest heart." He referred to the coming civil war as a "shedding of fraternal blood" and "fraternal strife" among "brethren," and he included in his speeches numerous references to "feelings" of patriotism and citizenship, which he hoped would combat the rising tide of disunion. He made appeals for calm amid the threatened disorder of secession, appeals that were more for national self-control than the rather unemotional appeals to reason he had made in the Lyceum address and elsewhere. "My advice, then, under such circumstances, is to keep cool," he declared. And he made clear his belief that "if we have patience; if we restrain ourselves; if we allow ourselves not to run off into a passion, I still have confidence that the Almighty . . . [will] bring us through this."[26]

During the trip east, he increasingly spoke in these terms, as a man sharing his feelings with others around him. "May I hope that the public expression which I have at this day given to my sentiments, may have contributed in some degree to your happiness," he told well-wishers in New York. "As far as I am concerned, the loyal citizens of every State, and of every section, shall have no cause to feel any other sentiment." He also spoke of the "good will" and "sincere feeling" he felt was evident in his listeners. Before Independence Hall in Philadelphia, he delivered extemporaneously what may have been the most emotion-laden speech of his entire career, admitting to his listeners that he was "filled with deep emotion at finding myself standing here in the place where were collected together the wisdom, the patriotism, the devotion to principle from which sprang the institutions under which we live." With uncharacteristic sentiment he referred to his desire to die for the principle of individual freedom embodied in the Declaration of Independence, and he made the eerie claim that "if this country cannot be saved without giving up that principle—I was about to say I would rather be assassinated on this spot than to surrender it."[27]

For this brief moment in his career, president-elect Abraham Lincoln spoke unabashedly of a sentimental America, a nation bound together by emotion as well as reason. He thanked delegations for their "renewed assurance of kind feeling," and he spoke of his own personal "sentiment" and his "heart."[28] The reasons were many: the pressures of the day, the imminent assassination plots and threats of violence, a national atmosphere charged with the threat of violent dissolution.

But there were limits to Lincoln's newfound American sentimentalism. Even as he found useful the language of national emotion, which to Jefferson Davis was second nature, he still approached his newly rediscovered American community essentially as a stranger, to be treated with friendship but also with a degree of distance. The reticence he had learned increased, and his reluctance to pry too deeply into the hearts of his fellow Americans continued. His appeals to white Southerners to remain in the Union were partially predicated on national fraternity—"We are not enemies, but friends. We must not be enemies," he said in his inaugural address—but he devoted an equal amount of time to reassuring Southerners that national unity did not necessarily require a heartfelt bonding. Rather, Southerners and Northerners need only obey the laws and abide by the results of the 1860 election; let the rest take care of itself in due time, with white Americans agreeing to disagree over all the thorny issues that had for years divided them. "If the Almighty Ruler of nations, with his eternal truth and justice, be on your side of the North, or on yours of the South, that truth, and that justice, will surely prevail," he declared.[29]

Like Lincoln—and every other American—Jefferson Davis felt the pressures of anxiety in the days leading up to the nation's final breakup. "The current of events rolls on with such rapidity that the conclusion of today may be inapplicable to the case of tomorrow," he wrote to a friend in January 1861. To Edwin De Leon, a fellow Democrat and soon-to-be Confederate ambassador, Davis observed rather wistfully, "We are advancing rapidly to the end of the 'Union.' The cotton states may now be regarded as having decided for secession."[30]

Davis wrote this on January 8, by then convinced that secession would indeed occur. His own loyalties were never in doubt; he would follow the wishes of Mississippi, come what may. He had said so on several occasions, and it seemed apparent to him and nearly everyone else that his home state would be among the first Southern states to leave the Union.[31]

Yet for a little while Davis seemed as confused in his loyalties as anyone else. He remained in Washington, D.C., despite the momentous events occurring in Mississippi and elsewhere; he thought that it was "possible that the state may choose to continue its senators here for purposes of defense against hostile legislation." He delivered a defiant speech in the Senate on the matter of Southern rights, which could not have failed to impress his listeners with his ardently prosecession sympathies. At the same time, however, he transacted routine business as if nothing was amiss. He wrote a letter of recommendation for a U.S. army officer in the Quartermaster's Department, he advised future Confederate general Joseph Johnston on the proper way to reimburse a regular army Indian scout for the loss of a horse struck by lightning, and he dutifully returned books he had borrowed from the Library of Congress.[32]

The break finally came on January 19, when he received a telegram officially informing him that Mississippi was now an independent state and that he should return home immediately. Davis dashed off a quick note to Clement Clay, a fellow Democrat from Alabama, in which he declared, "We have piped but they would not dance and now the Devil may care." After that, he reflexively and quite automatically shifted his national loyalty from America to the South, smoothly and without a hitch. "The hour is at hand which closes my connection with the United States," he announced on January 20. By January 30 he was already referring to the new Confederacy as his "country," even though only five of the eleven states that would eventually constitute the Confederacy had at that point seceded. He stopped giving advice to officers in the U.S. Army and told any Southerners who asked that their best plan of action was to quit their allegiances to the Union immediately and return home. He planned to do so himself.[33]

First, however, Davis felt the need to create for himself a supreme moment of truth, a dramatic farewell address to the Senate that would be his version of Lincoln's Springfield farewell. He did not need to do this. There was no pressing legal or political purpose to be served by a personal appearance before the Senate. He was ugently needed at home, and he was ill, suffering acutely from "dyspepsia neuralgia," a painful nerve condition in his face and eye that had left him bedridden for several days. Indeed, he was forced to summon a Herculean effort of will to drag his ailing body before the Senate. "Our medical attendant thought him physically unable to make his farewell," Varina remembered.[34]

The Senate chamber on January 21 was filled to bursting with curious spectators, journalists, diplomats, and government officials. "By nine [o'clock] there was hardly standing room in the galleries or in the passway behind the forum," Varina recalled. "The sofas and passways were full, and ladies sat on the floor against the wall where they could not find seats." She thought that "there brooded over this immense crowd a palpitating, expectant silence which was afterwards remarked as very unusual. . . . We felt blood in the air."

Her husband, "graceful, grave, and deliberate," rose to speak in a voice that Varina described as "at first low and faltering" but that soon gained strength so that it rang out across the Senate chamber "melodiously clear, like a silver trumpet."[35]

Davis steered his audience toward old, familiar ground: the Constitution, the law, states' rights. He drew a careful distinction between "nullification" and "secession," and he reiterated the Southern position on slavery, on race relations—"they were not put upon the footing of equality with white men," he said of "his people"—and on the proper reading of the Declaration of Independence, which "had no reference to the slave." He spoke of broken bonds of friendship between Northerners and Southerners, and he announced that the time had come for Mississippi to cut "all the ties of affection" binding her to the Union.[36]

Davis spoke often of fathers. John C. Calhoun, was a "great man who now reposes with his fathers." He further stated his belief that his fellow Mississippians and Southerners "are to be deprived in the Union of our rights which our fathers bequeathed to us." He invoked them as his trump card, the ace he held in his hand of constitutional arguments. Most of what he said was abstract and legalistic. For he had come to understand that neither he nor any other Southerner could rely on fraternity, friendship, feelings of affection from their Northern brethren. It just was not enough anymore; maybe it never had been.

But near the end Davis groped his way back toward sentiment. "I am sure I feel no hostility to you, Senators from the North," he said. "I see now around me some with whom I have served long; there have been points of collision; but whatever of offense there has been to me, I leave here; I carry with me no hostile remembrance." His last words sounded like the last rites in a divorce proceeding: "I have, Senators, in this hour of our parting, to offer you my apology for any pain which, in heat of discussion, I have inflicted. I go hence unencumbered of the remembrance of any injury received."[37]

There was nothing new here; it had all been said before. But it was a moment of high political drama, of excruciating emotion, and as such it suited Davis perfectly. It gave him a discernible moment in time, a bright, hard line that separated him physically, mentally, and emotionally from what his national loyalties had been before January 21, 1861, and what they would be afterward. His imagination needed a binary, before/after, either/or boundary, imbedded as deeply in sentiment as in constitutional argument and that could provide this man who so badly needed certainty with an absolute, indisputable referent point for what he had been and what he would now become. Lincoln could step off into the unknown, the blizzard of American diversity, where there were no clear lines and where loyalties and motives were shades of gray; Davis could not. He needed absolutes. And absolute his new national loyalty would be. He never once contemplated a return to the Union after January 21, and he would not admit defeat until it was crammed down his throat. He compared anyone who would consider reconstruction of the Union to "the Israelites of old . . . longing to turn back to the fleshpots they have left."[38]

Less than a month after he delivered his farewell address, Davis was inaugurated as the president of the new Confederate States of America. His ascendancy to the position was the product of a political process much different from the hurly-burly party maneuverings that propelled Lincoln to the White House. At the end of January, Davis went home to Brierfield and played no direct role in the events transpiring in Montgomery, Alabama. While delegates from the various seceding Southern states met in that city in February 1861 to hammer out the structure of a new national government, Davis at least feigned retirement from public life. "I feel the strongest desire to pass the remainder of my days in the peaceful useful toil of my cotton field," he wrote John Callan, a friend and former clerk in the War Department.[39]

Lincoln's days in late fall and early winter 1860–1861 were spent in anxious anticipation. Davis, on the other hand, seemed more relaxed and composed than at any other time in his life. He devoted himself to the comparatively mundane tasks of running his plantation; "in the homely but expressive language of [Henry] Clay to 'repair my fences,'" as he later wrote.[40] Lincoln, chafing with inactivity in Illinois, was still mentally in the hustle and bustle of American politics; he could readily imagine, and identify with, a rushing, swirling, politicking nation, even as he could have no active role in that process. He did not pretend to do otherwise and only reluctantly accepted the advice of friends that he should not appear in public during the campaign.

Davis, in contrast, affected the repose of the reluctant republican hero who rises above the muck of politics, who humbly and without ambition awaits his nation's bidding. "I would prefer not to have either place," as a president or a general, he wrote privately to a friend, "but in this hour of my country's severest trial will accept any place to which my fellow citizens may assign me."[41] Perhaps he was sincere in his expressed desire to remain an obscure farmer on his "little cotton field"; but he simultaneously revealed that he was keeping a careful (if discreet) eye on public events. "I have heard nothing from the Montgomery convention, and am waiting for news both from that and the one which was to assemble at Washington," he wrote.

These were odd interests from one who really wished to retire from public life, and Davis admitted that he was "daily expecting a summons to renew my . . . service to the public."[42] The issue here was not his sincerity, however, but the importantance he attached to imagining himself as the prototypical classical republican citizen and civic leader. He had to identify himself with the Roman heroes of old, like Cato, who proved his civic virtue by refusing to lower himself to the level of parties and politics and who unselfishly grasped the reins of power that were thrust into his hands. Such was the content of classical republicanism, a strain in American political thought since the days of the Revolution; and republicanism suffused much of white Southern political culture.[43]

A key component of that ideology was the virtue of unanimity, the image of a *polis* speaking with one voice as it summons forth a noble but reluctant hero to lead in a time of great trial. Varina wrote after the war that when the telegram arrived informing him of his appointment to the presidency, Davis "looked so grieved that I feared some evil had befallen our family. After a few minutes' painful silence he told me, as a man might speak of a sentence of death. As he neither desired or expected the position, he was more deeply depressed than before." According to Varina, her husband then "assembled his negroes and made them an affectionate farewell speech, to which they responded with expressions of devotion." This little story was entirely consonant with the way Davis wished to understand himself and his new national role. He later took pains in his memoirs to show that he had not engaged in "electioneering" for the presidency, that he did not really want the job, and that the decision of the Montgomery convention to make him their president had been entirely without opposition or dissent.[44]

Not that the political process by which Davis was chosen to be president was actually without rancor—far from it. Fire-eating Southern radicals wanted one of their own in the Confederate executive mansion and were generally disappointed with the choice of Davis, a man with a long-standing reputation as a moderate on Southern separatism. Georgia wanted one of its favorite sons—Howell Cobb, Robert Toombs, or Alexander Stephens—placed in the presidency, and the South Carolina delegation angled for the lead position to be awarded to Charleston firebrands Robert B. Rhett or Robert Barnwell. But Davis had a strong following, as well, particularly from those

Southerners who feared the extremism of the South Carolinians, the sus-pected lingering Unionism of Cobb and Stephens, and the open displays of drunkenness by the intemperant Toombs. Davis's support among moderates carried the day, though not without a good deal of grumbling from Rhett and other fire-eaters who felt they had been ignominiously shunted aside for a man who had often declared his reluctance to embrace secession.[45]

At the end of the day, however, Confederates put on the face of unity they felt they needed, and Davis quite happily accepted their narrative of events, claiming forever afterward that there had been no ugly behind-the-scenes maneuvering to award him the job. Lincoln, for his part, understood the rules of political propriety and the last vestiges of republicanism in American public life that required him to remain silent during the campaign. But he wanted the job. Everyone knew it, and he did not pretend otherwise. But Davis needed to convince himself that he was his nation's unanimous choice for a posi-tion he did not really desire.

The Confederacy's new president left his home at Davis Bend on Febru-ary 11, the same day Lincoln departed from Springfield. The Davis entou-rage, like its Northern counterpart, was large and filled with political and military allies of various stripes as well as family members (albeit Varina remained behind to tie up various loose ends at Brierfield). Unlike Lincoln, Davis was not accompanied by an apprehensive bodyguard, fearing for his safety, though he did receive honorary escorts of distinguished citizens who ostensibly were present to protect as well as to praise their new leader.[46]

The trip to the Confederacy's new capitol in Montgomery, Alabama, was shorter (two days) and consequently was marked by fewer speeches (about twenty-five) than Lincoln's journey.[47] Still, twenty-five speeches in two days was quite a feat. Like Lincoln, Davis wanted to see and be seen by as many of his new constituents as possible, to the point that he took a long, looping route to Montgomery by way of Georgia. He encountered throngs of well-wishers wherever he went. "I have been in a crowd of people and events from the time we reached Vicksburg," he wrote Varina on February 14. "The re-ception there and here was large and enthusiastic." The various townspeople along the way lit large bonfires, staged military drills and parades, and clam-ored for speeches at every stop of the Confederate president's train, how-ever brief. He did his best to comply with their wishes.[48]

Davis's tone in these whistle-stop speeches was different from Lincoln's. Lincoln tried to be conciliatory, not only toward other Northerners but to the recalcitrant South as well; and in so doing, his speeches possessed a reserved, even ambiguous quality as he tried to placate as many Americans as possible. Davis, on the other hand, felt no such compunction. He did not much care about influencing Northerners at this point, and he assumed that the denizens of his new Southern nation shared his sense of commitment and defiance. His speeches therefore carried a harsher, militant line of finality and irrevocability, even a degree of apocalyptic doom. "We have separated from them, and separated *forever,*" he declared. The Confederacy, he was certain, could lay the Northern economy waste by using its control of cotton to draw England in on its side; "Grass will grow in the northern cities where the pavements have been worn off by the tread of commerce." If necessary, he declared, they would take the war directly to the North, where "food for the sword and torch await the [Southern] armies."[49]

There was in all of this no sense of persuasion or debate; Davis seemed to believe he was preaching to the choir, speaking truth before fellow believers who shared his sentiments. Lincoln stood amid a bewildering swirl of faces; Davis, on the other hand, was beset by the familiar during his inaugural procession. Remnants of his old Mexican War regiment accompanied him on the journey, carrying with them their battle flag from Buena Vista and Monterrey. Brother Joe met the Davis entourage in Jackson and proudly attended Davis's speech in that city. Lincoln had his immediate family and friends with him as he crossed the new and unfamiliar territory to the White House, like an oasis of familiarity in a desert of anxiety and strangeness. Davis was met by his "family" of relatives and fellow war veterans en route, and he could be forgiven for thinking that his new Confederacy was, in some respects, an extension of that family.[50]

Still, Davis also encountered much that was unfamiliar. But even as he was discovering a new nation, he drew different conclusions from that of his Northern counterpart. Lincoln issued passionate, almost desperate calls for unity in a nation he knew full well was teetering on the brink of dissolution; Davis presumed that the unity was already present and that he need only ratify its existence by his official acknowledgment. "Our separation from the old Union is complete," he told a Montgomery crowd; "no compromise, no reconstruction will now be entertained." He assumed his audience, and the entire Confederacy, agreed with him on this point.[51]

Davis wanted to reimagine a new Southern national community whereby the past history of bickering and infighting among Southerners was forgotten in a newfound sense of national unity. He wanted a new nation of like-minded people with like-minded values; other American states that wished to join in the new Confederacy would have to do so "upon our own terms." This national unity would be rooted in many commitments: a shared sense of danger from the "hell born fanaticism" evident in the North, a common preparation for war, a slave-based cotton economy that "furnished indissoluble cords for binding together, in a grand homogenous Union, the States now making common cause with us." Primarily, his new Confederate imagined community had finally shed, once and for all, the pangs of guilt over slavery and white supremacy that had racked portions of the antebellum American populace and made it something less than a perfect community of sentiment. The North need not be troubled now by "the qualms of uneasy consciences"; but more important, the new Confederacy could openly embrace its status as a slave empire. Davis sketched for his listeners a glorious white future, a new manifest destiny for a united and confident Confederacy that could without reservation pursue an empire in "the West India Isles, which, under the old Union, were forbidden fruit to us, and there were the Northern parts of Mexico."[52]

This brave new world of the Confederacy was in many ways new to him. Like Lincoln, Davis was crossing new state borders and encountering places and people he had never seen before. But he carried into this new Confederate world the same essential values—the same imagination—that had characterized his prewar sense of community and nationhood. He needed and expected unanimity. He needed and expected heartfelt cooperation among citizens whose motives and values closely approximated his own. Above all, he needed and expected the nation he led to be composed of men and women who had made an irrevocable, final commitment to the Confederate cause. Lincoln would quickly grow comfortable presiding over his vast nation of strangers, but Davis needed a Confederate community of sentiment.

He clearly expressed this need in his inaugural address, delivered before a grand gathering of people around the entrance to the Alabama capitol building on February 18, 1861. The Confederates emulated the presidential inaugural ceremonies of their American forefathers, with overt religious symbolism (Davis swore his oath on a Bible, which he then kissed) and a ceremonial carriage ride, with Davis flanked by Vice President Alexander Stephens and Robert B. Rhett, men who were once his rivals for the presidency. "Put thy good Spirit into our whole people," prayed the Reverend Basil Manly in his opening invocation, as thousands of Southerners looked on from the capitol grounds and from the porticos and windows of nearby buildings.[53]

When Davis looked out upon this sea of upturned faces, he saw in effect one face, that of a steadfastly loyal Confederate whose commitment was no more wavering than his own. He responded accordingly. "It is joyous in the midst of perilous times, to look around upon a people united in heart, where one purpose of high resolve animates and actuates the whole," he said; "where the sacrifices to be made are not weighed in the balance against honor and right and liberty and equality." He assumed that his fellow Confederates had made precisely the same commitment to victory as their president. Commitment to one another, commitment to a common Southern national identity, and commitment to ultimate victory knit together the hearts of Davis and the citizens of his new community of sentiment, providing that bedrock of certainty he so badly needed. "Obstacles may retard, [but] they cannot long prevent the progress of a movement sanctified by its justice, and sustained by a virtuous people," he said. It was the confident declaration of a man who was sure he addressed a people of like hearts and minds.[54]

In his own inaugural address three weeks later, Lincoln also felt compelled to appeal to a sense of national unity but in a different vein. By this point he had seen and heard too much about secession, treason, seizures of federal property in the South, and assassination plots against him in the North to presume that he led a people "united in heart." Most of his address was a carefully prepared appeal to Southern reason and self-interest, suggesting to secession-minded slaveholders that their "property" was safer in the Union than without, even under a Republican president. This portion of his address was prepared with the help of Secretary of State William Seward. But at the very end, Lincoln added words peculiarly his own, and they spoke to the new president's newfound skill at evoking sentimental nationalism and to his desire—rather than Davis's self-assured certitude—that his nation could be held together by emotion as well as by reason: "Though passion may have strained, it must not break our bonds of affection. The mystic chords of memory, stretching from every battle-field, and patriot grave, to every living heart and hearthstone, all over this broad land, will yet swell the chorus of the Union, when again touched, as surely they will be, by the better angels of our nature."[55]

Lincoln looked to a future that would "yet swell the chorus of the Union" rather than to a present that had already done so; and his statement that "the better angels of our nature" would surely be touched by the "chorus of Union" sounded almost plaintive, particularly as it was delivered within close proximity to Americans carrying rifles and aiming cannon at Southerners and secessionist sympathizers who most manifestly had not experienced anything of the sort. Lincoln was making room for sentiment and emotion in a national imagination that had previously placed so strong an emphasis on reason, distance, and the dry rule of law. But even as he did so, he could not quite bring himself to Jefferson Davis's high degree of certainty that sentimental bonding was indeed present in his national audience and that it would be sufficient to carry the nation through the trials of the day. In 1861 Davis was a president who knew; Lincoln was a president who hoped.

FAITHS

In October 1862 Abraham Lincoln received a letter from God, or, to be more precise, "your Heavenly Father and God of all Nations," who informed the president that God himself was "the cause for the disruption between the North and the South for the sole purpose of breaking up the Kingdom divided against itself." God used long sentences; he did not use much punctuation, or perfect grammar: "I can readily explain to you that the best and only way for you to do under the existing state of things is to call together your mighty men the head officers and consider this whole thing whether there is not much time on both sides of the question whether you have not about as much evil in your system of things at the North as my people here at the South I wish you to weigh these things and see if there is not an equal balance the Devil has taught man that their neighbors was [sic] doing forever wrong and he himself was doing right." God directed Lincoln to gather "6 of your best men in the Army" and meet with Lydia Smith, a spiritual medium residing at a boarding house on Pennsylvania Avenue in Washington, D.C., who would then reveal a divine plan "to speedily terminate this Devilish war." Lincoln does not seem to have availed himself of the opportunity.[1]

With the war a year old, and with the madly percolating issues of military strategy and emancipation occupying the national conscience, Lincoln received a great deal of such unsolicited advice, both from those who presumed to speak in the name of God and from others who simply thought they were smarter or better informed than the president. In a typical four-day period, from September 3 to September 7, 1862, he received nine letters from various people with advice on how he should do his job. They ranged from high officials, including Minnesota governor Alexander Ramsey (who requested five hundred horses and had some points to offer on quelling the Sioux uprising in his territory), to a self-appointed expert on "the social characteristics of the South," to an unknown gentleman in Cincinnati, Ohio, who wrote a hasty note on hotel stationary informing Lincoln that he should replace Union general Don Carlos Buell with a "loyal man." Several bore overtly religious messages, including two resolutions condemning slavery from church congregations in Wisconsin and Ohio. "You have doubtless advisors and Saviours of the country enough," wrote William Stearns, president of Amherst College, who nevertheless offered Lincoln a detailed list of things to do to win the war, declaring, "We need a *national* acknowledgement of God."[2]

Lincoln bore the advice of these amateur counselors with relative good humor. They seemed so very sure of themselves. "*All* of the evils now threatening seriously the utter ruin of the country can be traced to the error consummated in the organization of your cabinet," wrote one man. Another writer who sent Lincoln a plan for reorganizing his cabinet confidently informed the president that "this [new] Cabinet would meet the expectations of the country and would end the War before spring."[3]

He could tolerate these people who thought they knew with absolute conviction which generals to fire, which regiments to deploy, and which plans of political action to pursue. Lincoln's forbearance was strained, however, when this presumption extended to a supposed knowledge of what was in the hearts of one's fellow Americans. His temper flared when he received a letter from Carl Schurz, an ebullient German-American general and a Republican loyalist, who accused Lincoln of appointing men to high public positions who really did not have their hearts in the struggle. Like Lydia Smith, Schurz seemed to fancy himself a seer, in his case, one who could divine men's loyalties and sympathies. Lincoln had absolutely no patience with this sort of attitude. "Be assured, my dear sir, there are men who have 'heart in it' that think you are performing your part as poorly as you think I am performing mine," he fumed. "I must say I need success more than I need sympathy, and that I have not seen the so much greater evidence of getting success from my sympathizers, than from those who are denounced as the contrary."[4]

Lincoln was similarly cool toward people who seemed overly confident in their claims to know the will of God. Benign resolutions from clergymen were one thing; self-appointed experts on God's great plan were something else. When a delegation from an organization calling itself the Progressive Friends called upon the president in June 1862 to inform him of a recent meeting during which they adopted a resolution of immediate emancipation, Lincoln (after uttering a brief word of thanks that they were not yet another collection of office seekers) told them that he agreed "that Slavery was wrong, but in regard to the ways and means of its removal, his views probably differed from theirs." One Friend, a William Bernard, assured Lincoln that, were he to free the slaves, "nations yet unborn would call him blessed, and, better still, he would secure the blessing of God." To this the president answered diplomatically, but a bit testily, "Perhaps, however, God's way of accomplishing the end which [you] have in view may be different [from your own]."[5]

Lincoln was not necessarily troubled by appeals for emancipation when the Progressive Friends delegation called upon him. He was bothered by the arrogant suggestion that there was an objective, divine will that had been discernible to those who seemed to think they possessed God's ear. "I hope it will not be irreverent to say that if it is probable that God would reveal his will to others ... it might be supposed he would reveal it directly to me," Lincoln told a group of Chicago Christians, who had presented him with yet another memorial about emancipation, "for, unless I am more deceived in myself than I often am, it is my earnest desire to know the will of Providence in this matter." Then, with some heat, he exclaimed, "*And if I can learn what it is I will do it!*" Lincoln was under no delusions on this score; he did not possess God's ear. "These are not, however, the days of miracles," he told the Chicagoans, "and I suppose it will be granted that I am not to expect a direct revelation."[6]

Despite his protestations of neutrality, God, or rather his erstwhile medium Lydia Smith, did not write to Jefferson Davis. That fall the Confederate president, like Lincoln, suffered his share of tribulations. The Union Army of the Potomac had advanced to the very outskirts of Richmond and was barely thwarted by the brilliant maneuvering of the Confederacy's newest military hero, Robert E. Lee. Lee's victories stabilized the situation in the east, but in the western half of the new nation the Confederacy's military losses had been staggering, culminating in the defeat and battlefield death of Davis's close friend, General Albert Sydney Johnston.

Critics of the Davis administration were growing louder throughout 1862; the honeymoon period of unity and harmonious cooperation had ended in the face of the war's growing pressures. Davis was finding that even in his newfound Confederate community of sentiment, there were those who disagreed with his decisions and who sometimes misconstrued his motives for political gain. "I have borne unjust criticism in silence and allowed vain men to shift the responsibilities of their grievous failures upon me," he wrote to one such critic in July. Lincoln was willing to respond, at times quite publicly, to critics like Carl Schurz. Davis preferred the role of silent martyr. He cited military security reasons for not responding to critics, such as those who called for offensive military measures—"If I could to-night issue orders to an army adequate to the work of invasion, how could I conscientiously gain the public applause by revealing [it] to the enemy?" he wrote—but one suspects that Davis remained silent at least as much because he wanted to understand himself as the honorably silent warrior, wounded by the slings and arrows of fellow countrymen who ought to understand that his heart was in the right place. "I love approbation and will toil on," he wrote, "though it be through evil report."[7]

Like Lincoln, Davis was beset by advisers as well as critics. During that same first week in September, when Lincoln was entertaining the suggestions of Minnesota's governor, the president of Amherst College, and others, Davis received a letter from a Southerner with the unlikely name of Gazaway Bugg Lamar, who advised Davis that the time had come to offer peace terms to the North and suggested that Davis deal with counterfeiters operating in his neighborhood. He was also contacted by the Southern journalist and diplomat Duff Green, who had some suggestions to offer concerning railroad construction, and by a group of citizens in Canton, Mississippi, who wanted Davis to declare martial law in their area for "the preservation of social order."[8]

Like Lincoln, Davis responded to these ministrations with patience, calmly endorsing the letters through their proper channels, and in the case of the Canton petition, writing in reply that "the law only authorizes the suspension of habeas corpus in places threatened by invasion." Publicly he seemed as sure of himself as ever. "We are destined to achieve our independence as sure as the sun rises and sets," he told an audience of well-wishers during a visit to Alabama. He also confidently predicted victory to Congress, giving "assurance to the friends of constitutional liberty of our final triumph." By late 1862, Davis had come to understand and respect the magnitude of the North's mobilization for war. He admitted that he might have underestimated the Yankees a bit. "The enemy have displayed more power and energy and resources than I had attributed to them," he said; nevertheless, "I am also one of those who felt that our final success was certain."[9]

He was just as confident of divine support, "trusting to the protection of a just God" for the Confederate cause. He often referred to the Confederate cause in overtly religious terms, speaking of the battlefield dead as having laid their lives on the "altar" of their country, for example, or invoking the "smile of Heaven upon the hearth-stones made desolate in this cruel and unjustifiable war." "On the assistance of God I confidently rely," he told a crowd of fellow Mississipians in December 1862.[10]

Both Civil War presidents were products of a nineteenth-century American political culture that expected, indeed required, professions of faith from its political leaders. Subsequently, Lincoln and Davis both invoked God's aid and intervention for their causes. But they did so in different ways. These distinctions were rooted partly in their personal religious differences, but they were also products of the particular ways each man approached national identity and the role of faith in promoting national cohesion.

Faith was always a difficult matter for Lincoln personally. He was born and raised in areas of Kentucky, Indiana, and Illinois that boasted strong traditions of Calvinist Protestantism. By all accounts the Lincoln household conformed to this standard; Lincoln's father was a devout Baptist, as was his mother and stepmother. But as an adult Lincoln avoided church, admitting that he was "not much of a judge of religion" and was also "a little shy of preachers." This reticence, along with his lack of formal church membership, caused some friends and neighbors to wonder whether he was a believer at all. His old law partner Billy Herndon went so far as to claim that Lincoln was an atheist who actually once wrote a book debunking Christianity (which, according to Herndon, he later discarded). Herndon seems to have overstated the extent of Lincoln's skepticism, and his claims were roundly denounced by many others. "However Lincoln's religious views may be disputed," wrote his friend Alexander McClure, "he had a profound belief in God and in God's immutable justice." But this belief was vague and shot through with ambivalence about what God meant to him personally and the role religious institutions should play in American society. Lincoln himself understood this, saying once, "I have often wished that I was a more devout man than I am."[11]

He knew that rumors of his religious skepticism could be a political liability. In 1846 he felt compelled to release a handbill publicly explaining his religious views. "That I am not a member of any Christian Church, is true; but I have never denied the truth of the Scriptures; and I have never spoken with intentional disrespect of religion in general, or of any denomination of Christians in particular," he declared. He did admit that "in early life I was inclined to believe in what I understand is called the 'Doctrine of Necessity'—that is, that the human mind is impelled to action, or held in rest by some power, over which the mind has no control." He added that he had not made such thoughts part of his public discourse, and "the habit of arguing this, however, I have, entirely left off for more than five years." Lincoln followed this rather awkward explanation with an equally awkward statement: "I do not think I could myself, be brought to support a man for office, whom I knew to be an open enemy of, and scoffer at, religion. Leaving the higher matter of eternal consequences, between him and his Maker, I still do not think any man has the right thus to insult the feelings, injure the morals, of the community in which he may live." It is a curious, quirky document with the convoluted, almost half-embarrassed tone of a man who would rather be talking about something else.[12]

Historians have closely scrutinized this handbill, seeking clues about Lincoln's private faith, for it is one of the very few times he chose to reveal anything at all about his religious beliefs.[13] Focusing merely on his personal convictions overlooks the larger point, however, that this proclamation was at least as much an expression of what he thought of public statements, public behavior, and the reaction of the community at large to matters of faith. The handbill also fit well within Lincoln's community ethos; in it he reveals nothing much about himself and still less does he presume to know much of anything about his audience beyond its basic adherence to Christianity.

The handbill seems to have worked, for thereafter questions about Lincoln's relationship with God faded to the background. In the meantime, he found other ways publicly to express his faith, or at least his acquiescence in a society imbued with faith, by using biblical phrases and imagery in his speeches.[14] He was quite familiar with the Bible, and though Shakespeare outranked Jehovah on his list of favorite authors, he learned the political value of trotting out an occasional biblical quote. His tendency to do so increased as the nation drew closer to civil war. Biblical phrases—the "house divided," for example—punctuated his statements concerning the moral content of national debates over slavery.[15]

God enjoyed quite a national revival in the wake of Fort Sumter, on both sides of the Mason-Dixon line. In the South, Christians of all denominations threw their support behind the new nation and used fervent appeals to do God's will as motivating factors for enlisting civilian support and filling the Confederate ranks. In the North, clergy helped rally Americans to the cause of restoring the Union, all the while painting the upcoming conflict in apocalyptic colors, as a grand showdown between the secessionist forces of evil and the Unionist Christian soldiers who were so plainly on God's side.[16]

Lincoln was not immune to this nationwide religious revival. When he became president, he began for the first time in his adult life regularly to attend church services at the New York Avenue Presbyterian Church in Washington, D.C., though he preferred to sequester himself in the pastor's study during the service, listening through a partially open door.[17] As he went to church, so did church come to him, as clergy of all denominations flocked to the White House. "He was visited almost daily by reverend gentlemen," recalled Ward Lamon; "he was a patient listener to the words of congratulation, counsel, admonition, exhortation, and sometimes reproof, which fell from the lips of his pious callers." Many of the ministers were affiliated directly or indirectly with an abolitionist cause that had always boasted a strong evangelical fervor, and Lincoln found himself constantly pressed from this quarter by ministers who believed the cause of ending slavery was the primary moral imperative presented by the war.[18]

The war galvanized a variety of religious groups, and not only those with an abolitionist bent. Lincoln often expressed his approbation for church organizations and assemblies that provided relief to soldiers and their families or otherwise supported the Union war effort. "It has been my happiness to receive testimonies of a similiar nature, from I believe, all denominations of Christians," he told a delegation of Presbyterians. "They are all loyal, but not perhaps in the same degree, or in the same numbers; but I think they all claim to be loyal." That was generally good enough for him. "Whatever shall be sincerely, and in God's name, devised for the good of the soldier and seaman, in their hard spheres of duty, can scarcely fail to be blest," he wrote the head of the U.S. Christian Commission.[19]

When Lincoln was confronted by this sudden outpouring of patriotism from the North's Christian communities, the temptation must surely have been strong for such a master politician to combine God and nation by reassuring his constituents that he knew God was on the side of the Union cause. He well understood the political uses of biblical imagery and employed it to good effect in his wartime speeches. He also understood that the Christian delegations that tramped almost incessantly in and out of his office represented powerful national constituencies.[20]

Lincoln responded by habitually and publicly acknowledging his reliance on God as a source of personal comfort. "By the help of an all-wise Providence, I shall endeavor to do my duty," he told a Methodist delegation in May 1862. He sometimes translated this into a vague sense that God was such a source for the entire nation. "I recommend that all patriots, at their homes, in their places of public worship, and wherever they may be, unite in common thanksgiving and prayer to Almighty God," he wrote in a press release, for Americans were reliant "upon, Him, without whom, all effort is vain."[21]

Lincoln also sounded themes of national sin and righteous suffering. "Nations like individuals are subjected to punishments and chastisements in this world," he believed, and the war was a form of divine retribution for national sins and shortcomings. He saw "the presence of the Almighty Father and the power of His hand equally in [our] triumphs and [our] sorrows," and he asked Americans to appeal to God to "subdue the anger, which has produced, and so long sustained, a needless and cruel rebellion."[22]

Emancipation and its relationship to God offered rare occasions for Lincoln to profess an understanding of God's plan for the American nation. Freeing the slaves had injected a degree of divine morality into a most immoral and dirty civil war; God cleansed the war, and the nation, through emancipation.[23] With emancipation and God linked closely in Lincoln's mind, he was apt to turn a deaf ear to callers who were at once Confederate sympathizers and outspoken Christians. When a woman from Tennessee lobbied Lincoln to free her husband, a rebel prisoner of war, because of his deep religious convictions, the president replied, "In my opinion the religion that makes men rebel and fight against their government is not the genuine article."[24] He was fairly sure slavery had no place in God's plan, and he was quite certain hypocrisy did not, particularly the hypocrisy practiced by white Christian slaveholders. "Those professed holy men of the South [who] . . . appealed to the christian world to aid them in doing to a whole race of men, as they would have no man do unto themselves, to my thinking, they contemned and insulted God and His church," he said. When a delegation of

Baptists called upon him to express their support for his policies, Lincoln thanked them for their aid to the cause of liberty and then added, "It is difficult to conceive how it could be otherwise with any one professing christianity, or even having ordinary perceptions of right and wrong. To read in the Bible, as the word of God himself, that 'In the sweat of *thy* face shalt thou eat bread,[']' and to preach therefrom that 'In the sweat of *other man's* faces shalt thou eat bread,' to my mind can scarcely be reconciled with honest sincerity."[25]

But immediately on the heels of these words, Lincoln followed the admonition that Northerners ought not inquire too closely into the purposes of the Almighty, even in the (for him) cut-and-dried truism that Christianity and slavery were fundamentally irreconcilable. "But let me forebear, remembering it is also written, 'Judge not, lest ye be judged.'"[26] This was typical of all his public pronouncements about God and the American nation God had made. He was reasonably certain that God provided a degree of personal and national comfort; he could see God's will in humbling a sinful nation through the scourge of civil war; and he believed that God's will and slavery were fundamentally incompatible. But these propositions constituted the sum of his certitude where God, the war, and the nation were concerned.

The list of subjects for which Lincoln was much less certain was far larger. For example, unlike the Garrisonian abolitionists, he would not quite consign to everlasting hellfire the souls of even the most hardened rebels. He prayed to God "in His infinite goodness to soften the hearts, enlighten the minds, and quicken the consciences of those in rebellion . . . that they may not be utterly destroyed."[27] He was no more certain of the fate of Unionist souls than those of secessionists. Whether the Union cause succeeded or failed was up to an unknowable God, and Lincoln carefully qualified his remarks concerning God's sanction of the Union cause or its adherents. When he issued one of his periodic proclamations for days of fasting and prayer, he prayed that the "existing rebellion may be speedily suppressed, and the supremacy of the Constitution and laws of the United States may be established throughout the States." But he prefaced this with the cautionary phrase, "if consistent with His will." He told a group of Lutherans, "If it please the Divine Being . . . this shall remain a united people."[28]

To the casual observer this response may have seemed like little more than an offshoot of Lincoln's personal humility. But his often professed need for personal and national humility before the sight of God was an expression of his own basic ambivalence, arrogance and the sin of pride being, after all, mistakes committed by the self-righteous and the self-assured. "We have

vainly imagined, in in the deceitfulness of our hearts, that [America's] blessings were produced by some superior wisdom and virtue of our own," he
declared; "intoxicated with unbroken success, we have become too self-
sufficient to feel the necessity of redeeming and preserving grace." Imbued
with a sense of religious fatalism from his Calvinist upbringing, Lincoln called
for the nation to "humble ourselves before the offended power" and place
faith "in the hope authorized by the Divine teachings, that the united cry of
the Nation will be heard on high."[29]

"Hope" is a fairly ambivalent feeling, a longing for events that may or may
not occur. Lincoln could never quite bring himself to tell the American people
that he was absolutely sure God was on the North's side. At best, he could
appeal to fellow Americans to "diligently apply the means, never doubting
that a just God, in his own good time, will give us the rightful result." This
was thin fare for those who wanted definitive assurances that a Union victory was clearly "the rightful result." Most of the time Lincoln would not give
his constituents even these rather faint assurances. "If God be with us, we
will succeed," he stated simply; "if not, we will fail."[30]

Perhaps the fundamental intellectual conundrum of the entire war for
Abraham Lincoln was his attempt to reconcile the devastating impact of the
war on the national community—North and South—with God's will. National
unity, Christian precepts of right and wrong, and the stark fact that American Christians on both sides of the Mason-Dixon line prayed to the same
God for diametrically opposite purposes played havoc with his imagination.
"In great contests each party claims to act in accordance with the will of God,"
he wrote in September 1862. "Both *may* be, and one *must* be wrong. God
can not be *for,* and *against* the same thing at the same time."[31]

Emancipation was a partial answer, a way of infusing the war with a high
enough moral plane to make national redemption for the sin of slavery seem
like an adequate explanation for God's divine plan for America. But even this
was not quite enough. As was evident with his remarks to the Progressive
Friends, Lincoln was not totally convinced that even the act of freeing millions of human beings necessarily placed the North on the right side of God
and the nation in general on the path to redemption. No American could
expect to know what God intended the war to do to the national fabric. "We
hoped for a happy termination of this terrible war long before this," he wrote
in fall 1864, "but God knows best, and has ruled otherwise. . . . We must work
earnestly in the best light He gives us, trusting that so working still conduces
to the great ends He ordains."[32]

So it was that in all the remarks Lincoln made concerning the Almighty during the Civil War, he almost never stated that he knew exactly what God's purpose might be regarding the American nation. Rather, he hedged his bets, reverting to the lawyerly language of his 1846 handbill. "I am conscious of no desire for my country's welfare, that is not in consonance with His will," he carefully observed in one such case. Or he gave the nation an inscrutable God, one whose purposes were so unfathomable and unknowable that even the burning issues of victory and defeat were largely beyond mankind's purview. Lincoln could give thanks for God's "mercy" and his "many and signal victories over the enemy, who is of our own household." He could follow such gratitude with a long list of blessings bestowed upon what seemed to many people to be obviously the winning side, which had enjoyed God's grace. Yet even then he could qualify his statements, saying only that the evidence offered "us reasonable hopes of an ultimate and happy deliverance from all our dangers and afflictions."[33]

This was curious leadership from a president charged with motivating a people to fight and die for the essentially abstract moral causes of the Union and freedom.[34] On a personal level, it reflected Lincoln's ongoing private ambivalence about the nature of God. As historian Allen Guelzo has put it, Lincoln was well aware of a "tremendous gap that yawned between him and this mysterious God." In his brilliant analysis of Lincoln's faith, Guelzo sees Lincoln's ambivalent God as a personal, intellectual issue, an uneasy combination of his psyche, his times, and his Calvinist background. In the end, Guelzo writes, Lincoln expounded a mysterious, complex God as "an intuitive, intellectual device for resolving his own hesitations and perplexities."[35] But what was ambivalent and rather confusing in Lincoln the leader and Lincoln the private man actually makes perfect sense for Lincoln the nationalist. His mysterious God meshed quite nicely with his national imagination of an American *polis* occupied by citizens whose motives were unapproachable and whose personal truths were as inscrutable as the purposes of the Almighty.

Unlike Lincoln, Davis does not seem to have wrestled with metaphysical demons or pondered very deeply the mysteries and contradictions of discerning God's will. Before the war he entertained an indifferent attitude toward religion. Like Lincoln, he did not regularly attend an organized church and was so lax in this regard that he was unsure whether or not he had actually been baptized during his childhood. Varina's descriptions of her husband's long conversations with Joseph in the office do not include matters of theology, and even though it is possible the brothers engaged in religious conversation, it seems fairly certain that such matters took a backseat to the high political and constitutional fare that dominated their intellectual lives.[36]

Politics and the Constitution preoccupied a great many white Southerners, but the region had always been host to passionate religious revivalism. The war put a more emotive, even desperate edge on Southern Christianity in general. Unlike the U.S. Constitution, the Confederacy's founding document contained explicit references to the Almighty, with the preamble invoking "the favor and guidance of Almighty God." The new nation witnessed recurrent waves of Christian evangelical fervor, particularly in the army camps, where chaplains prayed for Confederate victories or forgiveness for Confederate sins. Southerners consciously wove Protestant evangelism into their new national fabric.[37]

In this atmosphere some Southerners expressed discomfort with Davis's apparent lack of public devotion to God. Whether in response to this, or to privately felt needs during a time of enormous pressure, Davis allowed faith to play a more central role in his life. References to God began to appear more often in his speeches and letters. He regularly—and more openly than Lincoln—attended services at St. Paul's Episcopal Church in Richmond, where he was baptized and confirmed in May 1862. He issued faith-based calls for days of fasting and prayer, and he assured one Baptist minister that "my lips shall press the sacred volume" of the Bible during his inaugural ceremony. "All his messages and proclamations indicate that he is looking to a mightier power than England for assistance," wrote one observer.[38]

But Davis's professions of faith could be shunted aside by other, stronger facets of his personality. In response to a request from a Confederate citizen for an explicitly Christian day of fasting and prayer, Davis fell back on his well-worn strict constructionism in politely declining the request. "It might have been that our Constitution should not only have recognized a God, as it does; but the Saviour of Mankind also, that it should have had not merely a religious but a Christian basis," Davis wrote. "But such is not its character and my oath binds me to observe the Constitution as it is, not as I would have it, if in any respect I should wish it changed."[39]

Lincoln did not hesitate to put religious observances on an overtly Christian basis, and at any rate he most likely would not have indulged in this curious bit of legalistic pedantry.[40] If he had done so, he would surely have followed it with renewed assurances of his own essentially Christian character. With Northern clergy crowding his office on a daily basis, and the distant echoes of his rumored deism, he could not very well afford to take professions of faith for granted in a nation overwhelmingly Christian and desirous of public displays of faith. God was simply too deeply woven into the American national fabric for Lincoln either to extricate or ignore.

This belief was every bit as true for the Confederacy, of course; but Davis was more willing to take God for granted where his new nation was concerned. Though he made numerous references to God throughout the war, he employed fewer specifically biblical phrases or allusions than Lincoln. He did not create much in the way of a Confederate theology, a Southern equivalent to Lincoln's grand themes of national redemption, to explain the war or the Confederate nation's high moral purpose. For Davis, that purpose was essentially political, not theological, and in his wartime correspondence there was no equivalent to Lincoln's conflation of God, the nation, and an essentially religious-based moral imperative such as emancipation. Davis's Confederacy was conceived politically and constitutionally, to effect the political and constitutional ends that had always occupied the center of his national identity; unlike Lincoln, he simply assumed God had come along for the ride.

For Davis, God's benefaction toward a Confederate nation was a given. He did not speak of national sins that required divine forgiveness. "If we perform our duty and are true to ourselves, under the blessing of Providence, our victory [will] be complete," he told his fellow Confederates. The Confederacy enjoyed "the protection of the Almighty in this our day of trouble," he thought, and he told his constituents that they were engaged in a cause both "common and sacred." His reasoning was simple: the Confederate cause was just, God was just, and therefore God must be on their side. "Heaven so will prosper the Southern Confederacy," he stated, almost matter-of-factly. That Yankees as well as rebels prayed essentially to the same God for victory did not bother Davis nearly as much as it did Lincoln.[41]

Naturally when the war's fortunes turned in the Confederacy's favor, Davis was quick to point out God's hand in the work. "God I trust will shield you and soon give to our arms entire success," he wrote to his brother Joseph. He was well aware of the numerical odds favoring the Union, and when Confederate armies overcame these odds and produced victories, he was sure that "God has given them power over a much more numerous host." Battlefield victory was due to God's "blessing on our arms."[42] As those fortunes grew fainter, he still saw God's will, not in Confederate victory but in Confederate resistance to defeat. During the last winter of the war, with the news from nearly every battlefront increasingly bleak, he pointed out to the Confederate Congress, "When we revert to the condition of our country at the inception of the operations of the present year, to the magnitude of the preparations made by the enemy, the number of his forces, the accumulation of his war-like supplies, and the prodigality with which his vast resources have been lavished in the attempt to render success assured . . . we cannot fail, while rendering the full meed of deserved praise to our generals and soldiers, to perceive that a power higher than man has willed our deliverance."[43]

Lincoln was always circumspect in his references to God and the workings of divine will upon his fellow Americans. Davis, on the other hand, was confident that he followed God's plan for his fledgling new nation, and that if his fellow Confederates would simply put aside their petty differences and personal bickerings, they would realize that God's will, Davis's will, and the Confederacy's best interests were identical. When Edmund Kirby Smith, the Confederate commander of the Trans-Mississippi Department, balked at transferring men across the Mississippi River to meet the dire Confederate military emergencies in the East, Davis wrote that Smith should put the good of the entire country above his own or his department and ended his letter "with the hope that Divine Power may endow you with wisdom to see what is right."[44]

Davis knew, with a certainty that was utterly lacking in Lincoln, exactly what God had on his mind. "Mr. Davis had a childlike faith in the providential care of the Just Cause by Almighty God," Varina wrote, "and a doubt of its righteousness never entered his mind." The reverse was also true: Davis's God knew exactly what Southerners thought and felt. He "knew the hearts of man," Davis believed, and so would know that Confederates fought the war with pure hearts. "As for our motives, we meet the eye of Heaven," he declared.[45]

Even Davis's more innocuous references to God suggest this strong confidence. He signed one routine letter with "I trust that the Divine Omnipotence . . . will bless your efforts to serve our country" and closed another with "trusting that God will bless our good cause." Lincoln spoke often of "hope" in God's grace; Davis habitually spoke of "trust," in the sense of a calm assurance of God's blessing. "God will I trust give us wisdom to see and valor to execute the measures necessary to vindicate our just cause," he wrote Varina.[46]

Only on the rarest of occasions did Davis invoke Lincoln's inscrutable Almighty, and only in matters related to his personal life—the illness of one of his children in June 1862, for example—did he speak of a God of hope rather than certainty.[47] Like Lincoln, he asked God's benediction over the battlefield dead, and he asked for divine bestowal of "all the virtue, which is needed to save a suffering country and maintain a just cause." But Davis never seems to have once doubted God's willingness to recognize the necessity of his fledgling nation's existence or the justice of its cause. Even during the very lowest points of the war, he betrayed little despair that God had abandoned the South. In the wake of the Confederacy's devastating defeat at Gettysburg, he could still write, "I trust the prayers of the righteous will prevail . . . as to redound to the success of our people."[48]

Toward the very end of the war, Lincoln allowed himself a tiny bit of self-satisfaction. When three prominent Republican senators called on him in March 1865 to notify him formally that he had been elected to serve a second term, he replied with gratitude and "assured reliance on that Almighty Ruler who has so graceously [sic] sustained us thus far." By this point he was reasonably sure that his policies, particularly emancipation, were more or less in line with those of the Almighty. "The blessing of God and the efforts of good and faithful men will bring us an earlier and happier consummation than the most sanguine friends of the freedmen could reasonably expect," he wrote.[49]

A few days later, however, Lincoln reverted to form and delivered his second inaugural address, with its theme of national humility before God's unknowable plan. In language foreshadowed by four years of personal searching for some divinely sanctioned plan in the war, he essentially capitulated, admitting to his fellow Americans that he was not sure, even at the end, what God's purpose really was. "Each looked for an easier triumph, and a result less fundamental and astounding," he said. "Both read the same Bible, and pray to the same God; and each invokes His aid against the other." Lincoln injected his sense that slavery was at the heart of the matter, by saying (in words reminiscent of his earlier pronouncements on the subject), "It may seem strange that any men should dare to ask a just God's assistance in wringing their bread from the sweat of other men's faces; but let us judge not that we be not judged." He thought slavery must be an offense against God but in the end qualified even this, stating equivocally that "*if* we shall suppose American slavery is one of those offences . . . He now wills to remove . . . shall we discern therein any departure from those divine attributes which the believers in a Living God always ascribe to Him?"[50]

Davis could never have delivered this speech; indeed, in his last proclamation as Confederate president, with the Confederate nation in ashes, he declared his undimmed certainty that God was on their side: "Let us, then, not despond, my countrymen, but, relying on God, meet the foe with fresh defiance and with unconquered and unconquerable hearts."[51] In private matters of faith Davis not only lacked Lincoln's streak of Calvinist-inspired anguish, but he also could never allow himself to imagine a Confederate nation that was not unquestionably aligned with divine will. His imagination required a nation of like-minded men and women who in turn recognized and carried out the will of a like-minded God. Davis did not perceive the spaces between his fellow citizens' inner souls, their outward behavior, and their God.

Lincoln not only perceived these spaces, he dwelled upon them, perhaps was even obsessed with them—fitting behavior for a man whose nationalist imagination contained such deep-rooted uncertainty about the state of his fellow Americans' souls. It is a matter reminiscent of the passage in Romans 8:31, familiar alike to Northerner and Southerner in the trying times of war: "If God be for us, who can be against us?" Lincoln focused most of his energies on the "if." Davis did not.

WARS

President Lincoln made a relatively rare trip from Washington, D.C., on November 19, 1863, to bestow the presidential benediction on a new military cemetery in Gettysburg, Pennsylvania. Rituals for the honored dead, particularly for fallen soldiers, are key components of a nation's sense of itself, and any speeches or gestures offered in commemoration of wartime casualties tend to resonate through a nation's collective memory. Lincoln understood this well enough to prepare his address carefully and to measure his words with customary caution. "In my position it is somewhat important that I should not say any foolish things," he told a gathering of well-wishers at Gettysburg the evening before he gave his speech.[1]

For Lincoln's counterpart in the South, November 19 was a fairly typical day. Davis composed several anxious but relatively routine dispatches to various commanders concerning what had become a bleak Confederate military situation, particularly in the West. And while 180 miles away Lincoln spoke of a new birth of freedom, Davis dealt with the matter of who was responsible for removing African-American slaves from the path of the advancing Union army. He wrote a military official, "It was directed that owners should have their option as to whether they would retain control of the negroes so removed, or throw the responsibility of transportation and future care upon the Government."[2]

Davis's perspective on Gettysburg was certainly much different from Lincoln's. While Lincoln looked for fitting words to describe the Union victory, Davis scrambled to repair Lee's broken army and simultaneously either to minimize the battle's impact or ignore it entirely.[3] Gettysburg received only a passing mention in Davis's annual message to Congress that fall, as he put a positive spin on what was a stinging Confederate defeat. "In the hard-fought battle of Gettysburg [Lee] inflicted such severity of punishment as disabled [the Federals] from early renewal of the campaign" to take Richmond, he claimed. Perhaps sensing just how hollow this sounded, he then blamed the entire debacle on the weather. Lee's "supplies of munitions were interrupted by extraordinary floods, which so swelled the Potomac [River] as to render impassable the fords by which his advance had been made, and he was thus forced to a withdrawal."[4]

While Davis tried lamely to explain away the Confederacy's worst battlefield defeat, Lincoln gave a speech for the ages. The Gettysburg Address was many things. It was a moving piece of funeral oratory during a time when Americans made a fetish of finding appropriate words to speak over the dead. It was good politics, offering a unique opportunity for him to rise above the mundane wrack of parties and factions and speak to the higher issues of the Civil War. It was also a fine piece of propaganda, giving him an almost unassailable platform—the hallowed ground of the honored dead—upon which to stand and shape the conversation on the meaning of the war.[5]

Lincoln wanted to redeem the awful, bloody mess the war had become by making it a struggle for the noble, nationally enshrined ideals of liberty and equality contained in the Declaration of Independence. He "cleansed the morally infected air of Gettysburg," as Garry Wills has written.[6] In that brief moment, he imagined an American community, North and South, linked in multiple ways; united by a common political heritage—"our fathers brought forth on this continent a new nation, conceived in liberty and dedicated to the proposition that all men are created equal"; united in a common political and moral enterprise—"testing whether that nation or any nation so conceived and so dedicated can long endure"; and united in a common quest for the ultimate moral meaning of battlefield death itself. The Gettysburg Address was above all a transcendent quest for national meaning and a rhetorical unification of the nation in search of that meaning.[7]

Davis did not give such speeches, even in moments of Confederate triumph. This is not to say that he was oblivious of the need for shaping Confederate public opinion. Like Lincoln, Davis spoke in broad political and motivational terms of the war at numerous points during the contest, and like Lincoln, he often appealed to lofty political values. He told the Confederate Congress in fall 1861 that they were "fighting for the sacred right of self-government and the privileges of freemen." To an audience of fellow Mississippians the following year he claimed that Southerners "had chosen to exercise an indisputable right—the right to separate from those with whom we conceived association to be no longer possible." Later in the same speech he told his listeners, "The issue before us is one of no ordinary character. . . . The question for you to decide is, 'will you be slaves or will you be independent'? Will you transmit to your children the freedom and equality which your fathers transmitted to you?"[8]

This was an eloquent (if ironic) appeal to slaveholders who would not themselves be slaves. But it was much different from Lincoln's efforts at Gettysburg and elsewhere. At Gettysburg Lincoln spoke of a war that, if successful, would vindicate and even enlarge national moral principles. The war and the principles drew upon each other, fed off each other, in Lincoln's thought; at that moment, one was not more firm or more real than the other. There is no objective American truth in the Gettysburg Address. It contains, rather, a testing of propositions, "testing whether that nation, or any nation so conceived and so dedicated, can long endure." Lincoln believed in these high principles, but their viability, perhaps even their very reality, would be called into question should the Confederacy win the war.[9]

Davis, on the other hand, thought in terms of objective principles already established and true principles that did not require a war to validate. These principles—Calhounian localism, strict construction of the Constitution, and the right to separate from a political relationship with the North—were to Davis self-evidently correct. The only question was whether or not the war's outcome would permit white Southerners to exercise the inalienable rights of liberty and self-determination that he believed existed independently of victory and defeat. "The cause in which we are engaged is the cause of the advocacy of rights to which we were born," he declared; "the war which is waged to take from us the right of self-government can never attain that end."[10]

Davis subsequently spoke of the war's reasons, its causes, and its motives, as if they were debating points made in a polite conversation among friends in Brother Joe's office. Lincoln's war was more messy, its implications foggy and unclear. Davis was preaching to the choir; Lincoln was trying to persuade the jury. Davis spoke of yesterday—the American Revolution or the tumult of the 1850s—in an attempt to justify the Civil War of his present; Lincoln spoke of timeless American values that were larger than the actual war and reached at once to both the past and the future.

As a result, Davis's speeches about the nation and the war are largely forgotten while Lincoln's seem endlessly relevant. It is tempting to make of this merely another judgment concerning Davis's relative ineptitude as a presidential leader. Perhaps he just did not have the talent of an Abraham Lincoln to carry his listeners to the lofty heights of the Gettysburg Address. "Jefferson Davis did not—and probably could not—write anything like the Gettysburg Address, or anything else in the way of images and metaphors that Lincoln used to illustrate his points both great and small," James McPherson has observed.[11]

McPherson is right. Davis's efforts to communicate an inspiring vision of the war pale in comparison with Lincoln's, perhaps because Lincoln self-consciously reached forward to the hazy future—to us—in his eloquent groping for the war's ultimate national meaning. Davis was more likely to appeal to history, either the immediate past—the political crises of the 1850s—or to the principles of the American Revolution that he felt supported his cause. He said relatively little about the postwar future and less about global standards of human rights and freedom. Compared with Lincoln, Davis seems rather small, his Calhounianisms archaic and his thinking hopelessly outdated.

But the difference between the two men in this regard is perhaps not so great as one might suppose. The matter is reminiscent of the sometimes invidious comparisons made by contemporaries and historians between Edward Everett's keynote address at Gettysburg and Lincoln's shorter but more memorable speech. Garry Wills has rightly reminded us that Everett was a fine public speaker within the context of the nineteenth century, a respectable thinker and observer of his times who should not be dismissed out of hand for failing to measure up to Abraham Lincoln's lofty, indeed, revolutionary, standards.[12]

The same could be said of Davis. He performed capably, if not with Lincolnian brilliance, in his attempts to rouse the Confederate populace, and many of his motivational speeches were well received by Confederate audiences. During his inspection tour of the Army of Tennessee in fall 1863, for example, Davis was greeted by cheering throngs of soldiers and civilians and received praise from the Southern press for what a reporter called "one of those chaste, eloquent and appropriate fifteen minute speeches, for which he is so distinguished."[13]

Though Lincoln's efforts were sometimes acts of genius, Davis's speeches were at least appropriate and, apparently, at times inspiring. Moreover, the fact that Davis lacked Lincoln's profound grasp of language and his keen political and moral insight does not necessarily indicate that the Confederate president possessed a barren intellectual understanding of the war's meaning and its impact on the Confederate national community. What lay between Lincoln's and Davis's approaches to these matters was not so much a gulf of talent or perception but different assumptions concerning the role of war in creating and nurturing a sense of national community.

The antebellum roots of these assumptions are revealed in the different approaches Lincoln and Davis took toward the meaning of the American Revolution. For Davis, the Revolution was the national bedrock, a fundamental American communal experience that served as a permanent, objective force unifying North and South into one national community of sentiment. Lincoln, on the other hand, believed the glue of Revolutionary War–era nationalism was cracked and crumbling by the mid-nineteenth century, and he warned fellow Americans during his Lyceum address in 1837 that they should not place much confidence in the staying power of ancient wartime loyalties and friendships.

But then Lincoln never did care much for war and its trappings, and he was unwilling to face the possibility of a civil war in the months following his election in 1860. During his whistle-stop journey from Springfield to Washington, D.C., the president-elect hardly mentioned an impending war. "There is really no crisis except an *artificial one!*" he exclaimed. "Let the people on both sides keep their self-possession, and just as other clouds have cleared away in due time, so will this." A reasonable man who expected other Americans to behave reasonably, president-elect Lincoln thought reason would surely prevail and the possibility of civil war would recede "in due time." His speeches during the early months of the sectional crisis, and even his first message to Congress—made while the entire nation was arming itself for combat—are remarkably free of martial imagery and appeals to battlefield heroics. Lincoln sounded altogether like a man who fully expected to be a peacetime president, once Southerners had come to their senses.[14]

Unlike Lincoln (and even many Confederates), Jefferson Davis did expect war to come out of the secession crisis. If the border states entered the Confederacy, he wrote in early 1861, "there will probably be a peaceful separation." But Davis never had much faith in border-area Southerners and wrote, "If the cotton states are to maintain their position alone, war is probable." A few weeks later he wrote, "My mind has been for some time satisfied that a peaceful solution of our difficulties was not to be anticipated." In 1862 he told a crowd of Mississippians, "I was among those who, from the beginning, predicted war," though even he admitted that "the contest has assumed proportions more gigantic than I had anticipated."[15]

Lincoln was reluctant to imagine his new presidential duties and national standing in the context of war, but Davis embraced from the beginning the notion that his identity as a Confederate citizen, his presidency, and warfare were inseparable. He was in fact technically a soldier fighting for the Confederate cause before he was the new nation's president, having been made a major general in the Mississippi militia during the interlude between Lincoln's election and his own selection as the Confederacy's president. He believed that his tenure as chief executive would be temporary. "I thought myself better adapted to command in the field," he wrote; "I expected soon to be with the army of the Mississippi again."[16]

As late as 1863 he mused, "If I could take one wing and Lee the other, I think we could between us wrest a victory from those people."[17] The heavy burden of presidential duties made such thoughts increasingly fanciful, but he found ways to compensate. He vetoed a bill that would have created the office of Confederate commanding general, in large part because such an officer might impinge on Davis's involvement in military affairs. He tended to make big military decisions alone, reducing the various men who served as secretary of war to distinctly subordinate positions. He dabbled in the military minutiae of fortifications, ordnance, and gunpowder development, and he personally reconnoitered battlefields near Richmond whenever possible.[18]

In his youth Jefferson Davis the would-be lawyer was forced to become a soldier but clung to a legalistic mind-set. Now Jefferson Davis the would-be general was forced to become a president but clung to his martial identity by pursuing a hands-on approach to directing military affairs. The results were similiar in both cases: a bifurcated professional and public persona in which Davis sometimes annoyed colleagues by applying what seemed before the war to be an inappropriately rigid legalism to army affairs and politics, or during the war a tendency to meddle in military subordinates' purview and at times subvert the chain of command.

But there were boundaries to Davis's martial leanings. As a former soldier, Mexican War veteran, and secretary of war, he had an affinity for military topics and people that Lincoln never possessed, yet he did not necessarily glorify the violence of war itself. In 1848 he declared, "It is true that republics have often been cradled in war, but more often they have met with the grave than the cradle." He understood the pain warfare was inflicting on the South, referring to it as "a bleeding country" and telling Varina, "God help us, war is a dreadful calamity."[19]

Nevertheless, this firsthand sense of war's costs was leavened by factors of personal and regional pride, particularly as it related to his new nation's standing in the international community. Davis wanted foreign aid, like other Southerners, but he was pleased that his fledgling Confederate nation was able to create its own internal sense of patriotism and national purpose. He saw the war as central to this process. "This war is ours," he said in 1862; "we must fight it out ourselves, and I feel some pride in knowing that so far we have done it without the good will of anybody." He took pride in Southerners' reputation for militarism. "In Europe . . . they laugh at us because of our fondness for military titles and displays," he told a British visitor, "but the fact is, we are a military people." He was pleased to see the war creating a nation of veterans and experts in the arts of war. "When the war first began the teacher and the taught were in the condition of the blind leading the blind," he said in 1862, but "now this is all changed for the better. . . . In all respects, moral as well as physical, we are better prepared than we were a year ago."[20]

National glory and honor were recurrent themes in Davis's speeches; to him even the behavior of Confederate prisoners of war was evidence of "heroic constancy." "The suffering thus ruthlessly inflicted upon the people of the invaded Districts has served but to illustrate their patriotism," he believed. In the wake of Vicksburg's demise during summer 1863, he wrote one fellow Southerner that perhaps "our reverses may be the beginning of better efforts and brighter prospects." These opportunities to prove one's national pride redoubled on the battlefield. For Davis, combat was a chance for glory as much as it was a burden. "The day might not be far distant when [you] could have an opportunity to win renown on the battlefield, and to aid in driving the vandal foe from Confederate soil," he told a gathering of soldiers at Thunderbolt Battery in Savannah. To another crowd he asserted that a poor Confederate soldier who fought well, "although he could leave his children no other fortune, would leave them a rich inheritance of honor."[21]

Davis believed the war was a good and necessary ingredient for the Southern project of nationbuilding. "This is a new government, formed of independent States, each jealous of its own sovereignty," he told a Richmond crowd in 1863. "It is necessary that it should be tried in the severe crucible in which we are being tested." He described the war as a "common and sacred cause," a source of "proud memories," a great "struggle" or "contest," terms that implied positive attributes. To a Richmond audience he declared that Virginia was "the theater of a great central camp, from which will pour forth thousands of brave hearts to roll back the tide of [Northern] despotism." To Georgians he exclaimed that the battlefield was a place where Southerners forged "patriotism" and "martial spirit." Combat was a national honor, a "privilege," where Confederates might have an "opportunity to win renown."[22]

He was fond of the touching battlefield vignette, particularly those that created a direct mental connection in his listeners' minds between battlefield bravery and the Confederate national community. Flags were a particularly effective symbol of national ardor and patriotism, and he liked stories about soldiers risking their lives to save their regimental and national flags from dishonor. In Selma, Alabama, for example, he told his listeners of a battle flag that had been "pierced by more than fifty of the enemy's bullets; and that its gallant bearer . . . had just been promoted for his heroic conduct." A few days later in Mobile, he referred to the recent promotion of a color-bearer whose flag had been "pierced with eighty-three bullets and its staff shattered." He then employed a nice bit of subtle nationalist imagery, knitting together flags, battlefield bravery, devotion of the the old and the young, and his own romantic bent blended in a concoction of war and national imagination. Speaking of his recent review of Confederate troops, he told of "seeing among them young boys—some *very* young—and men whose heads were silvered with the frost of many winters. . . . They present a spectacle which the world has never before witnessed—the best population of the country poured into the army."[23]

Was this patriotic hyperbole from a man who needed soldiers to win battles? Certainly. But there is no indication that Davis did not believe his own rhetoric, and indeed this romanticization of war and connection between battlefields and national bonding far predated the Civil War in Davis's thinking. More important, his rhetoric provides an interesting contrast to Lincoln's. The Union's president needed resolute and impassioned patriotism from his soldiers as much as Davis, but his rhetoric concerning the war and its effect on the nation was much different.

Lincoln possessed none of his Confederate counterpart's private dreams of battlefield glory. His suggestions that he might himself try to command the Union—"May I borrow it for a while?" he once asked George McClellan of the Army of the Potomac—were Lincolnian specimens of wry humor. Lincoln was not altogether comfortable in military circumstances, especially at the beginning of the war. Davis the West Point graduate knew the intricacies of military protocol, such as allowing the lowest-ranking general officer to speak first at a formal council of war. Lincoln, on the other hand, sometimes offended soldiers with his lack of military decorum. He occasionally forgot to return the salutes of guards, some thought he dressed with inappropriate slovenliness during formal military events, and he could betray a lack of understanding for the problem of moving large armies of exhausted soldiers in the field.[24]

Where Davis habitually directed—some would say interfered with—his commanders in the field, Lincoln's tone was deferential. He developed into a sound military strategist, but he was careful to couch his views in the language of persuasion rather than as direct orders from the nation's commander in chief. As the war progressed, this sense of inferiority gradually faded away as he gained a more surefooted sense of military matters. But there was always for him a certain sense of distance from the professional soldiers with whom he interacted, a distance that at times shaded into a mild derision, aided by the foibles of men like George McClellan and Henry Halleck. "I who am not a specially brave man have had to sustain the sinking courage of these professional fighters in critical times," he privately observed.[25]

Davis was quite sure of himself where the letter of military rules and regulations were concerned, yet Lincoln often felt compelled, especially early in the war, to ask for advice on what would "violate the rules" and what would not on matters of military organization, procedure, and protocol. "Will the Secetrary of Navy please examine this, and inform me what, according to the rules of the Department I should do?" Lincoln wrote Gideon Welles about a request for reinstatement by a cashiered officer. Davis assumed he knew the answers to such questions, for he believed, unlike Lincoln, that all things military fell within his special area of expertise.[26]

This difference of course reflected their different professional backgrounds: Davis had once been a soldier, Lincoln had not. But there is something deeper here. Davis happily immersed himself in military paraphernalia, allowing the war to blend seamlessly into his ideas about personal and national pride and motivation. Lincoln kept the war at arm's length as much as possible on a personal level, and he was much less willing to fold the nation into the war and blur distinctions between the two.

There is little indication in Lincoln's speeches that he thought the Civil War, in and of itself, was creating a new and better American community. It was not creating a new and better America—as it was, in Davis's mind, creating a new and better Confederacy—and it was not uniting but fracturing a national polity that he never ceased to imagine in terms of both a Northern and Southern United States. For Davis, the war allowed Southerners to reimagine themselves in exciting new terms as a new union of Confederate citizens; for Lincoln, the war was creating distressing habits among the American people. "Actual war coming, blood grows hot, and blood is spilled," Lincoln wrote. "Thought is forced from old channels into confusion. Deception breeds and thrives. Confidence dies, and universal suspicion reigns. Each man feels an impulse to kill his neighbor, lest he be first killed by him. Revenge and retaliation follow. . . . Every foul bird comes abroad, and every dirty reptile rises up."[27]

This conflict was not Davis's war of opportunity for honor or glory. "War, at the best, is terrible," Lincoln declared. The numerous metaphors he employed to describe it contrast sharply with Davis's rhetoric of a grand and glorious national struggle. Lincoln's war was a "great difficulty," "our national troubles," an "affliction" of "burdens," "casualties and calamities," an "unhappy fraternal war," and a collection of "national difficulties." It was "unnecessary" and "injurious," begun by an act of "madness," and its incidents, such as calls for new volunteers, created not Davis's sense of community but the potential for "panics and stampedes." "I sincerely wish war was an easier and pleasanter business than it is," he wrote one correspondent, "but it does not admit of holy-days."[28]

In his numerous speeches and remarks on soldiers and battlefields, Lincoln did not echo Davis's direct, emotional connections between the war and the forging of a national community. He rarely referred to bullet-pierced flags and the like. His tone was rather more sad than triumphant when in the presence of combat veterans, and he was more apt to refer to soldiers' suffering and sacrifices than to their opportunities for glory. War was a matter of "toil and blood," he argued, and he prayed for God to relieve "those who, through the vicissitudes of marches, voyages, battles and sieges, have been brought to suffer in mind, body, or estate."[29]

He never told Union soldiers that the war had made them better people or more devoted patriots. His thinking was entirely the reverse of Davis's in this regard. Lincoln was more apt to notice battle wounds than battle flags, telling a gathering of soldier amputees in 1863 that "their crutches were orators; their very appearance spoke louder than tongues." Davis's recurrent word for his soldiers was "honor," but Lincoln often referred to soldiers' "suffering." Davis spoke to his soldiers of national glory; Lincoln was more likely to speak of national duty and sacrifice, of burdens born and responsibilities shared by Union soldiers, many of whom, Lincoln assumed, would rather be doing something else. "In my position I am environed with difficulties," he told a crowd of well-wishers in late 1862, "yet they are scarcely as great as the difficulties of those who, upon the battlefield, are endeavoring to purchase with their blood and their lives the future happiness and prosperity of this country." He even sympathized somewhat with those who wanted to avoid the draft, writing, "I do not say that all who would avoid serving in the war, are unpatriotic."[30]

Lincoln was also sensitive to those Americans who professed a moral aversion to warfare and the shedding of blood. Davis once dismissed a conscientious objector as a man who was afflicted with "a confusion of ideas" (though to his credit, he reacted less harshly than might have been expected, ordering that "if it be impossible to correct his error his Comdg. officer will no doubt find an appropriate duty for him"). When confronted with similiar ideas, particularly by representatives of the North's Quaker contingent, Lincoln sounded entirely sympathetic. "Your people—the Friends—are having a very great trial," he wrote one Quaker pacifist. "For those appealing to me on conscientious grounds, I have done, and shall do, the best I could and can, in my own conscience, under my oath to the law. That you believe this, I doubt not."[31]

Lincoln saw the war as an endless source of new problems that sorely tried the national character. Prior to 1860 he had imagined an American community of diverse citizens, held together by the complex latticework of a free enterprise economy and a political party system, all of which allowed Americans by and large to act both in their own self-interests and for the creation of a broadly moral national community. War and military matters played almost no role in this vision. But war was now an inescapable fact of American national life, the primary means by which Lincoln could exercise presidential power. He understood but was not pleased by this state of affairs. He believed the war was acting like a powerful stimulant, touching off

and highlighting the worst aspects of the American character. It had "radically changed for the moment, the occupations and habits of the American
people . . . [and] excited political ambitions and apprehensions," he declared.
He described wartime as "days of dereliction," which seemed to bring out
the worst in people who sought jobs and favors, avoided responsibilities,
peddled influence—in short, people who wanted to grow fat off the war's
tremendous social and economic upheavals.[32]

Lincoln fretted about the war's effects on the nation's finances, observ-
ing that it had "produced a national debt and taxation unprecedented." In
his 1864 annual message to Congress he spoke of the war's unfortunate distraction from beneficial projects like the transatlantic telegraph and stated,
"It is hoped that with the return of domestic peace the country will be able
to resume with energy and advantage its former high career of commerce
and civilization." Even at that late date, with victory near and the Northern
economy stronger than ever, Lincoln refused to concede that the war might
have provided a positive economic stimulus, stating only that the national
economy had proven "adequate" to the task of suppressing the rebellion.[33]

The North was flexing its muscles and creating an unprecedented rate
of industrial and technological growth. The war's various demands on the
nation's economic infrastructure were fueling the accumulation of vast
amounts of wealth and touching off the sort of entrepreneurial energy that
would most likely have made the antebellum Lincoln quite happy. His own
Treasury Department was realizing the long-standing Whig dream of a uniform national currency, as the war's monetary demands overrode ancient
Jacksonian shibboleths about a decentralized, "democratic" currency and
banking system. The war produced its share of economic hardships; yet on
the whole it was helping create the very sort of government-sanctioned release of entrepreneurial energy Lincoln had once dreamed about.[34]

Still, when Lincoln spoke of the economy in his annual speeches to Congress, he largely ignored this relationship between the war and economic
growth. Instead, he spoke in reserved tones about the North's wartime
economy, stating for example that "the national banking system is proving
to be acceptable to the capitalists and the people."[35] Or he worried about the
war's influence on the nation's money supply—"fluctuations in the value of
currency are always injurious"—the possible baleful effects of the blockade
on Americans' commercial relations with foreign powers, the embarrassing
accumulation of a large national debt, and the pressures placed by the war
on the government's pension office. He even expressed concern about the

war's effects on the wages of English textile workers.[36] The war "has destroyed property, and ruined homes," he told a crowd in 1864. "It has produced a national debt and taxation unprecedented."[37] These were legitimate concerns, but it is interesting to note that when presented ample opportunity to trumpet the North's vast economic ability to make war and the war's equally vast potential for remaking the American economy, he demurred, preferring instead to credit the nation's "abundant harvests" to God's grace.[38]

Lincoln gave the war little credit for national economic growth or development.[39] He equated it to a species of radical surgery in which a limb must be removed—slavery—to save the entire body. "While we must, by all available means, prevent the overthrow of the government," he wrote Secretary of War Edwin Stanton in 1864, "we should avoid planting and cultivating too many thorns in the bosom of society." The war cost too much, it diverted valuable resources, and it warped Americans' moral sensibilities into placing the need to pursue violent victory above other concerns, such as liberty and civil rights. As early as 1861 he worried about ways in which a relentless pursuit of victory, encompassing measures like property confiscation and martial law, might damage the very nation he wanted to save. "The Union must be preserved," he said, but "we should not be in haste to determine that radical and extreme measures, which may reach the loyal and the disloyal, are indispensable."[40]

At times, he also worried about what the war was doing to his personal standing in the eyes of the nation and the world. In response to a letter from a group of New England Quakers, he observed, "Engaged, as I am, in a great war, I fear it will be difficult for the world to understand how fully I appreciate the principles of peace." To a Massachusetts delegation that had presented Lincoln with a ceremonial whip, along with some comment about whipping the Confederacy, he replied, "Let us not think only of whipping rebels, or of those who seem to think only of whipping negroes, but of those pleasant days which it is to be hoped are in store for us, when, seated behind a good pair of horses, we can crack our whips and drive through a happy, peaceful, and prosperous land."[41]

Lincoln was troubled about the connections between himself, the war, and the nation. And unlike Davis, he rarely tried to make predictions about the war's eventual outcome. He lacked the Confederate president's certainty, at times an almost blinding certainty, as to what the war was about and what its consequences to the nation would be.[42]

Like Lincoln, Davis was well aware of the direct connection between battlefront and homefront, pointing out to Braxton Bragg, for example, that exposure of military shortcomings "impairs the public confidence." Like Lincoln, he described the conflict as a "war of the people,"and he sometimes collapsed entirely the distinction between "fellow-soldiers" and "fellow-citizens." As the war continued, he also could not fail to notice increasing discontent in some quarters of the Confederacy. He often attributed such behavior to "shirkers" and to that favorite Southern target, "speculators."[43]

Lincoln saw the war as the wellspring of such behavior, but for Davis, this behavior ran contrary to the true national patriotism that the war created. Calls for peace and reunion with the North were, he believed, the product of "a knot of traitors who have been conspiring at home" while the majority of Confederates were doing their duty. Davis drew a parallel to his beloved Revolutionary-era nationalism and suggested that in fact the Confederacy had created a stronger sense of national community, which made shirking and speculation quite the exception to the rule. "The tories of the Revolution were immensely more numerous than the disaffected among us," he claimed; "there was much division of sentiment among the people of the colonies, while we are a united people."[44]

Where Lincoln saw a war that threatened the nation's economic and business interests, Davis saw a war that could re-create and invigorate the Confederate economy, "complet[ing] the circle and diversify[ing] the productions of our industrial system." Lincoln tried to separate the war and American economic development; Davis enthusiastically collapsed the two, developing a political economy that viewed the war as an economic boon. "I can say with confidence that our condition is in every respect greatly improved over what it was last year," he declared at the end of 1862; "our manufactories have made rapid progress." To Congress he declared, "The manufacturing industry of the Confederate states was never so prosperous as now. The necessities of the times have called into existence new branches of manufactures, and given a fresh impulse to the activity of those heretofore in operation."[45]

If Lincoln was prone to downplay past the point of reason the war's stimulating effects on the Northern economy, it is fair to say that Davis's political economy often seemed to outrun common sense. He foresaw an almost unlimited Southern ability to make war, arguing, "If we husband our means and make a judicious use of our resources it would be difficult to fix a limit to the period during which we could conduct a war against the adversary whom we now encounter." Others saw a slowly diminishing Confederate capacity to make war in the face of rampant shortages and the tightening Union blockade, but Davis cheerfully asserted, "As long as hostilities continue the Confederate States will exhibit a steadily increasing capacity to furnish their troops with food, clothing and arms." He also thought he could practice a form of King Cotton Diplomacy on the North, telling a Mississippi audience in December 1862, "By holding that section of the [Mississippi] river between Port Hudson and Vicksburg . . . the people of the West, cut off from New Orleans, will be driven to the East to seek a market for their products, and will be compelled to pay so much in the way of freights that those products will be rendered almost valueless. Thus, I should not be surprised if the first daybreak of peace were to dawn upon us from that quarter."[46] Lincoln expected the war to expose people's foibles and shortcomings; at best it sometimes produced what he called "relieving coincidents," in the form of the Sanitary Commission and other such benevolent organizations. But Davis believed that the war had widespread beneficial economic effects on the South.[47]

If Davis discerned a new economy as a beneficial side effect of the war's robust Confederate nationalism, he saw the Confederate army as its incubating chamber. He thought army service could do for his fellow Confederates what his own Mexican War service had done for him: create a sense of communal bonding among officers, men, and their local communities, which in turn could only strengthen the national fabric. The best and brightest Confederate nationalists were in the army, Davis believed. "In the army the fire of patriotism needs no rekindling," he wrote. He contrasted "grumblers who sat around their firesides, finding fault with soldiers," with the demonstrable national ardor of the soldiers themselves, who were "confident of victory." "I can truly say that an army more pious and more moral in defending our liberties, I do not believe to exist," he declared. He understood that sometimes Confederate soldiers behaved "very badly" and that there were morale problems in the army, among "those who, skulking from their duty, go home with fearful tales to justify their desertion." But these were the exceptions to the rule; the center of gravity in the army was a patriotism other Confederates would do well to emulate.[48]

"From the camp comes the voice of the soldier patriots invoking each who is at home, in the sphere he may best fill, to devote his whole energies to the support of a cause, in the success of which their confidence has never faltered," Davis wrote in May 1864. The Confederate president believed the patriotic effects of army service could and should positively influence the homefront and help create a more viable national community. He thought military service could paper over what many observers saw as one of the

Confederate nation's most disturbing fault lines: class divisions between rich and poor, slaveholding and nonslaveholding whites. "When the war is over and our independence won," he declared, "who will be our aristocracy? I hope the limping soldier." In direct contrast to the "rich man's war, poor man's fight" complaints of poor whites, he believed that military service actually smoothed away distinctions between rich and poor. "We have no cause to complain of the rich," he told his fellow citizens. "All of our people have done well; and, while the poor have nobly discharged their duties, most of the wealthiest and most distinguished families of the South have representatives in the ranks."[49]

Lincoln thought the war brought out profiteers; Davis thought it should create patriots. "It would have gladdened my heart to have met you in prosperity instead of adversity," Davis told an audience in Macon, Georgia, *"but friends are drawn together in adversity."* He drew rhetorical connections between the national bonding prevalent in the shedding of blood during previous American wars and the similar shedding of Southern blood in defending the Confederacy. "Well, my friends, I can only say we will make the battlefields in Virginia another Buena Vista and drench them with blood more precious than that shed there. We will make a history for ourselves."[50] This was what war did for a nation; it created a history, a shared sense of personal sacrifice binding formerly disparate peoples together. Davis's war was not an affliction but an opportunity. "Revolutions develop the high qualities of the good and the great," he wrote Braxton Bragg. Davis acknowledged that the war "cannot change the nature of the vicious and the selfish," but in saying so he betrayed no sense that it made a people any worse: it could only elevate, or at worst, expose the characters who could not be elevated.[51]

Lincoln did not suggest the war was creating a national character or resolve. Rather, the reverse was true; character was needed to resist the difficulties and temptations caused by the war. He could see clearly that the war afforded certain opportunities; it allowed him to vanquish slavery. But he did not see the war as necessary to do this, at least not early on. When he pressed border state leaders voluntarily to emancipate their slaves, he suggested that in doing so they could mitigate the war's baleful effects: "The change [voluntary emancipation] contemplates would come gently as the dews of heaven, not rending or wrecking anything," as war was bound to do.[52]

Lincoln came to realize that the war was a useful vehicle for emancipation, and at times he sounded pleased that it had made the fighting worthwhile, becoming, as he put it, "a King's cure for all the evils" of the war. But he drew from this no grand sense of triumph. His tone was one of quiet, at times perhaps even reluctant, expediency. Yes, the war was going to destroy slavery and create a "new birth of freedom." He could describe the war as "the nation's days of trials, and also of its hopes," and battlefield death as having "laid so costly a sacrifice upon the altar of freedom." But one senses in Lincoln a pang of regret that it took a war to do so. "The incidents of the war cannot be avoided," he told border state politicians in 1862. "If the war continue[s] long . . . the institution [slavery] in your states will be extinguished by mere friction and abrasion." This was not John Brown's purifying violence, Frederick Douglass's righteous wrath of God, or for that matter Jefferson Davis's supreme test of national will. Lincoln's war did no more good for the country than an earthquake that happened to destroy some antiquated buildings.[53]

In fact, Lincoln sometimes turned the thinking of abolitionists on its head. They saw the war as a way to effect emancipation; Lincoln eventually agreed, but he also saw emancipation as a means of shortening the war. When he urged a program of gradual, compensated emancipation on Congress in December 1862, he presented it as a cost-effective way to end the bloodshed: "If, with less money, or money more easily paid, we can preserve the Union by this means, than we can by the war alone, is it not also economic to do it? . . . The war requires large sums, and requires them at once. The aggregate sum necessary for compensated emancipation, of course, would be large. But it would require no ready cash; nor bonds even." This was a politically effective means by which to urge emancipation on a skeptical American public, but it was also entirely consistent with Lincoln's personal perspective that the war was a dangerous and potentially damaging force to the nation, best shortened by any means necessary. "It is impossible to foresee all the incidents, which may attend and all the ruin which may follow," he said, early in the conflict.[54] "See our present condition," he told a group of African-American delegates; "our white men [are] cutting one another's throats, none knowing how far it will extend."[55]

Much of Lincoln's point of view was rooted in his keen emotional appreciation of the war's heavy human cost—what one observer called his "gushing sympathy for those who offered their lives for this country"—and perhaps particularly in his close relationship with ordinary Union soldiers and civilians.[56] The old Lincoln mythos about the frontier rail-splitter who had an affinity with the common man does contain this grain of truth: he made strenuous and consistent efforts to see and be seen by large numbers of ordinary Americans, at home and on the field of battle. Scholars see this as

evidence that he was a great communicator, a good steward of national bonding who was cognizant of his people's needs.[57] But perhaps he also did these
things because he felt that the bonds being created by the Civil War were as
transient as those created among Americans during the Revolution. In the
1830s he had spoken of national bonding from Revolutionary days that had
faded away. In his frequent visits to his men, his almost self-destructive willingness to see each visitor to the White House, even in the large number—
over forty—of likenesses he allowed to be taken of himself during the war,
Lincoln implied that he believed the people's national will to make war was
a fungible, transient thing with a relatively short shelf life.

Lincoln gave the Gettysburg Address and other speeches in that vein as a
way of reestablishing national faith, of creating links between the war and
national purpose.[58] But the unspoken assumption he brought to these tasks
was that Northerners needed him to do so, and to do so repeatedly, given a
debilitating civil war that did as much damage as good to the nation's sense
of itself as a community and given his own sense of the ephemeral quality of
wartime national bonding. Lincoln delivered the Gettysburg Address, and
engaged in similar public musings about the war's higher purpose, at least
in part because he saw whatever might have been the war's redeeming qualities for the nation as transitory and temporary. "Lincoln was one of the greatest repeaters in history," historian Roy P. Basler has pointed out, "stating
again and again some simple truths that needed repeating because, some-
how, people were in his day, as in ours, great forgetters."[59]

Otherwise, why make a speech like the Gettysburg Address? The volu-
minous literature on the address and his other famous speeches never really
explores why Lincoln thought his people needed to hear, repeatedly, his words
about the national meaning of the war. We assume the reason is self-evident:
to motivate the troops, to inspire the civilian homefront and the soldiers in
the field. But in fact there were serious political risks for Lincoln every time
he opened his mouth to comment on what it all meant. He knew this only
too well. "Everything I say, you know, goes into print," he told a crowd of
well-wishers. "If I make a mistake it doesn't merely affect me nor you but
the country."[60] He believed and he hoped that Americans would be inspired
by his talk of freedom and equality, but he was not certain.

Abraham Lincoln was not certain of anything, and it was this lack of certainty, and his fundamental lack of faith in the value of war itself, that compelled him to run the political risk of repeatedly and publicly trying to speak
to the war's higher meaning, at Gettysburg and elsewhere. He rarely missed

an opportunity, formal or informal, to do so because he imagined the national community to be one where motives, ideas, and ideals needed constant reinforcement and renewal.

For Davis, this approach was unnecessary; and in his actions, or lack thereof, we see the road not taken—not because he was not as bright or as astute as Lincoln, but because Davis's particular way of imagining his new Confederate nation made Lincolnian moments like the Gettysburg Address unnecessary, even superfluous. Davis needed no appeals to a higher power to make sense of the convergence of war and Confederate nationalism. Indeed, he believed not only that the Confederacy had been born in the cradle of war but also that it would continue to need a large army, even in peacetime. He told Varina that the Confederacy would most likely require an "immense standing army that would necessarily deplete the resources of the country if the slaves were still to be kept in bondage." He also thought the new nation would be subject to periodic intervals of hostilities with the North, the prospect of which should keep the Southern people permanently united and vigilant. "Cast your eyes forward to that time at the end of the war, when peace shall nominally be proclaimed," he told an audience in December 1862; "for peace between us and our hated enemy will be liable to be broken at short intervals for many years to come—cast your eyes forward to that time, and you will see the necessity for continued preparation and unceasing watchfulness." He then proposed what amounted to a system of peacetime conscription, with Southerners taking rotations of two or three years in the ranks. This would be a fine thing, Davis believed: "Serving among his equals, his friends, and his neighbors, [the Southerner] will find in the army no distinction of class." Lincoln always saw the war as a temporary aberration in the nation's life and history; for Davis, it was almost a permanent way of life, a "war of the people," which could create a stronger, more durable national community.[61]

Davis was not confused by the war; we find in his speeches and writings none of Lincoln's anguished musings about its greater meaning or purpose. "It is written in the book of fate that we shall whip them yet," Davis told his people in fall 1863, and he expected all Southerners to "be ready to make every effort, [and] make any sacrifice." "If we [are] unanimous . . . then our subjugation [will] be impossible," he declared.[62] He was not lacking in talent or ability, and it was not that he was unable to communicate effectively. But given his particular assumptions about the relationship between war and national bonding, he did not think he needed to try to do what Lincoln felt constantly impelled to do: speak to the national meanings of war that might transcend the strife itself.

To suggest that Davis lacked Lincoln's uncertainty about what the war meant may seem strange, since the popular vision of the two men suggests a surehanded Lincoln and a vacillating Davis.[63] And yet where the war's effect on national identity was concerned, rather the opposite was true. Lincoln's uncertainty about the war was a source of strength in his national imagina- tion, and Davis's certainty was in many ways a source of weakness, for it sometimes blinded him to the realities of class and social divisions within his nascent Confederacy. One could argue that Davis's apparent inability to recognize and address these divisions was a key difference of "talent" between himself and Lincoln.[64]

The weakness itself possessed limitations, but Davis's assumption that the war provided the requisite national bonding was not inherently wrongheaded; it was a reasonable premise for him. Indeed, given the relative strength of the South's postwar Lost Cause mythology in comparison with the short-lived commitment of white Northerners to African-American equality, perhaps Davis was more correct than Lincoln on this score. Conceivably, the war was indeed a more powerful nationalizing force than the Declaration of Independence.

13

OTHERS

By New Year's Day 1865 Confederate morale was deteriorating only slightly faster than the military situation, particularly in light of Lincoln's reelection two months earlier. Southerners had staked much of their dwindling hope on Lincoln's electoral defeat; although his opponent George McClellan had promised to continue the war for reunion, his own party's platform was much more ambivalent, calling for a cease-fire and negotiations with the Confederate government. This measure offered Southerners at least the possibility of a peaceful separation. With Lincoln reelected to a second term, and with subsequent military reversals in Georgia, Tennessee, and Virginia, even this slim hope was quickly disappearing.[1]

As he began the fourth year of his six-year term, Jefferson Davis faced the distinct possibility that his fragile country might disintegrate even sooner than the armies in the field. There was serious talk in South Carolina, North Carolina, Georgia, and elsewhere concerning the possibility of seeking a rapprochement with the North, irrespective of Richmond's wishes. Some disaffected Southerners even proposed outright secession from a Confederacy that was steadily disintegrating under the heels of Sherman's and Grant's victo-

rious Union armies. "Sherman marches always," commented Southern dia-
rist Mary Chesnut, "all [railroads] smashed. And if I laugh at any mortal thing,
it is that I may not weep."[2]

With these potentially disastrous developments in the back of Davis's mind,
his administration made a last-ditch effort to open peace negotiations with
President Lincoln. The instigator of this attempt was Vice President Alexander
Stephens, one of the more eccentric members of the administration. Just a bit
over five feet tall, weighing less than one hundred pounds, and afflicted with
a variety of ailments, Stephens was described by a contemporary as someone
who looked like "a boyish invalid escaped from some hospital." A lifelong bachelor who lived a moody, lonely existence surrounded by his books and his slaves
on a remote Georgia farm, he was hardly the prototypical white Southern
gentleman. Yet this wizened little man was also one the South's most brilliant
politicians, a sixteen-year veteran of the U.S. Congress and a highly respected
intellect on both sides of the Mason-Dixon line. "Stephens of Georgia is a smart
man," observed one Southerner. "Who denies it?" It was largely this respect
that garnered for him the Confederacy's second-highest office in 1861.[3]

It is hard to imagine two men as different as Jefferson Davis and Alexander
Stephens, and Stephens had in fact made his mark during the war as Davis's
gadfly. The vice president's support for secession was lukewarm at best—he
was "halfhearted clear through," according to Mary Chesnut—and he made
it clear that he would not sacrifice states' rights principles on the altar of
independence. As the Davis administration increasingly centralized power
at the expense of the states, particularly in areas of internal security and the
draft, Stephens's disenchantment with his own administration grew stronger, until by the middle of the war, he was the unofficial leader of a vocal
anti-Davis faction. Southerners were treated to the bizarre spectacle of a vice
president who avoided visiting his own nation's capital and who delivered a
widely publicized speech before the Georgia state legislature in 1864 that
accused the Davis administration of tyranny. Stephens avoided attacking his
boss too directly, but at one point he answered the suggestion that Davis was
an honorable man who would use his powers cautiously by saying, "Tell me
not to put confidence in the President. . . . The most ill-timed, delusive and
dangerous words that can be uttered are, can you not trust the President?"
Privately, Stephens was even less charitable, telling his brother that Davis
was "weak and vascillating, timid, petulant, peevish, obstinate but not firm."[4]

Lincoln would never have tolerated this sort of behavior in either of the
men who served as his vice president. Unlike Davis, who disdained overtly

political motives and men, Lincoln understood quite well that Hannibal Hamlin and Andrew Johnson were, each in his own way, political animals holding an office proffered them for explicitly political reasons. This insight gave Lincoln the means by which to manipulate and, when necessary, control them. He used Hamlin, an influential figure in New England politics, as a watchdog and an adviser for his New England political appointees, and he found Tennessean Johnson to be a useful sounding board for the progress of administration policies in his home state, particularly those pertaining to reconstruction. The nearly legendary ennui of the vice presidency notwithstanding, Lincoln knew the value of giving his second-in-command enough to do to keep him out of mischief, and he had the political savvy to listen to well-connected men like Hamlin and Johnson.[5]

But Jefferson Davis had little political leverage with Stephens. There was no party mechanism available either to make the fiery little Georgian toe the administration's line or bestow important political favors. After several abortive attempts to make use of Stephens's skills in the early months of the war, during which the vice president refused to perform the tasks assigned to him, Davis essentially gave up on him and thereafter never really tried to keep him busy or make him feel important. The Confederate president did not possess the Lincolnian political acumen necessary to recognize the need to do so; indeed, Davis would have been distressed at the very idea that someone so prominent in his Confederate community of sentiment required such attention.[6]

Even so, he realized that Stephens had his uses. In June 1863 the vice president asked Davis's leave to approach the Lincoln administration personally and negotiate a renewal of the prisoner exchange program, which had broken down completely. "I am at your service heart and soul," Stephens assured Davis, and there was a hint that Stephens might press further for some sort of "general adjustment," a peace settlement based on "the recognition of the Sovereignty of the States."[7] From the Confederate point of view, sending Stephens to negotiate made sense, for he and Lincoln were friends dating back to the 1840s, when both served together as Whig congressmen.[8]

Just as Lee's second invasion of the North was building toward its crescendo at Gettysburg, Lincoln received word that his old friend wished to contact him. Lincoln was inclined to meet with him, but several of his cabinet members talked him out of it, contending that Stephens was a "dangerous man" full of mischief and that such a meeting could do irreparable political damage to an administration insistent that the "so-called Confederate states" did not really exist. Lincoln refused to see Stephens or to accept his peace proposals.[9]

Eighteen months later, with the Confederacy now in a far worse military and economic position, Stephens wanted to make one more attempt at a negotiated settlement. Davis again gave the little Georgian permission to try, albeit with strict instructions to negotiate only on the basis of an armistice between "the two countries." This was not what Lincoln would have preferred; in the correspondence surrounding the negotiations he pointedly referred to "securing the peace to the people of our one common country." Nevertheless, this time he agreed to meet with Stephens face to face aboard a steamer anchored at Hampton Roads, Virginia. On February 3 the Union president, the Confederate vice president, and their delegations conferred for several hours in what proved to be a futile effort. The two sides disagreed on many things—emancipation, the restoration of confiscated property, the need for a temporary cease-fire while details of a peace agreement were hammered out—but the fundamental sticking point was Lincoln's insistence that the negotiation be treated as an agreement between a legitimate government and rebel insurgents, not between "the two countries." Stephens left Hampton Roads empty-handed.[10]

Perhaps Davis genuinely sought a settlement of some sort with the Lincoln administration, or perhaps he knew failure was likely and even wished it to be so as a way to discourage the growing peace movement in the South. Whatever the case may be, he was a better politician than many observers thought, for he seized upon the failure at Hampton Roads to solidify Confederate resistance and to call for a fight to the bitter end. He saw to it that the details of the conference were published, including in particular Lincoln's insistence on Southern ratification of the Thirteenth Amendment. And he even tried, unsuccessfully, to persuade Stephens to alter the language of his report and accuse Lincoln of attempted "subjugation" of the South. For Davis, the conference merely confirmed what he had been saying all along, that Lincoln's only desire was that "the Confederate States should surrender at discretion, admit they had been wrong from the beginning of the contest, submit to the mercy of their enemies, and avow themselves to be in need of pardon for their crimes." Here was proof positive that the Yankees and their leader were of such an ilk as to constitute what Davis called a "foreign people," who were bent on the utter ruin and subjugation of the South.[11]

Lincoln's point of view was rather different. Like Davis, he viewed the

Hampton Roads conference through the lens of public perception, worrying that he might be criticized by some people in the North for even meeting with Stephens. But where Davis saw a conspiracy of "foreigners" trying to subjugate his people, Lincoln treated the Stephens delegation in much the same manner as he treated any group of visitors to the White House. He cracked a gentle joke about Stephens's appearance; when the sickly little Georgian removed the oversized coat he wore to protect him from the chill, Lincoln quipped, "It was the biggest shuck and the littlest ear" he had ever seen. Ulysses S. Grant, who was present at the meeting, observed that Lincoln's demeanor throughout was relaxed and friendly, exhibiting a "generous and kindly spirit." Lincoln even agreed to look into the possibility of procuring a parole for Stephens's nephew, John A. Stephens, who was a prisoner of war. Lincoln treated this matter as he did hundreds of similar requests from hundreds of Northerners. He seems genuinely to have seen little difference in his dealings with the Stephens delegation and his dealings with Americans on his own side: same persona, same demeanor, same routine—it was all in a day's work for him.[12]

Davis instinctively grasped the fact that national identity has at least as much to do with who stands outside the national circle as who stands within it, who is a friend and who is an enemy. Patriots define themselves in relation to that which is unpatriotic; the loyal know who they are by understanding who is disloyal. Clearly delineating the enemy becomes particularly critical in wartime, as nations must justify the use of violence and the suppression of internal dissent.[13]

Lincoln did not draw sharp distinctions between North and South, retaining a sense of the American nation as a unified whole. There were sound reasons for doing so, not the least of which was the fact that a war for the "Union" would mitigate strongly in favor of blurring sectional lines. But there was a price to be paid for his unbifurcated nationalist imagination. In some ways, he might have done better to emulate Jefferson Davis, who understood quite well the value of defining and using the "enemy" in creating the negative spaces of nationalism, in creating a viable national community.

The two men said remarkably little to or about one another during the war. Lincoln never uttered a public derogatory comment about the Confederate president. In fact, he mentioned Davis infrequently, and when he did he referred to him in blandly neutral terms, such as "the insurgent leader."[14] Davis was more abusive, but not by much. He publicly derided Lincoln as an "ignorant usurper" on one occasion and on another called him a "baboon." During the Fort Sumter crisis he expressed dismay at Lincoln's "shifting and wavering policies," and he sometimes obliquely suggested that Lincoln was a dictator-in-the-making by describing Northern government policies as despotic. But this was rather mild fare, particularly from a man who was notorious for taking offense at even unintentional slights and who often personalized his political differences with other people.[15]

There was little direct correspondence between the two men, and all of it was one-sided, with Davis the instigator. The Confederate president composed stiff letters to Lincoln on a variety of war-related subjects—the prisoner exchange issue, for example—and one suspects Davis derived a bit of private satisfaction in closing these letters with "Presdt. and Commander in Chief of the Army and Navy of the Confederate States of America." The language of this correspondence was purposely tailored after formal diplomatic communiques, a subtle way of reinforcing the South's separation from the North, and Davis described one letter as "intended exclusively as one of those communications between belligerents which public law recognises [sic] as necessary and proper between hostile forces."[16]

Lincoln never communicated directly with the Davis administration. He could not do so and still convincingly maintain the legal and constitutional position that justified the Union war effort: that the "Confederate States of America" was a sham invented by American states that had never actually left the Union. One of the primary reasons he refused to meet with Stephens in 1864 was his belief that doing so might afford "quasi acknowledgment of the independence of the Confederacy."[17] Lincoln said he had "always thought the act of secession is legally nothing," and he carefully adhered to this position, referring to the war as an "insurrection," the Richmond government as "this illegal organization, in the character of Confederate States," and its supporters as "the rebels," "the people in revolt," the "disaffected portions of our fellow citizens, " "our own disloyal citizens," "our erring brethren," "insurgents," "mutineers," and even "lost sheep."[18]

But Lincoln's attitude went much deeper than questions concerning the legality of secession. There was no discernible difference between his public and private opinions on this matter. His legal position on the South seems to have reflected his personal position accurately; there is almost no contradiction at all between the two.

Before the war Lincoln believed Southerners were no different from Northerners, and he avoided a widespread habit in the North of defining itself as a region against the negative backdrop of the South's shortcomings. "We do not assume that we are better than the people of the South," he said in 1860; "neither do we admit that they are better than we." This attitude did not change after Fort Sumter. He continued to view Southerners, particularly ordinary whites, as Americans whose motives, aspirations, and attitudes were fundamentally similar to people living in other sections of the country.[19]

He was unable to fathom the depths of some white Southerners' sense of separation from the North and the American polity. He believed that the average, rank-and-file Confederate soldier was forced to enlist and did not have his heart in the war effort. "We are contending with an enemy who, as I understand, drives every able bodied man he can reach, into his ranks, very much as a butcher drives bullocks into a slaughter pen," Lincoln said. He understood the behavior of the "butchers," men like Davis who had gambled all on independence and could therefore be expected to fight with real resolve. "He cannot voluntarily accept the Union," Lincoln said of Davis; "we cannot voluntarily yield it. . . . It is an issue which can only be tried by war, and decided by victory."[20]

But when he was confronted with truly motivated "bullocks," Confederates who evinced the sort of genuine hatred and violence that indicated elemental alienation from the American mainstream, Lincoln was nonplussed. He simply did not know what to make of white Southerners whose sense of the Yankee enemy was so fundamental, whose loyalty to a united America was so completely compromised, that they felt justified in playing by a different set of rules from those that governed civilized behavior.

The bloody battleground of Missouri offers a telling example of Lincoln's limitations in this regard. Missourians' loyalties were at once confused and rigid; even though precise geographic boundaries between the combatants were nonexistent, each side categorized its enemies in shockingly vicious, even bigoted terms. Pro-Confederate Missourians were "pukes" to Unionists in the state; for their part, Confederates consigned their Unionist neighbors to the outer reaches of racial amalgamation and "nigger-stealing." Perhaps in no other section of the country did supporters of the Union and the Confederacy draw such stark, strict cultural and social (if not geographical) boundaries between "us" and "other."[21]

Lincoln did not know what to do about the situation in Missouri, where alienation between Confederate "pukes" and Union "nigger-stealers" ran so deeply that it threatened to destroy the legal and political institutions that guaranteed order. His entire sense of communal and national identity was wrapped around these institutions, and he thought that surely even Missouri Confederates—who to him had never ceased being Americans—agreed. His attempts to deal with the various outbreaks of violence and mayhem in Missouri were subsequently entirely inadequate, even naive. He convinced himself that "the Union men of Missouri [constituted], when united, a vast majority of the whole people," despite evidence of significant Confederate sentiment in the state. Appealing to a sense of reason and communal loyalty he thought must still exist, he repeatedly urged Union military commanders on the scene to appeal to that innate sense of law and order that he hoped and believed animated all Americans. "Please gather information, and consider whether an appeal to the people [in Missouri] to go to their homes, and let one another alone, recognizing as a full right of protection for each," would restore the peace, Lincoln wrote one commander there. On other occasions he suggested conferences. "Let neighborhood meetings be every where called and held," he wrote; "let all such meet and waiving all else pledge each to cease harassing others." Lincoln looked at Missouri Confederates, and he did not see violent denizens who had been removed from the American national community; rather, he saw neighbors who could still listen to reason.[22]

As Lincoln proved unable to cope with white Confederate extremists, so too did he place a sometimes overweening confidence in Southern Unionists. They were "the most valuable stake we have in the South," he believed. He was convinced that the vast majority of ordinary whites in the Confederacy were loyal to the national government; in his estimation they had been cowed by slaveholders to support a new regime, which offered them little and was inimical to their interests. He thought that Union armies would uncover cells of resistance to the Confederate government as they advanced southward, and he counted on white Southern Unionists to form the backbone of new state governments in the occupied regions.[23]

As Union forces overran large areas of the upper South and Louisiana, and as the issue of how best to reconstruct these states came to the nation's attention, Lincoln made it clear he wanted army-sanctioned free elections in occupied areas. If the Union army would just get out of the way and avoid "gratuitous hostility," he reasoned, Southerners would surely express the law-abiding and sensible qualities he knew they possessed and gravitate toward reunion with little trouble. "In all available ways give the people a chance to express their wishes at these elections," he wrote Union officials in Arkansas in November 1862. He wanted the elections in reconstructed Southern states to offer "conclusive evidence that respectable citizens . . . are willing to be members of congress and to swear support to the constitution; and that other respectable citizens there are willing to vote for them and send them." Union army officers and other Northerners in the occupied South might doubt that such evidence would be forthcoming; Lincoln did not.[24]

Lincoln could grow quite exasperated with Southern Unionists, particularly when they seemed willing to allow their Northern brethren to shoulder all the responsibility for winning the war. He wrote in frustration to an ally in Louisiana that Southern Unionists think "they are to touch neither a sail or a pump, but to be merely passengers,—dead heads at that—to be carried snug and dry, throughout the storm, and safely landed right side up."[25] Yet his faith in Southern Unionists never really wavered.[26] He thought he understood Southerners and reasoned that they should be capable of understanding him. Reports of vilification and distrust on their part perplexed and distressed him. His days as an attorney, and his personal inclination, led him to believe in a Union of reason, an America of calm, rational individuals; that white Southerners saw in him a tyrant struck him as absurd, rather like a convicted felon who blamed the prosecuting attorney. "The people of Louisiana—all intelligent people everywhere—know full well, that I never had a wish to touch the foundations of their society, or any right of theirs," he wrote in summer 1862.[27]

A few months later Lincoln did touch the foundations by issuing the Emancipation Proclamation, and at times he threatened to follow up emancipation with still more radical and harsh policies toward Southerners. "Broken eggs cannot be mended," he informed Southerners in Louisiana (and by extension the Confederacy), and there was "nothing to do now but to take her place in the Union as it was, barring the already broken eggs." Confederates needed to adjust to the harsh new realities of postemancipation America: "If they will not do this, should they not receive harder blows rather than softer ones?" Yet except for emancipation, Lincoln never followed through on the threat of "harder blows." "I am a patient man," he explained, and while he admitted he would not "surrender the game leaving any available card unplayed," he told all who would listen that he had no intention of acting out of malice and that he harbored no ill will toward the white South.[28]

Was this merely an expression of Lincoln's innate kindliness? A variety of people testified to his magnanimity, which has since become a staple of the Lincoln legend. "The president is without exception the most tender-hearted man I ever knew," said Judge Advocate General Joseph Holt, who watched Lincoln commute the sentences of hundreds of convicted men.

Lincoln himself contributed to the legend, with the famous reference in his second inaugural address to "malice towards none" and with repeated assurances given to Southerners that "I have not now, and never have had, any other than as kindly feelings towards you as the people of my own section." The Lincoln mythos tells us of a man so merciful and magnanimous that he could turn a blind eye to the sins of his Northern enemies and his Southern enemies, and like all myths, this one contains an element of truth.[29]

But Lincoln's kindness had its limits. Like all Americans of the day, he saw firsthand the price of war. He lost close friends to rebel bullets, and he carried the onerous burden of the war's many dead. He visited battlefields, gravesites, and hospitals, where he witnessed personally the wages of war. For many Northerners, these scenes were quite sufficient to read white Southerners right out of the American polity. At the very least, they developed harder hearts. Lincoln was not immune to this process. He pardoned many men, but he also allowed some to be executed. He expressed impatience with politicians, journalists, and generals who seemed unwilling to pursue the enemy with the proper intensity. "What would you do in my position?" he asked one fellow Northerner. "Would you drop the war where it is? Or would you prosecute it in [the] future, with elder-stalk squirts, charged with rose water?" He could speak of kind feelings toward the South, but he could also telegraph Ulysses S. Grant in summer 1864 to "hold on with a bull dog gripe, and chew and choke, as much as possible." And he understood the politics of revenge. During a cabinet meeting in the closing days of the war, the question was posed to him concerning what should be done with Davis and other high-ranking Confederate officials. Lincoln replied, "Now, if Jeff Davis and those other fellows will only get away, it will be all right. But if we should catch them, and I should let them go, '[Northerners] would give me hell.'"[30]

Lincoln's reaction to the South involved issues more complex than kindness or harshness. It involved, rather, a national imagination that simply could not consign any Americans to the status of excluded enemy, even Confederates.

His treatment of Southern petitioners is revealing in this regard, for he showed a truly remarkable, even reckless leniency toward Southerners and those who wished to traffic with them, blurring the lines between North and South in ways that cannot be accounted for by mere kindness. Lincoln offered to pardon high-ranking Confederate military officers in exchange only for their oaths of loyalty. He signed orders releasing imprisoned rebel soldiers who claimed to have been forcefully conscripted into the Confederate army. He authorized travel and commerce between Northerners and Southerners, despite objections from Union military leaders like Ulysses S. Grant. He even went out of his way to praise a journalist who wrote a flattering obituary for Stonewall Jackson. Lincoln rather sheepishly (and quite correctly) admitted that he possessed a "tendency to clemency for rebels and rebel sympathizers."[31]

He hoped to be able to persuade rather than berate white Southerners, as if they were a skeptical jury or courtroom audience. "We should urge [emancipation] *persuasively*, and not *menacingly*, upon the South," he wrote Horace Greeley in March 1862.[32] He was solicitous of Southerners' legal and constitutional rights, even those who were active in the rebellion. His primary objections to the Second Confiscation Act of 1862, for example, which would have allowed the government to seize property belonging to Confederate citizens, lay in the law's possible violations of constitutionally protected guarantees. "That to which I chiefly object . . . is the sum of those provisions which results in the divesting of title forever," Lincoln informed Congress, which to him would have violated constitutional language forbidding a "corruption of blood, or forfeiture, except during the life of the person attained." Three days after his display of hard resolve at the Hampton Roads conference, he wrote an interesting, and politically dangerous, suggestion to Congress that it adopt a policy of compensating Southerners for the expenses of the war and their loss of property.[33]

Politically, legally, and personally, Abraham Lincoln was unable to discern a Southern enemy. He thought of Southerns, at worst, as "a disloyal portion of the American people." He simply could not imagine a separated, bifurcated United States. "Physically speaking, we cannot separate," he pointed out. "A husband and wife may be divorced, and go out of the presence, and beyond the reach of each other; but the different parts of the country cannot do this." When he saw in his mind's eye the American landscape, the very foundation of national identity, he could not see a landscape divided North and South. "There is no line, straight or crooked, suitable for a national boundary, upon which to divide," he said. Surveying what he called "the great interior region" of the United States—the area between the Alleghenies and the Rocky Mountains—he said, "Separate our common country into two nations, as designed by the present rebellion, and every man of this great interior region is thereby cut off from some one or more of [river] outlets." This would be bad for commerce and bad for business; it would be, for Lincoln, inconceivable. "In all its adaptations," he believed, America "demands union, and abhors separation."[34]

If Lincoln had difficulty articulating a sense of a Confederate enemy, then he was equally unable to distinguish much of a Northern "us." He could be quite critical of his own section's sense of solidarity. "I don't believe there is any North. . . . *You* are the only Northern realities," a distraught Lincoln told soldiers arriving to strengthen Washington, D.C.'s defenses in the early days of the war. On another occasion he ruefully observed, "Some of our northerners seem bewildered and dazzled by the excitement of the hour."[35]

But these were rare pronouncements; generally, Lincoln did not speak of the "North" at all. He was much more likely to refer to Americans as "we, the loyal people," or simply, "our people," with no clear sectional referent. He also took particular offense over military dispatches that referred to "driv[ing] the invaders from our soil." There was no Northern "soil" distinct from a Southern soil for him; and to suggest otherwise left him, as he put it, "a good deal dissatisfied."[36]

When Lincoln went to war for the Union, he did so in defense of more than abstract constitutional principles or a political system. He waged war in the name of a nationalism that was an expression of a deep-seated inclusiveness that could not read the white South out of the American polity, even temporarily. This position was not a completely conscious or overtly ideological decision on his part; it was also an expression of the values inherent in a national imagination that discouraged deep investigation of the internal motives of one's neighbors and that placed a heavy emphasis on reason over emotion and institutions over sentimentality. Lincoln could afford to be inclusive where Southerners were concerned because he chose not to inquire too closely into their hearts, preferring to believe—and in some cases to be deluded—that ultimately Southern hearts differed very little from his own or from those of his Northern constituents.

Jefferson Davis, in contrast, was well able to redefine his former Northern neighbors as aliens and outcasts from his nationalist circle. This perspective was to some extent inherent in the task he inherited as a secessionist and as president of the Confederacy, for to secede was to separate in such a way that almost predisposed him to draw stark contrasts between Confederate friends and Union enemies. But his choices were also shaped by long-standing assumptions inherent in a nationalist imagination rooted in sentimentality and overt emotionalism.

The watershed event in Davis's mind was his fateful farewell address in January 1861. Before that point, he was willing to accept the idea that there were like-minded Northerners with whom Southerners like himself shared values and perspectives. Just four days before he gave his farewell, he wrote to a Massachusetts Democrat that he was "already mourning the fate which separates [me] from those friends of the Constitution—which is equivalent to saying those friends of the South—who have in the front rank of the battle been fighting the enemies of the Constitution and therefore of the South, in a manner which so well deserves success, but which unfortunately terminated in defeat."[37]

Davis's last real suggestion that there might be a common ground with Northerners came in his first official address as Confederate president a month later. In a convoluted appeal for peace, he said in his inaugural address, "I enter upon the duties of the office to which I have been chosen with the hope that the beginning of our career as a Confederacy may not be obstructed by hostile opposition to our enjoyment of the separate existence and independence which we have asserted and, with the blessing of Providence, intend to maintain." He then made a free-trade appeal for a peaceful commercial relationship between Confederates and what he termed "our late associates," suggesting a kind of North American free enterprise zone, involving more perhaps than would a mercantile trade agreement between foreign powers but falling short of that within a full-fledged nation. "There can be but little rivalry between ours and any manufacturing or navigating community, such as the Northeastern States of the American Union," he said; "it must follow, therefore, that a mutual interest would invite good will and kind offices." Davis brandished a stick with the carrot, however, declaring that the South was fully ready to defend itself from the "folly and wickedness" of an aggressive Northern foe.[38]

Three weeks later Confederate batteries bombarded Fort Sumter. After this, Davis made no more references to the "friends of the South" or to cooperative economic relationships.[39] Southerners were "freed from the shackles imposed upon us by our uncongenial association with a people who had proven themselves to be ten times worse than even [I] had supposed them to be."[40] The firing of shots united the South in Davis's mind, but it also united the North as well, whom he described as "maddened and now united for our subjugation." For him, the dividing line between North and South, his new nation and his former nation, "us" and "them" was now clear, bright, and easily distinguishable. The issues, he said, "were on the one hand freedom, independence, prosperity—on the other hand, subjugation, degradation and absolute ruin."[41]

Whereas Lincoln adopted a legal position that would not accede to the South's separation, even on a de facto basis, Davis moved quickly to establish precise legal boundaries between Confederates and Yankees. He supported and signed into law the Confederate sequestration act of August 1861, which confiscated the property of Northerners located in Confederate territory, thus placing beyond the pale of Confederate legal protection those who owned property in the South but would not aid in its defense. At the same time, he issued a proclamation requiring men fourteen years and older who did not wish to become citizens of the Confederacy to vacate the new nation's borders or be considered "alien enemies."[42]

Davis supplemented these proclamations with a deep repertoire of the "most monstrous crimes" visited upon his nation by that "foreign people." This was a particularly useful strategy for him to use in papering over what was perhaps the most difficult early nationbuilding issue for his Confederacy: the undeniable fact that many Southerners, starting with his own vice president, had been opposed to secession in 1860 and were, again like Stephens, "halfhearted clear through." Given Davis's own assumption that homogeneity was absolutely necessary for a viable nation, this matter was distressing.[43]

He got around it by claiming that the Yankees themselves had persuaded the fainthearted when they engaged in behavior that caused Southerners to "look with contemptuous astonishment on those with whom they have so recently been associated . . . [and] shrink with aversion from the bare idea of renewing such a connection." "Proud, honorable men may have opposed the act of secession," he conceded, "but can anyone not fit to be a slave, and ready to become one, think of passing under the yoke of such as the Yankees have shown themselves to be by their conduct in this war?" The issue was not so much the positive shared values that had created the Confederate national community but the unwillingness of any self-respecting Southerner to associate with people Davis had consigned to the borders of humanity. "Those people, when separated from the South and left entirely to themselves have, in six months, demonstrated their utter incapacity for self-government," he declared in late 1862, "and yet these are the people who claim to be your masters." The Yankees were the negative spaces of Confederate nationalism, he thought: "Contact [with] Yankees had thoroughly extinguished every spark of Union feeling wherever they had come."[44]

Perhaps his most frequent accusation was some variation on the theme of tyranny. He accused the North of "despotism," of pursuing "gratification of a lust of power and of aggrandizement," and of a "grasping ambition for power and greed of gain." Northerners instigated a "reign of terror," and their government was "the meanest despotism that ever disgraced the earth." Sometimes he coupled these accusations with popular stereotypes of Yankees as grasping, greedy merchants. In his first annual message to Congress he referred to the Union invasion of Virginia as "the wicked invasion which greed of gain and the unhallowed lust of power brought upon our soil." In a North Carolina speech he referred to "the Yankee nation of extortioners." On other occasions he revisited old antebellum arguments about the prerogatives of federal authority, accusing the Lincoln administration of "making war without the assent of Congress and "threaten[ing] judges . . . because they maintain the writ of habeas corpus."[45]

Davis couched these accusations in the language of individual rights, which was so important to white Southerners' self-image. Lincoln based his entire Reconstruction policy on the assumption that white Southerners could govern themselves, but Davis believed Northerners had proven incapable of properly running their political institutions. "These men, when left to themselves, have shown they are incapable of preserving their own personal liberty," he said. "They have destroyed the freedom of the press; they have seized upon and imprisoned members of State Legislatures and of municipal councils, who were suspected of sympathy with the South." He claimed that "men have been carried off into captivity in distant States without indictment, without a knowledge of the accusations brought against them, in utter defiance of all the rights guaranteed by the institutions under which they live." Davis saw such action as an instance of Northerners sullying their own heritage. To Joseph he wrote, "It was fortunate that we seperated [sic] from a people unfit to possess a free government before our people too become unworthy to possess the inheritance of community independence with civil and religious liberty."[46]

Davis closely coupled these assertions of Yankee tyranny with an endless catalog of "outrages" practiced by Lincoln's soldiers in the name of waging war. He lent credence to nearly every story circulating in the South concerning Union army depredations; his speeches are littered with accusations that Yankees committed "malignant outrages" and "base acts of the assassin and the incendiary" and that they "bombarded undefended villages without giving notice to women and children to enable them to escape" and waged war on "aged men, helpless women and children." Before a crowd in Wilmington, North Carolina, he declared that "he had found ruin and devastation marking the track of the vandal foes." For a man once labeled a "chaste speaker," Davis provided vivid imagery of Yankee abuses, describing "plunder and devastation of the property of noncombatants, destruction of private dwellings and even of edifices devoted to the worship of God," and declaring that "blackened chimneys alone remained to mark the spot where happy homes once stood, and smouldering ashes replaced the roofs that had sheltered the widow and the orphan." He asserted that Northerners were guilty of a "contempt of the usages of civilization, entirely unequalled in history" and that their invasions "pollute[d] the soil."[47]

Davis's rhetoric could shade off into visions of an apocalypse—the Yankees were trying to "subjugate or exterminate the millions of human beings" in the South—crude insults—Yankees were "like true dunghills"—and outright dehumanization of the enemy. He described Union soldiers as "murderers," "thieves and brutes in human form," and "outlaws and enemies of mankind."[48] In language familiar to Americans saddled with racist assumptions about African Americans, Native Americans, and other peoples of color, he suggested that his Union foes constituted a distinct species. "Our enemies are a traditionless and homeless race," he asserted during a lengthy speech in December 1862. "From the time of Cromwell to the present moment they have been disturbers of the peace of the world." Davis then embarked on a one-sided reading of early English and American history darkly reminiscent of Sir Walter Scott, telling his listeners, "Gathered together by Cromwell from the bogs and fens of the North of Ireland and of England, they commenced by disturbing the peace of their own country; they disturbed Holland, to which they fled, and they disturbed England on their return. They persecuted Catholics in England, and they hung Quakers and witches in America."[49]

Of all the members of this "homeless race," Benjamin F. Butler brought out the worst in Davis. Butler was the Union governor of New Orleans and, among other things, he promulgated the infamous "woman order" in spring 1862 that threatened the arrest of any demonstratively pro-Confederate New Orleans woman as "a woman of the town plying her avocation." It certainly did not help that Butler was also an outspoken abolitionist, widely rumored to be a war profiteer, and an abrasive man who tried even the limits of Abraham Lincoln's tolerance.[50]

On the heels of the "woman order," Davis took the unusual step of issuing a public proclamation singling out Butler by name as "a felon deserving of capital punishment" and "an outlaw and common enemy of mankind." When he heard the news that Butler had executed a New Orleans citizen, Davis suspended the practice of paroling Union officer prisoners of war and demanded that Butler be punished, declaring that he and his officers were "robbers and criminals deserving death." To a Richmond audience Davis declared, "Butler has exerted himself to earn the execrations of the civilised [sic] world, and now returns with his dishonors thick upon him to receive the plaudits of the only people on earth who do not blush to think he wears the human form." Here was Jefferson Davis at a superheated pitch, using language that had no counterpart in Lincoln's speeches.[51]

Davis was fully cognizant of the motivational qualities, the nationbuilding uses to which this language could be put, for when he embarked on his periodic sojourns into the Confederate heartland to boost morale, he used these lists of Yankee atrocities as special rallying points in his public speeches. His appeals to the negative equation of Confederate nationalism were explicit. "I wave the question of faith," he wrote a fellow Confederate, "and ask what could be hoped for from our brutal enemy . . . but such degradation as to a freeman would be worse than torture at the stake." To a crowd in Richmond he exclaimed, "By showing themselves so utterly disgraced that if the question was proposed to you whether you would combine with hyenas or Yankees, I trust every Virginian would say, give me the hyenas." This was an effective ploy; a reporter present recorded that this appeal elicited loud applause and cries of "Good! Good!"[52]

The legacy of the American Revolution is particularly palpable in these accusations. While Southerners were trying to defend the rights of self-government and liberty "for which our fathers of the Revolution bled," Northerners had "shown themselves so incapable of appreciating the blessings of the glorious institutions they inherited." Any Southern man who sought an accommodation with the Yankees was "fallen beneath the dignity of his ancestors."[53] With the same obtuse irony characterizing Revolutionary-era rhetoric about alleged British attempts to "enslave" slaveholding Americans, Davis appealed to his fellow slaveholders to rise up and throw off the shackles of Yankee bondage: "Will you be slaves; will you consent to be robbed of your property; to be reduced to provincial dependence?"[54]

This rhetoric was more than mere name-calling: it relied upon a fairly sophisticated set of political and cultural tools. It contained many of the elements used by white Southern slaveholders when they defined the black "other": the accusations of sexual impropriety, the suggestions of weak self-control ("they are incapable of preserving their own personal liberty"), a peculiar reading of history that consigns a people to an outlying border area of humanity. Davis's listeners would surely have recognized on some level the old wine of their own racism, even as he poured it into a new nationalist bottle. He could draw upon a dubiously rich heritage of white Southern slaveholders in defining and demonizing the "other," more so perhaps than Lincoln.[55]

There was also a strong sexual subtext underlying Davis's pronouncements concerning the Yankees, particularly the venom he aimed at Butler. Other Union generals committed depredations, and other Union generals executed Southern civilians. "Beast" Butler drew the special ire of Davis and other white Southerners because his "woman order" so egregiously violated Southern sexual mores. Butler "has been found of instincts so brutal," Davis said, "as to invite the violence of his soldiery against the women of a captured city."[56]

This was particularly disturbing, for Davis often praised the unanimous and selfless devotion to the cause displayed by the women of the Confederacy. Southern white women were in his mind uniformly chaste, patriotic, and loyal, "whose glorious example had inspired the heroism of their husbands." Davis saw women as the wellspring of Confederate patriotism, "whose past gives assurance of what you will do in the future . . . who have lined the wayside to minister to the feeble and pointed the dying to Heaven." He did not think he had to motivate Confederate women. "To the women no appeal is necessary. They are like the Spartan mothers of old," he claimed. He painted a heavily sentimentalized picture of their nationalist ardor. "Silently, with all [the] dignity and grandeur of patriotism, they have made their sacrifices," he said, "sacrifices which, if written, would be surpassed by nothing in history. . . . At the last moment when trampled upon and it became a necessity, they would not hesitate to strike the invader a corpse at their feet."[57]

White Confederate women were at the center of the Confederate "us," and it almost naturally followed that "Beast" Butler, who supposedly insulted and degraded the patriotic women of New Orleans, was a useful personification of the Yankee enemy.[58] Indeed, there is a sexual undertone to many of Davis's pronouncements about Yankee depredations. When he wrote the famous Confederate spy Rose O'Neal Greenhow after her release from a Union prison in 1863, he used subtle sexual imagery in alluding to the "bitter trials to which your free spirit was subjected while your person was in the power of a vulgar despotism." Elsewhere he accused Union soldiers of

"inflicting horrible outrages on women and children" and "insult[ing] helpless women." He believed that "some of the military authorities of the United
States seem to suppose that better success will attend a savage war in which
no quarter is to be given and no sex to be spared, than has hitherto been
secured by such hostilities as are alone recognised [sic] to be lawful by civilized men in modern times."[59]

Lincoln never suggested that Northern women were any more or less patriotic than the men, and in setting white Confederate women on such a high
pedestal, Davis had to practice upon himself a goodly bit of self-delusion.
Support for the Confederate cause was hardly universal among white Southern women.[60] Davis was given firsthand knowledge of this fact in spring 1863,
when a mob of hungry women looted downtown Richmond before his very
eyes. The Confederate president threw his spare pocket change at the women
to mollify them, and they relented only when he threatened to order militia-
men present to open fire if the mob did not disperse. Yet he continued to
talk of universal female support for the cause, and years later he dedicated
his history of the Confederacy to "the women of the Confederacy [who] shone
a guiding star undimmed by the darkest clouds of war." Imagination can
sometimes overpower reality, and for a man who defined group loyalty and
national identity in fundamentally sentimental terms, it made perfect sense
to place Confederate women and their allegedly universal patriotism near
the center of his Confederate national identity. Davis, like so many white
Southern men, combined notions of community, sentiment, masculinity, and
female identity in ways that were difficult to disentangle.[61]

The Confederate president was widely criticized, by contemporaries and
scholars, for his inability to motivate the Southern citizenry properly and
create a truly robust Confederate nationalism.[62] If one thinks only in terms
of positive nationalist attributes, this view may be valid. But in the negative
spaces of nationalism, Davis was all too effective. Indeed, he laid the groundwork for the Confederacy's ultimate triumph: not on the battlefield but in
the Confederate victory in absentia during Reconstruction. By portraying the
Yankees as grasping thieves with despotic intentions and murderous hearts,
and by contrasting this stereotype to that of the chaste and patriotic white
Southerner, Davis created some of the basic elements of the white South's
Lost Cause mythology long before it was truly lost. He showed fellow Southerners how to imagine the demonized, sexually depraved black man of Reconstruction by first applying these readily available cultural stereotypes to
the demonized, sexually depraved Yankee. His brand of sentimental, emo-

tive nationalism was perfectly suited to the white racial unity that bound defeated Confederates together after the war, a unity that transcended the death of the Confederacy itself and provided what amounted to a pan-Confederate national resistance to "carpetbagger rule" and attempts at achieving some form of racial equality.[63]

In 1881 Davis wrote *The Rise and Fall of the Confederate Government,* his particular contribution to the book battles waged by former Confederates to assess blame, point fingers, and take credit for the successes and defeats of the failed Southern nation.[64] But he was relatively generous to Lincoln's memory; it was the politically astute tone to assume toward a fallen national hero who was revered by so many in the North. In his book, Davis spared Lincoln even his relatively mild wartime epithets of "tyrant," "despot," and "baboon." He found much to criticize concerning Lincoln's administration policies, but he was wary of reproaching the man himself, his worst criticism being that Lincoln was guilty of a "series of usurpations" in his emancipation policies and of "malfeasance with traffic in human life" when he armed former slaves.[65] Like many white Southerners, Davis believed that postwar rule under Lincoln would have been decidedly preferable to that which had transpired under his successors. Lincoln's assassination "could not be regarded otherwise as a great misfortune to the South," Davis wrote. "He had power over the Northern people, and was without personal malignity toward the people of the South."[66]

Davis was in many ways a prophet of hate, and Lincoln has been widely praised for such magnanimity, his "malice towards none." But just as there was a price to be paid for Davis's use of the demonized enemy in the dubious "victory" of the Redeemer South, so too was there a price to be paid for Lincoln's inability to adequately construct a sense of a Southern enemy. In both cases the cost fell largely on African Americans; reconciliation was the freedmen's enemy, for it was effected on their backs. Protecting the freedmen required a leader willing accurately to assess the motives and minds of a potential Klansman. Reconstruction in general required a Northern sense of purpose united behind the idea that the South as a region needed fundamental political, social, and cultural reform because it had strayed from the national goal of equality and justice for all. Reconstruction required a president who could, at least for the short term, read recalcitrant white Southerners out of the national community. Lincoln was unwilling to do so during the war, and it is unlikely that he would have done so afterward.[67] He might have benefited from just a little malice toward some.

Conclusion

Sometime during the 1870s or 1880s Varina Davis heard a remarkable story about her husband, so remarkable that she included it in her memoirs. A clergyman named Harsha claimed that Jefferson Davis met Abraham Lincoln during the Black Hawk War in 1832, when Lieutenants Davis and Robert Anderson, the future commander of Fort Sumter, were dispatched to southern Illinois to swear into federal service several militia companies. Davis was "a very fascinating young man, of easy manners and affable disposition," Harsha said. "On the morning when the muster was to take place, a tall, gawky, slab-sided, homely young man, dressed in a suit of blue jeans, presented himself to the lieutenants as the captain of the recruits, and was duly sworn in." According to Harsha, "the homely young man was Abraham Lincoln." He was apparently fond of this dramatic little episode, for he repeated it to several people. When Harsha told it to a friend in a bookstore in New York, another clergyman who happened to be listening enthusiastically supported the story, saying he had been an army chaplain during the Black Hawk War and had witnessed the oath himself. Another bystander said he had even heard Lincoln joke in later years that his first oath of allegiance to the United States had been administered by Jefferson Davis.

But did it really happen? Varina had her doubts. She mentioned it to Davis, who could only vaguely remember swearing in some volunteers. He had no idea whether Lincoln was among them. Lincoln himself never corroborated the tale in writing, and Varina could only comment that it "seems a probable story."[1]

Had she been able to check the army's records, she would have discovered otherwise. Lieutenant Jefferson Davis was on furlough in Woodville, Mississippi, on May 29, 1832, when Lincoln and his fellow Illinois volunteers were mustered into service several hundred miles away. Harsha and his companions in the New York bookstore were most likely indulging a wish to contribute some little tidbit to the ever-growing Lincoln legend, concocting stories about him having become something of a national hobby in the decades following his assassination.[2] Davis was an old man by this time, so perhaps the volunteers he recalled mustering into service were the products of a faded memory. Whatever the reasons behind Harsha's story, the fact remains that Jefferson Davis never met Abraham Lincoln on that day or any other.[3]

It is a fascinating little lie, nevertheless. Harsha offered no value judgment concerning which of the two might be superior, implying that both were legitimate sides of a general American character, an Americanness stronger than region or profession that bonded the two men together and that never should have been broken. Davis was an upright young aristocrat, an officer, and a gentleman. His "easy manners" and " affable disposition" evoked the genteel Old South. Lincoln was ugly, rough, and even a little comical. He was the backwoods rail-splitter in his ill-fitting jeans; as such he represented the best of frontier America, equally as valuable as Davis's Dixie.

Americans North and South preferred to think of the war in these terms in the decades following the end of Reconstruction. Literally and figuratively, Harsha's contemporaries saw the war as a conflict between brothers, worthy adversaries from the same national family who exhibited tremendous martial bravery on the field of battle and who each brought valuable and distinctive cultural traits to the grand American enterprise. By the turn of the century Northerners and Southerners were making sincere efforts to heal the wounds of the war by telling themselves that neither side exhibited unworthy or dishonorable motives and that the war in some peculiar way demonstrated the best of America, North and South.[4]

It was a healing process with a decidedly white bandage, an undercurrent of national racial solidarity, as the grizzled old veterans of the blue and the gray met annually to shake hands on the fields of battles gone by. African Americans were read out of the war entirely, and the same nation that embraced Jim Crow and tossed its black denizens to the former Confederate wolves of the genteel South would strive earnestly to forget that slavery, racism, and inequality had played much of a role in the (white) brothers' war.[5]

A century later, historians thankfully have reversed this trend and in the process returned African Americans to their rightfully prominent place in the story of the Civil War. Myths like Harsha's have become almost unthinkable. Civil rights–minded Americans erect new statues to Abraham Lincoln, even as activists fight, in many cases successfully, to remove Jefferson Davis's name from places of honor throughout the country.

This is as it should be. I do not at all wish to suggest that we should return Lincoln and Davis to the same moral plane, and clearly we are well rid of the sense of white racial solidarity that underlay much of the national reconciliation of Harsha's day. But an excessive focus on the issues of slavery and victory, and on Lincoln's manifest superiority in both areas, obscures a subtle but fascinating dialectic lying beneath the surface in Lincoln's and Davis's nationalism, a dialectic between two separate but competing points of view, of equal viability and value, concerning the nature of an American national imagination.

Lincoln's imagined America was a nation of strangers, diverse men and women who were unable to know what was truly in one anothers' hearts. It was an imagination rooted in his complex personality, his relationships with his family and friends, and especially in his choice of the law as a profession. Lawyer Lincoln learned about the fragility of assumptions concerning the inner motives of one's neighbors and the dangers of placing excessive confidence in sentimental attachments. These lessons seeped into his general value system and worldview. He was casually acquainted with a great many people, but he was intimately attached to almost no one, and this was how he believed community relationships—local, state, and national—should best function.

Lincoln approached the sectional conflicts of the 1840s and 1850s from this perspective, believing that a majority of Americans shared his vision of the rational, detached Republic. He understood that there were some Americans who made political use of sentiment and emotion, but he did not much care for their stratagems. He relied on the rational procedures of the rule of law to corral sectional conflict, and he was reluctant to drag speculation about his fellow Americans' motives into the fray. As the nation slowly disintegrated around him, he found to his horror that many Americans—Stephen Douglas, slaveholders—did not necessarily share his feeling that slavery was un-American. Still, to the very end Lincoln hoped for a rational solution to the nation's sectional difficulties, a solution that would eschew overt emotionalism and appeal to peoples' innate sense of reason and, if that failed, to their political self-interest.

When he was elected president in 1860, Lincoln learned how to appeal to sentiment as well as to reason, and his national imagination made some room for an emotional dimension. But the center of gravity of his nationalism remained rooted in his lawyer's need for distance and circumspection. He could appeal to God for help but without presuming to know the will of God. He could speak of the war's broader national meaning, but he preferred to keep the war at arm's length. There was an essential tension here, a tension between his postulated objective set of universal truths—equality, progress, the sacred attributes of the Declaration of Independence—and an understanding that his fellow Americans were a fundamentally subjective, relativist lot who did not necessarily share his motives, desires, or even concerns.

The result was not the triumphalist nationalism now commonly associated with Lincoln but a national identity with limitations, uncertainties, and blind spots. Indeed, uncertainty was the hallmark of Lincoln's imagined America. It was at times a source of strength, but it could also—in the case of his dealings with a recalcitrant white South—become a source of weakness.

Certainty was key in Jefferson Davis's nationalist imagination, born of his personality, his training as a West Point and regular army officer, and the needs and fears of the white South in which he was raised. He believed that good white gentlemen, particularly those with military pedigrees, needed to surround themselves with people whose honor, motives, and comradeship (or, in the case of women and slaves, whose deference) was beyond question. This sentimentalist imagination was no impediment to the development of a strong nationalist identity. Indeed, Davis's nationalism before 1850 was intense precisely because it was rooted in the same values that cemented his loyalties to Mississippi and the South.

After 1850, however, the sentimental imagination that once had made Davis a strong American nationalist worked to produce in him a growing sense of alienation from his Northern neighbors. For him, the issue was one of mismatched expectations. He thought Americans in the North possessed fundamentally the same motives, feelings, and sentiments that animated white men like himself in the South. All good Americans, he believed, subscribed to an essentially Davisonian view of the Constitution, federal authority, states' rights, and white supremacy; and even as he could acknowledge the existence of transgressors like Stephen Douglas, still he tried to convince himself that a majority of Northerners thought and (most important) felt as he did. When this belief was no longer possible, he embraced secession.

As the new Confederacy's president, Davis continued to see national bonding as a matter of sentiment. He made overt appeals to his fellow white Southerners' hearts, painting an emotional mosaic of Confederate virtue and Yankee perfidy. He also continued to embrace that need for certainty, which was so important to his antebellum worldview. He needed to know, beyond a shadow of a doubt, that God was on the Confederacy's side and that victory was certain.

In Davis's nationalist thought, objective reality was a given, and it was an objective reality rooted ironically in the most subjective of phenomena—sentimentalism. The tensions in Lincoln's thought lay between high ideals and the hard, rational truth of American strangers; the tensions in Davis's imagined America (and imagined Confederacy) lay between his idealized community of sentiment and the realities of his fellow Confederates and Americans. Davis's nationalism was in many ways an ongoing confrontation between his need for emotional bonding to create a true national community, the fact that antebellum Americans fell far short in fulfilling this need, and his insistence that the Confederacy did indeed constitute a true community of sentiment.

This assessment turns traditional perspectives on Davis and Lincoln upside down. The Lincoln of myth is the sentimental nationalist, the devotee of the cult of the Union, who made overtly emotional appeals to the better angels of Americans' natures. But I have found that, in reality, his nationalist imagination construed America as a nation of aliens who could nevertheless function quite well without knowing one anothers' motives and innermost thoughts. Davis, on the other hand, is popularly perceived as a cold fish, one who eschewed sentimental ties to the Union and pursued an obdurately rational plan for secession and civil war. But I have found in Davis a sentimental nationalist who placed emotion at the foundation of his nationalist imagination and who needed to know what was in his fellow Americans' hearts in order to function properly in the American public square.

The importance of each man's imagined community transcends slavery and victory; it is the foundation of a general conversation about what it means to be an American, which is as relevant today as it was in the nineteenth century. Fundamentally, it is the ongoing question of how much each of us needs to know about one another to consider ourselves and our neighbors to be Americans. Lincoln could live with the fact that he did not know the hearts and minds of everyone in the American community; Davis could not.

One might argue that this need indicates a fatal weakness in Davis's nationalism, an unrealistic expectation of sentimental bonding, which, when carried to an extreme, could justify secession and civil war and render Davis unable to identify adequately the sources of true dissent in his short-lived Confederate nation. Conversely, Lincoln's point of view seems to be the more nuanced, the more mature vision of America, suitable for a diverse nation with a great many strangers who simply cannot be expected to bond in the manner Davis expected. There is truth in this view. But both Lincoln's strangers and Davis's sentiments are indispensable parts of a rich, complex, and at times contradictory American conversation about who we are and what we should expect of ourselves as a nation. Americans need Lincoln's sense of distance between one another; we need to keep ourselves at arm's length in our expansive, roiling *polis*. But we also need to believe in Davis's sentimental bonding, even as we perceive its limitations. The result is not a zero-sum game between a Lincolnian and Davisonian perspective on national identity; rather, the two together are necessary parts of that rich and complex American nationalism that has so often defied simple categorization. Strange as it may seem, we need Davis every bit as much as we need Lincoln if we are to possess a truly healthy, robust American imagination.

When the war began, Lincoln understood the shortcomings of his rationalist national imagination and made cautious appeals to sentiment as a way to bind his fractured nation together; and toward the very end of his life, Jefferson Davis seemed to understand, if only dimly, the limitations of his sentimental nationalism. In 1880 Davis invited one of Lincoln's closest friends, Alexander McClure, to visit him at his home in Beauvoir, Mississippi. Davis knew McClure from before the war. "He was not an especially genial gentleman," McClure recalled, "but [he was] always severely courteous."

McClure found the former Confederate president in an orange grove in front of his home, reading a newspaper with "two small boys playing tag all over him." McClure thought he was a pathetic figure, "an embittered and helpless old man," though he conceded that Davis "received me with great cordiality [and] I spent a most delightful day with him." As they talked, the discussion eventually turned to Lincoln, dead for fifteen years. Davis repeated the by-then common Southern benediction on the sorrow of Lincoln's passing. "Next to the day of the fall of the Confederacy," Davis said to McClure, "the South has known no darker day than the assassination of Lincoln."

But then Davis did something rather out of character for him. "In the course of the conversation he said he desired to know more about the character of Lincoln," McClure remembered; "he inquired very minutely as to his personal qualities, his habits, his feelings [and] his actions."[6] It was one of the few times in Jefferson Davis's life that he felt the need to ask such questions. White Southerners, army officers, slaves, Varina, fellow congressmen, fellow Americans, fellow Confederates—throughout his entire life he had presumed to know what was in their hearts, or earnestly hoped that he did so, anyway. Yet here, at the very end, Davis was confronted, if only briefly, with the realization that he had never known what motivated at least one of his fellow Americans. He had never really understood Abraham Lincoln.

Notes

Introduction

1. There are only two book-length, modern studies comparing Lincoln and Davis: William Catton and Bruce Catton, *Two Roads to Sumter* (New York: McGraw-Hill, 1963), written in the Cattons' inimical style, but valuable more for its narrative qualities than for its analysis; and Bruce Chadwick, *Two American Presidents: A Dual Biography of Abraham Lincoln and Jefferson Davis* (Secaucus N.J.: Birch Lane Press, 1999), which offers little at all in the way of serious scholarly insight.

2. Max Byrd, "Lincoln's Shadow," *New York Times Book Review,* December 3, 2000, 134; James M. McPherson, "How Lincoln Won the War with Metaphors," in *Abraham Lincoln and the Second American Revolution* (New York: Oxford University Press, 1990), 93–94; William C. Davis, *Jefferson Davis: The Man and His Hour* (New York: HarperCollins, 1992), 703; David M. Potter, "Jefferson Davis and the Political Factors in Confederate Defeat," in *Why the North Won the Civil War,* ed. David Donald (New York: Collier Books, 1960), 109; see also William J. Cooper Jr., *Jefferson Davis, American* (New York: Knopf, 2000), xiii. This is not to say that Davis has not had defenders vis-à-vis Lincoln; see Ludwell Johnson's thoughtful essay, "Jefferson Davis and Abraham Lincoln as War Presidents: Nothing Succeeds Like Success," *Civil War History* 27 (1981): 128–152. On the neo-Confederate extreme, Davis has been upheld in relation to Lincoln (in a very poor fashion) by Mildred Rutherford's *Jefferson Davis and Abraham Lincoln* (Athens: State Historian, Georgia Division, United Daughters of the Confederacy, 1916), and in Russell Hoover Quynn's *The Constitutions of Abraham Lincoln and Jefferson Davis: A Historical and Biographical Study in Contrasts* (New York: Exposition Press, 1959).

3. David Potter makes these various points in "Jefferson Davis and the Political Factors in Confederate Defeat," in Donald, ed., *Why the North Won the Civil War,* 105–109 and passim; see also Mark Neely's useful essay, "Abraham Lincoln vs. Jefferson Davis: Comparing Presidential Leadership in the Civil War," in *Writing the Civil War: The Quest to Understand,* ed. James M. McPherson (Columbia: University of South Carolina Press, 1998), and Frank Vandiver, *The Making of a President: Jefferson Davis, 1861* (Richmond: Virginia Civil War Commission, 1961), 13–14, and his useful essay, "The Shifting Roles of Jefferson Davis," in *Essays on Southern History, Written in Honor of Barnes F. Lathrop,* ed. Gary Gallagher (Austin: General Libraries, University of Texas at Austin, 1980), 125–127.

4. David M. Potter, "The Lincoln Theme and American National Historiography," in Potter, *The South and the Sectional Conflict* (Baton Rouge: Louisiana State Univer-

sity Press, 1968), 153; James A. Rawley, "The Nationalism of Abraham Lincoln," *Civil War History* 9 (1963): 283; Stephen B. Oates, *Abraham Lincoln: The Man Behind the Myths* (New York: HarperCollins, 1984), esp. parts 3 and 4; see also Nathaniel W. Stephenson, "Lincoln and the Progress of Nationality in the North," *Annual Report of the American Historical Association* (1919): 350–368; William B. Hesseltine, *Abraham Lincoln: Architect of the Nation* (Fort Wayne, Ind.: Fort Wayne Historical Society, 1959); and John P. Diggins, *On Hallowed Ground:Abraham Lincoln and the Foundations of American History* (New Haven: Yale University Press, 2000).

5. For a good historiographic overview of Lincoln's nationalism, see Mark E. Neely Jr., "Abraham Lincoln's Nationalism Reconsidered," *Lincoln Herald* 76 (spring 1974): 12–14.

6. Richard Bensel, *Yankee Leviathan: The Origins of Central State Authority in America, 1859–1877* (Cambridge, Mass.: Harvard University Press, 1991); Emory M. Thomas, *The Confederacy as a Revolutionary Experience*, 2d. ed. (Columbia: University Press of South Carolina, 1991), 58–78 and passim; Raimondo Luraghi, "The Civil War and the Modernization of American Society," *Civil War History* 28 (1972): 230–250; see also Frank Vandiver, *Jefferson Davis and the Confederate State* (Cambridge, Mass.: Oxford University Press, 1964).

7. Paul Escott, *After Secession: Jefferson Davis and the Failure of Confederate Nationalism* (Baton Rouge: Louisiana State University Press, 1978); Richard E. Beringer, Herman Hattaway, Archer Jones, and William N. Still Jr., *Why the South Lost the Civil War* (Athens: University of Georgia Press, 1986), 424–426 and passim.

8. Older examples of this straightforward, political nationalism include Ida M. Tarbell, *The Life of Abraham Lincoln*, Sangamon ed., 4 vols. (New York: Lincoln History Society, 1924); Carl Sandburg, *Abraham Lincoln: The War Years*, 5 vols. (New York: Harcourt Brace, 1939), esp. 1: 618; and Benjamin Thomas, *Abraham Lincoln: A Biography* (1952; reprint, New York: Barnes and Noble, 1994), esp. 196–198. More recent works are cognizant of the cultural and social contexts of Lincoln's nationalism, but it is fair to say that they are still grounded in traditional ideas of national identity as preeminently a matter of political institutions and ideology; see Richard N. Current, *What Is an American? Abraham Lincoln and "Multiculturalism"* (Milwaukee: Marquette University Press, 1993), 10, 21; David M. Potter, "The Lincoln Theme and American National Historiography," in Potter, *South and the Sectional Conflict*, 153; Rawley, "The Nationalism of Abraham Lincoln," 283; Oates, *The Man Behind the Myths*, esp. parts 3 and 4; and Jean H. Baker, "Lincoln's Narrative of American Exceptionalism," in *"We Cannot Escape History": Lincoln and the Last Best Hope on Earth*, ed. James M. McPherson (Urbana: University of Illinois Press, 1995), 33–42. For two rich studies that offer perhaps the best recent examples of this approach, see Phillip S. Paludan, *The Presidency of Abraham Lincoln* (Lawrence: University Press of Kansas, 1994), and Mark E. Neely, *The Last Best Hope of Earth: Abraham Lincoln and the Promise of America* (Cambridge, Mass.: Harvard University Press, 1993), esp. 35–39.

9. This literature of nationalism-as-imagination/culture is large; I have been influenced not only by Benedict Anderson, *Imagined Communities: Reflections on the Origin and Spread of Nationalism,* rev. ed. (London: Verso Press, 1991), but also by John Armstrong, "Towards a Theory of Nationalism," and John A. Hall, "Nationalism, Classified and Explained," in *Notions of Nationalism,* ed. Sukumas Periwal (Budapest: European University Press, 1995); Boyd C. Shafer, *Faces of Nationalism: New Realities and Old Myths* (New York: Harcourt Brace Jovanovich, 1972); Liah Greenfeld, *Nationalism: Five Roads to Modernity* (Cambridge, Mass.: Harvard University Press, 1992); Omar Dahbour and Micheline R. Ishay, eds., introduction, *The Nationalism Reader* (Atlantic Highlands, N.J.: Humanities Press, 1995); and David M. Potter's seminal "The Historian's Use of Nationalism and Vice Versa," in *The South and the Sectional Conflict,* 38. Also useful are David Miller, *On Nationality* (Oxford, U.K.: Clarendon Press, 1995), 10–11; Anthony Smith, *The Ethnic Origins of Nations* (Oxford, U.K.: Blackwell Press, 1986); Michael Walzer, "The New Tribalism: Notes on a Difficult Problem," *Dissent* (spring 1992): 164–171; and Wilbur Zelinsky, *Nation into State: The Shifting Symbolic Foundations of American Nationalism* (Chapel Hill: University of North Carolina Press, 1988), 4–5.

Prologue

1. See Davis's reference to "a serious and sudden attack of neuralgia" in his letter to Francis W. Pickens, January 13, 1861, in *Jefferson Davis, Constitutionalist: His Letters, Papers, and Speeches,* ed. Dunbar Rowland, 10 vols. (Jackson: Mississippi Department of Archives and History, 1923), 5: 36 (hereinafter *JDC*).

2. Varina Davis described this incident in *Jefferson Davis: A Memoir by His Wife,* 2 vols. (1890; reprint, Baltimore: Nautical and Aviation Company, 1990), 1: 575.

3. An account of Seward's visits to Davis can be found in ibid., 1: 579–581, and in William J. Cooper Jr., *Jefferson Davis, American* (New York: Knopf, 2000), 288–289; my characterizations of Seward are also based on Glyndon G. Van Deusen's biography, *William Henry Seward* (New York: Oxford University Press, 1967), esp. 260–261.

4. V. Davis, *Memoir,* 1: 580.

5. Ibid., 581.

6. David Donald, *Lincoln* (New York: Simon and Schuster, 1995), 270; Earl Schenck Miers and C. Percy Powell, eds., *Lincoln Day by Day: A Chronology, 1809–1865* (Dayton, Ohio: Morningside, 1991), 5 (1861).

7. See Van Deusen, *Seward,* 261.

8. Miers and Powell, eds., *Lincoln Day by Day,* 5 (1861).

9. List of visitors is based on a survey of Lincoln's daily activities over the preceding weeks; see ibid., 300–304 (1860), and 1–5 (1861).

10. Lincoln to James T. Hale, January 11, 1861, in *The Collected Works of Abraham Lincoln,* ed. Roy P. Basler, 8 vols. (New Brunswick, N.J.: Rutgers University Press, 1953), 4: 172 (hereinafter *CW*).

1. Fathers

1. Varina Davis, *Jefferson Davis: A Memoir by His Wife*, 2 vols. (Baltimore: Nautical and Aviation Company, 1990), 1: 11–12, 15; William C. Davis, *The Man and His Hour* (New York: HarperCollins, 1991), 8–11; William Cooper's fine biography, *Jefferson Davis, American* (New York: Knopf, 2000), was released just as this manuscript was nearing completion; though I have been able to make good use of Cooper's observations in several places, I have relied on William Davis's work as my standard reference biography for Jefferson Davis.

2. V. Davis, *Memoir*, 1: 15; W. Davis, *The Man and His Hour*, 13–14.

3. V. Davis, *Memoir*, 1: 17.

4. Ibid., 17.

5. Davis to Susannah Gartley Davis, August 2, 1824, in Lynda Lasswell Crist et al., eds., *The Papers of Jefferson Davis*, 10 vols. (Baton Rouge: Louisiana State University Press, 1971–1999), 1: 11; (hereinafter *PJD*). Contrast this response to Davis's emotional reaction to the death of his mother; see W. Davis, *The Man and His Hour*, 116, and V. Davis, *Memoir*, 1: 198.

6. W. Davis, *The Man and His Hour*, 3–5.

7. Samuel Emory Davis to Jefferson Davis, June 25, 1823, *PJD*, 1: 5.

8. Sarah Bush Lincoln, interview with William H. Herndon, September 8, 1865, in *Herndon's Informants: Letters, Interviews, and Statements about Abraham Lincoln*, ed. Douglas L. Wilson and Rodney O. Davis (Urbana: University of Illinois Press, 1998), 107 (hereinafter *HI*); Douglas L. Wilson, *Honor's Voice: The Transformation of Abraham Lincoln* (New York: Knopf, 1998), 56, is skeptical of Sarah's testimony on this matter, but for reasons that strike me as impressionistic; and Wilson—along with other scholars—takes Sarah to be a reliable witness in nearly every other regard.

9. David Donald, *Lincoln* (New York: Simon and Schuster, 1995), 1, 32.

10. Lincoln autobiography to John L. Scripps, c. June, 1860, 4: 61.

11. Lincoln to Joshua Speed, February 25, 1842, ibid., 1: 280.

12. Ibid., Lincoln to John D. Johnston, January 17, 1851, 2: 96–97; for other examples of Lincoln's feelings concerning Thomas, see Lincoln to John D. Johnston, December 24, 1848, 2: 15; Lincoln to Solomon Lincoln, March 6, 1848, 1: 455–456; and Lincoln to Jesse W. Fell, December 20, 1859, 3: 511. See also Marilyn G. Ames, "Lincoln's Stepbrother, John D. Johnston," *Lincoln Herald* 82 (spring 1980); 302–311, and Donald, *Lincoln*, 32–33; as Donald has pointed out, neighborhood rumors that Abraham was not in fact Thomas's child made matters even worse (605n).

13. See Anthony Rotundo, "American Fatherhood: A Historical Perspective," *American Behavioral Scientist* 29 (1985): 7–25, his *Fatherhood in America: A History* (New York: Basic Books, 1993), 11–16 and passim, and his section on nineteenth-century fatherhood images in *American Manhood: Transformations of Masculinity from the Revolution to the Modern Era* (New York: HarperCollins, 1993), 26–28.

14. See Donald, *Lincoln*, 27–28; W. Davis, *The Man and His Hour*, 7–8.

15. See esp. Lincoln to Thomas Lincoln and John D. Johnston, December 24, 1848, *CW*, 2: 15–16.

16. Samuel Davis to Jefferson Davis, June 25, 1823, *PJD,* 1: 5.

17. Herndon, quoted in Donald, *Lincoln,* 160.

18. V. Davis, *Memoir,* 1: 534, 566.

19. In using the term "ambition," I mean something different than that used by George Forgie in his well-known work on the psychological effects of the pursuit of ambition by the post-Revolutionary generation; Forgie has referred to the pursuit of immortal fame through heroic deeds, which he set in the context of psychological transference and guilt (see *Patricide in the House Divided: A Psychological Interpretation of Abraham Lincoln and His Age* [New York: W.W. Norton, 1979], chap. 2). I am here referring to ambition in less lofty terms, as simply the desire to move upward in economic, political, and social circumstances that were far removed from the farming lives of Lincoln's and Davis's families, or of ordinary Americans generally.

20. William H. Herndon and Jesse Weik, *Herndon's Life of Lincoln* (1889; reprint, New York: Da Capo Press, 1983), 304; Richard E. Beringer, "Jefferson Davis's Pursuit of Ambition: The Attractive Features of Alternative Decisions," *Civil War History* 38 (winter 1992): 9–11.

21. See, generally, Charles B. Strozier, "Lincoln's Quest for Union," in *The Historian's Lincoln: Pseudohistory, Psychohistory, and History,* ed. Gabor S. Boritt (Urbana: University of Illinois, 1996), 214–217; see also Michael Burlingame, *The Inner World of Abraham Lincoln* (Urbana: University of Illinois Press, 1994), 37–40, and Forgie, *Patricide in the House Divided,* 33–38.

22. Samuel Davis to Jefferson Davis, June 25, 1823, 1: 4–5, and Jefferson Davis to Susannah Gartley Davis, August 2, 1824, 1: 11, both in *PJD.*

23. See, e.g., ibid., Jefferson Davis to Varina Banks Howell, June 22, 1944, 2: 173.

24. On Joseph's life and personality, see, generally, Janet Sharp Hermann, *Joseph E. Davis, Pioneer Patriarch* (Jackson: University Press of Mississippi, 1990); see "tutor" quote at 164.

25. Ibid., 48, 52–60; on his political contacts and law practice, see 26, 31–36.

26. Ibid., 23–25; see also Frank E. Everett Jr., *Brierfield: Plantation Home of Jefferson Davis* (Hattiesburg: University and College Press of Mississippi, 1971).

27. See, e.g., Joseph Davis to Jefferson Davis, January 19, 1838, 1: 438, and Joseph Davis to Jefferson Davis, August 27, 1838, 1: 450, both in *PJD.*

28. On Joseph's interest in Owen and the relationship to his slaveholding practices, see Hermann, *Pioneer Patriarch,* 53.

29. V. Davis, *Memoir,* 1: 174–176.

30. This is Janet Hermann's argument, but I believe she greatly exaggerates this point in her somewhat overly flattering biography of Joseph (see *Pioneer Patriarch,* esp. 30–31).

31. See Joseph Davis to Jefferson Davis, January 19, 1838, *PJD,* 1: 438–439, for a good example of this shared racial paternalism.

32. Hermann, *Pioneer Patriarch,* 49–74; W. Davis, *The Man and His Hour,* 70–73.

33. Joseph Davis to Jefferson Davis, January 19, 1838, *PJD,* 1: 438.

34. V. Davis, *Memoir,* 1: 198.

35. Jefferson Davis to Joseph Emory Davis, January 2, 1838, 1: 435; Joseph Davis to Jefferson Davis, January 19, 1838, 1: 439; Joseph Davis to Jefferson Davis, February 19, 1838, 1: 442, all in *PJD*.

36. Ibid., Joseph Davis to Jefferson Davis, July 23, 1840, 1: 464–465.

37. V. Davis, *Memoir*, 1: 172.

38. On Davis's general veneration for the Founders, see *PJD* for eulogy on Andrew Jackson, July 1, 1845, 2: 272; speech on the Naturalization Laws and the Native American Party, December 18, 1845, 2: 390; and Davis to Alexander Hamilton Jr., February 9, 1848, 3: 267; see also Hermann, *Pioneer Patriarch*, 50–51.

39. V. Davis, *Memoir*, 1: 172–173; W. Davis, *The Man and His Hour*, 91–92.

40. On Joseph's dislike of party politics, see Hermann, *Pioneer Patriarch*, 33; V. Davis, *Memoir*, 1: 171.

41. Lincoln to John D. Johnston, December 24, 1848, 2: 16 (emphases in original), and Lincoln to Joseph D. Johnston, November 4, 1851, 2: 111, both in *CW*.

42. Ibid., Lincoln to Isham Reavis, November 5, 1855, 2: 327, and Lincoln to William H. Herndon, July 10, 1848, 1: 497.

43. Ibid., Lincoln to Isham Reavis, November 5, 1855, 2: 327; William H. Herndon, "Analysis of the Character of Abraham Lincoln: A Lecture," *Abraham Lincoln Quarterly* 1 (December 1941): 432; and William H. Tisdale, "Personal Orderly Gives Rare Glimpse of Lincoln," *St. Paul Pioneer Press*, February 12, 1904 (Lincoln Museum Newspaper Collection, Fort Wayne, Ind.), Michael Burlingame sets this in psychological terms, with the "Old Man" as an archetypal figure for Lincoln (*Inner World of Abraham Lincoln*, chap. 4).

44. Herndon and Weik, *Herndon's Lincoln*, 151.

45. Eulogy on Henry Clay, July 6, 1852, *CW*, 2: 127 (quote at 123).

46. Ibid., 2: 122, 124, 132.

47. Ibid., 2: 124, 126; see also Gabor S. Boritt, *Lincoln and the Economics of the American Dream*, 2d ed. (Urbana: University of Illinois Press, 1994), 99; Clay was not above exploiting his lowly origins for political gain, a practice that Lincoln may also have learned from his idol.

48. Lincoln, speech in Peoria, Illinois, October 16, 1854, 2: 251; see also his speech to Springfield Scott Club, August 26, 1854, 2: 137, and eulogy on Clay, 2: 124–126, all in *CW*.

49. Ibid., 2: 126, and Boritt, *Lincoln and the Economics of the American Dream*, 99, Burlingame, *Inner World of Abraham Lincoln*, 36, also makes the observation that Lincoln could well have been talking about himself when he eulogized Clay.

50. Lincoln, speech in Peoria, Illinois, October 16, 1854, 2: 282; speech in Bath, Illinois, August 17, 1858, 2: 543–544; see also Lincoln's ire toward "Black Democrats" in invoking Clay's name in speech in Bloomington, Illinois, May 29, 1856, 2: 341; and speech in Springfield, Illinois, July 17, 1858, 2: 519, all in *CW*.

51. Donald, *Lincoln*, 28, 126.

52. Eulogy on Clay, *CW*, 2: 130–132.

53. Herndon and Weik, *Herndon's Lincoln*, 36; Caleb Carman to William Herndon, December 8, 1866, *HI*, 504; see also Stephen Oates, *With Malice Toward None: The*

Life of Abraham Lincoln (New York: Mentor Books, 1977), 12, and William C. Davis, *Lincoln's Men: How President Lincoln Became Father to an Army and a Nation* (New York: Free Press, 1999), 1–5.

54. Lincoln, speech on the Sub-Treasury, December 26, 1839, 1: 170, 172–173; Lincoln's reply to Douglas, first debate, August 21, 1858, 3: 12, 18; reply to Douglas, third debate, October 7, 1858, 3: 220; Cooper Institute address, February 27, 1860, 3: 527, all in *CW*.

55. On Lincoln's ambivalence toward the Founders, see Harry V. Jaffa, *Crisis of the House Divided: An Interpretation of the Issues in the Lincoln-Douglas Debates*, 2d ed. (Chicago: University of Chicago Press, 1982), 207, 222; John P. Diggins, *The Lost Soul of American Politics: Virtue, Self-Interest, and the Foundations of Liberalism* (Chicago: University of Chicago Press, 1987), 171; Russ Castronovo, *Fathering the Nation: American Genealogies of Slavery and Freedom* (Berkeley: University of California Press, 1995), esp. 1–17; and Forgie, *Patricide in the House Divided*, 7–8, 33–34, 250.

56. Diggins, *Lost Soul*, 298.

57. See, e.g., his reference to the Revolution and "such a chief as Washington" during the race with Douglas; speech in Peoria, Illinois, October 27, 1854, 2: 283; reference to "Washington and his compeers," in speech in Leavenworth, Kansas, December 3, 1859, 2: 498, 502; his use of Washington in Cooper Institute address, February 27, 1860, 3: 536–537; his invocation of Washington alone during the sectional crisis in 3: 550; and speech in Manchester, New Hampshire, March 1, 1860, 3: 551, all in *CW*.

58. Ibid., Whig campaign circular, March 4, 1843, 1: 312; speech in Virginia, Illinois, February 22, 1844, 1: 333.

59. Lincoln also sometimes referred to Washington in the other capacities of civic fatherhood, breadwinner, and moral teacher; for example, he cited Washington as an example of the virtues of administrative frugality; see ibid., speech on the Sub-Treasury, December 26, 1839, 1: 173.

60. See also references linking Washington to "the Almighty" in ibid., Lincoln, speech to Congress, January 12, 1848, 1: 439.

61. Ibid., Lincoln, Cooper Institute address, February 27, 1860, 3: 550, and speech in Manchester, New Hampshire, March 1, 1860, 3: 551.

62. See, e.g., Diggins, *Lost Soul*, 304; a more interesting—if controversial—interpretation of the relationship may be found in Dwight G. Anderson's *Abraham Lincoln: The Quest for Immortality* (New York: Knopf, 1982); see also Robert V. Bruce's telling criticisms in "Commentary on 'Quest for Immortality,'" in Boritt, ed., *Historian's Lincoln*, 275–283, and W. Davis, *Lincoln's Men*, 1–5.

63. On the place Washington occupied in American political culture, see Richard Brookhiser, *Founding Father: Rediscovering George Washington* (New York: Free Press, 1996), esp. 185–194. Davis was also given to citing Washington as a controlling authority in numerous matters. But he tended more than Lincoln to lump Washington together with Jefferson and the other Founders; see, e.g., Davis to Malcolm G. Haynes, August 18, 1849, 4: 28, and Davis, speech in the U.S. Senate, January 24, 1850, 4: 60–61, both in *PJD*.

64. Jefferson Davis to Joseph E. Davis, September 22, 1855, *PJD*, 5: 122, See also W. Davis, *The Man and His Hour,* 185, 220; Jefferson and Joseph did have their share of quarrels, however (see 253).

2. Friends

1. William H. Herndon and Jesse Weik, *Herndon's Life of Lincoln* (New York: Da Capo Press, 1983), 25–39; see also David Donald, *Lincoln* (New York: Simon and Schuster, 1995), 32; the two anecdotes are in Francis Fisher Browne, *The Everyday Life of Abraham Lincoln* (1887; reprint, Lincoln: University of Nebraska Press, 1995), 53, 69.

2. Herndon and Weik, *Herndon's Lincoln,* 79.

3. Lincoln to Jesse W. Fell, December 20, 1859, *CW,* 3: 511–512; see also Joshua Speed, *Reminiscences of Abraham Lincoln and Notes of a Visit to California: Two Lectures* (Louisville, Ky.: John P. Morton, 1884), 23; Donald, *Lincoln,* 40–41; Benjamin P. Thomas, *Lincoln's New Salem* (New York: Knopf, 1954), 42–44, 60–64; and Herndon, and Weik, *Herndon's Lincoln,* 115, 187–189.

4. Thomas, *Lincoln's New Salem,* chap. 1 and passim; that Lincoln associated his work as postmaster with his circle of friends and acquaintances is indicated in a negative sense by one of the few surviving letters he wrote as postmaster, in which he informed George C. Spears that Spears had "wounded my feelings" concerning postage for a newspaper subscription fee; see Lincoln to Spears, July 1, 1834, *CW,* 1: 25.

5. For examples of these stories, see Thomas, *Lincoln's New Salem,* 95–97.

6. Herndon shrewdly perceived that Lincoln's "long[ing] to help someone else" was not just altruism; it won him some useful friends (see *Herndon's Lincoln,* 124–125).

7. William F. Herndon, "Analysis of the Character of Abraham Lincoln," *Abraham Lincoln Quarterly* 1 (September 1941): 411; for a judicious, balanced assessment of this aspect of Lincoln's character, see Michael Burlingame, *The Inner World of Abraham Lincoln* (Urbana: University of Illinois Press, 1994), 254–255.

8. William G. Greene to William Herndon, May 30, 1865, *HI,* 20.

9. Appraisal of an estray, December 16, 1830, 1: 3, and document drawn up for James Eastep, November 12, 1831, 1: 3, both in *CW;* examples of many similar transactions can be found at 1: 4, 13, 15, 16, 18, 19 and passim.

10. On Lincoln's motives in moving the capital as well as the rest of the "Long Nine," see Donald, *Lincoln,* 62.

11. There are innumerable examples in Lincoln's correspondence; see, e.g., Lincoln to John T. Stuart, January 29, 1840, 1: 200, January 22, 1840, 1: 195, and March 1, 1840, 1: 206; and Lincoln to Joshua F. Speed, June 25, 1841, 1: 258, all in *CW.*

12. Ibid., toast at public dinner, Springfield, Illinois, July 25, 1837, 1: 87; see also Wayne C. Temple, "Location of the Rural Hotel in Springfield Where Abraham Lincoln Drank a Toast," *Lincoln Herald* 81 (winter 1979): 3–4.

13. See John P. Diggins, *The Lost Soul of American Politics: Virtue, Self-Interest, and the Foundations of Liberalism* (Chicago: University of Chicago Press, 1987), 235–236.

14. Herndon suggested that Lincoln chose his occupation on the basis of providing time to meet "village celebrities, [and] exchange views with strangers" (Herndon and Weik, *Herndon's Lincoln,* 106, 126; see also his remarks about Lincoln "impress[ing] the force of his character" on others, 162). See Stephen B. Oates, *Abraham Lincoln: The Man Behind the Myths* (New York: HarperCollins, 1984), 40, on Lincoln's psychological dependence on his network of friends.

15. On Lincoln's ability to win over strangers quickly, see Burlingame, *Inner World of Abraham Lincoln,* 12.

16. Herndon and Weik, *Herndon's Lincoln,* 116.

17. For a somewhat different point of view, which emphasizes the Whiggish political atmosphere of Lincoln's early years, see Mark Neely, "The Political Life of New Salem," *Lincoln Lore* 1715 (January 1981): 3. Gabor S. Boritt, *Lincoln and the Economics of the American Dream,* 2d ed. (Urbana: University of Illinois Press, 1994), 98, points out that Lincoln did not share the Whigs' proclivities toward "cultural homogeneity."

18. Herndon and Weik, *Herndon's Lincoln,* 187–188; see also Speed, *Reminiscences of Abraham Lincoln,* 33. On Lincoln as party functionary, see Joel H. Silby, "'Always a Whig in Politics': The Partisan Life of Abraham Lincoln," *Journal of the Abraham Lincoln Association* 8 (1986): 21–42.

19. Herndon and Weik, *Herndon's Lincoln,* 115, 188.

20. Ibid.,107.

21. Speed, *Reminiscences of Abraham Lincoln,* 21–22.

22. See Thomas, *Lincoln's New Salem,* 60–63; see also promissory note to Reuben Bradford, October 19, 1833, *CW,* 1: 20.

23. See also Herndon's description of Lincoln's choosing him for a law partner in Herndon and Weik, *Herndon's Lincoln,* 266.

24. Ibid., 1; Lincoln to Alden Hull, February 14, 1843, 1: 306; Lincoln to Richard S. Thomas, February 14, 1843, 1: 307; Lincoln to Archibald Williams, March 1, 1845, 1: 344, all in *CW.*

25. L. M. Greene to William Herndon, July 30, 1865, in *HI,* 40–41; Herndon and Weik, *Herndon's Lincoln,* 76, 82–84; Browne, *Everyday Life of Abraham Lincoln,* 112–113: I agree with Professor Neely that the Clary's Grove story has received too much emphasis by scholars of the "frontier school," and yet it seems representative of the manner in which Lincoln in effect created his own political network (see Neely, "Political Life of New Salem," 1–2); see also Douglas L. Wilson's excellent treatment of the affair in *Honor's Voice* (New York: Knopf, 1998), 18–51.

26. Herndon and Weik, *Herndon's Lincoln,* 50, 55.

27. Speed, *Reminiscences of Abraham Lincoln,* 18.

28. Lincoln, second reply to James Adams, October 18, 1837, 1: 104–105 and 8: 429; see also the description of the legislative exchange between Lincoln and an opponent as "peculiarly sharp and personal" in 1: 238, all in *CW.* See Herndon's

description of Lincoln's "vindictive" belittlement of Jesse B. Thomas on the stump as well as similar incidents in Herndon and Weik, *Herndon's Lincoln,* 172, 194–195, 197–198. Burlingame, *Inner World of Abraham Lincoln,* xiv, 8, 155, has set this tendency of Lincoln to "hurt and belittle" opponents in the context of Jungian psychology and his relationship with his father (see also 150–155, 198 for a good descriptive overview of these incidents in Lincoln's early career).

29. The skunk story is quoted in Burlingame, *Inner World of Abraham Lincoln,* 152; Donald quite rightly characterized several of Lincoln's legislative speeches as "ad hominem" assaults (*Lincoln,* 62).

30. Herndon and Weik, *Herndon's Lincoln,* 190; temperance address, February 22, 1842, 1: 271, and speech on the Sub-Treasury, December 26, 1839, 1: 178, both in *CW.*

31. Speed, *Reminiscences of Abraham Lincoln,* 39; see also Burlingame, *Inner World of Abraham Lincoln,* 98–99, and Charles Strozier, "Lincoln's Quest for Union: Public and Private Meanings," in *The Historian's Lincoln,* ed. Gabor Boritt (Urbana: University of Illinois Press, 1996), 222, on Lincoln's fear of intimacy.

32. Charles Strozier suggested this as well, in the context of the Lyceum address; see "On the Verge of Greatness: Psychological Reflections on Lincoln at the Lyceum," *Civil War History* 36 (1990): 138.

33. Herndon and Weik, *Herndon's Lincoln,* 42 (quotes from teacher are at 34); David Donald, *Lincoln Reconsidered: Essays in the Civil War Era* (New York: Knopf, 1956), 67–68, argues that Lincoln's nature was "secretive."

34. Lincoln quoted in Herndon and Weik, *Herndon's Lincoln,* 79.

35. Ibid., 42.

36. Oates makes this point in *Man Behind the Myths,* 36; see also Donald, *Lincoln Reconsidered,* 167–186.

37. See, generally, Neely's astute observations about Lincoln transcending his environment in "Commentary on 'Abe Lincoln Laughing,'" 26, and observations by Lincoln's cousin John Hanks, both in Boritt, ed., *Historian's Lincoln,* 26. See also Burlingame, *Inner World of Abraham Lincoln,* 39. Herndon noted his partner's disdain for manual labor in *Herndon's Lincoln,* 42, as well as Lincoln's dislike for the alcohol-induced carousings of his friends (117). Boritt has made similar observations, albeit in the somewhat different context of Lincoln's political economy (see *Lincoln and Economics of the American Dream,* 79–89, and for Lincoln's ambivalence toward religious fervor, see 97). Browne, *Everyday Life of Abraham Lincoln,* 125, and Donald, *Lincoln,* 52, give anecdotes about Lincoln using farmwork to gain votes while older scholars and folklorists have in varying degrees seen him as a product of his frontier environment; see, e.g., Thomas, *Lincoln's New Salem,* vii, and Donald, *Lincoln Reconsidered,* 154–159.

38. Robert B. Rutledge to William Herndon, December 4, 1866, in *HI,* 498; also quoted by Herndon in *Herndon's Lincoln,* 111–112.

39. Herndon and Weik, *Herndon's Lincoln,* 112; Henry C. Whitney, *Life on the Circuit with Lincoln* (Boston: Estes and Lauriar, 1892), 139; see also Herndon and

Weik, *Herndon's Lincoln*, 84–85, and Robert B. Rutledge to William Herndon, November 30, 1866, in *HI*, 426.

40. See, e.g., speech on the Sub-Treasury, December 26, 1839, 1: 159–179, and speech in Tremont, Illinois, May 2, 1840, 1: 209–210, both in *CW*. See also Boritt, *Lincoln and the Economics of the American Dream*, who suggests that Lincoln's understanding of these matters was remarkable for his time. For Herndon's "head" remark, see "Analysis of the Character of Abraham Lincoln," 347.

41. See Burlingame, *Inner World of Abraham Lincoln*, 92–93, for an excellent collection of stories about Lincoln's mood swings. The neighbor is quoted in Herndon and Weik, *Herndon's Lincoln*, 114.

42. Samuel Davis to Jefferson Davis, June 23, 1823, *PJD*, 1: 5.

43. His attachment to his friends at Transylvania was strong; see Varina Davis, *A Memoir by His Wife*, 2 vols. (Baltimore: Nautical and Aviation Company, 1990), 1: 34; Davis's own description of the curriculum is at 26–27; and an autobiographical sketch is in *PJD*, 1: lxxviii.

44. William Davis, *The Man and His Hour* (New York: HarperCollins, 1992), 25, offers speculation that the family could not afford to send Jefferson to law school and wanted him to acquire a free public education at West Point; but if money was the primary reason behind Joseph's decision, then surely it would have been cheaper for Jefferson to study for the bar under Joseph's tutelage, a much more common arrangement in those days than law school.

45. See autobiographical sketch, 1: lxxviii, Davis to John C. Calhoun, 1: 10, and Davis to Susannah Gartley Davis, August 2, 1824, 1: 11–12, all in *PJD*.

46. Stephen Ambrose, *Duty, Honor, Country: A History of West Point* (Baltimore: Johns Hopkins University Press, 1966), 6–7, 18–19, and James L. Morrison, *"The Best School in the World": West Point, the Civil War Years, 1833–1860* (Kent, Ohio: Kent State University Press, 1986), 2–5.

47. Colonel Jonathan Williams, quoted in Ambrose, *Duty, Honor, Country*, 33, and Marcus Cunliffe, *Soldiers and Civilians: The Martial Spirit in America, 1775–1865* (Boston: Little, Brown, 1968), 156–157.

48. Morrison, *Best School in the World*, 64–66; Ambrose, *Duty, Honor, Country*, 74, 158.

49. Morrison, *Best School in the World*, 66–67, gives a description of one such trial.

50. Ibid., 64–66.

51. Ibid., 71–74.

52. Monthly Conduct Reports, February 28 to June 23, 1826, in *PJD*, 1: 48–50.

53. Quoted in V. Davis, *Memoir*, 1: 51.

54. Morrison, *Best School in the World*, 74.

55. Order no. 95, August 1, 1825, 1: 30, Military Academy Order no. 49, December 30, 1826, Order no. 3, December 31, 1826, and Court of Inquiry Proceedings, January 8, 1827, 1: 56, 58, 60, all in *PJD*. See also Davis, *The Man and His Hour*, 32–36.

56. Proceedings of General Court Martial, *PJD*, 1: 39.

57. Ibid., 1: 37.

58. Ibid., 1: 35–36.

59. Ibid., 1: 40.

60. Ibid., 1: 40–41.

61. Ibid., Order no. 14, February 8, 1827, 1: 82. Varina offered a highly biased account of the affair (see *Memoir*, 1: 54); see also W. Davis, *The Man and His Hour*, 36.

62. See, e.g., David S. Potter, "Jefferson Davis and the Political Factors in Confederate Defeat," in *Why the North Won the Civil War*, ed. David Donald (New York: Collier, 1960), 109, and Joseph Glatthaar, *Partners in Command: The Relationships Between Leaders in the Civil War* (New York: Free Press, 1994), 96.

63. Proceedings of Court Martial, August 4, 1825, *PJD*, 1: 40.

64. Quotes in Morrison, *Best School in the World*, 65; V. Davis, *Memoir*, 1: 20–22; see also W. Davis, *The Man and His Hour*, 20, on Davis's exposure to a variety of individuals at Transylvania.

65. Davis to Lucinda Farrar Davis Stamps, June 3, 1829, in Linda Lasswell, ed., "Jefferson Davis Ponders His Future, 1829," *Journal of Southern History* 41 (November 1975): 521; on Davis's lasting friendships with West Point comrades, see V. Davis, *Memoir*, 1: 54.

66. See, generally, Cunliffe, *Soldiers and Civilians*, 101–103, 105–110; Morrison, *Best School in the World*, 18–19, 25; Ambrose, *Duty, Honor, Country*, 32–33; and Charles Royster, *A Revolutionary People at War: The Continental Army and American Character, 1775–1783* (New York: W. W. Norton, 1979), 79–96. James Alden Barber Jr., "The Social Effects of Military Service," in *The Military and American Society: Essays and Readings*, ed. Stephen E. Ambrose and James A. Barber Jr. (New York: Free Press, 1972), 160–163, speculates on the effects military service has on soldiers' social attitudes and moral codes.

67. Here I disagree with Rotundo, who sees Lincoln's legal practice as having exclusivity at its roots; see E. Anthony Rotundo, *American Manhood* (New York: HarperCollins, 1993), 198–201.

68. Cunliffe, *Soldiers and Civilians*, 157–159, refers to the West Point cadets' "strong sense of gentlemanly camaraderie." For the social functions of camaraderie and fraternity among American men, see Clifford Putney, "Service over Secrecy: How Lodge-style Fraternalism Yielded Popularity to Men's Service Clubs," *Journal of Popular Culture* 27 (summer 1993): 182–183, and Ann Clawson, *Constructing Brotherhood: Class, Gender, and Fraternalism* (Princeton: Princeton University Press, 1989).

69. Quoted in Cunliffe, *Soldiers and Civilians*, 160.

70. Davis, letter to Lucinda Farrar Davis Stamps, June 3, 1829, in Lasswell, ed., "Jefferson Davis Ponders His Future," 517.

71. There is actually some dispute over the influence of the South at West Point, but Morrison disagrees, emphasizing the tremendous diversity of region, class, and so on among the cadets; his arguments are persuasive (*Best School in the World*, 61–62, 131–132, 177–179).

72. Jefferson Davis to Joseph Davis, January 12, 1825, *PJD*, 1: 18.

73. It is also interesting to note that when Davis described the people from various places in his early childhood neighborhood, he did not refer to them as Southerners (V. Davis, *Memoir, 1:* 8). One might argue that Davis's keenly developed sense
of personal honor was a Southern trait; but it seems to have been more the product
of his military education, since West Point had a highly developed code of honor
and since he spent much more time there and in the army than he did in the South
before 1838. There seems to be a general recent trend in the literature on honor to
move away from tying it to specific regions; see Joanne B. Freeman, "Dueling as
Politics: Reinterpreting the Burr-Hamilton Duel," *William and Mary Quarterly* 53
(April 1996): 289–329, and James McPherson's treatment of honor in the context
of Civil War soldiers in *For Cause and Comrades: Why Men Fought in the Civil War*
(New York: Oxford University Press, 1997).

74. V. Davis, *Memoir,* 1: 90. Nathaniel Stephenson, "A Theory of Jefferson Davis,"
American Historical Review 21 (October 1915): 73, makes a somewhat similar point,
suggesting that Davis in his early life possessed no close community relationships
with Mississippi or the South.

75. See, e.g., Davis to P. G. T. Beauregard, October 16, 1861, *PJD,* 7: 893; V. Davis,
Memoir 1: 54, quote at 90; Davis to Lucinda Farrar Davis Stamps, June 3, 1829, in
Lasswell, ed., "Jefferson Davis Ponders His Future," 520–521; and W. Davis, *The
Man and His Hour,* 34–38. Another interesting manifestation of this sense of mili-
tary community was his notion that the army was a melting pot for immigrants and
a strong argument against nativism (see Davis, speech in House of Representatives,
April 8, 1846, *PJD,* 2: 543).

76. Lasswell, ed., "Jefferson Davis Ponders His Future," 521.

3. Jobs

1. See will of Joshua Short, August 22, 1836, *CW,* 1: 51, and n. 1.

2. For a good discussion of the circumstances surrounding his decision to resign, see William C. Davis, *Jefferson Davis: The Man and His Hour* (New York:
HarperCollins, 1992), 199, 68–70. See also Matthew Arbuckle to Roger Jones, May
12, 1835, *PJD,* 1: 401–402. Davis was answering inquiries concerning his quartermaster duties as late as August of 1837 (see James Thompson to Jefferson Davis,
August 19, 1837, 1: 433–434).

3. On Lincoln's admission to the Illinois bar, see Albert A. Woldman, *Lawyer
Lincoln* (New York: Carroll and Graf, 1936), 23–24. William H. Herndon and Jesse
Weik, *Herndon's Life of Lincoln* (New York: Da Capo Press, 1983), 118, commented
on Lincoln's determination to become a lawyer but offered no reasons why.

4. Neighbors' recollections and Lincoln quote in Francis Fisher Browne, *The
Everyday Life of Abraham Lincoln* (Lincoln: University of Nebraska Press, 1995),
56; on the courtroom in antebellum frontier America, see Lawrence M. Friedman,
A History of American Law, 2d ed. (New York: Simon and Schuster, 1985), 160–
167; Maxwell Bloomfield, *American Lawyers in a Changing Society, 1776–1876*

(Cambridge, Mass.: Harvard University Press, 1976); and David J. Bodenhamer, "Law and Disorder on the Early Frontier: Marion County, Indiana, 1823–1850," *Western Historical Quarterly* 10 (1979): 323–327.

5. See, generally, cases listed in Lincoln Legal Papers, DVD–ROM database, and statistics summarized in *Lincoln Legal Briefs* (April–June 1998): 2–3; on Lincoln's circuit riding, see Earl C. Kubicek, "Lincoln's Friend: Kirby Benedict," *Lincoln Herald* 81 (winter 1979): 10–11.

6. There are innumerable examples of Lincoln's use of legal forms of various writs in the records of his law practice, many available in the Herndon-Weik Collection of Lincolnia, Library of Congress (microfilm); see, e.g., writ of trespass on the case *James Anderson Jr., et. al., v. Henry Garrett, et. al.,* March term, 1838, and writ of error, *Wiley Aville v. Spencer Field,* December term, 1841. Examples could be given almost ad infinitum from these files.

7. See, generally, John P. Frank, *Lincoln as Lawyer* (Urbana: University of Illinois Press, 1961), esp. chap. 1.

8. Ibid., 24–25, 85, 97; David Donald, *Lincoln* (New York: Simon and Schuster, 1995), 98.

9. Herndon noted Lincoln's steadily more austere speaking style during this time, although he did not explicitly tie this development to Lincoln's law practice (*Herndon's Lincoln,* 191). Quotes are in Browne, *Everyday Life of Abraham Lincoln,* 234, and Donald, *Lincoln,* 151.

10. William Herndon, "Analysis of the Character of Abraham Lincoln: A Lecture," *The Abraham Lincoln Quarterly* 1 (December 1941): 429. Several eyewitnesses who remarked on Lincoln's temper in court qualified their statements by attesting to their relative rarity; see, e.g., remarks by Logan and Whitney cited in Michael P. Burlingame, *The Inner World of Abraham Lincoln* (Urbana: University of Illinois Press, 1994), 148. Burlingame's general point about Lincoln's temper and tendency toward anger is quite valid, but I believe his own evidence shows Lincoln's largely successful attempts to control that anger in the courtroom. Herndon, the source of several anecdotes about Lincoln's temper, emphasized his self-control as a general thing (see "Analysis," 411, 419). Donald likewise emphasizes his self-control (*Lincoln,* 151–152), as does Frank, who argues that Lincoln outgrew his early hyperemotionalism at the bar (*Lincoln as Lawyer,* 76, 78).

11. The anecdote about the surgeon is in Burlingame, *Inner World of Abraham Lincoln,* 156; see Browne, *Everyday Life of Abraham Lincoln,* 216.

12. See Herndon and Weik, *Herndon's Lincoln,* 340–342, for a description of this case; see also Frank, *Lincoln as Lawyer,* 25; Woldman, *Lawyer Lincoln,* 249–250; and John E. Walsh, *Moonlight: Abraham Lincoln and the Almanac Trial* (New York: St. Martin's Press, 2000), 60–69.

13. Lincoln to Thomas J. Turner, December 21, 1853, *CW,* 2: 208.

14. Ibid., Lincoln to George B. Kinkead, September 13, 1853, 2: 203–204. There are many other such instances in Lincoln's practice; see, e.g., interrogatory in *Alton and Sangamon Railroad Company v. Joseph Klein,* July 21, 1857 (Herndon-Weik Collection of Lincolnia).

15. Herndon, "Analysis of the Character of Abraham Lincoln," 427.

16. "The Bear Hunt," September 6, 1846, *CW*, 1: 388 (emphasis in original).

17. Frank, *Lincoln as Lawyer*, 73–76; speech to jury, *Rock Island Bridge* case, September 22, 1857, *CW*, 2: 415 (see also analysis of this case in Frank, 84–87).

18. Incident and quote in Woldman, *Lawyer Lincoln*, 165; Lincoln to Joshua R. Stanford, May 12, 1853, *CW*, 2: 194.

19. On Lincoln as negotiator, see Woldman, *Lawyer Lincoln*, 157.

20. Lincoln to Abram Bale, February 22, 1850, 2: 76; see also arbitration proceedings involving Lincoln at 2: 326–327, both in *CW*.

21. Ibid., Fragments, notes for a law lecture, July 1, 1850, 2: 81; see also Woldman, *Lawyer Lincoln*, 154–155.

22. Examples of such cases could be cited almost endlessly from the Lincoln Legal Papers DVD–ROM database and from cases listed in the Herndon-Weik Collection; see, e.g., *Foster v. Foster*, fall term 1841 (divorce); *Gentry v. Gentry*, September 1841 (custody); *Goodall v. Taylor*, March term, 1842 (promissory note).

23. Fragments, notes for a law lecture, July 1, 1850, 2: 81; Lincoln to Joshua Speed, October 22, 1846, 389–391, Lincoln to C. U. Schlater, January 5, 1849, 2: 19, and Lincoln to Robert E. Williams, August 15, 1857, 1: 413, all in *CW*. Woldman likewise commented on Lincoln's dislike of sentiment in the courtroom (*Lawyer Lincoln*, 201). Chessboard quote is in A. K. McClure, *Abraham Lincoln and Men of War Times* (1892; reprint, Lincoln: University of Nebraska Press, 1996), 75.

24. See Frank, *Lincoln as Lawyer*, 62.

25. Speech in Congress, June 20, 1848, *CW*, 1: 484.

26. *Alger v. Alger*, 1844, and *Allen v. Allen*, 1854 (cases in Lincoln Legal Papers, DVD–ROM database); Anton-Herman Chroust, "Abraham Lincoln Argues a Proslavery Case," *American Journal of Legal History* 5 (October 1961): 299–308. Some of Lincoln's more earnest defenders have tried to imply that he was so halfhearted in his arguments for slavery before the Illinois bar that he purposely lost such cases (see, e.g., Woldman, *Lawyer Lincoln*, 70–71). But there is no evidence that he did anything of the sort, and this seems to be a case of wishful thinking (see Donald, *Lincoln*, 103–104, and Chroust, "Proslavery Case," 305–307). The Lincoln Legal Papers database shows Lincoln involved in fifteen cases involving slave property, and it is difficult to discern any moral pattern in them.

27. Remarks in Illinois legislature, January 25, 1839, 1: 138, and remarks in U.S. House, January 5, 1848, 1: 423 (emphasis in original), both in *CW*.

28. For examples of such phrases, see ibid., Lincoln to Robert Boal, January 7, 1846, 1: 353; Lincoln to Henry Dummer, November 18, 1845, 1: 350; Lincoln to John J. Hardin, December 18, 1844, 1: 343; Lincoln to Fillmore men, September 8, 1856, 1: 374; Lincoln to Usher F. Linder, March 22, 1848, 1: 457; Lincoln to Benjamin F. James, January 14, 1846, 1: 354; Lincoln to John Addison, July 22, 1849, 2: 59; Lincoln to John Addison, August 9, 1850, 2: 92.

29. Ibid., Lincoln to Edward D. Baker, January 26, 1839, 1: 129; Lincoln to Allen N. Ford, August 11, 1846, 1: 383; Lincoln to Usher F. Linder, February 20, 1848, 1: 453; and Lincoln to William Herndon, 1: 497; see also Lincoln to William Butler,

February 1, 1839, 1: 141, in which Lincoln criticizes actions based on "excitement" and "bad feeling."

30. Ibid., Lincoln to John J. Hardin, January 19, 1846, 1: 356.

31. Ibid., speech in Worcester, Massachusetts, September 12, 1848, 2: 1; see also speech in Rockport, Indiana, October 30, 1844, 2: 341.

32. On the general discontent of most army officers, see Marcus Cunliffe, *Soldiers and Civilians* (Boston: Little, Brown, 1968), 111–116, 130–140.

33. Davis to Stamps, June 3, 1829, in Linda Lasswell, ed., "Jefferson Davis Ponders His Future, 1829," *Journal of Southern History* 41 (November 1975): 521.

34. Varina Davis, *Jefferson Davis: A Memoir by His Wife,* 2 vols. (Baltimore: Nautical and Aviation Company, 1990), 1: 66–160, gives an exhaustive account of her husband's army sojourns; see also Davis, *The Man and His Hour,* chap. 3.

35. Davis quoted in V. Davis, *Memoir,* 1: 60; his stories about the frontier are collected at 59–81, 113–144, and 146–149. I have relied heavily on Varina's accounts here, since they are almost the only records of Davis's impressions of the West.

36. Ibid., 1: 85.

37. Ibid., 1: 100–101.

38. Davis to Thomas Jessup, February 3, 1831, *PJD,* 1: 174.

39. Ibid., 1: 174–176.

40. My descriptions are based on illustrations of these two forts in ibid., 1: 164, and 196, and on Davis's notes in a letter to Thomas S. Jessup, October 5, 1830, 1: 157–161; see also Francis Paul Prucha, *A Guide to the Military Posts of the United States, 1789–1846* (Madison: State Historical Society of Wisconsin, 1964).

41. V. Davis, *Memoir,* 1: 76–77.

42. For this one instance of Davis's roaming, see ibid., 1: 146–147.

43. Davis to Lucinda Farrar Davis Stamps, in Lasswell, ed., "Jefferson Davis Ponders His Future," 519. See also the anecdote about Davis in William T. Walthall, *Jefferson Davis: A Sketch of the Life and Character of the President of the Confederate States* (New Orleans: Times-Democrat, 1908), 6–7, and W. Davis, *The Man and His Hour,* 60.

44. Proceedings of a general court martial, February 12, 1835, 1: 358, and semiannual company muster roll, December 31, 1834, 1: 349, both in *PJD.*

45. Ibid., proceedings of court martial, February 12–17, 1835, 1: 358–381 (quote at 378).

46. Ibid., 1: 381.

47. Ibid., 1: 358, 381.

48. Ibid., Davis to Richard B. Mason, March 1, 1835, 1: 389. W. Davis points out that Davis never openly expressed disapproval of the verdict, but the timing of his leave and resignation strongly suggests his dissatisfaction (*The Man and His Hour,* 69).

49. Joseph Davis to Jefferson Davis, July 9, 1832, *PJD,* 1: 246.

50. Ibid., Matthew Arbuckle to Roger Jones, March 10, 1835, 1: 396; post return, Fort Gibson, March 31, 1835, 1: 400; Matthew Arbuckle to Roger Jones, May 12, 1835, 1: 403. W. Davis details his courtship of Sarah Taylor (*The Man and His Hour,* 52–54).

51. V. Davis, *Memoir,* 1: 165, 564; see also the incident with the soldier's wife described at 565. There are many examples in his correspondence of his disposition toward military men and the army; see, e.g., Davis to James K. Polk, April 10, 1846, 2: 547–548, and Jesse Sleight et al. to James K. Polk, June 3, 1846, 2: 636, both in *PJD.*

52. Walthall, *Jefferson Davis: A Sketch,* 47; Thomas H. Watts, *Life and Character of Ex-President Jefferson Davis;* speech delivered in Montgomery, Alabama, December 19, 1889 (copy in Mississippi Department of Archives and History), 5; on Davis's tendency to personalize attacks on the military, see V. Davis, *Memoir,* 1: 570.

53. On Davis's deep friendships with army comrades, see, e.g., his earnest support of old West Point friends in letters to William L. Marcy, May 5, 1848, 3: 316–317, and to James K. Polk, June 17, 1846, 2: 667–668, both in *PJD;* see also V. Davis, *Memoir,* 1: 37, for an example of animosities accrued while in the military. See Henry Dodge to George W. Jones, April 18, 1834, 1: 317, and evidence of his emotion-laden sense of military bonding may also be found in his eulogy on Andrew Jackson at 2: 269, both in *PJD.* Though these are examples drawn from his postarmy days, I would tend to disagree with William Davis's argument that Davis did not make an emotional commitment to the military until after leaving the service (*The Man and His Hour,* 126).

4. Homes

1. The classic study here is Bertram Wyatt-Brown's *Southern Honor: Ethics and Behavior in the Old South* (Cambridge, Mass.: Oxford University Press, 1982), and *Honor and Violence in the Old South* (Cambridge, Mass.: Oxford University Press, 1986); see also Kenneth Greenberg's quirky but informative *Honor and Slavery* (Princeton: Princeton University Press, 1997), a useful work even if one does not entirely agree with his central thesis that honor is rooted in slavery.

2. Notice of Organization of Mississippi Anti-Dueling Society, May 27, 1844, *PJD,* 2: 142–154.

3. See Davis's account of the affair in ibid., Davis to Howell Hinds, September 30, 1856, 6: 51–52.

4. Ibid., Davis to William Bissell, February 22, 1850, 4: 79–80; William H. Bissell to Davis, February 22, 1850, 2: 80–81; Davis to Bissell, February 23, 1850, 2: 81; Davis to Bissell, February 27, 1850, 2: 85, and February 27, 1850, 2: 86; William C. Davis, *Jefferson Davis: The Man and His Hour* (New York: HarperCollins, 1992), 196.

5. See, e.g., speech at Republican Banquet, Chicago, Illinois, December 10, 1856, 2: 384, and Lincoln to Lyman Trumbull, June 7, 1856, 2: 343, both in *CW.*

6. William H. Herndon and Jesse Weik, *Herndon's Life of Lincoln* (New York: Da Capo Press, 1983), 183; see also Douglas L. Wilson, *Honor's Voice: The Transformation of Abraham Lincoln* (New York: Knopf, 1998), 233–240, for his excellent treatment of the Shields affair; Lincoln to Joshua Speed, October 5, 1842, *CW,* 1: 302–303; for a good general account, see David Donald, *Lincoln* (New York: Simon and Schuster, 1995), 91–93. Common wisdom long held that Mary Todd was the

real author of the letters and that Lincoln claimed authorship to protect her, but Wilson has recently thrown significant doubt on this story (see *Honor's Voice*, 265–272).

7. Herndon and Weik, *Herndon's Lincoln*, 181; Joshua Speed, interview with William H. Herndon, c. 1865–1866, in *HI*, 475; see also Wilson, *Honor's Voice*, 291–292, 322; and Michael P. Burlingame, *The Inner World of Abraham Lincoln* (Urbana: University of Illinois Press, 1994), chap. 9; for a different interpretation of the Lincoln marriage, see Jean H. Baker, *Mary Todd Lincoln: A Biography* (New York: W.W. Norton, 1987).

8. Baker, *Mary Todd Lincoln*, 55–56.

9. William Jayne to William H. Herndon, August 17, 1887, in *HI*, 624; Baker, *Mary Todd Lincoln*, chaps. 4–5; Donald, *Lincoln*, 84–90, quote at 85.

10. William G. Greene, interview with William H. Herndon, May 30, 1865, *HI*, 21. The definitive discussion of the tangled historiography surrounding this relationship is Douglas Wilson's "Abraham Lincoln, Ann Rutledge, and the Evidence of Herndon's Informants," in his *Lincoln Before Washington: New Perspectives on the Illinois Years* (Urbana: University of Chicago Press, 1997), 74–93.

11. Greene interview, 21; Henry McHenry to William H. Herndon, January 8, 1866, 155–156; Benjamin F. Irwin to William H. Herndon, August 27, 1866, 325; Isaac Cogdal, interview with William H. Herndon, c. 1865–1866, 440, all in *HI*; see also Donald, *Lincoln*, 54–57, Burlingame, *Inner World of Abraham Lincoln*, 135–136, and John Y. Simon, "Abraham Lincoln and Ann Rutledge," *Journal of the Abraham Lincoln Association* 11 (1990): 23–40.

12. Isaac Cogdal, interview with William H. Herndon, c. 1865–1866, in *HI*, 440.

13. Herndon and Weik, *Herndon's Lincoln*, 105.

14. Ninian W. Edwards, interview with William H. Herndon, September 22, 1865, 133, and Joshua Speed, interview with William H. Herndon, c. 1865–1866, 475, both in *HI*. For an interesting psychobiographical account of Lincoln's courtship of Mary, see Charles B. Strozier, *Lincoln's Quest for Union: Public and Private Meanings* (Urbana: University of Illinois Press, 1997); see also Douglas Wilson, "Abraham Lincoln and 'That Fatal First of January,'" in *Lincoln Before Washington*, 99–125.

15. James H. Matheny, interview with William H. Herndon, May 3, 1866, in *HI*, 251; Lincoln to Joshua Speed, February 25, 1842, *CW*, 1: 280.

16. Lincoln to Samuel D. Marshall, November 11, 1842, *CW*, 1: 305; Herndon and Weik, *Herndon's Lincoln*, 180n; for a view that stresses the essentially positive nature of the marriage, see Baker, *Mary Todd Lincoln*, esp. chaps. 5–6; for a different point of view, see Mark E. Neely and R. Gerald McMurtry, *The Insanity File: The Case of Mary Todd Lincoln* (Carbondale: Southern Illinois University Press, 1986), and Burlingame, *Inner World of Abraham Lincoln*, 270–291.

17. See, generally, Baker, *Mary Todd Lincoln;* Donald, *Lincoln*, 82–83; Herndon and Weik, *Herndon's Lincoln*, 181; Wilson, *Honor's Voice*, 233–264; "policy match" quote in John T. Stuart, interview with William H. Herndon, June 1865, *HI*, 64.

18. Varina Davis, *Jefferson Davis: A Memoir by His Wife*, 2 vols. (Baltimore: Nautical and Aviation Company, 1990), 1: 200–203; Donald, *Lincoln*, 94–95.

19. This is Varina Davis's secondhand description; it is the only reliable extant description of Ms. Taylor; see V. Davis, *Memoir,* 1: 164.

20. Davis to Sara Knox Taylor, December 16, 1834, *PJD,* 1: 346; V. Davis, *Memoir,* 1: 94–95.

21. Marriage register, June 17, 1835, *PJD,* 1: 410; W. Davis, *The Man and His Hour,* 52–53; V. Davis, *Memoir,* 1: 95.

22. Sara Knox Taylor to Margaret Mackall Smith Taylor, June 17, 1835, *PJD,* 1: 407; V. Davis, *Memoir,* 1: 164.; W. Davis, *The Man and His Hour,* 74–76.

23. V. Davis, *Memoir,* 1: 164–166.

24. Ibid., 1: 202. In *PJD,* see Joseph Davis to Jefferson Davis, January 19, 1838, 1: 438, Davis to George W. Jones, February 9, 1839, 1: 455, Davis to William Allen, July 24, 1840, 1: 468, and census returns for 1840, 1: 463. The census listed twenty-nine of forty slaves involved directly in agriculture, the rest presumably acting as household servants.

25. Davis, speech on the Oregon bill, July 12, 1848, *PJD,* 3: 360.

26. V. Davis, *Memoir,* 1: 176–180; Davis, speech in Senate, April 20, 1848, *PJD,* 3: 315.

27. V. Davis, *Memoir,* 1: 79, 478; Davis, speech on the Oregon bill, July 12, 1848, *PJD,* 3: 358–363. I am not suggesting here that this sentiment was reciprocated, keeping in mind the observations of Steven Stowe and others that close proximity between masters and slaves does not imply intimacy (see Stowe, *Intimacy and Power in the Old South: Ritual and the Lives of Planters* [Baltimore: Johns Hopkins University Press, 1987], xvii).

28. V. Davis, 1: 171–172, and Davis to George W. Jones, February 9, 1839, 1: 455, both in *Memoir.*

29. I am following William C. Davis's excellent assessment here; see *The Man and His Hour,* 84–85.

30. V. Davis, *Memoir,* 1: 178.

31. Varina Banks Howell to Margaret K. Howell, December 19, 1843, *PJD,* 2: 52–53. W. Davis, speculates that Joseph engineered this encounter (*The Man and His Hour,* 96).

32. Varina Banks Howell to Margaret K. Howell, December 19, 1843, *PJD,* 2: 52–53.

33. V. Davis, *Memoir,* 1: 192; see also Carol K. Bleser, "The Marriage of Varina Howell and Jefferson Davis: 'I gave the best and all my life to a girdled tree,'" *Journal of Southern History* (February 1999): 5–6.

34. Jefferson Davis to Varina Davis, July 29, 1846, *PJD,* 3: 13.

35. Ibid., 3: 191–192.

36. Ibid., Jefferson Davis to Varina Davis, July 29, 1846, 3: 13–14, August 16, 1846, 3: 16, and April 18, 1848, 3: 302; Davis to George W. Jones, February 9, 1839, 1: 455; and Davis to Varina Davis, April 18, 1848, 3: 302 (emphasis in original).

37. Ibid., Jefferson Davis to Varina Davis, August 16, 1846, 3: 16, and December 10, 1846, 3: 94–95 (emphasis in original); Bleser, "Marriage of Varina Howell," 11.

38. Davis to Varina Davis, April 18, 1848, *PJD,* 3: 302–303.

39. Ibid., Varina Davis to Jefferson Davis, January 25, 1849, 4: 62, and July 25, 1852, 4: 291–292; Bleser, "Marriage of Varina Howell," 12–15.

40. For a critical look at the Lincoln marriage, see Burlingame, *Inner World of Abraham Lincoln,* 268–326, and Wilson, *Honor's Voice,* 291–292; for a different perspective, see Baker, *Mary Todd Lincoln,* esp. chap. 5.

41. James Gourley, interview with William H. Herndon, c. 1865–1866, *HI,* 453.

42. Baker, *Mary Todd Lincoln,* 99–101.

43. Harriet A. Chapman, interview with Jesse W. Weik, c. 1886–1887, *HI,* 646.

44. Burlingame, *Inner World of Abraham Lincoln,* 273–275; see also Baker, *Mary Todd Lincoln,* chap. 5, though Baker seems reluctant to discuss any domestic friction between the Lincolns at all.

45. James Gourley, interview with William H. Herndon. On Mary's domestic tribulations, see Baker's excellent description in *Mary Todd Lincoln,* chap. 5.

46. Margaret Ryan, interview with William H. Herndon, October 27, 1886, 597; Jesse K. DuBois, interview with William H. Herndon, c. 1883–1889, 692, and Stephen Whitehurst, interview with William H. Herndon, 722, all in *HI.*

47. Ibid., James Gourley, interview with William H. Herndon, 453, and Stephen Whitehurst, interview with William H. Herndon, 722.

48. Ibid., P. P. Enos, interview with William H. Herndon, c. 1865–1866, 449; Herndon and Weik, *Herndon's Lincoln,* 348.

49. P. P. Enos, interview with William H. Herndon, 449; Herndon and Weik, *Herndon's Lincoln,* 343–344.

50. James Gourley, interview with William H. Herndon, *HI,* 451.

51. See, generally, Burlingame, *Inner World of Abraham Lincoln,* 273–274.

52. Jefferson Davis to Varina Howell Davis, July 29, 1846, *PJD,* 3: 14.

53. Ibid., Varina Banks Howell Davis to Margaret K. Howell, June 6, 1846, 2: 642.

54. Baker, *Mary Todd Lincoln,* 99, 130–143 (Mary quote at 131).

55. Burlingame, *Inner World of Abraham Lincoln,* 323.

56. Bleser, "Marriage of Varina Howell," 11; Davis to George W. Jones, February 9, 1839, 1: 455, and see Davis's reference to family as being " affectionate faces" in letter to Joseph, April 30, 1847, 3: 170, both in *PJD.*

5. Speeches

1. Lincoln, speech in Jacksonville, Illinois, October 6, 1843, *CW,* 1: 329.

2. Davis, speech in Vicksburg, Mississippi, November 4, 1843, *PJD,* 2: 44–45.

3. Ibid., speech in Jackson, Mississippi, June 9, 1852, 4: 268; speech in Jackson, Mississippi, September 23, 1848, 3: 381; speech in Fayette, Mississippi, July 11, 1851, 4: 206.

4. Joel H. Silbey, "'Always a Whig in Politics': The Partisan Life of Abraham Lincoln," *Journal of the Abraham Lincoln Association* 8 (1986): 21–42; see also Daniel Walker Howe, *The Political Culture of the American Whigs* (Chicago: University of

Chicago Press, 1979); Lincoln to Samuel Haycraft, Springfield, Illinois, June 4, 1860, *CW*, 4: 70.

5. Davis to William Allen, March 25, 1844, *PJD*, 1: 131.

6. David Donald, *Lincoln* (New York: Simon and Schuster, 1995), 131–132. For a good, detailed description of Lincoln's appearance and gestures while giving a speech, see Harold Holzer's introduction to *The Lincoln-Douglas Debates: The First Complete, Unexpurgated Text* (New York: HarperCollins, 1993); see also Jeriah Bonham's account of a Lincoln speech in Francis Fisher Browne, *The Everyday Life of Abraham Lincoln* (Lincoln: University of Nebraska Press, 1995), 292. An interesting firsthand account may be found in James O'Donnell Bennett, "Soul of Lincoln Revealed in Words of 'Private Joe,'" *Chicago Sunday Tribune*, January 5, 1936 (Lincoln Museum Newspaper Collection, Fort Wayne, Indiana).

7. Joseph Gillespie to William H. Herndon, December 8, 1866, *HI*, 508.

8. See *PJD* for quotes from Davis, speech in Natchez, Mississippi, June 13, 1844, 2: 166, and speech in Port Gibson, Mississippi, July 1, 1844, 2: 176; see also Davis, speech in Vicksburg, Mississippi, November 4, 1843, 2: 45, and speech in Vicksburg, Mississippi, November 6, 1843, 2: 47.

9. Ibid., Davis, speech in Natchez, Mississippi, June 13, 1844, 2: 166; see also comments by an anonymous observer in "Franklin" to William A. Smyth, July 15, 1844, 2: 180.

10. Lincoln, speech on the Sub-Treasury, December 26, 1839, *CW*, 1: 159–179; Davis, eulogy on Andrew Jackson, July 1, 1845, 2: 279–280, and speech recommending John C. Calhoun, January 8, 1844, 2: 72, both in *PJD*; see petition for increase of tariff, May 12, 1842, *CW*, 1: 287. There were times when both men defied their party's positions, however; Davis, for example, opposed his party's stance on debt repudiation (see William C. Davis, *Jefferson Davis: The Man and His Hour* [New York: HarperCollins, 1992], 88–95).

11. Report and Resolutions in Relation to Purchase of Public Lands, January 17, 1839, *CW*, 1: 135; the best study of Lincoln's economics during this period is Gabor S. Boritt, *Lincoln and the Economics of the American Dream*, 2d ed. (Urbana: University of Illinois Press, 1994).

12. Proceedings of the State Democratic Convention, January 8, 1844, *PJD*, 2: 74.

13. Ibid., Davis to John Jenkins, July 5, 1845, 2: 287.

14. See, e.g., ibid., notes of a meeting of the Warren County Democratic Association, June 17, 1844, 2: 169; notice of a political meeting, July 10, 1844, 2: 178; notice of a political meeting, July 16, 1844, 2: 182; notice of a political meeting, July 26, 1844, 2: 187–188; meeting in Macon, Mississippi, August 7, 1844, 2: 196–197; meeting in Hinds, Mississippi, September 2, 1845, 2: 324–325.

15. Lincoln, speech on the annexation of Texas, May 22, 1844, *CW*, 1: 337.

16. See Donald M. Scott, "The Popular Lecture and the Creation of a Public in Mid-Nineteenth Century America," *Journal of American History* 66 (March 1980): 791–809.

17. Lincoln, Lyceum address, January 27, 1838, *CW*, 1: 108.

18. Ibid., 1: 109, 111.

19. Ibid., 1: 112, 114.

20. Lincoln's Caesar has been seen as an oblique reference to Andrew Jackson, an oblique reference to Stephen Douglas, an expression of the Whigs' distrust of executive power, an attempt to subconsciously repudiate the Founding Fathers, and a psychological projection of Lincoln's own ambition. See, generally, Michael Burlingame, *The Inner World of Abraham Lincoln* (Urbana: University of Illinois Press, 1994), 26; Charles Strozier, "On the Verge of Greatness," *Civil War History* 36 (1990): 137–147; and Major L. Wilson, "Lincoln and Van Buren in the Steps of the Fathers: Another Look at the Lyceum Address," *Civil War History* 29 (1983): esp. 201–203; all offer good overviews of this literature. For classic texts in this debate, see Charles Strozier, *Lincoln's Quest for Union: Public and Private Meanings* (New York: Basic Books, 1982); Dwight G. Anderson, *Abraham Lincoln* (New York: Knopf, 1982); George B. Forgie, *Patricide in the House Divided* (New York: W. W. Norton, 1979); and Edmund Wilson's older recitation of the "oedipal thesis" in *Patriotic Gore: Studies in the Literature of the Civil War Era* (New York: Oxford University Press, 1962). Good critical assessments of this literature may be found in Robert V. Bruce, Marcus Cunliffe, Major Wilson, and Kenneth Stampp's commentaries in *The Historian's Lincoln,* ed. Gabor S. Boritt (Urbana: University of Illinois Press, 1996), 275–285, 302–313, and in Burlingame, *Inner World of Abraham Lincoln,* 253–254, as well as in Richard O. Curry's judicious but in my judgment compelling critique, "Conscious or Subconscious Caesarism? A Critique of Recent Scholarly Attempts to Put Abraham Lincoln on the Analyst's Couch," *Journal of Illinois State Historical Society* 77 (1984): 67–71.

21. Lyceum address, *CW,* 1: 112, 115.

22. Donald makes this point as well, though in a somewhat different context (see *Lincoln,* 83).

23. Lyceum address, 1: 112, 113. Lincoln associated religion with emotion and lack of intellectual rigor; see, e.g., Lincoln to Mary Speed, September 27, 1841, 1: 261, both in *CW.* See also Joshua Speed, *Reminiscences of Abraham Lincoln and Notes of a Visit to California: Two Lectures* (Louisville: John P. Morton, 1884), 32.

24. Lyceum address, *CW,* 1: 110–112.

25. Ibid., 1: 112.

26. Ibid.

27. Davis to George Bancroft, December 12, 1845, 2: 381, and Bancroft to Davis, December 15, 1845, 2: 384, both in *PJD.*

28. See, e.g., ibid., Davis to Eli Abbott, December 21, 1845, 2: 399; Jesse Speight et al. to James K. Polk, December 27, 1846, 2: 400–401; presentation of petition of John L. Allen, December 30, 1845, 2: 404; petition concerning Joseph Bozeman, January 13, 1846, 2: 411; for remarks on "Mississippi's sons," see speech on the Oregon question, February 6, 1846, 2: 461–462.

29. Ibid., resolution concerning the establishment of military schools, December 19, 1845, 2: 393–394; notice of appointment to Select Committee, December 19, 1845, 2: 395–396; remarks concerning appropriations bill, April 22, 1846, 2: 563;

Varina Davis, *Jefferson Davis: A Memoir by His Wife,* 2 vols. (Baltimore: Nautical and Aviation Company, 1990), 1: 228.

30. Davis, speech before House, February 4, 1846, *PJD,* 2: 436.

31. Ibid., Davis speech in Benton, Mississippi, September 5, 1845, 2: 328; reply to William Sawyer, concerning the value of a military education, May 28, 1846, 2; 622, 625; speech in House, February 6, 1846, 2: 453; speech in Senate, September 23, 1848, 3: 386; remarks concerning Texas bill, February 4, 1846, 2: 436; Davis to John Jenkins, July 5, 1845, 2: 285; speech on Oregon bill, February 6, 1846, 2: 462.

32. Ibid., Davis, speech in Benton, Mississippi, 2: 327–328; speech in Senate, May 3, 1848, 3: 320; on Davis's expansionism, see also William Davis, *The Man and His Hour* (New York: HarperCollins, 1992), 175, 227, 251.

33. Davis, speech on Oregon bill, July 12, 1848, PJD 3: 369, and Davis to Hugh R. Davis, June 4, 1848, 3: 325, both in *PJD.*

34. Ibid., Davis, speech on the Harbors and Rivers bill, March 16, 1846, 2: 499, 514.

35. Ibid., speech on internal improvements, March 16, 1846, 2: 514.

36. Ibid., speech on the Oregon question, February 6, 1846, 2: 460, 463; speech on internal improvements, March 16, 1846, 2: 515.

37. On this matter of the South's political culture, see Christopher J. Olsen, *Political Culture and Secession in Mississippi: Masculinity, Honor, and the Antiparty Tradition, 1830–1860* (Cambridge, Mass.: Oxford University Press, 2000), 14–17 and passim.

6. Patriots

1. Davis, autobiographical sketches, November, 1889, *PJD,* 1: liii, lxix.

2. William C. Davis, *Jefferson Davis: The Man and His Hour* (New York: Harper-Collins, 1992), 49–50; excerpt from Black Hawk's autobiography, October 16, 1833, *PJD,* 1: 297.

3. Davis, speech in House of Representatives, February 6, 1846, *PJD,* 2: 439.

4. Ibid., 2: 462–463; speech on Oregon bill, July 12, 1848, 3: 366; see also Jefferson Davis, *The Rise and Fall of the Confederate Government,* 2 vols. (1881; reprint, New York: Da Capo Press, 1990), 1: 41.

5. On Lincoln's lack of knowledge concerning his family genealogy, see Lincoln to David Lincoln, March 24, 1848, 1: 459, and April 2, 1848, 1: 461–462, both in *CW.*

6. Ibid., Lincoln to Jesse W. Fell, December 20, 1859, 3: 511.

7. Ibid., Lincoln, Lyceum address, January 27, 1838, 1: 115.

8. Benjamin F. Irwin to William H. Herndon, September 22, 1866, *HI,* 352–353; a good general description of the events may be found in William C. Davis, *Lincoln's Men* (New York: Free Press, 1999), 7–9.

9. Davis, speech in House of Representatives, February 6, 1846, *PJD,* 2: 462–463.

10. Lincoln, Lyceum address, January 27, 1838, *CW,* 1: 115.

11. Davis, speech in House of Representatives, February 6, 1846, *PJD,* 2: 438.

12. Ibid., Davis, speech on Oregon, February 6, 1846, 2: 440–441; letter "To a Gentleman in Vicksburg," May 12, 1846, 2: 590.

13. See William W. Freehling, *The Road to Disunion: Secessionists at Bay, 1776–1854* (New York: Oxford University Press, 1990), 455–458, for a discussion of the Southern positions on this issue; see also Ernest McPherson Lander Jr., *Reluctant Imperialists: Calhoun, the South Carolinians, and the Mexican War* (Baton Rouge: Louisiana State University Press, 1980).

14. Quitman quoted in Eric Walther, *The Fire-Eaters* (Baton Rouge: Louisiana State University Press, 1992), 95.

15. See, e.g., *PJD*, for notice of political meeting, Vicksburg, Mississippi, November 4, 1843, 2: 44; notice of meeting of Vicksburg Anti-Dueling Society, March 25, 1844, 2: 151; and notice of political meeting, Vicksburg, Mississippi, June 17, 1844, 2: 168. On the use of military titles in Southern political culture, see Joseph E. Chance, *Jefferson Davis's Mexican War Regiment* (Jackson: University Press of Mississippi, 1991), 5–6.

16. Davis, speech in House of Representatives, May 28, 1846, *PJD*, 2: 621.

17. Ibid., 2: 615, and Jefferson Davis to James K. Polk, May 19, 1846, 2: 601.

18. Ibid., Davis, speech in the House of Representatives, May 28, 1846, 2: 615.

19. Ibid., 2: 617; exchange between Johnson and Davis, May 29, 1846, 2: 627–628, and May 30, 1846, 2: 630–633; see also W. Davis, *The Man and His Hour,* 130–131.

20. Davis, "To a Gentleman in Vicksburg," May 12, 1846, *PJD*, 2: 590.

21. Ibid., Varina Banks Howell Davis to Margaret K. Howell, June 6, 1846, 2: 641.

22. Ibid., Davis "To a Gentleman in Vicksburg," 2: 590; Samuel W. Oakey to Jefferson Davis, June 26, 1846, 2: 681; Chance, *Davis's Mexican War Regiment,* 20.

23. Davis, "To a Gentleman in Vicksburg," 2: 590, and Samuel W. Oakey to Jefferson Davis, June 26, 1846, 2: 681, both in *PJD;* Chance, *Davis's Mexican War Regiment,* 20; W. Davis, *The Man and His Hour,* 134–135.

24. Varina Davis, *Jefferson Davis: A Memoir by His Wife,* 2 vols. (Baltimore: Nautical and Aviation Company, 1990), 1: 284.

25. W. Davis, *The Man and His Hour,* 134–135. There were rumors that Davis chose for his personal staff only men whom he knew from the Vicksburg area (see Richard Bruce Winders, *Mr. Polk's Army: The American Military Experience in the Mexican War* [College Station: Texas A & M Press, 1997], 83).

26. Davis to Lucinda Farrar Davis Stamps, June 3, 1829, in Linda Lasswell, ed., "Jefferson Davis Ponders His Future, 1829," *Journal of Southern History* 41 (November, 1975): 520; V. Davis, *Memoir,* 1: 18–19; Davis to William Allen, July 24, 1840, *PJD*, 1: 467–468; on Davis's lack of firsthand experience of the South at this time, see W. Davis, *The Man and His Hour,* 203. William Davis also points out that Jefferson Davis's hustings tours left out significant portions of the state (see 111). On Davis as a westerner and an expert on western character prior to the Mexican War, see Davis, speech in House of Representatives, March 27, 1846, *JDC*, 1: 40, and Davis, speech in House of Representatives, March 16, 1846, *PJD*, 2: 512. He would later claim an early emotional attachment to the state, especially to his home county (see

speech in Fayette, Mississippi, July 11, 1851, *PJD,* 4: 184); but this strikes me as hindsight embellished by the sectional crisis of the time.

27. Chance, *Davis's Mexican War Regiment,* 24, 117; V. Davis, *Memoir,* 1: 286–287.

28. Jefferson Davis to Robert J. Walker, August 24, 1846, *PJD,* 3: 18; V. Davis, *Memoir,* 1: 288–290; W. Davis, *The Man and His Hour,* 137–139; Chance, *Davis's Mexican War Regiment,* 26–30.

29. See *PJD* for Davis, speech in Vicksburg, November 10, 1846, 3: 83 (emphasis in original); Davis to William P. Rogers, October 12, 1846, 3: 63; Davis's description of the battle in his report to Albert G. Brown, September 20, 1847, 3: 227–233; and his autobiography, 1: lv–lvii; see also Chance, *Davis's Mexican War Regiment,* 55–62.

30. Davis to William W. S. Bliss, March 2, 1847, *PJD,* 3: 141.

31. Ibid., Davis to Stephen Cocke, July 15, 1847, 3: 192.

32. V. Davis, *Memoir,* 1: 356; the "gratified" quote is from either Varina or the Mississippi *Picayune;* the text is confusing on this point. See also Chance, *Davis's Mexican War Regiment,* 128–129.

33. For Davis's rapid rise in reputation and consideration for political office after Buena Vista, see letter to him from Joseph E. Davis, May 13, 1847, *PJD,* 3: 172–173; see also W. Davis, *The Man and His Hour,* 154, 160, 163, 170; newspaper quote from *Natchez Courier and Journal,* June 16, 1847, quoted at *PJD,* 3: 183, and Davis, speeches in New Orleans and Natchez, at 3: 181–184.

34. Davis's description of Monterrey, 1846, undated typescript, Jefferson Davis Collection, Mississippi Department of Archives and History; Chance, *Davis's Mexican War Regiment,* 61–62.

35. Wilcox quote in Chance, *Davis's Mexican War Regiment,* 18.

36. Davis, speech in Vicksburg, Mississippi, November 10, 1846, *PJD,* 3: 82; Chance, *Davis's Mexican War Regiment,* 119.

37. Davis, speech in New Orleans, June 10, 1847, 3: 181–182; speech in Vicksburg, November 10, 1846, 3: 83 (emphasis in original); speech in Natchez, June 14, 1847, 3: 184; and Davis to Albert G. Brown, August 15, 1847, 3: 207, all in *PJD;* see also reference to Davis's pep talk with "three Mississippi cheers" in Chance, *Davis's Mexican War Regiment,* 86–87.

38. Davis, speech in Raymond, Mississippi, September 22, 1848, *PJD,* 3: 375; see also William C. Davis's interpretation of Jefferson Davis's handling of a dispute with one of his subordinates (W. Davis, *The Man and His Hour,* 154).

39. W. Davis, *The Man and His Hour,* 163.

40. Ibid., Davis, speech in Vicksburg, November 10, 1846, 3: 79; Davis to Albert G. Brown, August 15, 1847, 3: 207; Davis to Robert J. Walker, November 10, 1846, 3: 90.

41. Ibid., Davis, speech in Jackson, Mississippi, September 23, 1848, 3: 376.

42. See V. Davis, *Memoir,* 1: 473–475.

43. Davis, speech in Oxford, Mississippi, July 15, 1852, *PJD,* 4: 281–282.

44. It is worth noting here W. J. Cash's observation that white Southerners possess an "unusual proneness to sentimentality," though his attempt to locate this in

a white sense of guilt over slavery is, I think, misplaced; certainly there is no evidence to support the "guilt thesis" in Jefferson Davis; see Cash, *The Mind of the South* (1941; reprint, New York: Vintage Books, 1991), 82–83.

45. The notion of one "becoming Southern" is a relatively recent scholarly matter; see Christopher Morris, *Becoming Southern: The Evolution of a Way of Life, Warren County and Vicksburg, Mississippi, 1770–1860* (New York: Oxford University Press, 1995). Though his subject matter and theoretical framework are much different from my own, I am indebted to his suggestion—an accurate one—that regional identity might be acquired rather than taken as a given.

46. Davis, speech on the Oregon bill, July 12, 1848, *PJD*, 3: 339. See also W. Davis, *The Man and His Hour*, 166–167, 176, 185, who dates Davis's sense of himself as a Southern spokesman around the end of the Mexican War. See *PJD* for Davis to Charles J. Searles, September 19, 1847, 3: 225–226, and for Davis, speech in Jackson, Mississippi, September 23, 1848, 3: 381, on Mississippi as his "highest allegiance."

47. Davis, speech in New Orleans, June 10, 1847, 3: 181, and Davis's speech in House of Representatives, May 28, 1846, 2: 615, both in *PJD*.

48. Ibid., Davis, speech in New Orleans, June 10, 1847, 3: 182; K. Jack Bauer, *The Mexican War, 1846–1848* (New York: Macmillan, 1974), 216, and Windsor, *Mr. Polk's Army*, chap. 7.

49. On Hardin's involvement in the Shields affair, see Memorandum of Duel Instructions, September 19, 1842, *CW*, 1: 301n; William H. Herndon and Jesse Weik, *Herndon's Life of Lincoln* (New York: Da Capo Press, 1983), 149, 216–218; Lincoln to Benjamin F. James, November 17, 1845, 1: 349, and Lincoln, speech in House of Representatives, July 27, 1848, 1: 515, both in *CW*. On the complex political maneuvers surrounding Hardin and Lincoln's battle for the nomination, see David Donald, *Lincoln* (New York: HarperCollins, 1995), 111–114.

50. Lincoln, speech in House of Representatives, July 27, 1848, *CW*, 1: 515.

51. On Lincoln's attitude toward expansionism, see Gabor S. Boritt, *Lincoln and the Economics of the American Dream*, 2d ed. (Urbana: University of Illinois Press, 1994), 105–106, 258–259.

52. Lincoln to John M. Peck, May 21, 1848, *CW*, 1: 473.

53. Ibid., Spot resolutions, House of Representatives, December 22, 1847, 1: 421 (emphases in original).

54. Ibid., speech in House of Representatives, January 12, 1848, 1: 437–442.

55. Ibid., Lincoln to Josephus Hewett, February 13, 1848, 1: 450 (emphasis in original); Herndon and Weik, *Herndon's Lincoln*, 279; Democratic editor's quote in Donald W. Riddle, *Congressman Abraham Lincoln* (Westport, Conn.: Greenwood Press, 1979), 38.

56. Lincoln to Jesse Fell, December 25, 1859, 3: 511, and Lincoln to John L. Scripps, c. June, 1860, 4: 66, both in *CW*.

57. Ibid., speech on internal improvements, June 20, 1848, 1: 482.

58. Ibid., Lincoln to Jesse Lynch, April 10, 1848, 1: 463; see also Lincoln to Archibald Williams, April 30, 1848, 1: 468.

59. Ibid., speech in House of Representatives, July 27, 1848, 1: 505 (emphases in original).

60. Ibid., 1: 504.

61. Ibid., 1: 515.

62. The only exceptions I have found are at ibid., 1: 515, when Lincoln refers to Taylor as "the noblest Roman of them all," and Lincoln's speech in Worcester, Massachusetts, September 15, 1848, 2: 4–5, in which he declared that Taylor was "just the man" to whom the interests of the nation might be entrusted.

63. Mark Neely, "Lincoln and the Mexican War: An Argument by Analogy," *Civil War History* 28 (1978): 21–23, convincingly argues that Lincoln was not especially enamored of life as a Washington congressman.

64. Lincoln to William H. Herndon, January 8, 1848, *CW*, 1: 431.

65. Gabor Boritt, "A Question of Political Suicide: Lincoln's Opposition to the Mexican War," *Journal of Illinois State Historical Society* 67 (February 1974): 79–100, and Neely, "Lincoln and the Mexican War," 6–7, 19–23, argue that Lincoln's opposition to the war met with little criticism from Illinois Whigs and engendered no significant political costs for him and his party. Though Boritt and Neely provide a needed corrective to statements by Herndon and others that Lincoln's stance was "political suicide," I believe David Donald and Stephen Oates were correct in pointing out that the Whig press damned Lincoln with faint praise and that his antiwar stance, if not "suicide," was not without some political costs to him personally (see Donald, *Lincoln,* 125, and Stephen B. Oates, *With Malice Toward None* [New York: Mentor Books, 1977], 87).

66. Lincoln to William H. Herndon, February [?] 1848, *CW*, 1: 446; see also Donald, *Lincoln,* 124–126.

67. See *CW* for Lincoln to Jesse Fell, December 25, 1859, 3: 512; Lincoln to William Fithian, September 14, 1859, 2: 63; Lincoln to Thomas Ewing, April 7, 1849, 2: 40–42; Lincoln to William B. Preston, May 16, 1849, 2: 48–49; Lincoln to John M. Clayton, July 28, 1849, 2: 60–61, letters that are generally representative of his correspondence in the wake of Taylor's victory. See also Dwight G. Anderson, "Quest for Immortality: A Theory of Abraham Lincoln's Political Psychology," in *The Historian's Lincoln,* ed. Gabor Boritt (Urbana: University of Illinois Press, 1996), 261–262, and Michael Burlingame, *The Inner World of Abraham Lincoln* (Urbana: University of Illinois Press, 1994), 4.

68. Taylor to Davis, July 27, 1847, *PJD,* 3: 204, 208–214, and 217–223.

69. Ibid., Davis, speech in New Orleans, June 10, 1847, 3: 181; Davis's letter to citizens of Concordia Parish, September 24, 1847, 3: 236; and speech in Washington, D.C., June 13, 1848, 3: 327.

70. On the circumstances surrounding the proviso, see David M. Potter, *The Impending Crisis, 1848–1861* (New York: HarperCollins, 1977), 20–22; see also Freehling, *Road to Disunion,* 459–460.

71. See *PJD* for Davis to Malcolm D. Haynes, June 18, 1849, 4: 39; Davis to Charles J. Searles, September 19, 1847, 3: 225; and Davis's general remarks on Southern rights in the West in his speech in Fayette, Mississippi, July 11, 1851, 4: 193–195; J. Davis, *Rise and Fall of the Confederate Government,* 1: 10–14.

72. On Lincoln and the proviso in the context of Taylor's election, see his speech in the House of Representatives, July 27, 1848, 1: 505, speech in Taunton, Massachusetts, September [?] 1848, 2: 8, and speech in Peoria, Illinois, October 16, 1854, 2: 252; see also Lincoln to Joshua Speed, August 31, 1855, 2: 323, all in *CW*.

7. Declarations

1. Quote is from Judah P. Benjamin, future Confederate cabinet member; see Vincent C. Hopkins, *Dred Scott's Case* (New York: Fordham University Press, 1951), 61.

2. See Don Fehrenbacher's seminal work, *The Dred Scott Case: Its Significance in American Law and Politics* (New York: Oxford University Press, 1978); see also Kenneth M. Stampp, *1857: A Nation on the Brink* (New York: Oxford University Press, 1990), 93–101.

3. See Fehrenbacher, *Dred Scott,* 335–350, 351 and passim.

4. See *PJD* for Davis, speech in Jackson, Mississippi, November 4, 1857, 6: 159; speech in Portland, Maine, September 11, 1858, 2: 220; and "Address to the National Democracy," May 7, 1860, 6: 328; see also Jefferson Davis, *The Rise and Fall of the Confederate Government,* 2 vols. (New York: Da Capo, 1990), 1: 69–70.

5. Lincoln to James Steele and Charles Summers, February 12, 1857, *CW,* 2: 389; see, generally, cases listed for 1857 in the Lincoln Legal Papers DVD–ROM database; statistics on his practice compiled by the Lincoln Legal Papers Project in *Lincoln Legal Briefs,* 44 (October–December 1997 and July–September 1998).

6. See, e.g., Lincoln to Orville H. Browning, December 15, 1856, *CW,* 2: 386.

7. Ibid., fragment on formation of the Republican Party, c. February 28, 1857, 2: 391.

8. Ibid., Lincoln, speech on the Sub-Treasury, December 26, 1839, 1: 171; campaign circular from the Whig Committee, March 4, 1843, 1: 312.

9. Ibid., Lincoln, fragment on *Dred Scott* case [January 1857], 2: 387–388.

10. *Tribune* quote in Fehrenbacher, *Dred Scott Case,* 3.

11. See *CW* for notes for speech in Chicago, Illinois, February 28, 1857, 2: 390–391; fragment on formation of the Republican Party, c. February 28, 1857, 2: 391; speech in Springfield, Illinois, June 26, 1857, 2: 404.

12. See, generally, William E. Gienapp, *The Origins of the Republican Party, 1852–1856* (New York: Oxford University Press, 1987); Eric Foner, *Free Soil, Free Labor, Free Men: The Ideology of the Republican Party Before the Civil War,* 2d ed. (New York: Oxford University Press, 1995); James D. Bilotta, *Race and the Rise of the Republican Party, 1848–1865* (New York: Peter Lang, 1992). For a good local study, see Robert Cook, "Baptism of Fire: The Republican Party in Iowa, 1838–1878," *Journal of American Studies* 30, 1 (1996): 137–165.

13. Stephen Douglas made Lincoln's supposed participation in this meeting a campaign issue during their 1858 Senate race; see, e.g., first debate in Ottawa, Illinois, August 21, 1858, *CW,* 3: 4–7, 12–13.

14. Donald E. Fehrenbacher, *Prelude to Greatness: Lincoln in the 1850s* (New York: McGraw-Hill, 1962), 19–47; see also Michael F. Holt, *The Rise and Fall of the American Whig Party: Jacksonian Politics and the Onset of Civil War* (Cambridge, Mass.: Oxford University Press, 1999), 931–939.

15. On Lincoln's enthusiasm for the Republican Party, see Fehrenbacher, *Prelude to Greatness,* 94–95.

16. "A House Divided" speech in Springfield, Illinois, June 16, 1858, *CW,* 2: 468; Fehrenbacher gives a good discussion of Lincoln's sometimes hesitant move toward the Republican party once the Whigs fell apart (*Prelude to Greatness,* 40–45).

17. The best description of these events is still David M. Potter, *The Impending Crisis, 1848–1861* (New York: HarperCollins, 1977), chaps. 12–13; see also Fehrenbacher, *Prelude to Greatness,* 57–62, and Robert W. Johannsen, *Stephen A. Douglas* (Urbana: University of Illinois, 1997), chaps. 13–15.

18. See *CW* for Lincoln to Lyman Trumbull, December 28, 1857, 2: 430; fragments of a speech, c. May 18, 1858, 2: 448–449; letter to Elihu B. Washburne, May 27, 1858, 2: 455; and "House Divided" speech, Springfield, Illinois, June 16, 1858, 2: 467–468.

19. Ibid., fragments of a speech, c. May 18, 1858, 2: 450.

20. Ibid., Lincoln, speech in Peoria, Illinois, October 16, 1854, 2: 273.

21. Ibid., first debate, August 21, 1858, 3: 9; third debate, September 15, 1858, 3: 140.

22. Ibid., third debate, September 15, 1858, 3: 140; fourth debate, September 18, 1858, 3: 161.

23. Ibid., first debate, August 21, 1858, 3: 9.

24. See, e.g., Douglas's remarks at ibid., 3: 63, 280, 288.

25. Ibid., sixth debate, October 13, 1858, 3: 265.

26. Ibid., fourth debate, September 18, 1858, 3: 168.

27. Ibid., first debate August 21, 1858, 3: 19.

28. Ibid., third debate, September 15, 1858, 3: 117.

29. Ibid., fourth debate, October 13, 1858, 3: 253; first debate, August 21, 1858, 3: 22.

30. Ibid., third debate, September 15, 1858, 3: 122–127, 147.

31. Ibid., fourth debate, September 18, 1858, 3: 180.

32. He repeated this charge in many places; see, e.g., ibid., 3: 20–22.

33. Ibid., first debate, August 21, 1858, 3: 22 (emphases in original).

34. Ibid., second debate, September 2, 1858, 3: 83, 84 (emphasis in original).

35. Ibid., fragments, notes for speeches, c. October 1, 1858, 3: 205.

36. Ibid., sixth debate, October 13, 1858, 3: 252–254.

37. Ibid., fourth debate, October 7, 1858, 3: 233.

38. Ibid., first debate, August 21, 1858, 3: 13–14 (emphases in original).

39. See, e.g., Harold Holzer's remarks in his introduction, *The Lincoln-Douglas Debates: The First Complete, Unexpurgated Text* (New York: HarperCollins, 1993), 20–21; see also Potter, *Impending Crisis,* 333–334, and David Donald, *Lincoln* (New York: Simon and Schuster, 1995), 222. Stephen B. Oates, *Abraham Lincoln: The*

Man Behind the Myths (New York: HarperCollins, 1984), 48, aptly describes humor as "a potent political weapon" for Lincoln. See the seventh debate, October 13, 1858, *CW*, 3: 259, for a good example of Lincoln casting character aspersion on Douglas's habit of doing just that; here he says that Douglas would not, "like an honest man," admit that he had leveled false charges against him.

40. Fourth debate, September 18, 1858, *CW*, 3: 179.

41. On conspiracy theories, see Daniel Walker Howe's excellent analysis in *The Political Culture of the American Whigs* (Chicago: University of Chicago Press, 1979), 79–81; in arguing that such theories served a rational purpose for antebellum Americans and were not mere manifestations of paranoia, he has offered a convincing corrective to Richard Hofstadter's point of view (see Hofstadter, *The Paranoid Style in American Politics* [New York: Knopf, 1965]). See also David Zarefsky's helpful discussion concerning the uses of conspiracy theories in American political culture (*Lincoln, Douglas, and Slavery* [Chicago: University of Chicago Press, 1990], chap. 4).

42. The Declaration made a brief, transitory appearance in the Lyceum speech; see *CW*, 1: 112; he also made a brief reference to the document during his eulogy on Henry Clay in July 1852 (2: 121).

43. Ibid., Lincoln, speech in Peoria, Illinois, October 16, 1854, 2: 266; speech in Independence Hall, Philadelphia, February 22, 1861, 4: 240; speech in Peoria, October 16, 1854, 2: 255; speech in Lewistown, Illinois, August 17, 1858, 2: 547; fragment, notes for speeches, October 1, 1858, 3: 205.

44. On the Declaration's rising importance in the antebellum era, see Pauline Maier, *American Scripture: Making the Declaration of Independence* (New York: Knopf, 1997), chap. 4; Maier also suggests that Lincoln's interest in the Declaration was a response to assaults on it by Calhoun and others (see 202).

45. See *CW* for fragments on slavery, July 1, 1854 (?), 2: 222; for Douglas's responses, see first debate, Ottawa, Illinois, August 21, 1858, 9–10, quote at 3: 31; third debate, Jonesboro, Illinois, September 15, 1858, 3: 112–113; fourth debate, Charleston, Illinois, September 18, 1858, 3: 177; fifth debate, Galesburg, Illinois, October 7, 1858, 213–214, 216. On Lincoln's "problematic" reading of the Declaration's history, see Maier, *American Scripture*, 206.

46. On the place the Declaration and egalitarianism occupied in Lincoln's worldview, see Michael Burlingame, *The Inner World of Abraham Lincoln* (Urbana: University of Illinois Press, 1994), chap. 2; Oates, *Man Behind the Myths,* 59–61; and Gabor S. Boritt, *Abraham Lincoln and the Economics of the American Dream* (Urbana: University of Illinois Press, 1994), 158–160. See also Lincoln, speech in Springfield, Illinois, October 4, 1854, 2: 245, and speech in Peoria, Illinois, October 10, 1854, 2: 249, both in *CW*.

47. See especially reporter's summary of Lincoln's views during speech in Lewistown, August 17, 1858, 2: 546; Lincoln, speech in Peoria, Illinois, October 16, 1854, 2: 276; speech in Princeton, Illinois, July 4, 1856, 2: 346; speech in Springfield, Illinois, July 17, 1858, 2: 520–521, all in *CW*.

48. On Lincoln's reading of the Revolution, see Phillip Paludan, "Hercules Unbound: Lincoln, Slavery, and the Intentions of the Framers," in *The Constitution,*

Law, and American Life: Critical Aspects of the Nineteenth-Century Experience, ed. Donald G. Nieman (Athens: University of Georgia Press, 1992), 1–22, and Mark E. Neely Jr., "Abraham Lincoln's Nationalism Reconsidered," *Lincoln Herald* 76 (spring 1974), 15–18.

49. See, e.g., Harry V. Jaffa, *Crisis of the House Divided,* 2d ed. (Chicago: University of Chicago Press, 1982), chap. 17; also useful to Jaffa's perspective on these issues is his collection of arguments and critical responses in *Original Intent and the Framers of the Constitution: A Disputed Question* (Washington D.C.: Regnery Gateway, 1994). See also Glen E. Thurow, "Abraham Lincoln and American Political Religion," in *The Historian's Lincoln,* ed. Gabor S. Boritt (Urbana: University of Illinois Press, 1996), 124–143; John P. Diggins, *The Lost Soul of American Politics* (Chicago: University of Chicago Press, 1987), 295–311, and his more recent study, *On Hallowed Ground* (New Haven: Yale University Press, 2000); Sotorios Barber, *On What the Constitution Means* (Baltimore: Johns Hopkins University Press, 1984), 33–34; and J. David Greenstone, *The Lincoln Persuasion: Remaking American Liberalism* (Princeton: Princeton University Press, 1993).

50. Fragment on the Constitution and the Union, January, 1861 [?], 4: 169, and first inaugural address, March 4, 1861, 4: 253, both in *CW.* See also Greenstone, *Lincoln Persuasion,* 256–257, and Diggins, *Lost Soul,* 295–298.

51. I qualify this assertion with "broad sense" because Lincoln explicitly stated that he did see the Declaration as a legally binding instrument, to be obeyed and interpreted in a court of law (see Lincoln to James N. Brown, October 18, 1858, *CW,* 3: 327). I mean to suggest here that he saw the Declaration as performing some of the same general tasks in regulating community interaction that legal documents did for the courtroom (on this point, see Neely, "Lincoln's Nationalism Reconsidered," 16–17).

52. Lincoln, speech in Springfield, Illinois, July 10, 1858, *CW,* 2: 500–501, 520.

53. Ibid., eulogy on Henry Clay, July 6, 1852, 2: 130; speech in Springfield, Illinois, July 17, 1858, 2: 521; first debate, Ottawa, Illinois, August 21, 1858, 3: 16.

54. See, e.g., Fehrenbacher, *Prelude to Greatness,* 111.

55. See *CW,* first debate, Ottawa, Illinois, August 21, 1858, 3: 16, and speech in Springfield, Illinois, June 26, 1858, 2: 405.

56. Ibid., Lincoln, speech in Springfield, Illinois, June 26, 1857, 2: 404–406, and speech in Lewistown, Illinois, August 17, 1858, 2: 546–547.

57. For a good discussion of the high moral content of Lincoln's viewpoint, see Greenstone, *Lincoln Persuasion,* 250–251, and Maier, *American Scripture,* 208.

58. See *CW* for Lincoln, letter to Joshua Speed, August 24, 1855, 2: 323; speech in Paris, Illinois, September 7, 1858, 3: 90–91; speech in Lewistown, Illinois, August 17, 1858, 2: 547; speech in Chicago, July 10, 1858, 2: 500; eulogy on Henry Clay, July 6, 1852, 2: 130; speech in Peoria, Illinois, October 16, 1854, 2: 275; speech in Chicago, October 27, 1854, 2: 283; speech in Petersburg, Illinois, August 30, 1856, 2: 368; speech in Springfield, Illinois, June 26, 1857, 2: 407; speech in Monticello, Illinois, July 20, 1858, 527.

59. Ibid., sixth debate, Galesburg, Illinois, October 13, 1858, 3: 249.

60. Ibid., Lincoln, speech in Springfield, Illinois, June 26, 1857, 2: 407.

61. Ibid., speech in Chicago, July 10, 1858, 2: 500.

62. Ibid., speech in Bloomington, Illinois, September 4, 1858, 3: 89. Lincoln repeatedly used this phraseology; see, e.g., speech in Carlinville, Illinois, August 31, 1858, 3: 80; fifth debate, Galesburg, Illinois, October 7, 1858, 3: 234; and speech in Columbus, Ohio, September 16–17, 1859, 3: 424.

63. Ibid., speech in Philadelphia, February 22, 1861, 4: 240–241.

64. Davis, speech in Fayette, Mississippi, July 11, 1851, *PJD,* 4: 208.

65. Ibid., speech in Vicksburg, July 24, 1851, 4: 220.

8. Parties

1. Debates in the U.S. Senate, April 20, 1848, *PJD,* 3: 315.

2. See, generally, excerpts from Senate debates in *JDC,* 1: 219, 262–264, 372–374; 2: 24–29, 114, 171.

3. See ibid., 1: 262–263, and *PJD,* 2: 512–513, where Davis suggested Douglas's omnibus bill was "corrupt in morals."

4. Varina Davis to her parents, November 21, 1845, in *Jefferson Davis: Private Letters, 1823–1889,* ed. Hudson Strode (1966; reprint, New York: Da Capo Press, 1995), 34–35.

5. On Davis's personal enmity toward Douglas, see William C. Davis, *Jefferson Davis: The Man and His Hour* (New York: HarperCollins, 1992), 269, 271–274, 282; on blame for the war, see *JDC,* 1: xvii. Don Fehrenbacher has pointed out that a general hatred of Douglas among Southern Democrats was well nigh universal by 1858 (*Prelude to Greatness* [New York: McGraw-Hill, 1962], 141).

6. See *CW* for debates in Illinois legislature, December 21, 1836, in 1: 56–57, and for Lincoln et al. to the editor of the *Chicago American,* June 24, 1839, and Lincoln to John T. Stuart, November 14, 1839, 1: 151, 154.

7. Anecdote in Francis Fisher Browne, *The Everyday Life of Abraham Lincoln* (Lincoln: University of Nebraska Press, 1995), 175, and for third-party accounts suggesting that Lincoln/Douglas encounters in general were highly emotional, see 246–247.

8. See *CW* for Lincoln to William A. Minshall, December 7, 1837, 1: 107; Lincoln, speech to the Springfield Cotton Club, August 14, 26, 1852, 2: 136; and Lincoln to John T. Stuart, March 1, 1840, 1: 206. The "least man" quote is in Browne, *The Everyday Life of Abraham Lincoln,* 142.

9. Lincoln to John T. Stuart, December 23, 1839, *CW,* 1: 159; see also quote from *Manchester Mirror,* c. 1858, in which the writer points out that Lincoln's speeches did not "indulge in any personalities," except where Douglas was concerned; and Browne, *Everyday Life of Abraham Lincoln,* 319. On Lincoln and Douglas's "mutual annoyance" during debates, see Norman A. Graebner, "Commentary on 'Abe Lincoln Laughing,'" in *The Historian's Lincoln,* ed. Gabor S. Boritt (Urbana: University of Illinois Press, 1996), 22. Others suggest that it is impossible to tell exactly what Lincoln thought of Douglas; see George B. Forgie, "Lincoln's Tyrants," in Boritt, ed., *Historian's Lincoln,* 288. Still others emphasize Lincoln and Douglas's conge-

niality and philosophical similarities; see e.g., David M. Potter, *The Impending Crisis, 1848–1861* (New York: HarperCollins 1977), 333–334.

10. References to Davis by Lincoln are found in the seventh debate, Alton, Illinois, October 15, 1858, 3: 295, 324, and in his speech in Columbus, Ohio, September 16, 17, 1859, 423, 429, both in *CW*. Davis's earliest reference to Lincoln was in his speech in Washington, D.C., July 9, 1860, *PJD*, 6: 359.

11. Robert W. Johannsen, *Stephen A. Douglas* (Urbana: University of Illinois, 1997), 29; Lincoln, speech to the Springfield Cotton Club, August 14, 1852, *CW*, 2: 144.

12. Douglas quoted in Johannsen, *Douglas,* 244; on his views concerning slavery, see 233–237, 244, and passim. See also Harry V. Jaffa, *Crisis of the House Divided* (Chicago: University of Chicago Press, 1982), chap. 3.

13. William H. Herndon and Jesse Weik, *Herndon's Life of Lincoln* (New York: Da Capo Press, 1983), 247–248.

14. Lincoln to Edwin W. Bakewell, August 1, 1850, *CW,* 2: 91.

15. Ibid., Lincoln to Edward Seymour, July 17, 1854, 2: 224.

16. Ibid., Lincoln to George B. Kinkead, September 13, 1863, 2: 203–204.

17. Michael Burlingame, *The Inner World of Abraham Lincoln* (Urbana: University of Illinois Press, 1994), chap. 2; Lincoln, speech in Chicago, Illinois, July 10, 1858, *CW,* 2: 492.

18. Post office incident in Browne, *Everyday Life of Abraham Lincoln,* 119; Lincoln, speech at the Springfield Scott Club, August 14, 26, 1852, *CW,* 2: 157; Douglass quoted in Stephen B. Oates, *Abraham Lincoln: The Man Behind the Myths* (New York: HarperCollins, 1984), 118.

19. In suggesting that Lincoln did not give race much serious thought before 1852, I wish to steer a middle ground between scholars who paint him as remarkably enlightened on racial matters and those who see him as irredeemably racist. Representative views of the former are found in Oates, *Man Behind the Myths,* 21–31, 89–163; LaWanda Cox, *Lincoln and Black Freedom,* 2d ed. (Charleston: University of South Carolina Press, 1994), and James McPherson, *Abraham Lincoln and the Second American Revolution* (New York: Oxford University Press, 1990). Representative views of the latter are in Lerone Bennett Jr., *Forced into Glory: Abraham Lincoln's White Dream* (Chicago: Johnson, 2000); Vincent Harding, *There Is a River: The Black Struggle for Freedom in America* (New York: Harcourt Brace Jovanovich, 1992); Nathan Irving Huggins, *Slave and Citizen: The Life of Frederick Douglass* (Boston: Little, Brown, 1980); and George M. Frederickson, "A Man but Not a Brother: Abraham Lincoln and Racial Equality," *Journal of Southern History* 41 (February 1975): 39–58. The basic flaws on both sides, it seems to me, are twofold; first, that the only standard of racial enlightenment is a heart-and-soul conviction of complete racial equality, or lack thereof, and second, that Lincoln's racial views remained entirely static, either for better or for worse, and did not change over his lifetime. I will try to show that these presumptions are mistaken.

20. There are only three relatively famous cases related to slavery cited by Lincoln scholars; see Albert A. Woldman, *Lawyer Lincoln* (New York: Carroll and Graf, 1936), 60–63.

21. Protest in Illinois legislature on slavery, March 3, 1837, *CW*, 1: 75.

22. Ibid., Lyceum address, January 27, 1838, 1: 108–115; see also Fehrenbacher, *Prelude to Greatness*, 14.

23. On Stowe's sentimentalist critique of American law, see Greg D. Crane, "Dangerous Sentiments: Sympathy, Rights, and Revolution in Stowe's Antislavery Novels," *Nineteenth Century Literature* 51 (September 1996): 176–205. On the general approach of abolitionists to issues of inner motives and personal redemption, see Lawrence J. Friedman, *Gregarious Saints: Self and Community in American Abolitionism, 1830–1870* (New York: Cambridge University Press, 1982), 1–3 and passim; see also Robert W. Johannsen, *Lincoln, the South and Slavery: The Political Dimension* (Baton Rouge: Louisiana State University Press 1991), 66.

24. On Lincoln's prewar relationship with Chase, see John Niven, *Salmon P. Chase: A Biography* (Oxford: Oxford University Press, 1995), 222–223; on Sumner, see David Donald, *Charles Sumner and the Coming of the Civil War* (New York: Fawcett, 1960), 360–361; on the distinction between "antislavery" and "abolitionism," see James M. McPherson, *The Struggle for Equality: Abolitionism and the Negro in the Civil War and Reconstruction* (Princeton: Princeton University Press, 1964), 3.

25. Lincoln, speech in Chicago, July 10, 1858, *CW*, 2: 492.

26. Ibid., speech in Peoria, Illinois, October 10, 1854, 2: 255.

27. See, generally, Potter, *Impending Crisis*, chaps. 5–7.

28. Fragments on slavery, July 1, 1854 (?), *CW*, 2: 222–223 (emphasis in original).

29. Ibid., 2: 223 (emphasis in original).

30. Ibid., quotes from speech in Winchester, Illinois, August 26, 1854, 2: 227; see also speech in Carrollton, Illinois, August 28, 1854, 2: 227–228, and speech in Bloomington, Illinois, September 12, 1854, 2: 230–233.

31. Ibid., 2: 230–232; speech in Carrollton, Illinois, August 28, 1854, 2: 227; see also Fehrenbacher, *Prelude to Greatness*, 85.

32. Herndon and Weik, *Herndon's Lincoln*, 295; speech in Bloomington, Illinois, September 26, 1854, 2: 238–239, and in Peoria, Illinois, October 16, 1854, 2: 281, both in *CW*. Fehrenbacher rightly suggests that the act "amounted to a revolution" for Lincoln (*Prelude to Greatness*, 85) and Johannsen describes Lincoln as "stunned" and "confused" by the act (*Lincoln, the South and Slavery*, 24).

33. Lincoln to John M. Palmer, *CW*, 2: 228.

34. Ibid., Lincoln, speech in Peoria, Illinois, October 16, 1854, 2: 255 (emphasis in original).

35. Ibid., first debate, Ottawa, Illinois, August 21, 1858, 3: 29; Lincoln was here paraphrasing language used by Henry Clay.

36. On these points, see Johannsen, *Douglas*, 275–280, and Johannsen, *Lincoln, South, and Slavery*, chap. 2 and passim.

37. Lincoln, "House Divided" speech, June 16, 1858, *CW*, 3: 465–466.

38. W. Davis, *The Man and His Hour*, chaps. 9–11; William Freehling, *The Road to Disunion* (New York: Oxford University Press, 1990), 498–499.

39. See *PJD* for Davis, letter to Lowndes County citizens, November 22, 1850, 4: 145, 138–139, and speech in Jackson, Mississippi, September 23, 1848, 3: 376. On

Davis's somewhat touchy defense of Mississippi, see his remarks in the Senate, February 8, 1850, 4: 74, and his speech in Fayette, Mississippi, July 11, 1851, 4: 184–185, 212.

40. Ibid., Davis, speech in Holly Springs, Mississippi, October 25, 1849, 4: 49; remarks in Senate, May 6, 1850, 4: 99; speech in Senate, November 22, 1850, 4: 142–143; speech in Fayette, Mississippi, July 11, 1851, 4: 211.

41. W. Davis, *The Man and His Hour,* 213–216; see also correspondence related to campaign in *PJD:* Davis to Samuel A. Cartwright, September 23, 1851, 3: 234–235, and Reuben Davis to Jefferson Davis, [November 1851], 3: 232–233.

42. See *PJD* for Davis, speech in Jackson, Mississippi, September 23, 1848, 3: 382, and June 9, 1852, 4: 268; Davis to Barksdale and Jones, February 2, 1852, 4: 248. Davis was fairly typical in this for a Southerner of his time; see George C. Rable, *The Confederate Republic* (Chapel Hill: University of North Carolina Press, 1994), 9–12, and William Cooper, *Liberty and Slavery: Southern Politics to 1860* (New York: Knopf, 1983), 222. For Davis's appeal for Americans to rise above party, see his speech in Jackson, Mississippi, September 23, 1848, *PJD,* 4: 386.

43. Davis, speech in Senate, April 20, 1848, *PJD,* 3: 315.

44. Ibid., 3: 314–315.

45. Ibid., Davis, speech on Oregon bill, July 12, 1848, 3: 332.

46. See W. Davis, *The Man and His Hour,* 202–203.

47. Davis, speech in Senate, January 29, 1850, *PJD,* 4: 67.

48. Ibid., speech in Senate, March 14, 1850, 4: 87–90; speech, January 29, 1850, 4: 69; speech, May 15, 1850, 4: 107; see also Jefferson Davis, *The Rise and Fall of the Confederate Government,* 2 vols. (New York: Da Capo, 1990), 1: 9, 10.

49. Davis, speech in Senate, January 29, 1850, *PJD,* 4: 66–67; J. Davis, *Rise and Fall,* 1: 6–18.

50. Davis, speech in Senate, January 29, 1850, 4: 64, and speech in Raymond, Mississippi, October 26, 1850, 4: 136, both in *PJD.*

51. Ibid., Davis to Malcolm D. Haynes, August 18, 1849, 4: 40.

52. Ibid., Davis to Francis J. Lynch, February 27, 1850, 4: 84; Davis to Samuel A. Cartwright, June 10, 1849, 4: 23; speech in Senate, February 8, 1850, 4: 72.

53. Ibid., Davis to Charles J. Searles, December 20, 1849, 4: 53.

54. Ibid., Davis, speech in Raymond, Mississippi, September 22, 1848, 3: 374; speech in Fayette, Mississippi, July 11, 1851, 4: 185, 188, 194, 196.

55. Ibid., Davis, speech in Senate, March 14, 1850, 4: 88.

56. For good examples of this sense of the South as fearful and negative, see Cooper, *Liberty and Slavery,* 255; David L. Smiley, "The Quest for the Central Theme in Southern History," *South Atlantic Quarterly* 71 (summer 1972): 321; Freehling, *Road to Disunion,* esp. part 7; and Potter, *The Impending Crisis,* chap. 17.

57. Davis, speech in Senate, May 13, 1850, 4: 105; Davis to Malcolm D. Haynes, August 18, 1849, 4: 27, 30–32; speech in Senate, January 29, 1850, 4: 67; and speech in Jackson, Mississippi, May 7, 1849, 4: 20, all in *PJD.*

58. See Christopher J. Olsen, *Political Culture and Secession in Mississippi* (Cambridge, Mass.: Oxford University Press, 2000), 14–15 and passim.

59. Davis to Malcolm D. Haynes, August 18, 1849, *PJD,* 4: 31, 35.

60. Ibid., 4: 35; Davis to Malcolm D. Haynes, August 18, 1849, 4: 279–280; speech on Oregon bill, July 12, 1848, 4: 335.

61. Ibid., Davis, speech in Jackson, Mississippi, September 23, 1848, 3: 378–379; speech in Senate, April 20, 1848, 3: 315.

62. Ibid., Davis, speech in Senate, April 20, 1848, 3: 314; speech in Jackson, Mississippi, July 11, 1851, 4: 194–195, and June 9, 1852, 264.

63. Ibid., Davis to Malcolm D. Haynes, August 18, 1849, 4: 41; on the role of honor in secession politics, see Olsen, *Political Culture and Secession in Mississippi,* chaps. 2–3.

64. For a succinct rendering of Davis's critique of popular sovereignty, see *Rise and Fall of the Confederate Government,* 1: 25–36; on the complexities of Douglas's relationship with Southerners in general where these policies were concerned, see Freehling, *The Road to Disunion,* chaps. 30–31.

65. Speech in Senate, February 22, 1859, 6: 604, and May 17, 1860, 6: 296 and 336, both in *PJD.* On Davis's appeal to Douglas to withdraw from the nomination process in 1860, see W. Davis, *The Man and His Hour,* 283.

66. Many Southerners instinctively saw the party's division as a contest between Davis and Douglas; see letter from Collin S. Tarpley, October 1, 1858, in *PJD,* 6: 587.

67. Ibid., speech in Senate, May 17, 1860, 6: 336–337. The entire platform fight was in fact a political move on many Southern Democrats' part (including Davis) to hamstring Douglas's chances for the 1860 presidential nomination (see Johannsen, *Douglas,* 729–731).

68. Speech in Senate, February 22, 1859, *PJD,* 6: 604.

69. Ibid., speech in Senate, May 17, 1860, 6: 333, 336.

70. Ibid., Davis to John P. Hess, September 8, 1859, 6: 261.

71. Ibid., speech in Senate, May 17, 1860, 6: 334; Douglas's assertions are referred to at 6: 340.

72. For Davis's declaration that he bore Douglas no "personal animosity," see ibid., speech in Senate, December 19, 1859, 6: 622; on Davis's protestation of friendship, see 6: 331; on instances of their cooperation, see Douglas to Davis, June 24, 1854, and February 8, 1855, 5: 353, 407. For his part, Douglas would cite Davis when it suited his purposes; he even quoted Davis—calling him "that able and eloquent statesman"—during his debates with Lincoln see (*CW,* 3: 295).

9. Insurgents

1. Davis to John P. Heiss, September 8, 1859, and October 13, 1859, *PJD,* 6: 261, 263.

2. David M. Potter, *The Impending Crisis, 1848–1861* (New York: HarperCollins 1977), chap. 14; the first mention of Brown in Davis's correspondence was a letter related to Davis's participation in the investigation of Harpers Ferry (see Amos. A. Lawrence to Jefferson Davis, December 27, 1859, *PJD,* 6: 267–268).

3. Donald E. Fehrenbacher, *Prelude to Greatness* (New York: McGraw-Hill, 1962), chap. 7; Lincoln, speech in Leavenworth, Kansas, December 1, 1859, *CW*, 3: 496.

4. In a speech before the Senate, Davis declared, "I have some respect for a mere fanatic. If he is a mere fanatic, if his mind is absorbed with the idea of negrophilism, if he is sincere in struggling to overthrow the institutions of the South because he believes them to be a great wrong" (November 27, 1860, *JDC*, 4: 162). The speech contains references to Brown preceding this remark, but it is also possible Davis may have been referring to Caleb Cushing.

5. Jefferson Davis, *The Rise and Fall of the Confederate Government*, 2 vols. (New York: Da Capo Press, 1990), 1: 36.

6. Ibid., 1: 37.

7. Davis, speech in Senate, November 27, 1860, *JDC*, 4: 162.

8. Davis's newspaper statement mentioned in *PJD*, 6: 268n.

9. Davis, speech on the Harpers Ferry Resolutions, December 6, 1859, *JDC*, 4: 95.

10. Davis's actions in this regard are summarized in *PJD*, 6: 619–620.

11. Ibid., 6: 621.

12. Lincoln, speech in Leavenworth, Kansas, December 3, 1859, *CW*, 3: 502.

13. Ibid., second speech in Leavenworth, Kansas, December 5, 1859, 3: 503.

14. For reference to Brown as an "insurrectionist," see ibid., Lincoln's second Leavenworth speech, 3: 503, and for Brown as a sign of general decay, see the notes for a speech at Hartford, Connecticut, March 5, 1860, 4: 1.

15. Ibid., Lincoln, second speech in Leavenworth, 3: 503.

16. Ibid., speech in Hartford, Connecticut, March 5, 1860, 4:13.

17. Ibid., speech in Dover, New Hampshire, 3: 553.

18. Ibid., speech in Bloomington, Illinois, April 10, 1860, 4: 42.

19. Ibid., speech at Cooper Union, February 27, 1860, 3: 541–542.

20. See *PJD* for Davis to Malcolm D. Haynes, August 18, 1849, 4: 35; speech in Fayette, Mississippi, July 11, 1851, 6: 212; Davis to commissioners of Gulf and Ship Island Railroad, August 28, 1858, 6: 210–211.

21. J. Davis, *Rise and Fall*, 126.

22. See *PJD* for Davis, reply to Stephen A. Douglas, May 17, 1860, 6: 298, 317; Davis, reply to William H. Seward, February 29, 1860, 6: 281, 304, 336; remarks on the ten-regiment bill, January 3, 1848, 3: 354; letter to Lowndes County citizens, November 22, 1850, 4: 139; speech in Jackson, Mississippi, September 23, 1848, 4: 384; speech on Harbors and Rivers bill, March 16, 1846, 2: 510; remarks on Cumberland Island dam bill, April 14, 1848, 3: 296–297; and Davis, *Rise and Fall*, 1: 130, 143–144.

23. See *PJD* for Davis, speech in Philadelphia, July 12, 1853, 5: 29; Davis to William H. Bissell, February 14, 1854, 5: 57; Davis to John E. Wool, April 24, 1854, 5: 63–64.

24. Ibid., reply to William H. Seward, February 29, 1860, 6: 280.

25. Ibid., Davis to Malcolm D. Haynes, August 18, 1849, 4: 26; speech in Benton, Mississippi, November 22, 1850, 4: 143.

26. J. Davis, *Rise and Fall,* 1: 143–144; see speech in Portland, September 11, 1858, *PJD,* 6: 216, where he explicitly compared the commercial relations between the states to the laying of a telegraph line between the United States and Britain.

27. See *PJD* for Davis, speech in Portland, New Jersey, September 11, 1858, 6: 223; remarks on the New York resolutions, 4: 7; speech in Mississippi City, Mississippi, October 2, 1857, 6: 139.

28. Ibid., Davis's farewell address to the Senate, January 21, 1861, 7: 20; see also speech in Portland, Maine, September 11, 1858, 6: 214, where he referred to himself as an American citizen, then as a "stranger" in the North; Davis to William L. Ellsworth, June 5, 1856, 6: 25, reference to "best interests of the country," followed by recitation of sectional grievances; speech in Fayette, Mississippi, July 11, 1851, 4: 207, reference to service to United States, "heart beat for the Union," followed by statements of primary allegiance to Mississippi and the South; speech in Mississippi City, Mississippi, October 2, 1857, 6: 149, reference to "people of the United States," which he immediately breaks down into state and sectional interests; speech in Jackson, Mississippi, May 29, 1857, 6: 120–121, with references to "whole country," followed by devotion to Mississippi. He also sometimes referred to an American "people" when speaking of American relations with other countries; but even then sectional interests often crept into his perceptions of such foreign policy issues. See remarks on bill to protect rights of American settlers in Oregon, April 17, 1846, 2: 554; amendment and remarks on compromise bill, May 15, 1850, 4: 103; remarks on guano trade, March 29, 1860, 6: 144–146, 287.

29. Ibid., Davis, speech in Oxford, Mississippi, July 15, 1852, 4: 275–277, 283.

30. Ibid., speech in Jackson, May 29, 1857, 6: 124; reply to William H. Seward, February 29, 1860, 6: 283; Davis, reply to Stephen Douglas, May 17, 1860, 6: 311.

31. Ibid., Davis, speech in Jackson, Mississippi, September 23, 1848, 3: 381; speech on Oregon bill, July 12, 1848, 3: 352, 361–362. During a speaking tour in New England in summer 1848, Davis was greeted with warm applause and approval wherever he went and responded with profusely nationalistic speeches, declaring "the whole confederacy is my country . . . I love it all." Paul Escott has seen this as evidence of Davis's antebellum nationalism, arguing that he "became a fervid advocate of patriotism and national unity" (see *After Secession* [Baton Rouge: Louisiana State University Press, 1978], 7). But as the evidence just cited indicates, this burst of nationalist fervor was isolated and short-lived. It is significant that Davis did not expect to find anyone who thought like him at all; he wrote former president Franklin Pierce with surprise that "the difference is less than I supposed," indicating that he initially approached New England as if it were a strange and inhospitable environment (see Davis to Franklin Pierce, January 17, 1859, in *JDC,* 3: 498).

32. Davis to Arthur C. Halbert, August 28, 1858, *PJD,* 6: 205.

33. Ibid., Davis to Charles J. Searles, September 19, 1847, 3: 226.

34. Ibid., speech in Benton, Mississippi, November 2, 1850, 4: 137; Davis to Stephen Cocke, August 2, 1849, 4: 36; on Southern citizens, rights, and so on, see Davis to Francis J. Lynch, February 25, 1850, 4: 84; remarks on admission of California, March 14, 1850, 4: 87; reply to Lewis Cass, February 20, 1850, 4: 78; amend-

ments and remarks on compromise bill, May 15, 1850, 4: 105; Davis to Arthur C. Halbert, August 22, 1858, 6: 206; speech in Mississippi City, Mississippi, October 2, 1857, 6: 149; and remarks on admission of California, March 14, 1850, 4: 89.

35. Ibid., Davis, speech in Fayette, Mississippi, July 11, 1851, 4: 209; Davis, letter to Lowndes County, Mississippi, citizens, November 22, 1850, 4: 145; see also Davis's farewell address to the Senate, January 21, 1861, 7: 19, for statement that Mississippi's actions were paramount. At the same time, however, Davis strongly urged his state to refrain from secession if it could not do so as part of a united Southern front (see speech in Vicksburg, July 24, 1851, 4: 220).

36. Ibid., speech in Fayette, Mississippi, July 11, 1851, 4: 199; see also William Freehling, *The Road to Disunion* (New York: Oxford University Press, 1990), 6, who characterized Davis as "an expert on southern divisions."

37. Davis to Horatio J. Harris, April 17, 1851, 4: 178–179, and speech in Fayette, Mississippi, July 11, 1851, 4: 197, 205, both in *PJD*.

38. Ibid., Davis to Horatio J. Harris, April 17, 1851, 4: 179.

39. Ibid., speech in Benton, Mississippi, November 22, 1850, 4: 141; Davis to John P. Heiss, June 18, 1860, 6: 353; speech in Fayette, Mississippi, July 11, 1851, 4: 190; reply to Stephen Douglas, May 17, 1860, 6: 323. See also Davis, *Rise and Fall*, 1: 34. One might have expected Davis therefore to endorse Lewis Cass's "squatter sovereignty," in which the first ten thousand people to settle a territory, of whatever political persuasion, could form a state government and vote on slavery or freedom. Davis argued that this left the entire issue of sovereignty to the whims of chance, a foot race, as it were, between slave owners and non–slave owners who "without authority or law, have gathered together." Davis wanted a time of mature reflection, during which that "conglomerated mass" could form a community of sentiment, considering carefully what sort of character, slave or free, the community would acquire (Davis, reply to Lewis Cass, February 22, 1850, *PJD*, 4: 77–78).

40. See *PJD* for Davis's speech in Jackson, Mississippi, May 7, 1849, 4: 19; Davis to commissioners of the Gulf and Ship Island Railroad, August 26, 1858, 6: 211–212; Davis's farewell address to the Senate, January 21, 1861, 7: 18; and speech in Oxford, Mississippi, July 15, 1852, 4: 282. This need for unanimity was not unique to Davis; Southerners in general felt a need for total agreement on key issues, especially matters related to race and slavery (see, generally, Clement Eaton, *Freedom of Thought in the Old South* [Durham, N.C.: Duke University Press, 1940]).

41. Article from *Vicksburg Southern Intelligencer*, August 9, 1845, 2: 310, and Davis's remarks on state resources being transferred out of state; Davis to commissioners of the Gulf and Ship Island Railroad, August 28, 1858, 6: 209–210, all in *PJD*.

42. Ibid., Davis to William R. Gannon, January 8, 1850, 4: 55; speech in Fayette, Mississippi, July 11, 1851, 4: 187.

43. Cooper, *Jefferson Davis, American*, 237–239. 19,443.

44. Ibid., speech in Fayette, Mississippi, July 11, 1851, 4: 184; Davis to Patrick W. Tompkins, December 25, 1847, 3: 253.

45. Ibid., Davis to David L. Yulee, July 18, 1851, 4: 218; speech in Jackson, Mississippi, June 9, 1852, 4: 268; speech in Fayette, Mississippi, July 11, 1851, 4: 192.

46. The role of slavery as a unifying force for the white South has been postulated by many scholars; the two seminal works are Edmund S. Morgan, *American Slavery, American Freedom: The Ordeal of Colonial Virginia* (New York: W. W. Norton, 1975), and George M. Fredrickson, *The Black Image in the White Mind: The Debate on Afro-American Character and Destiny* (New York: Harper and Row, 1971).

47. Speech on Oregon bill, July 12, 1849, *PJD*, 3: 355, and William C. Davis, *Jefferson Davis: The Man and His Hour* (New York: HarperCollins, 1992), 80–81.

48. W. Davis, *The Man and His Hour*, 176–182; speech in Jackson, Mississippi, May 7, 1849, 4: 19, and speech in Senate, February 8, 1850, 4: 74–75, both in *PJD*.

49. Speech in Fayette, Mississippi, July 11, 1851, *PJD*, 4: 204.

50. Ibid., speech in Jackson, Mississippi, November 4, 1857, 6: 162; speech in Corinth, Mississippi, September 21, 1860, 6: 365; J. Davis, *Rise and Fall*, 1: 120, 129.

51. J. Davis, *Rise and Fall*, 1: xxvii, 121, and W. Davis, *The Man and His Hour*, 82.

52. Davis, speech in Portland, September 11, 1858, 6: 220, and on Oregon bill, July 12, 1848, 3: 341, both in *PJD*; see also Davis's speech in *JDC*, 3: 99.

53. J. Davis, *Rise and Fall*, 1: 67; resolutions on the relations of the states, February 2, 1860, *PJD*, 6: 273.

54. Davis, speech in Senate, January 10, 1861, *JDC*, 5: 24; see also *PJD* for speech in Fayette, Mississippi, July 11, 1851, 4: 213, and Davis to Lowndes County citizens, November 22, 1850, 4: 138, 140.

55. Varina Davis, *Jefferson Davis: A Memoir by His Wife*, 2 vols. (Baltimore: Nautical and Aviation Company, 1990), 1: 231.

56. Davis to George Lunt, January 17, 1861, *PJD*, 7: 14; W. Davis, *The Man and His Hour*, 276.

57. Lincoln, speech in Indianapolis, Indiana, February 11, 1861, *CW*, 4: 196.

10. Presidents

1. See Jean Baker, *Mary Todd Lincoln* (New York: W. W. Norton, 1987), 165–166; see also David Donald, *Lincoln* (New York: Simon and Schuster, 1995), 270–272.

2. Elizabeth Keckley, *Behind the Scenes; or, Thirty Years as a Slave, and Four in the White House* (Buffalo, N.Y.: Stansill and Lee, 1931), 82–83.

3. Ibid., 66–67.

4. Ibid., 70–71.

5. See, generally, Ira Berlin, *Slaves Without Masters: The Free Negro in the Antebellum South* (New York: New Press, 1992).

6. Davis to George Lunt, January 17, 1861, *PJD*, 7: 14.

7. Keckley, *Behind the Scenes*, 79.

8. See, generally, Donald, *Lincoln*, 282–283; see also Ward Hill Lamon, *Recollections of Abraham Lincoln, 1847–1865* (1895; reprint, Lincoln: University of Nebraska Press, 1994), 53–54.

9. See James Thomas Flexner, *George Washington and the New Nation, 1783–1793* (Boston: Little, Brown, 1969), 173–181.

10. Ibid., 174; compare Washington's speech here with Lincoln's farewell address (see Lincoln, farewell address, February 11, 1861, *CW,* 4: 190–191).

11. On the distance and days, see Donald, *Lincoln,* 273.

12. Lamon, *Recollections of Abraham Lincoln,* 34.

13. Lincoln, speech in Poughkeepsie, New York, February 19, 1861, *CW,* 4: 228.

14. Ibid., remarks in Painesville, Ohio, February 1861, 4: 218; remarks in Westfield, New York, February 16, 1861, 4: 219; on his general concern with his physical appearance, see Lincoln to James F. Babcock, September 13, 1860, 4: 114, and Samuel R. Weed, "Hearing the Returns with Mr. Lincoln," *New York Times Magazine,* February 14, 1932 (Lincoln Museum Newspaper Collection, Fort Wayne, Indiana).

15. See *CW* for Lincoln to Zachariah Chandler, August 31, 1860, 4: 102–103; Lincoln to George G. Fogg, August 14, 1860, 4: 94 (emphases in original); Lincoln to George Bliss and others, August 22, 1860, 4: 99.

16. Ibid., Lincoln, speech in Poughkeepsie, New York, February 19, 1861, 4: 228; see also remarks at Republican rally in Springfield, Illinois, August 8, 1860, 4: 91; speech in Buffalo, New York, 4: 220; reply to mayor of Philadelphia, February 21, 1861, 4: 238; remarks in Jersey City, New Jersey, February 21, 1861, 4: 233.

17. Ibid., Lincoln to Thurlow Weed, February 4, 1861, 4: 185.

18. Lamon, *Recollections of Abraham Lincoln,* 33; see *CW* for address to the Pennsylvania General Assembly, February 22, 1861, 4: 245; speech in Pittsburgh, Pennsylvania, February 15, 1861, 4: 210–211; see also speech in Buffalo, New York, February 18, 1861, 4: 221; address to the state legislature of New York, February 18, 1861, 4: 226.

19. Michael Burlingame and John R. Turner Ettlinger, eds., *Inside Lincoln's White House: The Complete Civil War Diary of John Hay* (Carbondale: Southern Illinois University Press, 1997), 11 ("shut pan" remark at 241); see also A. K. McClure, *Abraham Lincoln and Men of War Times* (Lincoln: University of Nebraska Press, 1996), 77; McClure also recorded Lincoln's reference to being "shut pan" (see 78).

20. Lincoln to George D. Prentice, October 29, 1860, 4: 135, and Lincoln to Oliver P. Morton, September 29, 1861, 4: 541, both in *CW.*

21. Ibid., Lincoln to Abraham Jonas, July 21, 1860, 4: 86; see also Lincoln's worries about appearing weak to the South; Lincoln to George T. M. Davis, October 27, 1860, 4: 133; Lincoln to Simon Cameron, January 13, 1861, 4: 174–175; Lincoln to Nathaniel P. Paschall, November 16, 1860, 4: 140; Lincoln to Truman Smith, November 10, 1860, 4: 138.

22. Ibid., Lincoln to Lyman Trumbull, April 29, 1860, 4: 46; Lincoln to John Hanks, August 24, 1860, 4: 100; Lincoln to John Coulter, September 4, 1860, 4: 109; Lincoln to Hannibal Hamlin, September 4, 1860, 4: 110.

23. Ibid., Lincoln to Samuel Haycraft, June 4, 1860, 4: 69–70.

24. Ibid., memorandum on Fort Sumter, March 18, 1861, 4: 289; first inaugural address, March 4, 1861, 4: 250, 256; reply to Andrew J. Curtin, February 22, 1861, 4: 243; reply to Mayor James G. Berret, February 27, 1861, 4: 246; Lincoln to

L. Montgomery Bond, October 15, 1860, 4: 128; message to Congress, July 4, 1861, 4: 432–433; speech in Philadelphia, February 22, 1861, 4: 241.

25. Ibid., Lincoln, speech in Pittsburgh, Pennsylvania, February 15, 1861, 4: 210; speech before Ohio legislature, February 13, 1861, 4: 204; speech in Cincinnati, Ohio, February 12, 1861, 4: 199; see also speech at the Astor house, New York, February 19, 1861, 4: 230; and reply to Mayor Alexander Henry of Philadelphia, February 21, 1861, 4: 238.

26. Lincoln, remarks in Springfield, Illinois, November 20, 1860, 4: 143; speech at Independence Hall, Philadelphia, February 22, 1861, 4: 241; reply to Governor Andrew J. Curtin, Harrisburg, Pennsylvania, February 22, 1861, 4: 243; speech in Cincinnati, Ohio, February 13, 1861, 4: 199; address to Pennsylvania General Assembly, February 22, 1861, 4: 244; speech in Columbus, Ohio, February 13, 1861, 4: 205; speech in Pittsburgh, Pennsylvania, February 15, 1861, 4: 211; speech before the New York legislature, February 18, 1861, 4: 226; see also appeals for patience in the first inaugural address, March 4, 1861, 4: 260–261; keeping national "composure" in speech in Buffalo, New York, February 18, 1861, 4: 221; and reference to his own "sincere heart" in his reply to Mayor Alexander Henry of Philadelphia, February 21, 1861, 4: 238.

27. Ibid., Lincoln, reply to New York delegation, March 4, 1861, 4: 272; speech in Pittsburgh, Pennsylvania, February 15, 1861, 4: 210; speech at Independence Hall, Philadelphia, February 22, 1861, 4: 240–241; see also speech in Indianapolis, February 11, 1861, 4: 193.

28. Ibid., Lincoln, reply to Massachusetts delegation, March 5, 1861, 4: 274.

29. Ibid., Lincoln, first inaugural address, March 4, 1861, 4: 270–271.

30. Davis to Alexander M. Clayton, January 30, 1861, PJD, 7: 27, and to Edwin De Leon, January 8, 1861, 7: 6.

31. See, e.g., his statement that he would stand with Mississippi "for good or for evil," in speech to U.S. Congress, January 10, 1861, JDC, 5: 34.

32. Davis to Edwin De Leon, January 8, 1861, PJD, 7: 6; speech to U.S. Congress, January 10, 1861, JDC, 5: 1–35; see PJD for Davis to Joseph Holt, January 19, 1861, 7: 16; Joseph E. Johnston to Jefferson Davis, January 16, 1861, 7: 14; Library of Congress loan record, January 1861, 7: 30–31; see also Jefferson Davis, The Rise and Fall of the Confederate Government, 2 vols. (New York: Da Capo, 1990), 1: 189.

33. Davis to Franklin Pierce, January 20, 1861, PJD, 7: 17, and to Clement C. Clay, January 19, 1861, 7: 16.

34. Ibid., Joseph E. Davis to Jefferson Davis, January 2, 1861, 7: 3; Davis to Francis W. Pickens, January 13, 1861, 7: 10; Varina Davis, Jefferson Davis: A Memoir by His Wife, 2 vols. (Baltimore: Nautical and Aviation Company, 1990), 1: 696.

35. V. Davis, Memoir, 1: 696–697.

36. Davis, farewell address, Senate, January 21, 1861, PJD, 6: 21.

37. Ibid., 6: 22.

38. Speech in Columbia, South Carolina, October 6, 1864, JDC, 6: 350.

39. Davis to John F. Callan, February 7, 1861, PJD, 7: 35; for an account of the events in Montgomery, see William C. Davis, "A Government of Our Own": The Making of the Confederacy (New York: Free Press, 1994).

40. Davis, *Rise and Fall,* 1: 197.

41. Davis to Alexander M. Clayton, January 30, 1861, *PJD,* 7: 28.

42. Ibid., Davis to John F. Callan, February 7, 1861, 7: 35.

43. On the role of republicanism in Southern political culture, see George C. Rable, *The Confederate Republic: A Revolution Against Politics* (Chapel Hill: University of North Carolina Press, 1994), esp. chap. 1, and Drew Gilpin Faust, *The Creation of Confederate Nationalism: Ideology and Identity in the Civil War South* (Baton Rouge: Louisiana State University Press, 1988), 30–32.

44. V. Davis, *Memoir,* 2; 19; J. Davis, *Rise and Fall,* 2: 203–206; see also speech in Vicksburg, Mississippi, February 11, 1861, *PJD,* 7: 38.

45. W. Davis, *"A Government of Our Own,"* 55, 94–97, 98–102 and passim; W. Davis, *The Man and His Hour,* 302–305.

46. V. Davis, *Memoir,* 2: 22.

47. W. Davis made an estimate of the number (*The Man and His Hour,* 305).

48. Davis to Varina Howell Davis, February 14, 1861, *PJD,* 7: 40; J. Davis, *Rise and Fall,* 1: 198.

49. Davis speech in Stevenson, Alabama, February 14, 1861, 7: 42 (emphasis in original) and speech in Jackson, Mississippi, January 11, 1861, 7: 38, both in *PJD.*

50. W. Davis, *The Man and His Hour,* 304–305.

51. Davis, speech in Montgomery, Alabama, February 16, 1861, *PJD,* 7: 45.

52. Ibid., speech in Montgomery, Alabama, February 16, 1861, 7: 45; speech in Cartersville, Georgia, February 15, 1861, 7: 42; speech in Atlanta, Georgia, February 16, 1861, 7: 43–44.

53. W. Davis, *"A Government of Our Own,"* 160–162; Manly quote at 162.

54. Davis, inaugural address, February 18, 1861, *PJD,* 7: 50.

55. Lincoln, inaugural address, March 4, 1861, *CW,* 4: 271.

11. Faiths

1. Lydia Smith to Abraham Lincoln, October 4, 1862, in *Dear Mr. Lincoln: Letters to the President,* ed. Harold M. Holzer (Reading, Mass.: Addison-Wesley, 1993), 343–344.

2. William Stearns to Lincoln, September 3, 1862 (emphasis in original); Samuel Galloway to Lincoln, September 4, 1862; William W. Weeks to Lincoln, September 4, 1862; resolutions of the New Hampshire General Assembly of Congregational and Presbyterian ministers, September 5, 1862; William De Love to Lincoln, September 5, 1862; Samuel Shellabarger to Lincoln, September 5, 1862; Alexander Ramsey to Lincoln, September 6, 1862; J. W. Chaffin to Lincoln, September 6, 1862; Francis Thomas to Lincoln, September 6, 1862; all in Abraham Lincoln Papers, Library of Congress (reel 41).

3. Ibid., Francis Thomas to Lincoln, September 6, 1862; anonymous to Lincoln, December [?] 1862, in Holzer, ed., *Dear Mr. Lincoln,* 56.

4. Lincoln to Carl Schurz, November 24, 1862, *CW,* 5: 509–510.

5. Ibid., remarks to delegation of Progressive Friends, June 20, 1862, 5: 278–279.

6. Ibid., remarks to Chicago delegation, September 13, 1862, 420 (emphases in original).

7. Davis to John Forsyth, July 18, 1862, *PJD,* 8: 293, 295.

8. Ibid., Gazaway Bugg Lamar to Jefferson Davis, September 5, 1862, 8: 377; Duff Green to Jefferson Davis, September 6, 1862, 8: 378; petition from Canton, Mississippi, citizens, September 7, 1862, 8: 382.

9. Ibid., Davis, speech in Mobile, Alabama, December 30, 1862, 8: 588; Davis to Canton, Mississippi, citizens, September 8, 1862, 8: 382; Davis, message to Congress, August 18, 1862, *JDC,* 5: 321; speech in Jackson, Mississippi, December 26, 1862, *PJD,* 8: 575.

10. See PJD for Davis, speech in Mobile, Alabama, December 30, 1862, 8: 588; speech in Macon, Georgia, October 10, 1862, 10: 43; speech in Jackson, Mississippi, December 26, 1862, 8: 574, 579; see also speech at Missionary Ridge, October 9, 1863, 10: 21.

11. On Lincoln's early religious background, see Allen C. Guelzo, *Abraham Lincoln: Redeemer President* (Grand Rapids, Mich.: William B. Eerdman's, 1999), 36–39; story written for Noah Brooks, December 6, 1864, *CW,* 8: 155; "Preachers" quote in Ward Hill Lamon, *Recollections of Abraham Lincoln, 1847–1865* (Lincoln: University of Nebraska Press, 1994), 94; A. K. McClure, *Abraham Lincoln and Men of War Times* (Lincoln: University of Nebraska Press, 1996), 101; Lincoln, reply to Baltimore Presbyterian Synod, October 24, 1863, *CW,* 6: 535.

12. Lincoln handbill replying to charges of infidelity, July 31, 1846, *CW,* 1: 382.

13. See, e.g., Elton Trueblood, *Abraham Lincoln: Theologian of American Anguish* (New York: Harper and Row, 1973), 14–17; Richard N. Current, *The Lincoln Nobody Knows,* 2d ed. (New York: Greenwood, 1980), chap. 3; Earl C. Kubicek, "Abraham Lincoln's Faith," *Lincoln Herald* 85 (fall 1983): 188–190: W. Emerson Reck, "Mr. Lincoln's Growth in Faith," *Lincoln Herald* 92 (spring 1990): 6–11.

14. Trueblood, *Theologian of American Anguish,* chap. 3.

15. Guelzo, sees Lincoln's use of biblical quotations as "more a cultural habit than a personal one" (*Redeemer President,* 193, 313).

16. See James H. Moorhead, *American Apocalypse: Yankee Protestants and the Civil War* (New Haven: Yale University Press, 1978); Phillip Shaw Paludan, "Religion and the American Civil War," and George M. Fredrickson, "The Coming of the Lord: The Northern Protestant Clergy and the Civil War Crisis," in *Religion and the American Civil War,* ed. Randall M. Miller, Harry S. Stout, and Charles Reagan Wilson (New York: Oxford University Press, 1998), 21–42, 110–130.

17. Trueblood, *Theologian of American Anguish,* 73–74; Michael Burlingame, ed., *Lincoln Observed: Civil War Dispatches of Noah Brooks* (Baltimore: Johns Hopkins University Press, 1998), 13.

18. Lamon, *Recollections of Abraham Lincoln,* 91.

19. See *CW* for Lincoln to Alexander Reed, February 22, 1863, 6: 114; see also reply to members of the Presbyterian General Assembly, June 2, 1863, 6: 245; reply

to Baltimore Presbyterian Synod, October 24, 1863, 6: 535–536; reply to delegation of Baptists, May 28, 1864, 7: 365; response to Methodists, May 18, 1864, 7: 350–351; and Lincoln to George B. Ide, James R. Doolittle, and A. Hubbell, May 30, 1864, 7: 368. On the other hand, Lincoln found annoying any sectarian competition in ministering to wartime needs (see Lincoln to Edwin M. Stanton, September 29, 1862, 5: 445).

20. Guelzo, *Redeemer President,* 372–373.

21. See *CW* for Lincoln to I. A. Gere, A. A. Reese, and George D. Chenowith, May 15, 1862, 5: 215; Lincoln "to the Friends of Union and Liberty," May 9, 1864, 7: 333; reply to members of the Presbyterian General Assembly, June 2, 1863, 6: 246.

22. Ibid., proclamation of thanksgiving and prayer, July 15, 1863, 6: 332; proclamation of thanksgiving, October 3, 1863, 6: 497; see also proclamation of national fast day, August 12, 1861, 4: 482; and David R. Murph, "Abraham Lincoln and Divine Providence," *Lincoln Herald* 73 (spring 1971): 8–13.

23. On the relationship between God, emancipation, and the war, see Kenneth W. Stampp, "One Alone? The United States and National Self-Determination," in *Lincoln the War President: The Gettysburg Lectures,* ed. Gabor S. Boritt (Cambridge, Mass.: Oxford University Press, 1992), 140–141, and Guelzo, *Redeemer President,* 336.

24. Lamon, *Recollections of Abraham Lincoln,* 90.

25. Lincoln to George B. Ide, James R. Doolittle, and A. Hubbell, May 30, 1864, *CW,* 7: 368.

26. Ibid., 7: 368; these words echo his more famous pronouncement of forbearance ten months later in the second inaugural address.

27. Ibid., proclamation of a day of prayer, July 7, 1864, 7: 431–432.

28. Ibid., 7: 431; response to Evangelical Lutherans, May 13, 1862, 5: 212–213.

29. Ibid., proclamation appointing a national fast day, March 30, 1863, 6: 156.

30. Ibid., Lincoln to James Conkling, August 26, 1863, 6: 410; remarks to New School Presbyterians, October 22, 1863, 6: 531.

31. Ibid., Lincoln, meditation on divine will, September 2, 1862, 5: 403–404.

32. Ibid., Lincoln to Eliza P. Gurney, September 4, 1864, 7: 535; see also remarks to her in earlier interview, October 26, 1862, 5: 478, and similiar phrase in his message to Congress, December 1, 1862, 5: 518; response to serenade, September 24, 1862, 5: 438; see also reply to Chicago delegation of Christians, September 13, 1862, 5: 419–421.

33. Ibid., Lincoln to Caleb Russell and Sallie A. Fenton, January 5, 1863, 6: 39–40; proclamation of thanksgiving, October 20, 1864, 8: 55.

34. On the connection between God, nation, and the Civil War, see Frank Klement's thoughtful essay, "Nationalism and the Writing of Civil War History," in *Lincoln's Critics: The Copperheads of the North,* ed. Steven K. Rogstad (Shippensburg, Pa.: White Mane Books, 1999), 165–167.

35. Guelzo, *Redeemer President,* 328, 398.

36. Clement Eaton, *Jefferson Davis* (New York: Free Press, 1977), 14; Varina believed Davis had a personal affinity for Catholicism, due to his early education at a

Catholic school; see Varina Davis, *Jefferson Davis: A Memoir by His Wife,* 2 vols. (Baltimore: Nautical and Aviation Company, 1990), 2: 445.

37. See Drew Gilpin Faust, *The Creation of Confederate Nationalism* (Baton Rouge: Louisiana State University Press, 1988), 22–34; Gardiner H. Shattuck Jr., *A Shield and a Hiding Place: The Religious Life of Civil War Armies* (Macon, Ga.: Mercer University Press, 1987); Mark E. Neely Jr., *Southern Rights: Political Prisoners and the Myth of Confederate Constitutionalism* (Charlottesville: University Press of Virginia, 2000).

38. Arthur H. Edey to Jefferson Davis, March 6, 1865, *JDC,* 6: 504–506; John B. Jones, *A Rebel War Clerk's Diary,* 2 vols. (Philadelphia: J. B. Lippincott, 1866), 1: 104, quote; Davis to J. R. Graves, December 26, 1861, *PJD,* 7: 444; proclamation of fasting and prayer, in CSA *Messages,* 1: 103–104 (for public gossip about Davis's religious views, see 120); an account of his baptism may be found in V. Davis, *Memoir,* 2: 269, and in Hudson Strode, *Jefferson Davis,* 3 vols. (New York: Harcourt, Brace and World, 1959), 2: 243.

39. Davis to J. W. C. Watson, March 8, 1865, *JDC,* 6: 512.

40. For examples, see Lincoln's order for Sabbath observance, November 15, 1862, *CW,* 5: 497.

41. See *PJD* for Davis, speech in Savannah, Georgia, October 31, 1863, 10: 44; Davis to Varina Howell Davis, June 2, 1862, 8: 210; Davis to Earl Van Dorn, May 20, 1862, 8: 193; see also inaugural address, February 18, 1861, 7: 48; Davis to Congress, April 29, 1861, *JDC,* 5: 84; and V. Davis, *Memoir,* 2: 373.

42. See *PJD* for Davis to Joseph Davis, May 7, 1863, 9: 167; Davis to William Stamps, July 5, 1862, 8: 278; speech in Richmond, Virginia, July 23, 1861, 7: 260; and message to Congress, May 2, 1864, 10: 383.

43. Davis message to Congress, November 7, 1864, *JDC,* 6: 384.

44. Ibid., Davis to Edmund Kirby Smith, December 24, 1864, 6: 428.

45. V. Davis, *Memoir,* 2: 493; see *PJD* for Davis, inaugural address, February 18, 1861, 7: 47; interview with William H. Russell, May 7, 1861, 7: 154; and message to Congress, November 18, 1861, 7: 419.

46. Davis to T. H. Watts, September 18, 1863, *JDC,* 6: 41; see *PJD* for Davis to Robert W. Johnson, July 14, 1863, 9: 277; Davis to Varina Howell Davis, June 2, 1862, 8: 209; speech in Savannah, Georgia, October 31, 1863, 10: 44; and Davis to Charles Todd Quintard, June 5, 1864, 10: 449; Davis to George W. Jones, January 20, 1861, *JDC,* 5: 39.

47. I have found only one instance of Davis's appealing to an inscrutable deity; see *PJD,* Davis to Robert W. Johnson, July 14, 1863, 9: 276; on his child's illness, see Davis to Varina Howell Davis, June 13, 1862, 8: 243; and Davis to Varina Howell Davis, June 2, 1863, 8: 210.

48. Ibid., Davis to Narcissa Smith Barksdale, July 24, 1863, 9: 304; Davis to Robert E. Lee, July 28, 1863, 9: 308; Davis to Eliza Cannon, July 18, 1863, 9: 287.

49. See *CW* for Lincoln, reply to notification committee, March 1, 1865, 8: 326, and Lincoln to Thomas W. Conway, March 1, 1865, 8: 325.

50. Lincoln, second inaugural address, March 4, 1865, *CW,* 8; 333 (emphasis added).

51. Jefferson Davis, *The Rise and Fall of the Confederate Government,* 2 vols. (New York: Da Capo, 1990), 2: 574.

12. Wars

1. Lincoln, remarks to citizens of Gettysburg, Pennsylvania, November 18, 1863, *CW,* 7: 17; see also, generally, Garry Wills, *Lincoln at Gettysburg: The Words That Remade America* (New York: Simon and Schuster, 1992), and Harold Holzer, "Lincoln's 'Flat Failure': The Gettysburg Myth Revisited," in Holzer, *Lincoln Seen and Heard* (Lawrence: University Press of Kansas, 2000), 191–198. For the central role of funeral rituals in national identity, see Benedict Anderson, *Imagined Communities: Reflections on the Origin and Spread of Nationalism,* rev. ed. (London: Verso Press, 1991).
2. Davis to Charles Clark, November 19, 1863, in U.S. Government, *War of the Rebellion: A Compilation of the Official Records of the Union and Confederate Armies,* 127 vols. (Washington, D.C.: Government Printing Office, 1880–1901), ser. 1, vol. 31, pt. 3, 763, (hereinafter *OR*).
3. See Davis to Robert E. Lee, July 21, 1863, *PJD,* 10: 294–295.
4. Davis, message to Congress, December 7, 1863, *OR,* 4, 2: 1025.
5. On these points, see, generally, Wills, *Lincoln at Gettysburg,* chap. 1 and passim; Phillip S. Paludan, *"The Better Angels of Our Nature": Lincoln, Propaganda and Public Opinion During the American Civil War,* Fifteenth Annual R. Gerald McMurtry Lecture (Fort Wayne: Lincoln Musuem, 1992).
6. Wills, *Lincoln at Gettysburg,* 177.
7. On the various issues of the Gettysburg Address and its meaning, see ibid., esp. chap. 3; James McPherson, "How Lincoln Won the War with Metaphors," in *Abraham Lincoln and the Second American Revolution* (New York: Oxford University Press, 1990), 110–112; Stephen Oates, "The Man for our Redemption," in *Abraham Lincoln: The Man Behind the Myths* (New York: HarperCollins, 1984), 114; Joseph R. Fornieri, "Abraham Lincoln and the Declaration of Independence," in *Abraham Lincoln: Sources and Style of Leadership,* ed. Frank J. Williams (New York: Greenwood Press, 1994), 45–70.
8. See *PJD* for Davis, address to Congress, November 18, 1861, 7: 413; Davis, speech in Jackson, Mississippi, 8: 566, 573; Davis to Zebulon Vance, January 8, 1864, 10: 161.
9. Gettysburg Address, November 19, 1863, *CW,* 6: 23; Allen C. Guelzo makes a somewhat similiar point—at least in terms of Lincoln's basic uncertainty in the address—see *Abraham Lincoln: Redeemer President* (Grand Rapids, Mich.: William B. Eerdman's, 1999), 371–372.
10. Davis, speech in Richmond, Virginia, June 1, 1861, 7: 184, and address to Congress, November 18, 1861, 7: 419, both in *PJD;* see also speech in Augusta, Georgia, October 10, 1864, *JDC,* 6: 357.
11. McPherson, *Abraham Lincoln and the Second American Revolution,* 112; see also Guelzo, *Redeemer President,* 454.

12. See Wills, *Lincoln at Gettysburg,* 32–36 and passim.

13. *Charleston Mercury,* October 13, 1863; see also reporter's description of a typical motivational speech by Davis in *JDC,* 6: 75; on the beneficial effects of Davis's troop reviews, see Steven E. Woodworth, *Davis and Lee at War* (Lawrence: University Press of Kansas, 1995), 67.

14. On Lincoln's antiwar leanings, particularly before 1860, see Gabor S. Boritt, "War Opponent and War President," in *Lincoln the War President: The Gettysburg Lectures* (Cambridge, Mass.: Oxford University Press, 1992), 179–211; see *CW* for Lincoln, speech in Cleveland, Ohio, 5: 216 (emphases in original); speech in New York, 4: 227; speech in Pittsburgh, Pennsylvania, 4: 211; and message to Congress, December 3, 1861, 5: 35–53. See also David Donald, *Lincoln* (New York: Simon and Schuster, 1995), 275–277, and Joseph George Jr., "Philadelphia's *Catholic Herald* Encounters President Lincoln," *Lincoln Herald* (fall 1980): 448–449.

15. See *PJD* for Davis to Alexander M. Clayton, January 30, 1861, 7: 28; Davis to Francis W. Pickens, February 20, 1861, 7: 55; speech in Jackson, Mississippi, December 26, 1862, 8: 566 and 575; see also Davis's rather apocalyptic early views of the war in letter to John A. Campbell, 7: 92. See also Robert V. Bruce, "The Shadow of a Coming War," in Boritt, ed., *Lincoln the War President,* 27–28.

16. Varina Davis, *Jefferson Davis: A Memoir by His Wife,* 2 vols. (Baltimore: Nautical and Aviation Company, 1990), 2: 9,18; see *PJD* for John J. Pettus to Jefferson Davis, January 23, 1861, 7: 27; on Davis's desire for a military commission, see letter to William M. Brooks, March 15, 1862, 8: 102; see also Davis to Alexander M. Clayton, January 30, 1861, 7: 27–28.

17. V. Davis, *Memoir,* 2: 397; see also Woodworth, *Davis and Lee,* 63.

18. James D. Richardson, ed., *Messages and Papers of the Confederacy,* 2d ed., 2 vols. (New York: Chelsea House–R. Rector, 1966), 1: 215–216; Davis to Joseph E. Johnston, August 13, 1861, *PJD,* 7: 282; V. Davis, *Memoir,* 2: 284, 317, 498; Davis to Braxton Bragg, April 3, 1861, *PJD,* 7: 86; on his love of military company, see Woodworth, *Davis and Lee,* 67. Anne J. Bailey, *The Chessboard of War: Sherman and Hood in the Autumn Campaigns of 1864* (Lincoln: University of Nebraska Press, 2000), 174, makes the point that Davis made most strategic decisions alone by 1864.

19. Davis, speech in House of Representatives, February 6, 1846, 2: 439, and speech in Wilmington, North Carolina, 10: 50, both in *PJD;* V. Davis, *Memoir,* 2: 10; see also interview with Arthur J. Fremantle, June 17, 1863, in *PJD,* 9: 229, in which Davis vividly describes the horrors of war.

20. See *PJD* for Davis, speech in Jackson, Mississippi, December 26, 1862, 8: 576; interview with Lord Russell, May 7, 1861, 7: 153–154; and speech in Jackson, Mississippi, December 26, 1863, 8: 575–576.

21. Ibid., Davis, message to Congress, May 2, 1864, 10: 379; Davis to Reuben Davis, July 20, 1863, 9: 291; speech in Savannah, Georgia, November 2, 1863, 10: 44; speech in Wilmington, North Carolina, 10: 50; see also speech in Richmond, Virginia, July 23, 1861, 7: 662, speech in Charleston, South Carolina, November 3, 1863, *JDC,* 6: 77; and reference to war's "role of honor" in letter to Eliza Cannon, July 18, 1863, *PJD,* 9: 287.

22. See *PJD* for Davis, speech in Macon, Georgia, October 30, 1863, 10: 43; speech in Richmond, Virginia, January 5, 1863, 9: 14; message to Congress, May 2, 1864, 10: 380; speech in Richmond, June 1, 1861, 7: 184; speech in Savannah, Georgia, October 31, 1863, 10: 44.

23. Ibid., Davis, speech in Selma, Alabama, October 17, 1863, 10: 29; speech in Mobile, Alabama, October 24, 1863, 10: 33 (emphasis in original); for other examples of his fascination with flags, see Davis to Samuel Cooper, July 21, 1861, 7: 259; Davis to Robert E. Lee, September 28, 1862, 8: 409; speech in Richmond, Virginia, March 16, 1864, 10: 281; V. Davis, *Memoir,* 2: 382; speech in Demopolis, Alabama, October 18, 1863, *PJD,* 9: 29.

24. Woodworth, *Davis and Lee,* 65; Guelzo, *Redeemer President,* 273; I am here referring particularly to Lincoln's lack of understanding evinced for the Army of the Potomac following the Gettysburg campaign; for his reaction to their "slowness," see Michael Burlingame and John R. Turner Ettlinger, eds., *Inside Lincoln's White House* (Carbondale: Southern Illinois University Press, 1997), 62.

25. See *CW* for examples of this deferential tone; Lincoln to David Hunter, October 24, 1861, 5: 1; Lincoln to Joseph Hooker, June 5, 1863, 6: 249; Lincoln to William S. Rosecrans, February 17, 1863, 6: 109; Lincoln to Lorenzo Thomas, July 8, 1863, 6: 322; Lincoln to Edwin D. Morgan, May 20, 1861, 4: 375; Lincoln to George B. McClellan, July 4, 1862, 5: 306; Lincoln to Agenor-Etienne de Gasparin, August 4, 1862, 5: 355; Lincoln to Don C. Buell, January 6, 1862, 5: 91; see also Burlingame and Ettlinger, eds., *Inside Lincoln's White House,* 191.

26. See *CW* for Lincoln to Gideon Welles, December 5, 1861, 5: 59; for other examples, see Lincoln to Joseph R. Smith, October 6, 1862, 5: 451; Lincoln to Edwin M. Stanton, September 29, 1862, 5: 446; Lincoln to Henry W. Halleck, January 7, 1863, 5: 43; Lincoln to John F. Lee, 5: 116; Lincoln to Winfield Scott, June 18, 1861, 4: 411.

27. Ibid., Lincoln to Charles D. Drake and others, October 5, 1863, 6: 500.

28. Ibid., Lincoln, proclamation of thanksgiving for victories, April 10, 1862, 5: 186; Lincoln to I. A. Gere et al., 5: 216; reply to Joseph Bertinatti, July 30, 1864, 7: 473; order for observance of the death of Martin Van Buren, July 25, 1862, 340; Lincoln to Eliza P. Gurney, October 26, 1862, 5: 478; call for new volunteers, July 1, 1862, 5: 297; Lincoln to John E. Bouligny, April 14, 1863, 6: 172; Lincoln to Thomas H. Clay, October 8, 1862, 5: 452; Lincoln, message to Congress, December 1, 1862, 5: 519; message to Congress, December 8, 1863, 7: 41; Davis to Earl Van Dorn, May 20, 1862, *PJD,* 8: 193. For other examples, see also Lincoln's reply to Notification Committee, March 1, 1865, 8: 326; Lincoln to Matthew Birchard and others, June 29, 1863, 6: 301; Lincoln, proclamation of thanksgiving, July 15, 1863, 6: 332; Lincoln, remarks to Baltimore Presbyterian Synod, October 24, 1863, 6: 535; Lincoln to Augustus W. Bradford, November 2, 1863, 6: 557; Lincoln to John P. Usher, August 24, 1863, 6: 405. See also Michael Burlingame, ed., *Lincoln Observed* (Baltimore: Johns Hopkins University Press, 1998), 43. There were times when Davis referred to war in negative terms (see, e.g., Davis to John Forsyth, July 18, 1864, *PJD,* 8: 293).

29. See *CW* for Lincoln, opinion on the draft, September 14, 1863, 6: 447; proclamation of thanksgiving, July 15, 1863, 6: 332; Lincoln, endorsement concerning Henry Andrews, January 7, 1864, 7: 111. I have found only two references by Lincoln to the patriotic qualities of flags; see speech at Dunkirk, New York, February 16, 1861, 4: 220, and Lincoln to Mrs. Hutter, Miss Lager, and Miss Claghorn, August 10, 1863, 6: 375.

30. Ibid., Lincoln, speech to the "One-Legged Brigade," 6: 226; Lincoln, response to serenade, September 24, 1862, 5: 438; Lincoln, opinion on the draft, September 14, 1863, 6: 447; for various examples of Lincoln referring to some form of soldierly suffering, see proclamation of thanksgiving and prayer, September 3, 1864, 7: 533; Lincoln, speech at Union League Club, June 16, 1864, 7: 397; remarks at closing of Sanitary Fair, March 18, 1864, 7: 253–254; letter to "the New England Kitchen," March 2, 1864, 7: 220; response to serenade, October 19, 1864, 8: 53; Lincoln to Sarah B. Meconkey, May 9, 1864, 7: 333; Lincoln to Clara and Julia Brown, March 21, 1864, 7: 258; Lincoln to Mrs. Hutter, Miss Lager, and Miss Claghorn, August 10, 1863, 6: 375–376. Davis sometimes spoke of duty as well; see speech in Savannah, Georgia, November 2, 1863, in *PJD,* 10: 44. But he would more likely couch such appeals in terms of overall battlefield glory. Lincoln sometimes—but rarely—spoke of glory to soldiers (see Lincoln to the Managing Committee of the Sailor's Fair, November 8, 1864, *CW,* 8: 95).

31. Joel B. Ragsdale to Jefferson Davis, July 4, 1864, *PJD,* 10: 497; Lincoln to Eliza P. Gurney, September 4, 1864, *CW,* 7: 535. Davis received a request from Quaker conscientious objectors as well, which he merely passed on to his secretary of war without comment (see Nereus Mendenhall, Isham Cox, and Jonathan Harris to Jefferson Davis, March 16, 1864, *PJD,* 10: 281).

32. See *CW* for Lincoln, speech to the Great Sanitary Fair, Philadelphia, June 16, 1864, 7: 394; annual message to Congress, December 1, 1862, 5: 519; Lincoln to John M. Clay, August 9, 1862, 5: 364; see also message to Congress, December 8, 1863, 7: 52.

33. Ibid., Lincoln to Edwin M. Stanton, March 18, 1864, 7: 255; Lincoln, message to Congress, December 6, 1864, 8: 139; for a similiar understated assessment of the wartime economy, see message to Congress, December 8, 1863, 7: 41–42; on the war's expense, see Lincoln, appeal to border state representatives, July 12, 1862, 5: 318; Lincoln, annual message to Congress, December 1, 1862, 5: 532–534.

34. See, generally, Guelzo, *Redeemer President,* 379–382; Lincoln, annual message to Congress, December 1, 1862, *CW,* 5: 522–523; Lincoln also used the war as an excuse to effect various internal improvements (see annual message to Congress, December 3, 1861, 5: 37).

35. Ibid., Lincoln, annual message to Congress, December 6, 1864, 8: 143.

36. Ibid., Lincoln, 1862 annual message to Congress, 5: 519, 522; message to Congress, January 17, 1863, 6: 60–61; annual message to Congress, December 3, 1861, 5: 45; Lincoln to the workingmen of Manchester, England, January 19, 1863, 6: 63–64; see also Burlingame and Ettlinger, eds., *Inside Lincoln's White House,* 217.

37. Lincoln, speech at Great Central Sanitary Fair, June 16, 1864, *CW,* 7: 394.

38. Ibid., Lincoln, 1864 annual message to Congress, 8: 136. I have found only one exception to these characterizations: in his 1863 annual message to Congress, December 8, 1863, 7: 40, Lincoln states that "under the sharp discipline of civil war, the nation is beginning a new life," but even in this speech this mild praise is buried under reticence or gloomy assessments of the war's economic costs.

39. Mark E. Neely Jr., "'Civilized Belligerents': Abraham Lincoln and the Idea of Total War," in *New Perspectives on the Civil War,* ed. John Y. Simon and Michael E. Stevens (Madison, Wis.: Madison House, 1998), 4–5, points out that Lincoln lacked a modern understanding of the relationship between war and economic development.

40. See *CW* for remarks at the Great Central Sanitary Fair, Philadelphia, June 16, 1864, 7: 394; Lincoln to Albert G. Hodges, April 4, 1864, 7: 281; on Lincoln's sense of the war's tremendous cost, see Lincoln to Henry J. Raymond, March 9, 1862, 5: 152–153; message to Congress, December 1, 1862, 5: 532; and message to Congress, December 3, 1861, 5: 49; on the consequences of the war for laboring classes, see Lincoln's address to the New York Workingmen's Democratic Republican Association, March 21, 1864, 7: 259–260.

41. Ibid., Lincoln to Samuel B. Tobey, March 19, 1862, 5: 165; remarks to a Massachusetts delegation, March 13, 1862, 5: 158.

42. See ibid. for Lincoln's remarks on his own unwillingness to make predictions about the war in his speech at the Great Sanitary Fair, June 16, 1864, 7: 395–396.

43. See *PJD* for Davis to Braxton Bragg, October 3, 1863, 10: 6; speech in Savannah, Georgia, October 31, 1863, 10: 44; speech in Mobile, Alabama, December 30, 1862, 8: 587. See also Davis to W. F. Leak, March 26, 1864, *JDC,* 6: 217.

44. See *PJD* for Davis to Zebulon Vance, February 29, 1864, 10: 268, and Davis, speech in Mobile, Alabama, December 30, 1862, 8: 588. See also Davis, message to Congress, February 3, 1864, *JDC,* 6: 165–167.

45. See *PJD* for Davis, speech in Jackson, Mississippi, December 26, 1862, 8: 579; message to Congress, November 18, 1861, 7: 412, 416, 419; see also speech in Mobile, Alabama, December 30, 1862, 8: 588; message to Congress, 8: 59, 61; inaugural address, February 18, 1861, 7: 49. See also speech in Augusta, Georgia, October 10, 1864, *JDC,* 6: 357.

46. Davis, message to Congress, November 18, 1861, 7: 416, and speech in Jackson, Mississippi, December 26, 1862, 8: 577, both in *PJD.*

47. Lincoln, speech at the Great Sanitary Fair, Philadelphia, June 16, 1864, *CW,* 7: 394; see also Davis, message to Congress, November 7, 1864, *JDC,* 6: 389; on the Davis administration's nationalizing tendencies, see Raimondo Luraghi, "The Civil War and the Modernization of American Society," *Civil War History* 18 (1972); 230–250, and Frank Vandiver, Hardwick Hall, and Homer L. Kerr, *Essays on the Civil War* (Austin: University of Texas Press, 1968), 73–81.

48. Davis, speech in Goldsboro, Georgia, November 7, 1863, *PJD,* 10: 58; Davis to Henry D. Capers, February 27, 1864, *JDC,* 6: 192; Davis to William W. Avery, *OR,* 1, 9; 436; see *PJD* for speech in Jackson, Mississippi, December 26, 1862, 8: 578, 579;

interview with North Carolina delegation, January 23, 1864, 10: 200 (reference to "best of them [North Carolina citizens] in the army"); speech at Missionary Ridge, October 10, 1863, 10: 21; Davis to Robert E. Lee, August 11, 1863, 9: 337 (reference to newspapers failing to judge "true sentiment" of the army).

49. Davis, speech in Macon, Georgia, September 29, 1864, *JDC*, 6: 342–343; see *PJD* for Davis, annual message to Congress, May 2, 1864, 10: 379; Davis to Joseph E. Johnston, February 28, 1862, 8: 69; speech in Jackson, Mississippi, December 26, 1862, 8: 569; speech in Richmond, Virginia, January 5, 1863, 9: 14; and Davis to James M. Howry, August 27, 1863, 9: 358.

50. *PJD*, 7: 185.

51. Davis, speech in Macon, Georgia, September 29, 1864, *JDC*, 7: 341 (emphases in original), and Davis to Braxton Bragg, August 5, 1862, 8: 322.

52. Proclamation revoking General Hunter's order, May 19, 1862, *CW*, 5: 223.

53. See CW for response to serenade, February 1, 1865, 8: 254; Lincoln, speech to 113th Ohio, June 11, 1864, 7: 388; Lincoln to Mrs. Lydia Bixby, November 21, 1864, 8: 117; appeal to border state representatives, July 12, 1862, 5: 318.

54. Ibid., Lincoln, message to Congress, March 7, 1862, 5: 145–146.

55. Ibid., address on colonization, August 14, 1862, 5: 372.

56. Ibid., interview with Alexander W. Randall and Joseph T. Mills, August 16, 1864, 7: 507.

57. This point is made particularly by William C. Davis, *Lincoln's Men* (New York: Touchstone Books, 2000), esp. chap. 5; see also Lincoln's own reference to his many appearances before soldiers in his speech to the Twelfth Indiana Regiment, May 13, 1862, *CW*, 5: 213.

58. On this point, see especially Davis, *Lincoln's Men,* esp. chap. 9; Glen Thurow, *Abraham Lincoln and American Political Religion* (Albany, N.Y.: 1976); Hein J. Morganthau and David Heln, eds., *Essays on Lincoln's Faith and Politics* (Lanham, Md.: University Press of America, 1983).

59. Roy P. Basler, "Abraham Lincoln: An Immortal Sign," in *The Enduring Lincoln,* ed. Norma A. Graebner (Urbana: University of Illinois Press, 1959), 1.

60. Lincoln, response to a serenade, April 10, 1865, *CW*, 8: 394. Lincoln constantly expressed his concerns about being misconstrued or of saying anything too divisive (see, e.g., speech of April 11, 1865, 8: 402–403).

61. V. Davis, *Memoir,* 2: 12; see PJD for speech in Jackson, Mississippi, December 26, 1862, 8: 573, and speech in Savannah, Georgia, October 31, 1863, 10: 44.

62. Speech in Savannah, Georgia, October 31, 1863, *PJD,* 10: 44, and in Wilmington, North Carolina, November 5, 1863, 10: 49.

63. On Davis's vacillation, see Richard E. Beringer, "Jefferson Davis's Pursuit of Ambition: The Attractive Features of Alternative Decisions," *Civil War History* 38 (winter 1992): 12–15.

64. This point has been made by Paul Escott, among others, in *After Secession* (Baton Rouge: Louisiana State University Press, 1978), and also by Richard E. Beringer, Herman Hattaway, Archer Jones, and William N. Still Jr., *Why the South Lost the Civil War* (Athens: University of Georgia Press, 1986).

13. Others

1. On the general circumstances of the 1864 election, see David E. Long, *The Jewel of Liberty: Abraham Lincoln's Re-Election and the End of Slavery* (New York: Stackpole Books, 1994); for the Confederate perspective on the election, see Larry E. Nelson, *Bullets, Ballots, and Rhetoric: Confederate Policy for the United States Presidential Contest of 1864* (Tuscaloosa: University of Alabama Press, 1980).

2. C. Vann Woodward, ed., *Mary Chesnut's Civil War* (New Haven: Yale University Press, 1983), 705; for Davis's reaction to the suggestion that Southern states might negotiate a separate peace, see his speech in Columbia, South Carolina, October 6, 1864, *JDC,* 6: 352–353, and his letter to A. R. Wright et al., November 17, 1864, in 6: 404–405.

3. Woodward, ed., *Mary Chesnut's Civil War,* 786 and 437; Thomas E. Schott, *Alexander H. Stephens: A Biography* (Baton Rouge: Louisiana State University Press, 1988), quote at 20.

4. On the differences and similarities between Davis and Stephens, see James Z. Rabun, "Alexander Stephens and Jefferson Davis," *American Historical Review* 58 (1958): 291–293; on his disagreements with Davis, see 299–316 (Stephens quotes are at 309–310); Woodward, ed., *Mary Chesnut's Civil War,* 332; Schott, *Alexander Stephens,* 407–408.

5. See *CW* for Lincoln to Hannibal Hamlin, May 6, 1861, *CW,* 4: 357–358; memoranda, appointment of Mark H. Dunnel, March 15, 1861, 4: 284; and Lincoln to Hannibal Hamlin, July 11, 1861, 4: 445. On Lincoln's relationship with Hamlin, see H. Draper Hunt, "President Lincoln's First Vice President: Hannibal Hamlin of Maine," *Lincoln Herald* 88 (winter 1986): 137–144; on Lincoln's relationship with Johnson and Tennessee's reconstruction issues, see William C. Harris, *With Charity for All: Lincoln and the Restoration of the Union* (Lexington: University Press of Kentucky, 1997), 50–53; on his overtly political motives and calculations concerning the vice presidency, see A. K. McClure, *Lincoln and Men of War Times* (Lincoln: University of Nebraska Press, 1996), 115–130.

6. William C. Davis, *Jefferson Davis: The Man and His Hour* (New York: Harper-Collins, 1992), 573, and Rabun, "Alexander Stephens and Jefferson Davis," 294–297; on the political ramifications of the absence of political parties in the Confederacy, see Eric L. McKitrick, "Politics and the Union and Confederate War Efforts," in *The American Party Systems: Stages of Political Development,* ed. William N. Chambers and Walter D. Burnham (Cambridge, Mass.: Oxford University Press, 1967), 120–153. Richard Bensel, *Yankee Leviathan* (Cambridge, U.K.: Cambridge University Press, 1990), 229–234, and George C. Rable, *The Confederate Republic* (Chapel Hill: University of North Carolina Press, 1994), 344–345, tend to disagree with McKitrick's conclusions. But where Davis's relationship with Stephens is concerned, especially vis-à-vis Lincoln, I think the lack of a party system was detrimental.

7. Alexander Stephens to Jefferson Davis, June 12, 1863, *JDC,* 5: 513–515; Schott, *Alexander Stephens,* 375–377.

8. See Waldo W. Braden, "A North-South Friendship: Abraham Lincoln and Alexander H. Stephens," *Lincoln Herald* 91 (fall 1989): 104–109: Ward Hill Lamon later claimed that Lincoln seriously considered Stephens for a cabinet position prior to Georgia's secession (see *Recollections of Abraham Lincoln, 1847–1865* [Lincoln: University of Nebraska Press, 1994], 286).

9. Schott, *Alexander Stephens,* 377–380; see also Lincoln to Samuel P. Lee, July 4, 1863, *CW,* 6: 314–315; Davis to Alexander Stephens, July 2, 1863, *JDC,* 5: 515–516; and Stephens to Jefferson Davis, in Gideon Welles, *The Diary of Gideon Welles: Secretary of the Navy Under Lincoln and Johnson,* 2 vols. (Boston: Houghton-Mifflin, 1911), 1: 286–290.

10. See *CW* for Lincoln to Francis P. Blair Sr., January 18, 1865, 8: 221; see also endorsement concerning Francis P. Blair Sr., January 28, 1865, 8: 243; Lincoln to William H. Seward, January 31, 1865, 8: 250–251; and message to House of Representatives, February 10, 1865, 8: 274–285. A useful account may also be found in F. B. Carpenter, *The Inner Life of Abraham Lincoln: Six Months at the White House* (1866; reprint, Lincoln: University of Nebraska Press, 1995), 212–214; Schott, *Alexander Stephens,* 443–447; W. Davis, *The Man and His Hour,* 589–591; and Harris, *Charity for All,* 238–240. A good recent description of the events leading up to the conference may be found in Charles W. Sanders Jr., "Jefferson Davis and the Hampton Roads Peace Conference: 'To secure peace to the two countries,'" *Journal of Southern History* 63 (November 1997): 802–822.

11. Davis quoted in Jefferson Davis, *The Rise and Fall of the Confederate Government,* 2 vols. (New York: Da Capo Press, 1990), 2: 516 (for his perspective of the Hampton Roads affair, see 516–519); and Davis to Congress, February 6, 1865, *JDC,* 6: 465–466. A good example of Davis's general attitude about peace negotiations can be found in his letter to Zebulon Vance, January 8, 1864, *PJD,* 10: 160–162; Schott sees the Hampton Roads episode as a species of political intrigue on Davis's part (*Alexander Stephens,* 447), but W. Davis takes a rather more charitable approach to Davis's motives, though he likewise sees in Davis's handling of Hampton Roads a rare public relations victory (*The Man and His Hour,* 590–593). Sanders argues that Davis was sincere in his efforts to seek peace ("Jefferson Davis and the Hampton Roads Peace Conference," 811, 816–817, 821–824). For another example of Davis's use of peace-mission failures to bolster morale, see his interview with the North Carolina delegation, January 23, 1864, *PJD,* 10: 200.

12. Schott, *Alexander Stephens,* 447; Ulysses S. Grant, *Ulysses S. Grant: Memoirs and Selected Letters, 1839–1865* (New York: Library of America, 1990). Lincoln's sensitivity to public perception is suggested by his letter to Ulysses S. Grant, February 8, 1865, *CW,* 8: 269, and by his remarks to Francis Carpenter (quoted in *Inner Life of Abraham Lincoln,* 210). Lincoln made good on his promise to parole Stephens's nephew (see Lincoln to Charles W. Hill, February 4, 1865, *CW,* 8: 259, and Lincoln to Alexander H. Stephens, February 10, 1865, 8: 287).

13. Benedict Anderson, *Imagined Communities* (London: Verso Press, 1991); Ellis Cose, *A Nation of Strangers: Prejudice, Politics and the Populating of America* (New York: William Morrow, 1992); Ernest Gellner, *Encounters with Nationalism* (Cam-

bridge, Mass.: Oxford University Press, 1994). I have also been influenced by Michael Fellman's thinking on this matter in *Inside War: The Guerrilla Conflict in Missouri During the American Civil War* (Cambridge, Mass.: Oxford University Press, 1989), and by John Dowers's masterful discussion of the cultural constructions of the Japanese other during World War II, in *War Without Mercy: Race and Power in the Pacific War* (New York: Pantheon Books, 1987).

14. Michael Burlingame and John R. Turner Ettlinger, eds., *Inside Lincoln's White House* (Carbondale: Southern Illinois University Press, 1997), 71, 188; see *CW* for Lincoln, address to Congress, December 6, 1864, 8: 151; see also Lincoln's joking reference to Davis in memorandum concerning J. Wesley Greene, December [?] 1862, 5: 517. Lincoln did keep a close eye on Davis's movements (see Lincoln to William T. Sherman, September 27, 1864, 8: 27).

15. See *PJD* for Davis, speech in Richmond, Virginia, June 1, 1861, 7: 184; Davis to Zebulon Vance, January 8, 1864, 10: 160; interview March [?] 1861, 7: 84; speech in Mobile, Alabama, December 30, 1862, 8: 589. For his reaction to emancipation, see Davis to Congress, January 12, 1863, *OR*, 1, 2: 341, and remarks in Murfreesboro, Tennessee, December 13, 1862, *PJD*, 8: 548.

16. Davis to Alexander Stephens, July 2, 1863, *JDC*, 5: 515–516; Davis to Abraham Lincoln, July 6, 1861, *PJD*, 6: 222; see also Davis, message to Congress, July 20, 1861, *JDC*, 5: 115.

17. Lincoln to Horace Greeley, August 9, 1864, *CW*, 7: 489–490.

18. Ibid., Lincoln, message to Congress, July 4, 1861, 4: 423, and reply to nominating committee, June 9, 1864, 7: 380; Michael Burlingame, ed., *Lincoln Observed* (Baltimore: Johns Hopkins University Press, 1998), 44; Burlingame and Ettlinger, eds., *Inside Lincoln's White House*, 38; see *CW* for Lincoln, reply to a New York delegation, March 4, 1861, 4: 272; proclamation suspending the writ of habeas corpus, September 24, 1862, 5: 436; speech to the 140th Indiana Regiment, March 17, 1865, 8: 360; proclamation of the Act to Suppress Insurrection, July 25, 1862, 5: 341; letter to the Senate, February 10, 1865, 8: 286; Lincoln to Cuthbert Bullitt, July 28, 1862, 5: 345; annual message to Congress, December 1, 1862, 5: 518–519; reference to "seceded States, so called" in last public address, April 11, 1865, 8: 403; and Burlingame and Ettlinger, eds., *Inside Lincoln's White House*, 218. See also James M. McPherson, "Lincoln and the Strategy of Unconditional Surrender," in *Lincoln the War President*, ed. Gabor S. Boritt (Cambridge, Mass.: Oxford University Press, 1992), 41. The closest Lincoln came to an admission of legitimacy for the Confederacy was a stray reference to it as an "embryo state" (see resolution on slavery, April 15, 1863, *CW*, 6: 176).

19. See *CW* for Lincoln, speech in Hartford, Connecticut, March 5, 1860, 4: 3; Lincoln, reply to Mayor James G. Berret, February 27, 1861, 4: 246; reply to emancipation memorial, September 13, 1862, 5: 423; see also Lincoln, speech in Hartford, Connecticut, March 5, 1860, 4: 3; Allen C. Guelzo, *Redeemer President* (Grand Rapids, Mich.: Eerdman's, 1999), 254; see also Richard N. Current, *Speaking of Abraham Lincoln: The Man and His Meaning for Our Times* (Urbana: University of Illinois Press, 1983), 146–171; Stephen B. Oates, "'My Dissatisfied Fellow Country-

men': Abraham Lincoln and the Slaveholding South," in *Essays on Southern History, Written in Honor of Barnes F. Lathrop,* ed. Gary W. Gallagher (Austin: General Libraries of the University of Texas at Austin, 1980), 97–106; on Northerners' use of the South as a negative other, see Susan-Mary Grant, *North over South: Northern Nationalism and American Identity in the Antebellum Era* (Lawrence: University Press of Kansas, 2000), 41–47, 154.

20. Lincoln to Horatio Seymour, August 7, 1863, 6: 370, and Lincoln, message to Congress, December 6, 1864, 8: 151, both in *CW.*

21. Fellman, *Inside War,* 11–22.

22. See *CW* for Lincoln to John M. Schofield, May 27, 1863, 6: 234; Lincoln to Grenville M. Dodge, January 15, 1865, 8: 217; Lincoln to Thomas C. Fletcher, February 20, 1865, 8: 308.

23. Ibid., Lincoln to Don C. Buell, January 6, 1862, 5: 91; Harris, *Charity for All,* 8, 57, and passim. For an interesting perspective on Lincoln's perception of the white Southern aristocracy, see Ethan Fishman, "Under the Circumstances: Abraham Lincoln and Classical Prudence," in *Abraham Lincoln: Sources and Style of Leadership,* ed. Frank J. Williams (New York: Greenwood Press, 1994), 3–15.

24. See *CW* for Lincoln to Stephen A. Hurlbut, November 14, 1864, 8: 107; Lincoln to Frederick Steele, John S. Phelps, and others, November 18, 1862, 5: 500; Lincoln to George F. Shepley, November 21, 1862, 5: 504–505.

25. Ibid., Lincoln to Cuthbert Bullitt, July 28, 1862, 5: 345.

26. Here I draw a different conclusion from that of James M. McPherson, who suggests that Lincoln actually did lose faith in Southern Unionists (see McPherson, "Lincoln and the Strategy of Unconditional Surrender," 47). But recent scholarship on Lincoln's Reconstruction policies suggests a continued faith in white Southerners, at least enough for him to pursue what William C. Harris called a policy of Southern "self-reconstruction" (see Harris, *Charity for All,* 4, 9, 129 and passim; see also Harris, "Abraham Lincoln and Southern White Unionism," in Williams, ed., *Sources and Style of Leadership,* 125–127).

27. Lincoln to Reverdy Johnson, July 26, 1862, *CW,* 5: 342.

28. Ibid., 5: 342–343; Lincoln to August Belmont, July 31, 1862, 5: 350; see also Lincoln's call for "vigorous measures" in remarks to Unionist Kentuckians, November 21, 1862, 5: 504; and Harris, *Charity for All,* 76.

29. Holt quoted in Carpenter, *Inner Life of Abraham Lincoln,* 33; see also Burlingame and Ettlinger, eds., *Inside Lincoln's White House,* 246; see *CW* for Lincoln, reply to Mayor James G. Berret, February 27, 1861, 4: 246; Lincoln to Cuthbert Bullitt, July 28, 1862, 5: 346; and speech in Frederick, Maryland, October 4, 1862, 5: 450; on Lincoln's general magnanimity, see McClure, *Lincoln and Men of War Times,* 277; Lamon, *Recollections of Abraham Lincoln,* 137, 243–246; J. David Greenstone, *The Lincoln Persuasion: Remaking American Liberalism* (Princeton: Princeton University Press, 1993), 217–218.

30. Lincoln to Cuthbert Bullitt, July 28, 1862, 5: 346, and Lincoln to Ulysses S. Grant, August 17, 1864, 7: 499, both in *CW;* Lamon, *Recollections of Abraham Lincoln,* 248–249.

31. Lamon, *Recollections of Abraham Lincoln,* 187; See *CW* for Lincoln to James S. Rollins, August [?] 1863, 6: 360; Lincoln to Edwin M. Stanton, September 7, 1863, 6: 436; letter to Stanton, August 19, 1863, 6: 398; Lincoln, pass for Mrs. Willis F. Jones, February 12, 1865, 8: 292; Lincoln, authorization for Charles H. Ray, February 15, 1865, 8: 299; see also memorandum concerning Herman Koppel, January 22, 1863, 6: 72; Lincoln to John W. Forney, May 13, 1863, 6: 214; and Lincoln to Benjamin F. Butler, August 9, 1864, 7: 487.

32. Lincoln to Horace Greeley, March 24, 1862, *CW,* 5: 169 (emphases in original).

33. Ibid., Lincoln, message to Congress, July 17, 1862, 5: 330–331; Lincoln to the Senate and House of Representatives, February 6, 1865, 8: 260–261.

34. Ibid., Lincoln, message to Congress, December 3, 1861, 5: 36; Lincoln, message to Congress, December 1, 1862, 5: 528–529.

35. Burlingame and Ettlinger, eds., *Inside Lincoln's White House,* 3, 11, 19 (emphasis in original).

36. Lincoln, last public address, April 11, 1865, *CW,* 8: 401; Lincoln to Henry W. Halleck, July 6, 1863, also *CW,* 6: 318; see also Burlingame and Ettlinger, eds., *Inside Lincoln's White House,* 62. For a different perspective on Lincoln and Northern nationalism, see S. Grant, *North over South,* esp. 30–32, 159–160. Michael F. Holt, "Abraham Lincoln and the Politics of Union," in John L. Thomas, ed., *Lincoln and the American Political Tradition* (Amherst: University of Massachusetts Press, 1986), 117–118, puts a party-politics face on this matter, suggesting that Lincoln wanted actually to destroy the Republican party of 1860 to create a new, national party embracing North and South.

37. Davis to George Lunt, January 17, 1861, 7: 14, and Davis to John A. Campbell, April 6, 1861, 7: 92–93, both in *PJD;* Davis to George W. Jones, January 20, 1861, *JDC,* 5: 39.

38. Davis, inaugural address, February 18, 1861, *PJD,* 7: 47–48; see also Davis's remarks about his desire to preserve peaceful economic and social relations in his speech to the U.S. Senate, January 10, 1861, *JDC,* 5: 32.

39. Davis later expressed surprise that economic pressures did not win the Confederacy more sympathy in the North; see Davis to Joseph E. Davis, June 18, 1861, *PJD,* 7: 203.

40. Ibid., Davis, speech in Wilmington, North Carolina, November 5, 1863, 10: 51. Davis could draw internal distinctions between various peoples within the North (see remarks about Massachusetts in interview with Arthur J. L. Freemantle, June 17, 1863, 9: 228–229).

41. Ibid., Davis to Joseph E. Davis, June 18, 1861, 7: 203; Davis, speech in Wilmington, North Carolina, November 5, 1863, 10: 49; see also Davis, message to Congress, July 20, 1861, *JDC,* 5: 116.

42. Davis, proclamation, August 14, 1861, *OR,* 2, 2: 1369–1370.

43. Davis message to Congress, August 18, 1862, *JDC,* 5: 322.

44. See *PJD* for Davis to Robert W. Johnson, July 14, 1863, 9: 277; Davis, speech in Jackson, Mississippi, December 26, 1862, 8: 574; message to Congress, Novem-

ber 18, 1861, 7: 416; speech in Wilmington, North Carolina, November 5, 1863, 10: 50; see also remarks about Southern Unionists in Davis's speech at Missionary Ridge, October 10, 1863, 10: 21; speech at Augusta, Georgia, October 10, 1864, *JDC,* 6: 357.

45. See *PJD* for Davis to Zebulon Vance, January 8, 1864, 10: 160; speech in Jackson, Mississippi, December 26, 1862, 8: 566; Davis, speech at Missionary Ridge, October 10, 1863, 10: 21; speech in Savannah, Georgia, October 31, 1863, 10: 44; Davis to E. Kirby Smith, July 28, 1862, 8: 305; message to Congress, November 18, 1861, 7: 413, 416; Davis, speech in Raleigh, North Carolina, January 3, 1863, 9: 8; see also message to Congress, July 20, 1861, *JDC,* 5: 112–113, and letter to Samuel J. Person, December 15, 1864, also in *JDC,* 6: 421.

46. See *PJD* for Davis, speech in Jackson, December 26, 1862, 8: 574; Davis to Joseph E. Davis, June 18, 1861, 7: 203; see also Davis to Congress, April 29, 1861, 5: 70.

47. Ibid., Davis to Joseph E. Davis, May 31, 1863, 9: 200; Davis, message to Congress, November 18, 1861, 7: 413; Davis, speech in Richmond, Virginia, June 1, 1861, 7: 185; message to Congress, November 18, 1861, 7: 416–417; message to Congress, May 2, 1864, 10: 378; Davis, speech in Wilmington, North Carolina, November 5, 1863, 10: 50; Davis, speech in Jackson, Mississippi, December 26, 1862, 8: 566; speech in Savannah, Georgia, October 31, 1863, 10: 45; Davis to Robert E. Lee, July 31, 1862, 8: 310; see also message to Congress, July 20, 1861, *JDC,* 5: 114.

48. Davis, speech in Augusta, Georgia, October 10, 1864, *JDC,* 6: 357, Davis to Varina Howell Davis, June 25, 1862, *PJD,* 8: 269, and message to Congress, November 18, 1861, also in *PJD,* 7: 417.

49. See *PJD* for Davis, message to Congress, May 2, 1864, 10; 380; Davis, speech in Raleigh, North Carolina, January 3, 1863, 9: 8; Davis, speech in Jackson, Mississippi, December 26, 1862, 8: 567; see also his reference to "extermination" in excerpt from C. C. Clay and James P. Holcombe, July 25, 1864, 10: 560, and similar reference in message to Congress, April 29, 1861, *JDC,* 5: 79. See also Davis, speech in Richmond, Virginia, January 5, 1863, *PJD,* 9: 13, and reference to Yankee "crimes" in letter to Joseph Davis, May 31, 1863, also in *PJD,* 9: 200.

50. On Butler's career, see Howard P. Nash Jr., *Stormy Petrel: The Life and Times of Benjamin F. Butler, 1818–1893* (Rutherford, N.J.: Fairleigh Dickinson University Press, 1969).

51. Davis, proclamation in *OR,* 1, 15: 906–908; see also message to Congress, August 18, 1862, *JDC,* 5: 320–322; Davis, speech in Richmond, Virginia, January 5, 1863, *PJD,* 9: 13; and speech in Macon, Georgia, September 29, 1864, *JDC,* 6: 343. Butler's behavior also contributed to the breakdown of the exchange system that Stephens wanted to repair; see J. Davis, *Rise and Fall,* 2: 499–501 (for other examples of Davis's attitude toward Butler, see 2: 64, and 241–244); see also Varina Davis, *A Memoir by His Wife,* 2 vols. (Baltimore: Nautical and Aviation Company, 1990), 2: 276.

52. See *PJD* for Davis to Robert W. Johnson, July 14, 1863, 9: 277, and Davis, speech in Richmond, Virginia, January 5, 1863, 9: 43.

53. Davis to Braxton Bragg, September 10, 1863, *OR,* 1, 52, pt. 2: 524. See *PJD* for speech in Richmond, Virginia, June 1, 1861, 7: 184, and Davis to Zebulon Vance, January 8, 1864, 10: 160.

54. See *PJD* for Davis, speech in Jackson, Mississippi, December 26, 1862, 8: 574; for similiar references to the Revolution, see 8: 573; and speech in Charleston, South Carolina, November 3, 1863, *JDC*, 6: 76.

55. There is a large body of literature on the ways in which white Southerners defined the racial "other": see, e.g., George M. Fredrickson, *The Black Image in the White Mind* (New York: Harper Books, 1971); Winthrop D. Jordan, *White over Black: American Attitudes Toward the Negro, 1550–1812* (Chapel Hill: University of North Carolina Press, 1968); Thomas F. Gossett, *Race: The History of an Idea in America,* 2d ed. (Cambridge, Mass.: Oxford University Press, 1997); Eugene D. Genovese, *Roll, Jordan, Roll: The World the Slaves Made* (New York: Random House, 1976); Lawrence J. Friedman, *The White Savage: Racial Fantasies in the Postbellum South* (Englewood Cliffs, N.J.: Prentice Hall, 1970); Grace Elizabeth Hale, *Making Whiteness: The Culture of Segregation in the South, 1890–1940* (New York: Pantheon, 1998).

56. Davis, message to Congress, August 18, 1862, *JDC*, 5: 322.

57. Davis, speech in Savannah, Georgia, October 31, 1863, *PJD*, 10: 45; see *JDC* for speech in Augusta, Georgia, October 10, 1864, 6: 359; speech in Macon, Georgia, September 29, 1864, *PJD*, 6: 342; speech in Columbia, South Carolina, October 6, 1864, *PJD*, 6: 354; see also speech in Richmond, Virginia, January 5, 1863, *PJD*, 9: 43; Davis to Sara E. Cochrane, June 5, 1862, *JDC*, 5: 269.

58. See Mary P. Ryan's excellent analysis of the gendered content of the Butler controversy in *Women in Public: Between Banners and Ballots, 1825–1880* (Baltimore: Johns Hopkins University Press, 1992).

59. See *PJD* for Davis to Rose O'Neal Greenhow, May 26, 1863, 9: 191; speech in Richmond, Virginia, June 1, 1861, 7: 185; see also interview with Arthur J. L. Fremantle, July 17, 1863, 9: 229; message to Congress, May 2, 1864, 10: 378; Davis to Robert E. Lee, July 31, 1862, 8: 310.

60. On this issue, see Drew Gilpin Faust, *Mothers of Invention: Women of the Slaveholding South in the American Civil War* (New York: Vintage Books, 1997), and Faust's essay, "Altars of Sacrifice," in *Divided Houses: Gender and the Civil War,* ed. Catherine Clinton and Nina Silber (Cambridge, Mass.: Oxford University Press, 1992).

61. On the Richmond bread riot, see Emory M. Thomas, *The Confederate Nation, 1861–1865* (New York: HarperCollins, 1979), 203–204; J. Davis, *Rise and Fall,* 2: prefatory page.

62. Davis's primary scholarly critics in this regard have been Paul Escott, *After Secession* (Baton Rouge: Louisiana State University Press, 1978), and Richard E. Beringer et al., *Why the South Lost the Civil War* (Athens: University of Georgia Press, 1986). Carl Degler also seems to suggest this when he points out that Lincoln was closer to Otto von Bismarck than to Davis; see Degler, "One Among Many: The United States and National Unification," in Boritt, ed., *Lincoln the War President,* 91–119.

63. On the nature of this Lost Cause mythos, see Hale, *Making Whiteness,* 67–84; Dewey W. Grantham, "The South and the Politics of Sectionalism," in *The Regional Imagination: The South and Recent American History* (Nashville: Vanderbilt University Press, 1979), 1–22.

64. J. Davis, *Rise and Fall,* 2: esp. chap. 38; for a general discussion of the circumstances surrounding the book's publication, see V. Davis, *Memoir,* 2: 825–826; and W. Davis, *The Man and His Hour,* 676–678.

65. V. Davis, *Memoir,* 2: 152–154, 162; he did tend toward direct criticism of Lincoln in his discussion of the president's amnesty proclamation (see 250).

66. J. Davis, *Rise and Fall,* 2: 580; for similiar comments by Davis, see his letter to Crafts J. Wright, May 11, 1876, *JDC,* 7: 514; for Lincoln's postwar transformation to a Southern hero, see Donald E. Fehrenbacher, *Lincoln in Text and Context: Collected Essays* (Stanford: Stanford University Press, 1987), 97.

67. For a different perspective on Lincoln's possible reconstruction policies, see Christopher Dell, "Reconstruction, Had Lincoln Lived," *Lincoln Herald* 81 (winter 1979): 257–267, and Stephen B. Oates, "Towards a New Birth of Freedom: Abraham Lincoln and Reconstruction, 1854–1865," *Lincoln Herald* 82 (spring 1980): 287–296.

Conclusion

1. Varina Davis, *Jefferson Davis: A Memoir by His Wife,* 2 vols. (Baltimore: Nautical and Aviation Company, 1990), 1: 131–132. Francis Fisher Browne also printed this story in his eclectic collection of Lincoln anecdotes (see *The Everyday Life of Abraham Lincoln* [Lincoln: University of Nebraska Press, 1995], 111–112).

2. For a discussion of the creation of the Lincoln myth during this time, see Merrill D. Peterson, *Lincoln in American Memory* (New York: Oxford University Press, 1994), esp. chap. 4.

3. See *PJD* for Order no. 65, March 26, 1832, 1: 236; for a detailed discussion of Davis's movements around this time, see note 4, 1: 241; see also muster roll of Lincoln's company, May 27, 1832, *CW,* 1: 10–12, Lincoln reenlisted two days later, the time when Davis supposedly was present. See also Browne, *Everyday Life of Abraham Lincoln,* 111 (quote from the captain of Lincoln's company giving exact date and location of Lincoln's reenlistment). On the general issue of Lincoln and Davis never having met, see V. Davis, *Memoir,* 1: 268. See also Irving Werstein, *Abraham Lincoln vs. Jefferson Davis* (New York: Crowell, 1959), 20.

4. See, generally, Gaines M. Foster, *Ghosts of the Confederacy: Defeat, The Lost Cause, and the Emergence of the New South* (Cambridge, Mass.: Oxford University Press, 1989), and Alan T. Nolan, "The Anatomy of the Myth," in *The Myth of the Lost Cause and Civil War History,* ed. Gary W. Gallagher and Alan T. Nolan (Bloomington: Indiana University Press, 2000). For sheer entertainment value, nothing beats Hattie Semons, *Duel with Destiny* (Radford, Va.: Commonwealth Press, 1976), who claims that Lincoln and Davis were both the bastard sons of John C. Calhoun.

5. On this issue of the war and white racial solidarity, see Grace Elizabeth Hale, *Making Whiteness: The Culture of Segregation in the South, 1890–1940* (New York: Pantheon, 1998).

6. Reminiscences of A. K. McClure, unidentified newspaper clipping, 1909 (Lincoln Museum Newspaper Collection, Lincoln Museum, Fort Wayne, Indiana).

Bibliography

Note on Sources

For this book I have relied largely on printed primary sources, particularly those that are available in three major collections: the eight-volume *Collected Works of Abraham Lincoln,* the ten-volume *Papers of Jefferson Davis* (an ongoing project that as of this writing had progressed to fall 1864), and the older ten-volume *Jefferson Davis, Constitutionalist: His Letters, Papers, and Speeches.* My reliance on these sources is partly a testament to their thoroughness—the *Papers of Jefferson Davis,* for example, offers nearly an exhaustive collection of known Davis materials—partly a matter of convenience, but also in large part a conscious decision. The purpose of this book was never to provide a completely comprehensive dual biography of both men but to target those source materials that best illuminate their nationalist identities. Since nationalism is preeminently a public phenomenon, I have thought it best to focus most of my attention on sources with a public content, particularly speeches and public correspondence, and these sources are most readily available in these collections.

I have also relied on eyewitness accounts of Lincoln and Davis by their contemporaries, particularly those written by William H. Herndon and Varina Davis. Each presents unique challenges. Herndon's reputation has been quite uneven with historians. Although providing invaluable descriptions of Lincoln during his early career, he tended to make overly self-serving claims that exaggerated his influence on the president's thinking, and several scholars have suggested that he distorted Lincoln's views on religion and the state of his marriage (Herndon detested Mary Lincoln). Varina Davis has sometimes been criticized for her overt attempts to resurrect her husband's public reputation after the war, a crusade that may have distorted the evidence she presents about Davis in her memoirs. With these caveats in mind, I have made cautious but extensive use of both Herndon and Davis, simply because they provide information and insights that are available from no other source.

Primary Sources

Abraham Lincoln Papers. Library of Congress (microfilm).

Angle, Paul M., ed. "The Recollections of William Pitt Kellog," *Abraham Lincoln Quarterly* 3 (September 1945).

Basler, Roy P., ed. *The Collected Works of Abraham Lincoln.* 8 vols. New Brunswick, N.J.: Rutgers University Press, 1953.

Browne, Francis Fisher, *The Everyday Life of Abraham Lincoln*. 1887. Reprint, Lincoln: University of Nebraska Press, 1995.

Burlingame, Michael, ed. *Lincoln Observed: Civil War Dispatches of Noah Brooks*. Baltimore: Johns Hopkins University Press, 1998.

Burlingame, Michael, and John R. Turner Ettlinger, eds. *Inside Lincoln's White House: The Complete Civil War Diary of John Hay*. Carbondale: Southern Illinois University Press, 1997.

Carpenter, F. B. *The Inner Life of Abraham Lincoln: Six Months at the White House*. 1866. Reprint, Lincoln: University of Nebraska Press, 1995.

Crist, Lynda Lasswell et al., eds. *The Papers of Jefferson Davis*. 10 vols. Baton Rouge: Louisiana State University Press, 1971–1999.

Daniel, John W., ed. *Life and Reminiscences of Jefferson Davis by Distinguished Men of His Time*. Baltimore: R. H. Woodward, 1890.

Davis, Jefferson. *The Rise and Fall of the Confederate Government*. 2 vols. 1881. Reprint, New York: Da Capo Press, 1990.

Davis, Varina. *Jefferson Davis: A Memoir by His Wife*. 2 vols. 1890. Reprint, Baltimore: Nautical and Aviation Company, 1990.

Grant, Ulysses S. *Ulysses S. Grant: Memoirs and Selected Letters, 1839–1865*. New York: Library of America, 1990.

Herndon-Weik Collection of Lincolnia. Library of Congress (microfilm).

Herndon, William H. "Analysis of the Character of Abraham Lincoln: A Lecture." *Abraham Lincoln Quarterly* 1 (December 1941).

Herndon, William H., and Jesse Weik. *Herndon's Life of Lincoln*. 1889. Reprint, New York: Da Capo Press, 1983.

Holzer, Harold M., ed. *Dear Mr. Lincoln: Letters to the President*. Reading, Mass.: Addison-Wesley, 1993.

Hunt, Eugenia Jones. "My Personal Recollections of Abraham and Mary Todd Lincoln." *Abraham Lincoln Quarterly* 3 (March 1944–December 1945).

Jones, John B. *A Rebel War Clerk's Diary*. 2 vols. Philadelphia: J. B. Lippincott, 1866.

Keckley, Elizabeth. *Behind the Scenes; or, Thirty Years as a Slave, and Four in the White House*. Buffalo, N.Y.: Stansill and Lee, 1931.

Lamon, Ward Hill. *Recollections of Abraham Lincoln, 1847–1865*. 1895. Reprint, Lincoln: University of Nebraska Press, 1994.

Lasswell, Linda, ed. "Jefferson Davis Ponders His Future, 1829." *Journal of Southern History* 41 (November 1975).

Lincoln Legal Papers, DVD–ROM Database.

Lincoln Museum Newspaper Collection, Fort Wayne, Indiana.

McClure, A. K. *Abraham Lincoln and Men of War Times*. 1892. Reprint, Lincoln: University of Nebraska Press, 1996.

Richardson, James D., ed. *Messages and Papers of the Confederacy*. 2d ed., 2 vols. New York: Chelsea House–R. Rector, 1966.

Rowland, Dunbar, ed. *Jefferson Davis, Constitutionalist: His Letters, Papers, and Speeches*. 10 vols. Jackson: Mississippi Department of Archives and History, 1923.

Speed, Joshua. *Reminiscences of Abraham Lincoln and Notes of a Visit to California: Two Lectures.* Louisville: John P. Morton, 1884.

Stevens, Walter B. *A Reporter's Lincoln.* St. Louis: Missouri Historical Society, 1916.

Strode, Hudson, ed. *Jefferson Davis: Private Letters, 1823–1889.* New York: Da Capo Press, 1995.

U.S. Government. *War of the Rebellion: A Compilation of the Official Records of the Union and Confederate Armies.* 127 vols. Washington, D.C.: Government Printing Office, 1880–1901.

Watts, Thomas H. *Life and Character of Ex-President Jefferson Davis.* Speech delivered in Montgomery, Alabama, December 19, 1889 (copy in Mississippi Department of Archives and History, Jackson).

Welles, Gideon. *The Diary of Gideon Welles: Secretary of the Navy Under Lincoln and Johnson.* 2 vols. Boston: Houghton-Mifflin, 1911.

Whitney, Henry C. *Life on the Circuit with Lincoln.* Boston: Estes and Lauriar, 1892.

Wilson, Douglas L., and Rodney O. Davis., eds. *Herndon's Informants: Letters, Interviews, and Statements About Abraham Lincoln.* Urbana: University of Illinois Press, 1997.

Woodward, C. Vann, ed. *Mary Chesnut's Civil War.* New Haven: Yale University Press, 1981.

Books

Ambrose, Stephen. *Duty, Honor, Country: A History of West Point.* Baltimore: Johns Hopkins University Press, 1966.

Ambrose, Stephen, and James A. Barber Jr., eds. *The Military and American Society: Essays and Readings.* New York: Free Press, 1972.

Anderson, Benedict. *Imagined Communities: Reflections on the Origin and Spread of Nationalism.* Rev. ed. London: Verso Press, 1991.

Anderson, Dwight G. *Abraham Lincoln: The Quest for Immortality.* New York: Knopf, 1982.

Angle, Paul M. *"Here I Have Lived": A History of Lincoln's Springfield, 1821–1865.* New Brunswick. N.J.: Rutgers University Press, 1950.

Bailey, Anne J. *The Chessboard of War: Sherman and Hood in the Autumn Campaigns of 1864.* Lincoln: University of Nebraska Press, 2000.

Baker, Jean H. *Mary Todd Lincoln: A Biography.* New York: Norton, 1987.

Barber, Sotorios. *On What the Constitution Means.* Baltimore: Johns Hopkins University Press, 1984.

Bartley, Numan V., ed. *The Evolution of Southern Culture.* Athens: University of Georgia Press, 1988.

Bauer, K. Jack. *The Mexican War, 1846–1848.* New York: Macmillan, 1974.

Bennett, Lerone Jr. *Forced into Glory: Abraham Lincoln's White Dream.* Chicago: Johnson, 2000.

Bensel, Richard. *Yankee Leviathan: The Origins of Central State Authority in America, 1859–1877*. Cambridge: Harvard University Press, 1991.

Berlin, Ira. *Slaves Without Masters: The Free Negro in the Antebellum South*. New York: New Press, 1992.

Bilotta, James D. *Race and the Rise of the Republican Party, 1848–1865*. New York: Peter Lang, 1992.

Bloomfield, Maxwell. *American Lawyers in a Changing Society, 1776–1876*. New York, 1976.

Boritt, Gabor S. *Lincoln and the Economics of the American Dream*. 2d ed. Urbana: University of Illinois Press, 1994.

———. *Lincoln the War President: The Gettysburg Lectures*. Cambridge, Mass.: Oxford University Press, 1992.

———. ed. *The Historian's Lincoln: Pseudohistory, Psychohistory, and History*. Urbana: University of Illinois Press, 1996.

Bozett, Frederick W., and Shirley H. M. Hanson, eds. *Fatherhood and Families in Cultural Context*. New York: Springer, 1991.

Brookhiser, Richard. *Founding Father: Rediscovering George Washington*. New York: Free Press, 1996.

Burlingame, Michael. *The Inner World of Abraham Lincoln*. Urbana: University of Illinois Press, 1994.

Cash, W. J. *The Mind of the South*. New York: Vintage, 1991.

Castronova, Russ. *Fathering the Nation: American Genealogies of Slavery and Freedom*. Berkeley: University of California Press, 1995.

Catton, Bruce, and William Catton. *Two Roads to Sumter*. New York: McGraw-Hill, 1963.

Chadwick, Bruce. *Two American Presidents: A Dual Biography of Abraham Lincoln and Jefferson Davis*. Secaucus, N.J.: Birch Lane Press, 1999.

Chambers, William N., and Walter D. Burnham, eds. *The American Party Systems: Stages of Political Development*. Cambridge, Mass.: Oxford University Press, 1967.

Chance, Joseph. *Jefferson Davis's Mexican War Regiment*. Jackson: University Press of Mississippi, 1991.

Clawson, Ann. *Constructing Brotherhood: Class, Gender and Fraternalism*. Princeton: Princeton University Press, 1989.

Clinton, Catherine, and Nina Silber, eds. *Divided Houses: Gender and the Civil War*. Cambridge, Mass.: Oxford University Press, 1992.

Cobb, James C. *The Most Southern Place on Earth: The Mississippi Delta and the Roots of Regional Identity*. Oxford: Oxford University Press, 1992.

Cooper, William J. Jr. *Jefferson Davis, American*. New York: Knopf, 2000.

———. *Liberty and Slavery: Southern Politics to 1860*. New York: Knopf, 1983.

Cose, Ellis. *A Nation of Strangers: Prejudice, Politics and the Populating of America*. New York: William Morrow, 1992.

Cox, LaWanda. *Lincoln and Black Freedom*. 2d ed. Charleston: University of South Carolina Press, 1994.

Cunliffe, Marcus. *Soldiers and Civilians: The Martial Spirit in America, 1775–1865*. Boston: Little, Brown, 1968.

Current, Richard N. *The Lincoln Nobody Knows*. 2d ed. New York: Greenwood Press, 1980.

———. *Speaking of Abraham Lincoln: The Man and His Meaning for Our Times*. Urbana: University of Illinois Press, 1983.

———. *What Is an American? Abraham Lincoln and "Multiculturalism."* Milwaukee: Marquette University Press, 1993.

Dahbour, Omar, and Micheline R. Ishay, eds. *The Nationalism Reader*. Atlantic Highlands, N.J.: Humanities Press, 1995.

Davis, William C. *"A Government of Our Own": The Making of the Confederacy*. New York: Free Press, 1994.

———. *Jefferson Davis: The Man and His Hour*. New York: HarperCollins, 1991.

———. *Lincoln's Men: How President Lincoln Became Father to an Army and a Nation*. New York: Free Press, 1999.

Diggins, John P. *The Lost Soul of American Politics: Virtue, Self-Interest, and the Foundations of Liberalism*. Chicago: University of Chicago Press, 1987.

———. *On Hallowed Ground: Abraham Lincoln and the Foundations of American History*. New Haven: Yale University Press, 2000.

Donald, David. *Charles Sumner and the Coming of the Civil War*. New York: Fawcett, 1960.

———. *Lincoln*. New York: Simon and Schuster, 1995.

———. *Lincoln Reconsidered: Essays on the Civil War Era*. New York: Knopf, 1956.

———. *Lincoln's Herndon: A Biography*. New York: Da Capo, 1988.

———. *Why the North Won the Civil War*. New York: Collier, 1960.

Dower, John, *War Without Mercy: Race and Power in the Pacific War*. New York: Pantheon, 1987.

Eaton, Clement, *Freedom of Thought in the Old South*. Durham, N.C.: Duke University Press, 1940.

———. *Jefferson Davis*. New York: Free Press, 1977.

Ellis, Joseph, and Robert Moore. *School for Soldiers: West Point and the Profession of Arms*. New York: Oxford University Press, 1974.

Escott, Paul D. *After Secession: Jefferson Davis and the Failure of Confederate Nationalism*. Baton Rouge: Louisiana State University Press, 1978.

Everett, Frank E. Jr. *Brierfield: Plantation Home of Jefferson Davis*. Hattiesburg: University and College Press of Mississippi, 1971.

Faust, Drew Gilpin. *The Creation of Confederate Nationalism: Ideology and Identity in the Civil War South*. Baton Rouge: Louisiana State University Press, 1988.

———. *Mothers of Invention: Women of the Slaveholding South in the American Civil War*. New York: Vintage, 1997.

Fehrenbacher, Donald E. *The Dred Scott Case: Its Significance in American Law and Politics*. New York: Oxford University Press, 1978.

———. *Lincoln in Text and Context: Collected Essays*. Stanford: Stanford University Press, 1987.

————. *Prelude to Greatness: Lincoln in the 1850s.* New York: McGraw-Hill, 1962.

Fellman, Michael. *Inside War: The Guerrilla Conflict in Missouri During the American Civil War.* Cambridge, Mass.: Oxford University Press, 1989.

Flexner, James Thomas. *George Washington and the New Nation, 1783–1793.* Boston: Little, Brown, 1969.

Foner, Eric. *Free Soil, Free Labor, Free Men: The Ideology of the Republican Party Before the Civil War.* 2d ed. New York: Oxford University Press, 1995.

Forgie, George B. *Patricide in the House Divided: A Psychological Interpretation of Lincoln and His Age.* New York: Norton, 1979.

Foster, Gaines M. *Ghosts of the Confederacy: Defeat, the Lost Cause, and the Emergence of the New South.* Cambridge, Mass.: Oxford University Press, 1989.

Frank, John P. *Lincoln as Lawyer.* Urbana: University of Illinois Press, 1961.

Fredrickson, George M. *The Black Image in the White Mind: The Debate on Afro-American Character and Destiny.* New York: Harper and Row, 1971.

Freehling, William W. *The Road to Disunion.* Vol. 1 *Secessionists at Bay, 1776–1854.* New York: Oxford University Press, 1990.

Friedman, Lawrence J. *Gregarious Saints: Self and Community in American Abolitionism, 1830–1870.* Cambridge, Mass.: Cambridge University Press, 1982.

————. *The White Savage: Racial Fantasies in the Postbellum South.* Englewood Cliffs, N.J.: Prentice-Hall, 1970.

Friedman, Lawrence M. *A History of American Law.* 2d. ed. New York: Simon and Schuster, 1985.

Gallagher, Gary, ed. *Essays on Southern History, Written in Honor of Barnes F. Lathrop.* Austin: General Libraries of the University of Texas, Austin, 1980.

Gallagher, Gary, and Alan T. Nolan., eds. *The Myth of the Lost Cause and Civil War History.* Bloomington: Indiana University Press, 2000.

Galloway, K. Bruce, and Robert Bowie Johnson Jr. *West Point: America's Power Fraternity.* New York: Simon and Schuster, 1973.

Gellner, Ernest. *Encounters with Nationalism.* Cambridge, Mass.: Oxford University Press, 1994.

Genovese, Eugene D. *Roll, Jordan, Roll: The World the Slaves Made.* New York: Random House, 1976.

Gienapp, William E. *The Origins of the Republican Party, 1852–1856.* New York: Oxford University Press, 1987.

Glatthaar, Joseph. *Partners in Command: The Relationships Between Leaders in the Civil War.* New York: Free Press, 1994.

Gossett, Thomas F. *Race: The History of an Idea in America.* 2d ed. Cambridge, Mass.: Oxford University Press, 1997.

Graebner, Norma A., ed. *The Enduring Lincoln.* Urbana: University of Illinois Press, 1959.

Grant, Susan-Mary. *North over South: Northern Nationalism and American Identity in the Antebellum Era.* Lawrence: University Press of Kansas, 2000.

Grantham, Dewey W. *The Regional Imagination: The South and Recent American History.* Nashville, Tenn.: Vanderbilt University Press, 1979.

Greenberg, Kenneth. *Honor and Slavery*. Princeton: Princeton University Press, 1997.

Greenfeld, Liah. *Nationalism: Five Roads to Modernity*. Cambridge, Mass.: Harvard University Press, 1992.

Greenstone, J. David. *The Lincoln Persuasion: Remaking American Liberalism*. Princeton: Princeton University Press, 1993.

Griswold, Robert L. *Fatherhood in America: A History*. New York: HarperCollins, 1993.

Guelzo, Allen C. *Abraham Lincoln: Redeemer President*. Grand Rapids, Mich.: William B. Eerdman, 1999.

Hale, Grace Elizabeth. *Making Whiteness: The Culture of Segregation in the South, 1890–1940*. New York: Pantheon, 1998.

Harding, Vincent. *There Is a River: The Black Struggle for Freedom in America*. New York: Harcourt Brace Jovanovich, 1992.

Harris, William C. *With Charity for All: Lincoln and the Restoration of the Union*. Lexington: University Press of Kentucky, 1997.

Hermann, Janet Sharp. *Joseph E. Davis, Pioneer Patriarch*. Jackson: University Press of Mississippi, 1990.

Hesseltine, William B. *Abraham Lincoln: Architect of the Nation*. Fort Wayne, Ind.: Fort Wayne Historical Society, 1959.

Hofstadter, Richard. *The Paranoid Style in American Politics*. New York: Knopf, 1965.

Holt, Michael F. *The Rise and Fall of the American Whig Party: Jacksonian Politics and the Onset of Civil War*. Cambridge, Mass.: Oxford University Press, 1999.

Holzer, Harold. *Lincoln Seen and Heard*. Lawrence: University Press of Kansas, 2000.

———. *The Lincoln-Douglas Debates: The First Complete, Unexpurgated Text*. New York: HarperCollins, 1993.

———. *The Mirror Image of Civil War Memory: Abraham Lincoln and Jefferson Davis in Popular Prints*. Seventeenth R. Gerald McMurtry Lecture. Fort Wayne, Ind.: Lincoln Museum, 1996.

———. ed. *Dear Mr. Lincoln: Letters to the President*. Reading, Mass.: Addison-Wesley, 1993.

Hopkins, Vincent C. *Dred Scott's Case*. New York: Fordham University Press, 1951.

Howe, Daniel Walker. *The Political Culture of the American Whigs*. Chicago: University of Chicago Press, 1979.

Huggins, Nathan Irving. *Slave and Citizen: The Life of Frederick Douglass*. Boston: Little, Brown, 1980.

Jaffa, Harry V. *Crisis of the House Divided: An Interpretation of the Issues in the Lincoln-Douglas Debates*. 2d. ed. Chicago: University of Chicago Press, 1982.

———. *Original Intent and the Framers of the Constitution: A Disputed Question*. Washington, D.C.: Regnery Gateway, 1994.

Johannsen, Robert W. *Lincoln, The South and Slavery: The Political Dimension*. Baton Rouge: Louisiana State University Press, 1991.

———. *Stephen A. Douglas*. Urbana: University of Illinois Press, 1997.

Jordan, Winthrop D. *White over Black: American Attitudes Toward the Negro, 1550–1812*. Chapel Hill: University of North Carolina Press, 1968.

Lander, Ernest McPherson Jr. *Reluctant Imperialists: Calhoun, the South Carolinians, and the Mexican War*. Baton Rouge: Louisiana State University Press, 1980.

LaRossa, Ralph. *Modernization of Fatherhood: A Social and Political History*. Chicago: University of Chicago Press, 1997.

Long, David E. *The Jewel of Liberty: Abraham Lincoln's Re-Election and the End of Slavery*. New York: Stackpole, 1994.

Maier, Pauline. *American Scripture: Making the Declaration of Independence*. New York: Knopf, 1997.

McPherson, James M. *Abraham Lincoln and the Second American Revolution*. New York: Oxford University Press, 1990.

———. *Battle Cry of Freedom*. New York: Ballantine, 1988.

———. *Drawn with the Sword: Reflections on the American Civil War*. New York: Oxford University Press, 1996.

———. *For Cause and Comrades: Why Men Fought in the Civil War*. New York: Oxford University Press, 1997.

———. *The Struggle for Equality: Abolitionism and the Negro in the Civil War and Reconstruction*. Princeton: Princeton University Press, 1964.

———. *"We Cannot Escape History": Lincoln and the Last Best Hope on Earth*. Urbana: University of Illinois Press, 1995.

———, ed. *Writing the Civil War: The Quest to Understand*. Columbia: University of South Carolina Press, 1998.

Miers, Earl Schenck, and C. Percy Powell, eds. *Lincoln Day by Day: A Chronology, 1809–1865*. Dayton, Ohio: Morningside, 1991.

Miller, David. *On Nationality*. Oxford, U.K.: Clarendon Press, 1995.

Miller, Marion M., ed. *A Life of Lincoln*. 2 vols. New York: Baker and Taylor, 1908.

Miller, Randall M., Harry S. Stout, and Charles Reagan Wilson, eds. *Religion and the American Civil War*. New York: Oxford University Press, 1998.

Moorhead, James H. *American Apocalypse: Yankee Protestants and the Civil War*. New Haven: Yale University Press, 1978.

Morgan, Edmund S. *American Slavery, American Freedom: The Ordeal of Colonial Virginia*. New York: Norton, 1975.

Morganthau, Hans J., and David Heln, eds. *Essays on Lincoln's Faith and Politics*. Lanham, Md.: University Press of America, 1983.

Morris, Christopher. *Becoming Southern: The Evolution of a Way of Life, Warren County and Vicksburg, Mississippi, 1770–1860*. New York: Oxford University Press, 1995.

Morrison, James L. *"The Best School in the World": West Point, the Civil War Years, 1833–1860*. Kent, Ohio: Kent State University Press, 1986.

Nash, Howard P. Jr. *Stormy Petrel: The Life and Times of Benjamin F. Butler, 1818–1893*. Rutherford, N.J.: Fairleigh Dickinson University Press, 1969.

Neely, Mark E. *The Last Best Hope of Earth: Abraham Lincoln and the Promise of America*. Cambridge: Harvard University Press, 1993.

————. *Southern Rights: Political Prisoners and the Myth of Confederate Constitu-tionalism.* Charlottesville: University Press of Virginia, 2000.

Neely, Mark E., and R. Gerald McMurtry. *The Insanity File: The Case of Mary Todd Lincoln.* Carbondale: Southern Illinois University Press, 1986.

Nelson, Larry E. *Bullets, Ballots, and Rhetoric: Confederate Policy for the United States Presidential Contest of 1864.* Tuscaloosa: University of Alabama Press, 1980.

Nieman, Donald G., ed. *The Constitution, Law, and American Life: Critical Aspects of the Nineteenth-Century Experience.* Athens: University of Georgia Press, 1992.

Niven, John. *Salmon P. Chase: A Biography.* Oxford: Oxford University Press, 1995.

Oates, Stephen B. *Abraham Lincoln: The Man Behind the Myths.* New York: Harper-Collins, 1984.

————. *With Malice Toward None: The Life of Abraham Lincoln.* New York: Mentor Books, 1977.

Olsen, Christopher J. *Political Culture and Secession in Mississippi: Masculinity, Honor, and the Antiparty Tradition, 1830–1860.* Cambridge, Mass.: Oxford University Press, 2000.

Paludan, Phillip S. *"The Better Angels of Our Nature": Lincoln, Propaganda and Public Opinion During the American Civil War.* Fifteenth Annual R. Gerald McMurtry Lecture. Fort Wayne, Ind.: Lincoln Museum, 1992.

————. *The Presidency of Abraham Lincoln.* Lawrence: University Press of Kansas, 1994.

Pappas, George S. *To the Point: The United States Military Academy, 1802–1902.* Westport, Conn.: Praeger, 1993.

Periwal, Sukumas, ed. *Notions of Nationalism.* Budapest: European University Press, 1995.

Peterson, Merrill D. *Lincoln in American Memory.* New York: Oxford University Press, 1994.

Potter, David M. *The Impending Crisis, 1848–1861.* New York: HarperCollins, 1977.

————. *The South and the Sectional Conflict.* Baton Rouge: Louisiana State University Press, 1968.

Pressly, Thomas J. *Americans Interpret Their Civil War.* New York: Free Press, 1962.

Prucha, Francis Paul. *A Guide to the Military Posts of the United States, 1789–1846.* Madison: State Historical Society of Wisconsin, 1964.

Quynn, Russell Hoover. *The Constitutions of Abraham Lincoln and Jefferson Davis: A Historical and Biographical Study in Contrasts.* New York: Exposition Press, 1959.

Rable, George C. *The Confederate Republic: A Revolution Against Politics.* Chapel Hill: University of North Carolina Press, 1994.

Reid, John Shelton. *Southerners: The Social Psychology of Sectionalism.* Chapel Hill: University of North Carolina Press, 1983.

Remini, Robert V. *Henry Clay: Statesman for the Union.* New York: Norton, 1991.

Riddle, Donald W. *Congressman Abraham Lincoln.* Westport, Conn.: Greenwood Press, 1979.

Rogstad, Steven K., ed. *Lincoln's Critics: The Copperheads of the North.* Shippensburg, Pa.: White Mane Books, 1999.

Ross, Ishbel. *First Lady of the South: The Life of Mrs. Jefferson Davis.* Westport, Conn.: Greenwood Press, 1973.

Rotundo, E. Anthony. *American Manhood: Transformations of Masculinity from the Revolution to the Modern Era.* New York: HarperCollins, 1993.

———. *Fatherhood in America: A History.* New York: Basic Books, 1993.

Royster, Charles. *The Destructive War: William Tecumseh Sherman, Stonewall Jackson, and the Americans.* New York: Knopf, 1991.

———. *A Revolutionary People at War: The Continental Army and American Character, 1775–1783.* New York: Norton, 1979.

Rutherford, Mildred. *Jefferson Davis and Abraham Lincoln.* Athens: State Historian, Georgia Division, United Daughters of the Confederacy, 1916.

Ryan, Mary P. *Women in Public: Between Banners and Ballots, 1825–1880.* Baltimore: Johns Hopkins University Press, 1992.

Sandburg, Carl. *Abraham Lincoln: The War Years.* 5 vols. New York: Harcourt Brace, 1939.

Schott, Thomas E. *Alexander H. Stephens: A Biography.* Baton Rouge: Louisiana State University Press, 1988.

Semons, Hattie. *Duel with Destiny.* Radford, Va.: Commonwealth Press, 1976.

Shafer, Boyd C. *Faces of Nationalism: New Realities and Old Myths.* New York: Harcourt Brace Jovanovich, 1972.

Shattuck, Gardiner H. Jr. *A Shield and a Hiding Place: The Religious Life of Civil War Armies.* Macon, Ga.: Mercer University Press, 1987.

Simon, John Y., and Michael E. Stevens, eds. *New Perspectives on the Civil War.* Madison, Wis.: Madison House, 1998.

Smith, Anthony. *The Ethnic Origins of Nations.* Oxford, U.K.: Blackwell Press, 1986.

Stampp, Kenneth M. *1857: A Nation on the Brink.* New York: Oxford University Press, 1990.

Stowe, Steven. *Intimacy and Power in the Old South: Ritual and the Lives of Planters.* Baltimore: Johns Hopkins University Press, 1987.

Strode, Hudson. *Jefferson Davis.* 3 vols. New York: Harcourt, Brace and World, 1959.

Strozier, Charles B. *Lincoln's Quest for Union: Public and Private Meanings.* Urbana: University of Illinois Press, 1997.

Tarbell, Ida M. *The Life of Abraham Lincoln.* Sangamon ed. 4 vols. New York: Lincoln History Society, 1924.

Taylor, William R. *Cavalier and Yankee: The Old South and American National Character.* New York: G. Braziller, 1963.

Thomas, Benjamin. *Abraham Lincoln: A Biography.* New York: Barnes and Noble, 1994.

———. *Lincoln's New Salem.* New York: Knopf, 1954.

Thomas, Emory M. *The Confederacy as a Revolutionary Experience.* 2d ed. Columbia: University Press of South Carolina, 1991.

———. *The Confederate Nation, 1861–1865*. New York: HarperCollins, 1979.

Thomas, John L., ed. *Lincoln and the American Political Tradition*. Amherst: University of Massachusetts Press, 1986.

Thurow, Glen. *Abraham Lincoln and American Political Religion*. Albany, N.Y.: Suny Press, 1976.

Trueblood, Elton. *Abraham Lincoln: Theologian of American Anguish*. New York: Harper and Row, 1973.

Van Deusen, Glyndon G. *William Henry Seward*. New York: Oxford University Press, 1967.

Vandiver, Frank. *Jefferson Davis and the Confederate State*. Cambridge, Mass.: Oxford University Press, 1964.

———. *The Making of a President: Jefferson Davis, 1861*. Richmond: Virginia Civil War Commission, 1961.

Vandiver, Frank, Hardwick Hall, and Homer L. Kerr. *Essays on the Civil War*. Austin: University of Texas Press, 1968.

Viroli, Maurizio. *For Love of Country: An Essay on Patriotism and Nationalism*. Oxford, U.K.: Clarendon Press, 1995.

Walsh, John E. *Moonlight: Abraham Lincoln and the Almanac Trial*. New York: St. Martin's Press, 2000.

Walthall, William T. *Jefferson Davis: A Sketch of the Life and Character of the President of the Confederate States*. New Orleans: Times-Democrat, 1908.

Walther, Eric. *The Fire-Eaters*. Baton Rouge: Louisiana State University Press, 1992.

Waugh, E. D. J. *West Point*. New York: Macmillan, 1944.

Werstein, Irving. *Abraham Lincoln vs. Jefferson Davis*. New York: Crowell, 1959.

Weston, Ernest James. *Campaign Lives of Abraham Lincoln, 1860*. Springfield: Illinois State Historical Society, 1937.

Williams, Frank J., ed. *Abraham Lincoln: Sources and Style of Leadership*. New York: Greenwood Press, 1994.

Wills, Garry. *Lincoln at Gettysburg: The Words That Remade America*. New York: Simon and Schuster, 1992.

Wilson, Douglas L. *Honor's Voice: The Transformation of Abraham Lincoln*. New York: Knopf, 1998.

———. *Lincoln Before Washington: New Perspectives on the Illinois Years*. Urbana: University of Illinois Press, 1997.

Wilson, Edmund. *Patriotic Gore: Studies in the Literature of the Civil War Era*. New York: Oxford University Press, 1962.

Winders, Richard Bruce. *Mr. Polk's Army: The American Military Experience in the Mexican War*. College Station: Texas A&M Press, 1997.

Woldman, Albert A. *Lawyer Lincoln*. New York: Carroll and Graf, 1936.

Woodworth, Steven E. *Davis and Lee at War*. Lawrence: University Press of Kansas, 1995.

Wyatt-Brown, Bertram. *Southern Honor: Ethics and Behavior in the Old South*. Cambridge, Mass.: Oxford University Press, 1982.

Yellin, Jean Fagan, and John C. Van Horne, eds. *The Abolitionist Sisterhood: Women's Political Culture in Antebellum America.* Ithaca, N.Y.: Cornell University Press, 1994.

Zarefsky, David. *Lincoln, Douglas, and Slavery.* Chicago: University of Chicago Press, 1990.

Zelinsky, Wilbur. *Nation into State: The Shifting Symbolic Foundations of American Nationalism.* Chapel Hill: University of North Carolina Press, 1988.

Articles

Ames, Marilyn G. "Lincoln's Stepbrother, John D. Johnston." *Lincoln Herald* 82 (spring 1980).

Bartley, Numan V. "Social Change and Sectional Identity." *Journal of Southern History* 61 (February 1995).

Beringer, Richard E. "Jefferson Davis's Pursuit of Ambition: The Attractive Features of Alternative Decisions." *Civil War History* 38 (winter 1992).

Bleser, Carol K. "The Marriage of Varina Howell and Jefferson Davis: 'I gave the best and all my life to a girdled tree.'" *Journal of Southern History* (February 1999).

Bodenhamer, David J. "Law and Disorder on the Early Frontier: Marion County, Indiana, 1823–1850." *Western Historical Quarterly* 10 (1979).

Boritt, Gabor. "A Question of Political Suicide: Lincoln's Opposition to the Mexican War." *Journal of Illinois State Historical Society* 67 (February 1974).

Braden, Waldo W. "A North-South Friendship: Abraham Lincoln and Alexander H. Stephens." *Lincoln Herald* 91 (fall 1989).

Byrd, Max. "Lincoln's Shadow." *New York Times Book Review,* December 3, 2000.

Chroust, Anton-Herman. "Abraham Lincoln Argues a Proslavery Case." *American Journal of Legal History* 5 (October 1961).

Cook, Robert. "Baptism of Fire: The Republican Party in Iowa, 1838–1878." *Journal of American Studies* 30, 1 (1996).

Crane, Greg D. "Dangerous Sentiments: Sympathy, Rights, and Revolution in Stowe's Antislavery Novels." *Nineteenth-Century Literature* 51 (September 1996).

Curry, Richard O. "Conscious or Subconscious Caesarism? A Critique of Recent Scholarly Attempts to Put Abraham Lincoln on the Analyst's Couch." *Journal of Illinois State Historical Society* 77 (1984).

Dell, Christopher. "Reconstruction, Had Lincoln Lived." *Lincoln Herald* 81 (winter 1979).

Frederickson, George M. "A Man but Not a Brother: Abraham Lincoln and Racial Equality." *Journal of Southern History* 41 (February 1975).

Freeman, Joanne, B. "Dueling as Politics: Reinterpreting the Burr-Hamilton Duel." *William and Mary Quarterly* 53 (April 1996).

George, Joseph Jr. "Philadelphia's *Catholic Herald* Encounters President Lincoln." *Lincoln Herald* (fall 1980).

Hunt, H. Draper. "President Lincoln's First Vice President: Hannibal Hamlin of Maine." *Lincoln Herald* 88 (winter 1986).

Johnson, Ludwell. "Jefferson Davis and Abraham Lincoln as War Presidents: Nothing Succeeds Like Success." *Civil War History* 27 (1981).

Kubicek, Earl C. "Abraham Lincoln's Faith." *Lincoln Herald* 85 (fall 1983).

———. "Lincoln's Friend: Kirby Benedict." *Lincoln Herald* 81 (winter 1979).

Luraghi, Raimondo. "The Civil War and the Modernization of American Society." *Civil War History* 18 (1972).

Murph, David R. "Abraham Lincoln and Divine Providence." *Lincoln Herald* 73 (spring 1971).

Neely, Mark. "Abraham Lincoln's Nationalism Reconsidered." *Lincoln Herald* 76 (spring 1974).

———. "Lincoln and the Mexican War: An Argument by Analogy." *Civil War History* 28 (1978).

———. "The Political Life of New Salem." *Lincoln Lore* 1715 (January 1981).

Oates, Stephen B. "Towards a New Birth of Freedom: Abraham Lincoln and Reconstruction, 1854–1865." *Lincoln Herald* 82 (spring 1980).

Paludan, Phillip S. "The American Civil War Considered as a Crisis in Law and Order." *American Historical Review* 77 (October 1972).

———. "Lincoln, the Rule of Law, and the American Revolution." *Journal of Illinois State Historical Society* 70 (February 1977).

Putney, Clifford. "Service over Secrecy: How Lodge-Style Fraternalism Yielded Popularity to Men's Service Clubs." *Journal of Popular Culture* 27 (summer 1993).

Rabun, James Z. "Alexander Stephens and Jefferson Davis." *American Historical Review* 58 (1958).

Rawley, James A. "The Nationalism of Abraham Lincoln." *Civil War History* 9 (1963).

Reck, W. Emerson. "Mr. Lincoln's Growth in Faith." *Lincoln Herald* 92 (spring 1990).

Riley, Harris D. "Jefferson Davis and His Health, Part I." *Journal of Mississippi History* 49 (August 1987).

Rotundo, E. Anthony. "American Fatherhood: A Historical Perspective." *American Behavioral Scientist* 29 (1985).

Sanders, Charles W. Jr. "Jefferson Davis and the Hampton Roads Peace Conference: 'To secure peace to the two countries.'" *Journal of Southern History* 63 (November 1997).

Scorr, Kenneth. "Lincoln's Home in 1860." *Journal of Illinois State Historical Society* 44 (spring 1953).

Scott, Donald M. "The Popular Lecture and the Creation of a Public in Mid-Nineteenth-Century America." *Journal of American History* 66 (1980).

Silby, Joel H. "'Always a Whig in Politics': The Partisan Life of Abraham Lincoln." *Journal of the Abraham Lincoln Association* 8 (1986).

Simon, John Y. "Abraham Lincoln and Ann Rutledge." *Journal of the Abraham Lincoln Association* 11 (1990).

Smiley, David L. "The Quest for the Central Theme in Southern History." *South Atlantic Quarterly* 71 (summer 1972).

Stephenson, Nathaniel W. "A Theory of Jefferson Davis." *American Historical Review* 21 (October 1915).

———. "Lincoln and the Progress of Nationality in the North." *Annual Report of the American Historical Association* (1919).

Strozier, Charles. "On the Verge of Greatness: Psychological Reflections on Lincoln at the Lyceum." *Civil War History* 36 (1990).

Temple, Wayne C. "Location of the Rural Hotel in Springfield Where Abraham Lincoln Drank A Toast." *Lincoln Herald* 81 (winter 1979).

Walzer, Michael. "The New Tribalism: Notes on a Difficult Problem." *Dissent* (spring 1992).

Wilson, Major L. "Lincoln and Van Buren in the Steps of the Fathers: Another Look at the Lyceum Address." *Civil War History* 29 (1983).

Index